D1569913

WERTHEIM PUBLICATIONS
IN INDUSTRIAL RELATIONS

The French Labor Movement

VAL R. LORWIN

HARVARD UNIVERSITY PRESS
CAMBRIDGE, MASSACHUSETTS
1966

DISTRIBUTED IN GREAT BRITAIN BY
OXFORD UNIVERSITY PRESS
LONDON

Library of Congress Catalog card number 54-7062

PRINTED IN THE UNITED STATES OF AMERICA

CONTENTS

TABLES

FIGURES

FOREWORD

France is a vexing problem to the average American, even to the intelligent and literate American, burdened as he is with the unwelcome responsibilities of a divided world. A glance at our seventh grade atlas reveals why France is an indispensable element in any system of defense of western Europe, why this vital area must be both available and secure, why western Germany can be successfully added to our strength only in a setting of French acceptance and coöperation. And yet thus perilously placed in this perilous world, the French periodically act in ways which seem to some Americans not only irresponsible but at times almost wilfully recalcitrant and uncoöperative.

If France is to play the key role which geography has fashioned for her, it has become increasingly clear that she must shore up certain of her fundamental social weaknesses: she must produce more and distribute it more equitably; she must win for the Republic the convinced support of vast numbers of alienated workers—Communists, fellow travelers, disillusioned deserters of their unions, men who feel they have no real stake in the state in peace or war. At the heart of this problem are weak and divided labor unions faced by an arrested and often intransigent business leadership, which has learned little in a period when learning was neither compulsory nor immediately profitable.

This is the subject of Mr. Lorwin's admirable book, which is at once a history of the French labor movement and an analysis of the structure and functioning of French unions as they have existed since Liberation, and especially since 1947. To this complicated task Mr. Lorwin brings important credentials—a period of graduate study in the *atelier* of the late Carl Becker (and his writing shows the impress of this experience), two decades of concern with France and French labor problems, and repeated and extended contacts with French unions in recent years. In the latter connection, he has sought particularly to tap the grass roots, to get down to the lowest echelons of union leadership.

First, for history, Mr. Lorwin finds the logical beginning of his story in the French Revolution of 1789 when the triumphant middle class stated the individualist credo which the French working class has yet to challenge with anything like the success of workers in various other industrialized countries. He follows the labor movement through the nineteenth-century decades of alternate weakness and repression to its emergence as "revolutionary syndicalism" before the first war, which precipitated both its breakdown and the rise of Communism. With the latter came the division of the movement in the twenties and the all too brief coalescence of the Popular Front era, followed by the suppression by Vichy and the rebirth in the Resistance, with the Communists, become patriots, exploiting to the full the superb advantages of a mature and highly articulated underground apparatus.

The significant "discontinuity" of Liberation offers the author an occasion to present a much fuller account of the way in which the Communists took over the dominant national labor organization, the CGT, only to precipitate a new and tragic division when they turned to the large-scale manipulation of the unions for the political ends of Moscow. At the same time hundreds of thousands of disillusioned workers deserted the unions entirely, and the high hopes of labor unity and a new day for the worker were left a shambles.

This is the historical picture. But the author is even more concerned to give us, in the latter half of the book, a rounded and rather detailed account of how French unions function and in general what "makes them tick." This is the freshest, the most novel part of the book for the American reader. Mr. Lorwin shows us with discrimination much that is similar and more that is different from American organization and practice, and seeks to avoid the fallacies he believes beset the foreign observer of another shore—Pago-Pago, Victoria's lady-in-waiting, Judy O'Grady.

The sources of union weakness are etched in bold relief. Unions suffer from the constriction of indefensibly low dues, irregularly collected and adversely affected by massive inflation. In the face of labor organizations weakened by division and drastic decline in numbers, employers have seen no reason to coöperate to contribute, for instance, to the effective functioning of the collective bargaining law of 1950; hence few agreements have been reached. The law itself is far from being a useful instrument in any case: the obligatory clauses cover a wide range of subjects, but they are accompanied by no requirements that the parties bargain. The worker seems on the surface to find an important supplementary source of income in so-called "social wages" (family allowances and various other benefits), but in actual fact these very substantial additions come not out of business profits but from a redistribution of working class income (for instance, bachelors are penalized to increase the share of larger families). The strike is "misused"—irresponsibly for minor objectives, as a symbol for the affirmation of class consciousness, as a political weapon (by the Communists).

Labor relations at the plant level are least satisfactory of all; ingrained employer hostility takes full advantage of worker confusion arising from the blurred jurisdictions of competing unions, shop stewards, and plant committeemen (members of the now emasculated *comités d'entreprise* created after Liberation). Finally, the Communist domination of the CGT has sought to make its component organizations puppets of Moscow, introducing a political motive which is foreign to the traditions of French syndicalism and a further source of confusion and weakness.

But no such rapid enumeration of elements in Mr. Lorwin's analysis can be a substitute for a direct reading of his wide-ranging and perceptive treatment of the nature of the French labor movement and the various facets of French life which it penetrates and affects. No one who has a serious interest in the ills which have beset France in these recent years of crisis and who would find his way through the travail of this gifted but harassed people can afford not to read and ponder this book's findings.

DONALD C. McKAY

PREFACE

Many of the threads of French labor history run along in rather continuous patterns from the early years of industrialization to the present. Others are suddenly interrupted, and the pattern seems to run off in quite a new direction. The liberation of France in 1944 marked the latest of these apparent discontinuities. The trade union movement that emerged after the war is a far different movement from anything France had seen before. Despite much writing about French labor, it is not surprising therefore that, eight years after the second World War, there is still no adequate description and analysis of the unions which, even in their present weakened condition, are the most important mass movement in France.

The discontinuities—notably the rapid Communist Party seizure of control of the major segment of the trade union movement after 1944—have clear origins in the past. Some history is necessary to make intelligible the present of any social movement. Much history is necessary to understand a movement not only historically conditioned but historically minded. The attitudes of social, economic, and political life derive from the past everywhere, but in France, to an extraordinary degree, they spring consciously from the past. The patterns of labor's thinking are haunted by revolutionary reminiscences of 1789 and other "great years" between the French Revolution and the Russian Revolution, and by nostalgia for 1936.

In the first part of this study I have sketched the historical background and origins of the contemporary movement or, to put it more accurately, movements. That every generation must rewrite history for itself is a precept most often honored in the breach. The precept seems particularly valid today for labor history. (These pages may also indicate why the writer hopes to return at greater length to a number of aspects of the first century of French labor history.)

One must submit to the discipline of available space even in the discussion of origins which are endlessly ramified. For obvious reasons I have begun in 1789, with the political revolution which created the modern France to which the industrial revolution came. The first six chapters (Part One), carrying the history down to 1944, aim primarily to throw light on the factors most important for an understanding of the contemporary unions. The accent is mainly on the national unions and the confederations, not always as the seat of power, but as the meeting place of currents of action and ideas, and as the vantage point from which, in a necessarily short account, we may see the movement as a whole.

Part Two gives the history of the unions from the liberation (that is, the liberation of Paris in 1944) to mid-1953. These two chapters are the longest of the historical chapters, because they break the newest ground.

Part Three describes and discusses the structure and functioning of the unions, their relative strength and influence, their collective bargaining relationships, their role within the shop, and their relationships to the political parties. I have tried to show the relationships of union structure, ideologies, and bargaining patterns, and to get at the attitudes of the rank and file and lower rank leadership, as well as those of the top leadership. Rank-and-file attitudes challenge our attention in any country. They are doubly important in France, where leadership views do not mold, or reflect, those of the rank and file half as much as they do, for example, in the United States.

In this complex area, a foreigner must be humble about his achievements. In three or four years' work he can probe a vast and baffling surface, and experience a few insights, thanks to friendships and acquaintances, work and luck. In my most recent long period of work in France, during most of the year 1950, it was my chief preoccupation to get down to the lowest echelons of union leadership, the paid and usually the unpaid local officers, shop stewards, and plant committeemen; to try to enter into their attitudes toward higher union leadership, employers, and the institutions of industrial and political government.

There is no need to reiterate the importance of France in the world, the labor organizations in France, the Communists in the labor organizations. I shall disclaim what Ford Madox Ford once called the desire of every Anglo-Saxon to reform the economic system of France. Nor shall I here urge what we ourselves can learn from French experience —although I think there is much to learn. For dissimilar though the backgrounds are, more fortunate one land than another, human experience illuminates human problems.

If I speak of many of the contradictions in French trade unionism and French life, it is not to indicate that the French are queer people because their national life is full of contradictions. All nations, all groups, all individuals have their contradictions. I have wanted to avoid the single-explanation theories of complex historical development which are the weakness of some of the most brilliant observers of national life.

Along with a statement of the author's high resolve to be objective should go some warning to readers of what may get in the way of his objectivity: what he is objective for and—like the legendary neutral Irishman—against? One could not for several years have been a close disciple of the great historian, Carl Becker, without appreciating some of the limitations and responsibilities of "objectivity." Objectivity cannot be indifference or neutrality to values when the subject is a living social movement and indeed a whole society, which we cherish because it is so close to us and yet so intriguingly different from ours. Objectivity in such a study as this consists of an awareness of one's own values and preferences and those of one's own environment, and scrupulous care that those values and preferences cloud one's observation and deform one's judgment as little as possible.

I might specify prepossessions and values which are relevant. I share the conventional belief in vigorous, democratic, and responsible unionism and in collective bargaining as desirable and inevitable in a free industrial society. The unions' role in society—which finds other definition in France than in the United States—must go beyond collective bargaining with employers. Government may need to intervene in setting some of the conditions of employment and some of the conditions of collective bargaining and of collective organization itself. But the maintenance of centers of power and voluntary associations independent of the state—for example, trade unions—is indispensable to democracy.

Objectivity is less difficult if one recognizes that phenomena which one finds unpleasant are not perforce unnatural. It is important to understand how millions of perfectly normal and run-of-the-mill citizens of another democracy can belong to Communist-run unions and vote the Communist ticket. French employers and employer association officials apparently find this state of affairs "normal" and tell one, in so many words or more elegantly, "If I were a worker, I might be a Communist too." Or, even more commonly, "If I were a worker, I'd be a member of the General Confederation of Labor too, even if it is Communist-dominated."

Three special hazards or fallacies beset those who report on foreign labor movements and social systems, whether upon brief tours of inspection or after overlong research. The first might be called the Pago-Pago fallacy. It is that of describing everything like a South Sea isle, in terms of what is strange and different. Fascinated by narrow streets, unaccustomed politics, and strange bargaining practices, we magnify the odd and picturesque.

From the touristic wonders of the Pago-Pago variety, it is easy to slide into moral judgments in which different means wrong. This second related pitfall may be called the fallacy of Queen Victoria's lady-in-waiting, taking the name from an account of remarks in the royal box during a performance of Shakespeare's *Antony and Cleopatra*. As the unhappy Egyptian monarch pressed the fatal asp to her bosom, one of Victoria's ladies-in-waiting sighed and murmured, "How different from the home life of our own dear Queen!" So it is in some of the reporting from abroad, for example by visitors returning to a comfortable nation from a mission to tell a less comfortable people how to manage its affairs. How different from our own labor movement, and how quaintly wrong. Often fact finding becomes fault finding.

A third, altogether different deformation results from the Judy O'Grady or sisters-under-the-skin fallacy. Of course, we say, there are obvious differences between this foreign movement and the comparable American development. But all these differences are only superficial; they must not obscure the basic identity of problems and institutions. The same appetites and drives, the same resistances and insecurities move individuals and groups under whatever flag they live and in whatever tongue they organize and bargain. Explanations which are valid here must be valid everywhere; forms of action which have proved themselves here are the forms for elsewhere.

Into each of these fallacies I may have lapsed at times. If I have fallen into the Pago-Pago error, I hope that at least I have had some of the perceptions that go with what Jean Fourastié has called "that essential faculty of the scientific spirit: astonishment." If I have lapsed into any moral judgments and any of the complacence of Queen Victoria's lady-in-waiting, it is despite an effort not to judge but to evaluate, and that in terms of the professed aims of the unions and their possibilities of action. If I have generalized—and who would not add a cubit to his stature by generalizing?—I trust it has been with an appreciation of the differences between nation and nation, between social situation and very different situation.

One of the pleasures of finishing a manuscript is the opportunity it gives to acknowledge aid, criticism, encouragement in many generous forms. I thank Professor John T. Dunlop for persuading me in December 1949 to join his Harvard University project of foreign trade union studies. For critical questions and comments I am happily indebted to him and my two colleagues on the Harvard study: Daniel L. Horowitz and Professor Walter Galenson. I owe a special debt of thanks to Professor Maurice F. Neufeld for many things, among them a thoughtful and painstaking reading of an early version of the manuscript. My thanks go also to Professors John W. McConnell, Vernon H. Jensen, and Charles A. Gulick. Great thanks go to a number of Americans with a sympathetic understanding of French problems, who have read parts of the manuscript in one stage or another: Professor Henry W. Ehrmann, William Chaikin, Warren Baum, Professor Adolf Sturmthal, Professor John E. Sawyer, Lenore Epstein, Kenneth Douty, Otto Kirchheimer, and, for many ideas, James L. Houghteling, Jr. My greatest debt, for numerous insights, is to Richard Eldridge. There are many people in France to whom I am indebted. They include members, staff, and officials of Force Ouvrière and the Confederation of French Catholic Workers; employers and officials of employer associations; government officials in Paris and the provinces. They also include personal friends, some once but no longer active in trade union or employer organizations. I shall not attempt to name them here, but they would know that my thanks go to them for patience and understanding, for frankness and fellowship. No reader will hold any of those mentioned responsible for errors of fact or personal interpretation.

To the American Philosophical Society I am grateful for a grant which enabled me to spend most of the summer of 1953 in France, observing at first hand some of the changes since my previous stay and notably the recent operations of the collective bargaining law of 1950. The Rockefeller Foundation provided earlier assistance through the support of the Harvard foreign labor project.

To Curt and Lise Hansen of Copenhagen I give thanks for finding for us the tranquility beside a Danish fjord where I did the final revising of this manuscript.

Finally, and most inadequately, my thanks go to my spouse, Madge Lorwin, for many forms of help. Here my thanks are most of all for her asking many of the questions to which, until she asked them, I had assumed I had satisfactory answers.

Skovnaes
Frederikssund, Denmark
August 24, 1953

V. R. L.

PART ONE

DEVELOPMENT OF THE UNIONS (1789-1944)

CHAPTER I

THE EARLY PRECURSORS (1789-1871)

> The ridiculous thing about this new industrial bourgeoisie . . . is this
> fear which it does not at all hide, which it expresses at every turn with a
> singular naiveté. Let three men get together in the street to talk about
> wages, let them ask the employer, whom their work has made rich, for
> one sou's increase in wages, and the bourgeois becomes panic-stricken
> and calls for the help of the soldiery.
>
> Jules Michelet, *Le Peuple,* 1846.

> I believe as you do that the workers of Paris are intelligent, and I
> thank you for your good opinion of them. But how can one reconcile this
> intelligence with this inertia. . . ? There is only one way, that is to tell
> us: You are free, organize yourselves; carry on your own affairs, we will
> not put any obstacles in the way.
>
> —Henri Tolain, bronze engraver, letter to
> *L'Opinion Nationale,* October 17, 1861.

A French engineer, exasperated by the excessively historical thinking he encountered in his efforts at modernization of his country's industry and agriculture, exclaimed, "I wish I could kill off some of the
ancestors of these people." But the ancestors will not be killed off, even
though their descendants repudiate them or torture their history for
present justification. To see the unions as they are now, it is necessary
to look at their ancestors, to retrace briefly the development of the
unions across more than a century and a half of wars, revolutions, and
slow economic growth since the revolution of 1789.[1]

Modern industry came later, and far more slowly, to France than to

---

[1] Part One of this book does not attempt a full history of the trade union movement
before 1944. It is concerned with bringing out the factors and memories which have
conditioned the current movement, its structure and philosophy, its relations with
employers and government. (The bibliographical appendix lists the most important
historical works upon which I have drawn. A complete or satisfactory history remains
to be written.) Part Two is devoted to trade union history since the liberation in 1944,
which is recounted in greater detail. A chronology of major events in labor history
and related political history is given in Appendix A.

THE FRENCH LABOR MOVEMENT

England. The workers of Paris who in 1789 were the "infantry of the revolution" were not an industrial proletariat, but artisans and handi-craftsmen. The revolution did not bring them the emancipation it brought the peasantry and the middle classes. Their attempts to associate for economic ends met with repeated government prohibitions and repressions that were to hamper, though not altogether prevent, organization for three quarters of a century.

The revolution abolished the guilds in the name of economic liberty, and declared citizens free to practice any trade they pleased. It gave them freedom to assemble as they chose. But it soon withdrew most of this new freedom. When journeymen combined to meet rising food prices, demanded higher wages, and went out on strikes, the Constituent Assembly quickly voted the Le Chapelier Law. In reporting out his bill, Le Chapelier (a deputy of the Third Estate) reiterated the individualist conception which was in theory to preside over the next century's economic growth: "There are no more guilds in the state, there are only the particular interest of each individual and the general interest. No one is permitted to bring the intermediate interest of a guild between the citizens and the commonweal."

Workers, entrepreneurs, and storekeepers alike were forbidden, if they assembled, to "select officers, keep minutes, pass resolutions, or adopt regulations" on what the law called "their pretended common interests." If, "against the principles of liberty and the Constitution," employers attempted to agree on wages to offer, or workers on wages they would accept, they were subject to heavy fines. The Assembly reassured tradesmen that it did not intend the law to apply to their chambers of commerce, since, as Le Chapelier said, "You can be sure that none of us intends to prevent the merchants from discussing their common interests."[2]

To these provisions of the revolutionary assembly, the Napoleonic penal code in 1810 added criminal penalties for workers' combinations. Employers' combinations were in theory also subject to criminal prosecution, but only if they tended to lower wages "unjustly and abusively." Workers were required to carry work-books to "guarantee workshops against desertion, and contracts against violation," and, although this was not proclaimed, to facilitate police controls. In disputes over wage claims, the employer's word was given credence over the worker's, a distinction which added social insult to economic injury.

---

[2] For the interesting committee report of Le Chapelier, and text of the law and discussion, see *Archives Parlementaires,* I série, vol. 27, pp. 210-213. The text of the law is given in English by John Hall Stewart, *A Documentary Survey of the French Revolution* (New York, 1951), pp. 165-166.

Such was the law until well past the middle of the century. Its enforcement was uneven and capricious. Government attitudes varied with the whims and fears of the moment and with the ties, suspected or real, between workers' associations and political dissent. Intermittently the workers were permitted to organize, only to have the police come down upon them later. Tolerance alternated with prosecutions, fines, and jailings.

EARLY FORMS OF ORGANIZATION

The precursors of the modern trade unions, in the order of their appearance, were the *compagnonnages,* the mutual aid societies, and the societies of resistance. Naturally the lines of difference between them were often blurred.

The compagnonnages, going back at least to the fifteenth century, formed a link between medieval guild society and modern unionism. Secret societies of bachelor workmen, they admitted new members—in guild fashion—on practical demonstrations of skill. Some of their journeymen members graduated to the ranks of masters or employers. The compagnonnages were organized not along craft lines, although these were recognized, but in three main orders called "devoirs."[3] Each included a number of craft groupings, with the building crafts predominating. Each "devoir" had a network of arrangements to receive, house, and find jobs for young men as they worked their way from one city to another, learning the trade, in what was called the "Tour de France." Thus they fostered a workers' solidarity which went beyond a single craft and a single locality. The journeymen's loyalty to their organizations and their pride of craftsmanship were, unfortunately, accompanied by bloody rows with rival "devoirs," bullying of their own junior members, and a snobbish refusal to admit those they considered working in the less noble crafts.

Exerting a considerable control over local labor markets for their members, the compagnonnages were the only effective organization of workingmen in the first third of the century. Although illegal, they were tolerated much of the time, with the police intervening when they fell to brawling too violently among themselves. In 1841, Agricol Perdiguier estimated that there were 100,000 compagnons in France.[4] Perdiguier, a compagnon cabinetmaker and one of the finest spirits of the early workers' movement, tried to reform the compagnonnages to keep their solidarity and craftsmanship, but eliminate their sectarianism

---

[3] "Devoir" is literally "duty" or "obligation." The orders took their quaint names from the building of the Temple of Solomon, to which they traced their origins.

[4] *Le Livre du compagnonnage,* 2d ed. (Paris, 1841), p. 68.

and feuds. The institution was doomed, however, by the first onrush of industrial progress and the spirit of a new age.

The railroads made obsolete the elaborate travel arrangements of the Tour de France. Craft lines were being shifted by machines, to the detriment of some of the proud old crafts. Moreover, organization by single trades or industries had more economic rationale and seemed more natural than the heterogeneous multi-trade organization of the "devoirs." Secret rites, ornate insignia and costumes, and religious observances no longer appealed to workmen's tastes. Nevertheless some compagnonnages survived, especially in the building trades,[5] down to the end of the century. One may still meet workers who in their youth followed the Tour de France before that term came to denote only an annual bicycle race. And a few vestigial antiquarian organizations of artisans persist.[6]

Less picturesque were the mutual aid societies, which had some roots in the last years of the Old Régime. Like the English friendly societies, they insured their members against illness, work accidents, or unemployment. The government watched the mutual aid societies with a careful eye. It wanted workers to acquire habits of thrift and providence, lest they manifest discontent or become public charges. On the other hand, it was dangerous to permit workmen to get together regularly, for they might concert action against the government or against their employers. To discourage their striking, the government at one time ruled that the mutuals must include the members of more than one trade. Organization by a single trade came more easily, however. In 1823 the printers of Paris alone had 30 mutuals numbering over 2600 members. As happened so often, the printers were in the lead over other trades, and Paris over other regions.

The resistance societies were secret organizations for defense, not against ill fortune, but against employers. They resisted wage cuts, tried to fix wage rates and reduce the hours of work, and occasionally attempted to bar new machinery. Some also carried on mutual aid activities, for the line between mutual aid and resistance to employers could hardly remain clear or constant.

Industrialization, barely started in the time of Napoleon and the Bourbon restoration, went forward more rapidly under the bourgeois

---

[5] The building trades are a "group which economic historians are astonishingly apt to neglect," J. H. Clapham remarks. *The Economic Development of France and Germany, 1815-1914,* 4th ed. (Cambridge, 1936, reprinted 1948), p. 75.

[6] For an idealized version of the modern survival, see *Compagnonnage, par les compagnons du Tour de France* (Paris, 1951), introduction, pp. i-vi. This anthology contains a valuable detailed bibliography, a work of love, by Roger Lecotté, pp. 271-417.

monarchy of Louis Philippe. The textile industry was, as in other countries, the first to develop factory conditions. Cotton, wool, silk, and linen spinning and weaving, coal and iron mining, and iron foundries were the most rapidly expanding industries. The tempo of industrial expansion was still comparatively slow. Indeed the distinguished economic historian, Clapham, holds that:

in the course of the nineteenth century most French industries were remodelled, but it might be said that France never went through an industrial revolution. There was a gradual transformation, a slow shifting of her economic center of gravity from the side of agriculture to that of industry, and a slow change in the methods of industrial organization. In the first half of the century the movement is barely perceptible, in spite of the noise and controversy which accompanied it.[7]

Louis Philippe's minister, Guizot, was urging, "Enrich yourselves." Needless to say, this counsel was not addressed to the wage earners. Upon them and their children were laid all the cruelties of the early industrial revolution—miserable factory conditions, foul overcrowded housing, the labor of little children and women for long hours at wages even lower than those of men, widespread pauperism. Ameliorative legislation was slow in coming. The first factory act was passed in 1841. It forbade the employment of children under eight years of age and night work for those under twelve. It set an eight-hour day for children from eight to twelve, and a twelve-hour day for those from twelve to sixteen. But it applied only to establishments using power-driven machinery or employing twenty or more workers. Thus it did not even try to cover the vast majority working in the smaller shops and in homes. Enforcement was entrusted to ex-manufacturers, serving without pay, instead of the paid inspectors originally proposed. This ineffectual child labor act was, except for the transitory laws of the 1848 revolution, the only protective legislation until 1874.

Philanthropists, physicians, and government officials—many of Catholic inspiration—were reporting at length and with anxiety on the growing pains of industry. A contemporary summed up their efforts:

The pauperists and philanthropists have analyzed with care and minutely described *the effects* of misery. Then they have counselled to the rich alms and charity; to the poor patience, resignation, continence, and thrift (savings for those who do not even earn enough to live on!).[8]

---

[7] *The Economic Development of France and Germany, 1815-1914*, p. 53.

[8] F. Vidal, *De la répartition des richesses, ou de la justice distributive en économie sociale* (Paris, 1846), p. 461. Italics in original.

After the revolution of 1830 in which the workers of Paris played a leading part, there was a brief flourishing of labor organization and of the first workers' newspapers. The workers soon discovered that the revolution had brought neither political nor economic liberty. In 1831 one of the epic struggles of the workers' movement took place in Lyon, the Manchester of France. Like so many of the epics of French labor history, it was a confused, lost fight, its meaning clearest in its repression. It was the doing, not of the lowest-paid proletarians, but of the working subcontractors of the silk industry, who operated machines themselves and hired other hands as well. The subcontractors' organization, in effect both a mutual aid and resistance society, for a brief moment obtained from the employers what was probably the first wage scale agreement in French industry. When some employers refused to respect the new scale, a strike broke out, turning from rioting to an incoherent insurrection. After the royal troops had restored order, the Premier pointed out that the "workers must realize that there are no remedies for them but patience and resignation."[9] Two Lyon men summed up the situation, "Despotism, driven from the chateaux, has taken refuge in the workshops."[10]

Despite stricter laws against unauthorized associations, workers' societies revived in the 1840's. In aim they combined varying degrees of economic aspiration and republicanism; in form, both open and secret organization. It was the more prosperous craftsmen rather than the more depressed new factory laborers who organized. The printers were the most successful of those who banded in mixed mutual aid and "resistance" activities. In Paris the typographers' society, founded in 1839, although technically illegal, enrolled about half the trade and secured a wage scale agreement with its employers which lasted two decades.

Along with such limited efforts, social reformers were proposing utopias unlimited, new systems of social organization: communal societies, producers' and credit coöperatives, and romantic socialism. Since undemocratic government in western Europe then was nothing like modern dictatorship, it was possible to write of a better world under the noses of those who governed the imperfect one. In no country were social questioning and utopia building more active than in France in the second quarter of the nineteenth century. "We became firmly convinced we were living during the last days of a dying civilization," Bakunin

---

[9] Edouard Dolléans, *Histoire du mouvement ouvrier,* 4th ed. (Paris, 1948), vol. 1, p. 69.

[10] Bernard and Charnier, *Rapport fait et présenté à M. le Président du Conseil des Ministres sur le causes générales qui ont amené les évènements de Lyon,* 1832, cited by Dolléans, vol. 1, p. 60.

wrote. "Two months on the boulevards of Paris was enough to turn a liberal into a socialist."[11]

1848: REVOLUTION AND COUNTERREVOLUTION

The hopes of the optimistic forties seemed about to be fulfilled in the February revolution of 1848. The heavy manual labor of revolution this time was supplied not only by artisans and handicraftsmen, as in 1789 and 1830, but also by factory workers. The surprising ease with which they tumbled the monarchy was matched by the workers' mildness in victory. They insisted only on the proclamation of a republic and the "right to work," for the revolution came in the wake of acute unemployment.

To give effect to the "right to work," the government set up the so-called "national workshops."[12] They were nothing more than gigantic versions of the old charity workshops, "work-alms." The promise of work for all was impossible to realize. In a few months there were over 100,000 men in the Paris workshops, occupied only two days a week at the most obvious and demoralizing make-work. Their growing discontent and then rioting alarmed the government, composed of men bewildered by the exercise of unexpected power.

In June the government decided to close down the national workshops. Faced with starvation, the workers demonstrated in spontaneous and leaderless protest. The government took fright, and ordered its Minister of War, General Cavaignac, to clear the streets. In the four days of fighting known as the "June Days," General Cavaignac wiped out the unorganized but determined protest.

The June Days were to remain a bitter memory among French workers. Modern social warfare was making its hateful and memorable entry on the French scene. The victorious general glimpsed the consequences. "In Paris I see victors and vanquished," said Cavaignac in a proclamation. "Accursed be my name if I consent to seeing victims."[13] There were victims: not only the several thousand killed and many more thousands arrested, but also the nascent workingmen's and socialist movements. Soon one of the victims was the republic itself. When in 1851 Louis Napoleon swept aside the republic, only scattered resistance came

---

[11] Lewis L. Lorwin, *Labor and Internationalism* (Washington, 1929), p. 23.
[12] The English term "workshops" makes the "ateliers nationaux" sound more constructive than they were. As the leading authority on this episode points out, "national workshops" is "at best an awkward rendering of an untranslatable term." Donald C. McKay, *The National Workshops* (Cambridge, 1933), p. vii.
[13] Charles Schmidt, *Des ateliers nationaux aux barricades de juin* (Paris, 1948), p. 57. On the numbers killed and arrested, Schmidt prefers to "remain imprecise to be correct."

from the workers. The frightened republican assembly had withdrawn the universal suffrage first granted in 1848; Napoleon III felt it was safe to restore it.

The Second Empire—the decades of the fifties and sixties—saw a speedier pace in the industrialization of France, an increased growth of urban life and factory conditions, and the beginnings of the modern unions. The factory did not displace the small workshop or the home worker. But it was beginning to create a new type of industrial life in many cities and in the midst of rural or semirural communities. This was the period of railroad building, unrestrained speculation, and the growing use of the joint stock company form.

Lines of class were hardening. Henceforth few workers were to graduate into the employer class; henceforth the classes were to live apart physically. The spectacular renovation of Paris which Baron Haussmann directed, the great increase in the city's wealth, and the building of whole new neighborhoods broke up the close proximity in which rich and poor had often lived, and separated them in lavish bourgeois neighborhoods and mournful workers' suburbs. The separation was even greater in the industrial cities of the north.[14]

In this period the alienation of most of the working class from the church of its fathers was consummated. The church was an established church, associated with authority, with the monarchy earlier and now with the empire to which it rallied, and with the hard-fisted employer. Liberal French Catholics—talented writers and forward-looking prelates —were repudiated by Pope Pius IX. As one Catholic writer recently put it, the workers "thought they saw God behind the employers, the gendarmes, the judges, all arrayed against the hungry strikers. Could this God be the good Lord? And if he was not good, could he even be true?"[15]

Despite the tempo of economic activity, the movement of workers' association lapsed for a decade after the blows of the June Days and the coup d'état of Napoleon III. The workers' producer coöperatives, which had proliferated in 1848, were suspected by Napoleon's police of republicanism and socialism; most survived only a short time.

The last years of the empire, however, saw the rise of the first trade unions. Napoleon III had ideas, albeit vague and contradictory, about doing things for the working classes. On his road to power, he had "fooled everybody because he was sincere." Now he needed popular support to make up for the loss of following in other classes. In 1862 he

[14] Georges Duveau, *La Vie ouvrière en France sous le second empire* (Paris, 1946), pp. 343-351.

[15] Edmond Pognon, "Sociologie de l'athéisme contemporaine," *Témoignages, Cahiers de la Pierre-Qui-Vire,* no. 28, January 1951, p. 15.

allowed a delegation of workers freely elected by the various trades to go to the London Exposition. (International expositions were great occasions in the past century for workers to get around and compare conditions in different countries.) The delegates were impressed with the better conditions of English workers and with their trade unions. On their return they quite boldly asked for freedom of association and the right to strike. Another result of this trip was the activity of French workers in the creation of the International Workingmen's Association (the First International) in London in 1864.

GROWTH OF UNIONS IN THE 1860's

In the year of the delegation to the London Exposition took place the first big strike the empire had seen. The Paris typographical workers demanded a new wage scale to replace that fixed with their employers in 1843, and protested the employment of women. Their leaders were convicted under the antistrike law, but the emperor pardoned them. Clearly, as his ministers complained in a confidential report, the empire was enjoying "neither the advantages of a severe penal legislation, nor the honor and benefit of a liberal legislation."[16] In 1864, therefore, a law gave the workers the right to strike. This was the first great breach in the anticombination legislation inherited from the individualistic tradition of the revolution and the police tradition of the first empire.

Workers did not yet have the right of free assembly or of association. In 1868 the government let it be known that it would permit workers' organizations, as it permitted employers' organizations. It did not embody this tolerance in legislation. Nor did the practice of the "liberal Empire" fully respect this promise.

Organization grew rapidly in the late 1860's, as if to make up for lost time. Local unions sprang up in Paris and in other cities. These were for the first time called "chambres syndicales ouvrières" or—the term that was to survive—"syndicats."[17] As in the 1840's, the skilled trades were in the forefront—the printing trades, the building crafts, hat workers, bronze founders, bakers, cabinetmakers, shoemakers, tailors, machinists, goldsmiths, jewelers, and coopers.[18] They were on the whole the trades least touched by technological change or factory conditions.

---

[16] Edmond Villetard de Prunières, *Histoire de l'internationale* (Paris, 1872), p. 41.

[17] Many writers, including some of the best, have translated "syndicat" as "syndicate." A "syndicat" in French may be a trade union ("syndicat ouvrier"), an employer organization ("syndicat patronal"), or a farmers' organization ("syndicat agricole"). The context usually makes clear which without the adjective. In English, however, the word "syndicate" does not mean a trade union.

[18] A list of dates of foundation of the first unions in various trades is given by Jean Montreuil, *Histoire du mouvement syndical en France des origines à nos jours* (Paris, 1946), pp. 112-115.

unorganized groups began organizing, notably metallurgical
nd store clerks. By 1870, there were some sixty to seventy
nion members in Paris and a like number in the provinces.
unions launched several attempts at regional and national craft
federations, and, more successfully, their first horizontal federations. In
1869 a city central was set up in Paris, with Marseille, Lyon, and Rouen
following its lead in 1870.

Many of the unions were affiliated with the First International, and
they formed the largest national section of that organization. By 1870,
there were over 200,000 "members" of the International in France.
Affiliation was loose and transient; disaffiliation as easy and informal.
The 200,000 included not only members of unions but also political
study clubs, coöperatives, and other groups. At first the French section
of the International had much of the spirit of Proudhon and hardly any
of Marx's. One could find almost anything one wanted in Proudhon's
diffuse and voluminous writings. In general the Proudhonists believed
in the workers' own economic action through unions, credit mutuals,
and producer coöperatives rather than political action or collective
ownership. They emphasized voluntarism and local autonomy as against
the central role of the state. They were humanitarian and not determin-
istic; gradualist rather than revolutionary. Actually, the majority of reflective and articulate workers appeared more interested in republican
ideas than in either coöperatives or unions.

In the International the practical British unionists stressed the dangers of competition from abroad of lower-paid workers and imported
strike breakers. The French replied in more general terms: since "capital was concentrating in mighty financial and industrial combinations,"
the workers of the world must look for "satisfaction through solidarity."[19] At the 1866 and 1867 congresses of the International, the French
delegates and the Proudhonist program won out. By 1868 and 1869,
when the Marxian collectivist program was endorsed, the French delegates were no longer Proudhonist "mutualists," but more radical in
spirit.

After permitting the International to function freely for several years,
the government prosecuted its Paris leaders as an unauthorized association. In the first trial the court's penalties were mild, almost nominal.
But the convictions in that and two succeeding trials brought more radical leadership into the organization. An unsympathetic contemporary
could write of "the rule which inevitably leads to demogogy: influence
escaped from the moderates, and it was the most violent and the craziest

---

[19] Quoted in Lewis L. Lorwin, *Labor and Internationalism*, p. 35.

who inherited it."[20] Perhaps it was the government's repression rather than a rule of demogogy which turned the moderate and promising French labor movement of the late 1860's into revolutionary channels.[21] After the legal persecution came the senseless war with Prussia.

The war into which Napoleon III allowed himself to be provoked swallowed up his throne and gave the occasion for German unification. It submerged the French unions. A by-product, as Marx guessed, was to take from the French and give to the Germans and to Marx and the Marxists the dominant role in the international labor and socialist movement.[22]

THE COMMUNE

The war was followed in 1871 by the tragic struggle between the Paris Commune and the Provisional Government under Thiers at Versailles. The uprising known as the Commune[23] began when the Parisians refused to surrender the arms they had accumulated against the Prussians. Some of the Paris Council of the First International were among the leaders of the Commune. But the Commune was not the doing of the International. Nor was the Commune specifically socialist or overwhelmingly proletarian.[24] As often happens when radical organizations are involved, the International claimed the rebels and the martyrs for its own, and the conservatives were glad to blame it for the violence and villainy. Thus was created the legend of the Commune as the work of the International, which frightened good citizens long after the International had died out.

The origins of the Commune were indeed mixed: wounded national patriotism (the feeling that true Jacobin republicanism could have won the war against Prussia); local autonomy (Paris against the central state); the demand for a "social" republic rather than the conservative

---

[20] Villetard de Prunières, *Histoire de l'internationale,* p. 202.

[21] The report of the General Council to the 1868 Congress of the International could observe with much basis: "The harassments of the government, far from killing the International, have given it a new lease on life by cutting short the unwholesome flirtation between the Empire and the working class." *Ibid.*

[22] Marx wrote Engels soon after Napoleon III's declaration of war against Prussia: "The French need a sound thrashing. If the Prussians win . . . the weight of German power will transfer the center of gravity of the labor movement in Western Europe from France to Germany . . . The German working class is superior to the French from the standpoint of theory and of organization. Its preponderance over the French on the world scene would at the same time be the preponderance of our theory over Proudhon's." July 20, 1870, Karl Marx—Friedrich ·Engels, *Briefwechsel* (Berlin, Abteilung 3, Band IV, 1931), p. 339.

[23] The term "commune" comes from the name given the free chartered town of the Middle Ages, and taken up again during the French Revolution; not from communism.

[24] See especially Edward S. Mason, *The Paris Commune: An Episode in the History of the Socialist Movement* (New York, 1930).

regime seemingly ahead; and a number of needless vexations inflicted by the Versailles authorities on the city which had just bravely stood four months' Prussian siege.

The Commune went down in the burning of monuments and the shooting of hostages. The repression was bloodier, vaster, more cold-blooded. Between ten and fifteen thousand Communards were killed in the streets or by summary courts martial.[25] Over four thousand were transported to New Caledonia, and several thousand more imprisoned in France. In its repression the Commune acquired its legendary form of another battle in the social war. Its legend lived in hatred. Images of the Commune are as vivid in France as those of the Civil War in America's South. It is not only the defeated who remember, however, but the victors too.

---

[25] This is the estimate of Mason, *The Paris Commune*, pp. 292-294, after examination of the extreme claims on both sides. Writing in 1930, before the full flowering of modern dictatorship, he could call this "the most extensive judicial repression of modern times."

Even the moderate founder of the Catholic trade union movement wrote (as late as 1937) of the Commune's "110,000 victims: dead, wounded, deported; women, children, or old people left without support." Jules Zirnheld, *Cinquante années de syndicalisme chrétien* (Paris, 1937), p. 19.

CHAPTER II

THE ORIGINS OF MODERN UNIONISM (1871-1914)

> The unions, now that they can be sure of the future, will be able to bring together the resources necessary to create and multiply those useful institutions which have produced such worth-while results among other nations: retirement funds, credit unions, educational courses, libraries, coöperatives, bureaus of information, of placement, and of wage statistics.
>
> Certain nations, less favored by nature than France and which are her serious competitors, owe much of their commercial, industrial, and agricultural prosperity to the vitality of these institutions. Under pain of national decline, France must hasten to follow this example.
>
> —Waldeck-Rousseau, Minister of the Interior, circular to prefects of all departments, August 25, 1884.

The period between 1871 and 1914 is one to which many Frenchmen now look back as an age of peace, prosperity and artistic creation, an age when things were "normal." For workers it was a period of generally moderately rising standards of living, of increasing expansion of factory production, of the formation of the modern unions and socialist parties.

Economic development, slow for a generation, quickened its pace between the turn of the century and the outbreak of the first World War. The iron and steel industry grew significantly, as did the machinery and chemical industries; pioneering work was done in the automobile industry. Only in mining and heavy industry, however, did the large factory come to predominate. Other industries were still characterized by small and medium-sized shops and even home work. In 1896, 64 per cent of all industrial employees, and in 1906, 59 per cent worked in establishments of fewer than one hundred employees. Shops with only one to ten employees still accounted for a third of all industrial employment in 1906. A large part of France's industrial life centered on luxury articles —silks, lace, gloves, perfumes, jewelry, china, leather crafts, cutlery, women's fashions, "articles of Paris," which lent themselves to the little workshop. Urbanization moved at a moderate pace too, except for

Paris, which was the only city with over a million population. Marseille and Lyon just exceeded the half-million figure and only two others (Bordeaux and Nantes) the 200,000 mark in 1911.

Even in many of the larger scale enterprises, and in industries in which factory production dominated, family structured business remained important. The heads of family concerns carried with them into industry the values and habits of a tight-fisted peasantry and a cautious commercial middle class. They put their emphasis on security rather than risk-taking.

Back in 1862, the worker delegates to the London International Exposition had seen contrasts with their own industries that inspired a disquiet increasingly justified in the next generations. "We look ahead of us with misgivings in our hearts," said the French porcelain decorators.

We see skillful manufacturers offering consumers excellent and beautiful products. But this force which comes from large sums of capital, handled with breadth and intelligence, this force which does not hesitate at expense to develop the best workers and to acquire supremacy in industry—that we look for in vain.[1]

French enterprise was neither as vigorous nor as adaptable as that of the young capitalist powers, the United States and Germany, or even that of older Britain. Many of the hardiest plants of capitalist growth elsewhere have been fertilized by government benefits, but in France the requirements in tariffs and subsidies seemed larger and more continuous than those of its principal competitors.[2] After the one free trade experiment under Napoleon III, and low duties during the 1870's and 1880's, the nation in 1892 enacted a tariff which was "one of the stiffest in the world though not so stiff as those of Russia and the United States."[3]

The agricultural interests obtained their protection against lower-cost foreign foodstuffs. Freed from the pressure to adopt newer methods, they fell farther behind other countries in the modernization of farming. For urban workers, artifically high food prices meant that money wages had to be fairly high in terms of the international competitive position of French manufactures, even though modest in terms of domestic purchasing power.

Protectionism probably helped stimulate the industrial spurt around the century's turn. In the long run, however, it reduced the stimulus to

---

[1] Cited by Dolléans, *Histoire du mouvement ouvrier*, vol. 1, pp. 271-272.

[2] The dramatically absurd illustration was the government's continuing subsidy for the construction of sailing vessels well after steamships had come to stay.

[3] Clapham, *The Economic Development of France and Germany*, p. 264. See also Eugene O. Golob, *The Méline Tariff: French Agriculture and Nationalist Economic Policy* (New York, 1944).

modernization of method and equipment and inhibited the development of domestic markets. Lack of competition behind tariff walls permitted French manufacturers to make good profits from small sales, largely off the top of the home market, without the necessity to develop markets in depth. In manufacture and merchandising the nation accepted the limiting and almost static frontiers of social class rather than striking out on the broader path pointed by its political democracy.

Government financial policy encouraged the close *rentier* mentality rather than the expansive entrepreneurial spirit. Early in the Third Republic the government ceased to rely on tax revenue to meet its current budgetary needs and went in for borrowing, even in prosperous years. Frenchmen's fear of going into debt was not projected into the French government's habits: an instance of what André Siegfried calls the difference between private and public morality. The habit of saving was strong among the people. But the search for security and the reliance on government guaranties led chiefly to investment in French and foreign government securities rather than to investment in French industry. Foreign loans absorbed about 70 per cent of the capital subscribed in France in the decade before the war.[4]

The growth of population between the Franco-Prussian War and the first World War was almost imperceptible. The demographic decline was relative, not absolute: what a Scottish historian has called "a great and distressing historical event—the rapid decline of the proportion of Frenchmen to other Europeans."[5] The population increase was too small to dramatize the possibilities of an expanding domestic market or offer an obviously cheap labor supply. Almost alone of European countries, France did not send its sons to America in any appreciable numbers. From the poorest and most populous rural regions, such as Brittany, emigration flowed into the cities, especially Paris and its industrial suburbs. In other areas, such as the Lorraine iron and steel complex and the northern coal fields, especially after the turn of the century, manpower came from poorer and more crowded countries—Italy, Belgium, and Spain. French North Africans came into the foundries, chemical plants, and other unpleasant jobs.

The repression of the Commune and the flight of Communards abroad halted working class organization and decimated a generation of leadership. Yet organization soon resumed, guardedly at first, in Paris and then in the provinces. For a brief period, emphasis was on producers' coöperatives and mutual credit societies. By 1876 it was possible to

---

[4] Beau de Loménie, *Les responsibilités des dynasties bourgeoises* (Paris, 1943-1947), vol. 2, p. 333.

[5] D. W. Brogan, *The Development of Modern France* (New York, 1940), p. 418.

hold the first "national workers' congress" in France, bringing together representatives of unions and coöperatives; as yet there was no national organization. With the leaders keeping an eye out for possible police intervention, its tone was moderate.

One of the notes struck by the congress was that of a manual workers' exclusiveness which was to be a continuing theme of the unions:

All the systems of ideas, all the utopias for which the workers have been blamed have never come from them at all. They have all come from middle class people (bourgeois), no doubt well-intentioned, who have sought the remedies for our ills in their own ideas, burning the midnight oil instead of looking at our needs and at reality.[6]

In 1876 this "ouvriérisme," this affirmation of workers wanting to go it on their own without benefit of bourgeois intellectuals, was a counsel of moderation; later it was to be one of extremism.

Local unions were growing up again in all the cities of France. The first trades to organize successfully included the printers, coopers, silversmiths, bronzeworkers, carriage workers, saddlers, all still in an artisanal stage. They also included semi-industrialized trades like those of the hatters; the industrialized mining and textile industries; and the railroad workers. By 1881, there were 500 local unions, 150 in Paris alone, with some 60,000 members. The first national union was formed by the hatters in 1879; the second by the typographers two years later. In 1883 the miners, not in the vanguard of organization before, established a regional federation in the South.

FREEDOM OF ASSOCIATION

The unions were still in a twilight zone of tolerance. Unions in a single trade were hardly disturbed, but the authorities often banned gatherings of representatives from different trades. When the republicans finally came into control of the Republic after 1877, they responded to the three most insistent demands of the workers. They set up a system of universal free public secular education; they granted amnesty to the Communards; and in 1884[7] they voted the right of freedom of association. The 1884 law[8] obliged unions, like other associations, to register

---

[6] Fernand Pelloutier, *Histoire des bourses du travail* (Paris, 1901), p. 77. References are to the 1946 reprinting of this classic.

The French delegates, chiefly Proudhonists, at the first congress of the International in 1866 had pressed for, and almost carried, a resolution to exclude all but manual workers as delegates.

[7] The year in which France sent the United States the Statue of Liberty.

[8] French laws are referred to ordinarily by the date of their passage, rather than by the names of their legislative parents: e.g., law of March 21, 1884, rather than "the Waldeck-Rousseau law." The text of the law is in the appendix to Pelloutier, *Histoire des bourses du travail*, pp. 265-269.

their constitutions and by-laws and the names of their officers. For years revolutionary unions attacked these provisions as a police trap; many refused to register. "It puts us in the same situation as street walkers," complained one unionist in 1886. But by the late 1890's most unions had reconciled themselves to the forms of compliance.

The politicians who put through the law hoped the unions might develop along peaceful, nonrevolutionary and nonsocialist lines. Waldeck-Rousseau, one of the most capable political figures of the Third Republic, then Minister of the Interior, had been a sponsor of the law. Now he instructed the prefects[9] to help the unions get started—in the right direction:

The government and Parliament have not let themselves be frightened by the hypothetical peril of an anti-social federation of all the workers . . . The association of individuals along occupational lines is less an arm of combat than an instrument of material, moral and intellectual progress.

Help the unions to organize, he said, but "leave the initiative to the people concerned . . . A generous but imprudent zeal would only arouse suspicion."[10]

The law of 1884 recognized a state of fact: the unions existed. But difficulties in the exercise of freedom of association did not disappear with the legal recognition of the right. Employers had not manifested any great concern when the law was voted, but for two generations to come they made life difficult for union organizers. Blacklists, firing of unionists, lockouts, *agents provocateurs,* and spies were some of the familiar devices used. Efforts to add to the law some protection against arbitrary dismissal or discrimination in hiring had no success.

Company unions enjoyed a brief prominence. The first appeared in 1899 after a strike at the great Schneider-Creusot iron and steel works. Forming a national federation, the "yellow unions"[11] made claims of 200,000 members at their first convention in 1902. There one of the "yellow" leaders thanked the benefactors of the organization: "The

[9] For the text of his interesting instruction, see Waldeck-Rousseau, *Questions sociales,* (Paris, 1907), pp. 303-319.

The prefect is the representative of the central government in each department. Immediately responsible to the Minister of the Interior, he administers most affairs of the department. The elected council of each department plays a minor role.

"Département" cannot be translated either as state or county. The department is the next unit of government below the national level. There are 90 departments within the present boundaries of metropolitan France.

[10] *Ibid.,* p. 306.

[11] The name, which the company unionists themselves used, came from the yellow paper which the members of the Montceau-les-Mines company union pasted over its windows after strikers smashed all the panes. Georges Weill, *Histoire du mouvement social en France* (Paris, 1924), p. 425, n. 1.

money we need we have found . . . The donors are all good Frenchmen
and big industrialists."[12] Despite—or because of—this support, the
movement practically died out before 1914.

SOCIALISTS AND THE UNIONS

Another danger to the unions came not from their enemies but from
their declared friends, the Socialists. The warm but nebulous humanitarian socialist writing of the previous generation was succeeded by the
business of party organization. But the Socialists began splitting almost
as soon as they formed their first party. Clashes of personality and
shocks of doctrine produced four splits in 1880-1882, and five national
parties by the century's end. A generation of fratricidal combat was
ended only by the unification into a single party in 1905. Even that
party, although the best organized in France, was not as solid a party
of mass membership as a number of other European countries created.
It appeared, as Daniel Halévy said, that "socialist enthusiasm is of
French origin. But the institution of (socialist) parties is German and
Belgian."[13]

Each socialist group in the 1880's and 1890's naturally went to the
unions to get support for the one true socialism and its candidates for
office. Unions affiliated with parties; members of opposing parties split
off; new unions were formed on the basis of party affiliation or opposition; strikes were lost because of political splits in the unions.

The first party to establish itself in the unions was that of Jules
Guesde, the dour and domineering figure who was of all French socialist
leaders the closest to Karl Marx in program, temper, and personal ties.
At the national workers' congress of 1879, where socialist clubs as well
as unions were represented, the moderate unionists were swamped by
the Guesdist socialists.[14] For the first time a French workers' congress
went on record in favor of collective ownership and the class struggle.

The first nationwide federation of unions in different trades, the
National Federation of Trade Unions ("Fédération Nationale des Syndicats et Groupes Corporatifs"), was founded in 1886. It was almost
immediately captured by the Guesdist Socialists. The Federation and

---

[12] Jules Zirnheld, *Cinquante années de syndicalisme chrétien*, p. 144.

[13] Daniel Halévy, *Essais sur le mouvement ouvrier en France* (Paris, 1901), p. 253.

[14] For years the lines of differentiation between political party and trade union
organization were blurred. As late as 1899 unions were represented at the political
"Congress of Socialist Organizations." The word "socialist" had not yet become a
monopoly of the political party and the distinguishing word "unionist" ("syndicaliste")
had not yet become current. Many unions not committed to political action regarded
themselves as just as much bearers of the socialist tradition and hopes as the socialist
parties.

the Guesdist party held their annual conventions in the same city, one immediately after the other; many of the delegates were the same. To the Guesdists—most nearly the forefathers of present-day French Communists—the economic gains of unionism were secondary to the political conquest of the state; the trade unions were to be satellites of the party.

Control by a socialist party might have been endurable. What was unendurable was the competition of rival socialist parties for control of the struggling young unions. In self protection many unionists washed their hands of all socialist parties. The antisocialist current was strengthened when in the 1890's a considerable number of anarchists went into the unions.

THE BOURSES DU TRAVAIL

In most trades and industries national unions were being formed. But the heart of union life beat in the local union and in the local federation of trades known as Bourse du Travail. The first Bourse was set up in Paris in 1886. By the 1890's, the chief center of organizing activity and labor philosophy was generally the Bourse du Travail. It is best to use the French term, for it defies translation. The Bourse du Travail was a combination of a labor exchange (the literal meaning of the term), a workers' club and cultural center, and—increasingly—a central labor union. Seeking to direct placement, it brought together information on labor supply and demand and wage rates. In a period when men still traveled in search of work, it helped find the out-of-town unionist a job or gave him a modest cash grant to take him on to another town with better job opportunities. Its library, vocational training, and cultural courses enlarged the earning capacity and the mental horizon of workers.[15]

The competition between local or regional organization and national organization is a recurring feature of trade union development. In few countries did local organization attain the importance it had in France. The Bourses combined day-by-day economic services with the aims of "complete" emancipation of the workers. The unusual combination is best seen in the work of the chief organizer, theoretician, and historian of the Bourses. Fernand Pelloutier was originally a Guesdist Socialist. He turned his back on political action when the Guesdists refused to follow him and his friend Aristide Briand on the principle of the general strike. In 1895, at the age of 27, he became secretary of the National

---

[15] The range of Bourse activities was often even more extensive. Some Bourses carried on a neo-Malthusian propaganda for "procreation prudence" against the pressures of population on wages and employment.

Federation of Bourses du Travail, which fourteen of the Bourses had set up in 1892. The national committee of the Federation, of which he was secretary, was, as he said, "only a slow and imperfect correspondence bureau."[16] He himself was desperately ill and poor. But in his few tuberculosis-ravaged years he built the Bourses into the most important labor institution of the day, and deeply marked the methods and philosophy of union action.

He was never so preoccupied with his meticulous instructions on the housekeeping or placement work of the Bourses as to forget the "social revolution" which he, like most of the working class élite of the time, advocated. But he was never so enamored of utopia as to put aside the day's grubby work of keeping accounts or compiling statistics on the labor market.

Pelloutier was one of the rare spirits in French labor leadership who knew how to work for the future by creating in the present. The future, he was sure, belonged to the freely-federated societies of producers of which Proudhon and Bakunin had written. These he saw in the local unions and Bourses, whose numbers were growing steadily. He saw too the importance of shorter hours, minimum wages, old age security, and "all the demands which can—by improving, no matter how slightly, the immediate condition of the proletariat—liberate it from demoralizing worries about the day's bread."[17] It is easy for a workers' leader to stress the workers' claims. Pelloutier also stressed their obligations, as a class and as individuals, to themselves and to society. This was the more responsible side of the anarchism of the period. Workers had to "pursue more actively, more methodically, and more persistently the work of moral, administrative and technical education necessary to make viable a society of free men."

By the 1890's, for the first time, the unions were becoming truly free of the political parties. Pelloutier had no use for the collectivist political program which, "demanding no reflection, no study, offered an easy career to any ambitious mediocrity who had a ready tongue on the platform."[18] He expressed his scorn for the socialist politicians, whether parliamentary or revolutionary, as

the parliamentary doctors, who have taught that any social transformation is subordinated to the conquest of political power, the revolutionary doctors who have taught that no socialist effort is possible before the redeeming cataclysm.[19]

---

[16] Pelloutier, *Histoire des bourses du travail*, p. 245.
[17] *Ibid.*, p. 17.
[18] *Ibid.*, p. 96.
[19] *Ibid.*, pp. 247-248.

Candor obliged him, however, to say that the idea of federating the Bourses had an origin "more political than economic."[20] For it had come from some of the Paris Bourse members who wanted to offset the Guesdist-controlled National Federation of Labor Unions because they themselves belonged to a rival socialist party.

On principle he objected to government subsidies, which had enabled the Bourses to exist from the beginning. He himself was forced to take a job for a time with the Labor Bureau of the Ministry of Commerce to keep alive. For this, at his last Federation convention, Pelloutier, deathly ill, had to defend himself against suspicion and insinuation. A year later, in 1901, at the age of 32, working to the last from his sickbed, he died.

The Federation of Bourses had by then grown to 65 affiliated Bourses, numbering 782 dues-paying local unions. A few more Bourses were unaffiliated. There are no reliable figures for union membership. Government figures are subject to great caution, since many unions in this period refused to register. Total union membership probably passed the 100,000 mark in 1886; the 200,000 mark in 1890; 300,000 by the following year, and 400,000 the year after that; then grew more slowly to reach half a million by the close of the century. By 1905, it was 780,000; it reached its prewar peak of 1,064,000 in 1912.[21]

ORGANIZATION OF THE CGT

Two years after the founding of the Federation of Bourses, the National Federation of Trade Unions breathed its uneasy last. Its structure had left a gap between locals and over-all federation. It had never created any horizontal local or regional groupings, nor any vertical industrial groupings between it and the local unions which made up its membership. It performed no services for its affiliates, and it was obviously a tail to the Guesdist party kite. A split in its ranks on the question of the general strike finished its existence.

The organization which succeeded in creating a national trade union center was the General Confederation of Labor (*Confédération Générale du Travail*). The CGT, as it is commonly called, dates its founding back to 1895. Its first years, like those of national federations in many countries, were weak and uncertain. Its structure was a hodge-podge of directly affiliated locals, regional and national bodies. Weak in leader-

---

[20] *Ibid.,* pp. 113-114.

[21] Up to 1893, I have used the estimates made by John Bowditch III in his excellent Harvard University thesis, *A History of the General Confederation of Labor in France* (*to 1914*) (unpublished, 1948), p. 67. For later years I have used the figures reported by the government.

ship, bereft of financial support, its very existence was in doubt until it fused with the more vigorous Federation of Bourses. When that fusion was made firm in 1902, the CGT entered upon the half dozen or so years of its "heroic period," when it firmed up its structure, extended its organization, and defied employers and government with the gospel of revolutionary syndicalism. In the decade before the war the initials CGT caused right-thinking people in France and other lands to tremble for the future of the social order.

In structure the CGT was a "bicephalous creature." The section of national unions (the original CGT) and the section of Bourses (the old Federation of Bourses) were co-equal components of the confederation. Their executive bodies meeting together constituted the CGT executive. In conventions of the CGT the unit of representation was the local union, each with a single vote, regardless of its size.

The Bourses might cover an area from a small locality to a department (the unit of governmental administration) or a region. By 1912 there were some 153 Bourses, many of them small and out of contact with the movement as a whole. The 1912 convention instructed the Bourses to complete their metamorphosis or merger into department-wide federations ("unions départementales"); some shrank into the much less significant role of city centrals ("unions locales").[22] This move toward rationalization of the CGT's horizontal structure was also a move, only partly successful, toward making the department federations administrative units of the confederation rather than independent centers of power. Between 1902 and 1914, Bourses and department federations often played a more important role than national union headquarters or the CGT executive.

Both horizontal and vertical organization was permeated by the spirit of "federalism," that is, decentralization and autonomy at each echelon of union government. Disagreeable decisions of the CGT executive or even its convention, or of national union executives, were often ignored by the local units.

The chief focus of action continued to be the local trade union.[23] The typical local was small, with an average membership (in 1912) of 204. Most locals lived on modest dues and collected those irregularly. Few could afford paid officials. Of its dues income, the local gave small fractions to the Bourse, to the national union, and far less and more grudgingly to the confederation. Officials were generally subject to recall, and there were constant attempts to make them ineligible for reëlection lest

---

[22] For discussion of union structure, see *infra,* Chapter IX.
[23] The term "trade union" is used here synonymously with labor union, not in the sense of a unionism of narrowly economic preoccupations.

they lose the common touch. Nevertheless, as the years went on, something of a union bureaucracy did develop at various levels of the movement.

The classic issue of craft versus industrial unionism was debated for years. Many of the first vertical organizations were unions of crafts or specialized subcrafts. Gradually most joined larger units. At its 1906 convention, the class-conscious CGT voted to admit no more craft unions and to promote the amalgamation of its existing craft affiliates into industrial unions. Naturally the delimitation of industrial boundaries continued to give trouble. But the building trades, although retaining many craft locals, fused in a single national union. So did most of the metallurgical, metal, and foundry workers, together with many of the machinists. The various railway organizations amalgamated during the first World War.

INDUSTRIAL RELATIONS

The printers, hatters, and machinists were almost alone in having friendly society or benefit features by which to tie the member to his union. Few unions had any real collective bargaining relations. The printers, who maintained the only highly centralized national union, with national supervision of bargaining and strike aid, had the longest experience of trade agreements. For a generation before 1914, the trade's conditions were governed by collective agreements on a local or regional basis. From 1895 on, there was a national union-employer commission, which kept an eye on local agreements. Local joint arbitration committees functioned effectively, though of course not avoiding all strikes. In the mines of the north collective bargaining was introduced by the famous "Arras agreement," which covered the nation's chief coal basin. First signed in 1891, the agreement was renewed with modifications until 1914. The hatters had continuous bargaining relations with their employers; in this industry, with its long-established unionism, both employers and union were sensitive to the play of export considerations. There were a few regional agreements for the building trades, textiles, and for dock labor, plus scattered local agreements.

Employer organizations became much more active in the 1890's and early 1900's, in response to the growth of unions, the increase of strikes, and fears of increasing intervention by the state. The chief historian of French industrial relations remarks, "If the industrialists and merchants organized, it was above all to protect traditional laissez-faire and individualism."[24] The northern coal mine operators' association, signer of

---

[24] Pierre Laroque, *Les Rapports entre patrons et ouvriers* (Paris, 1938), p. 135.

the Arras agreement, was a rare exception in industry. Most employer associations were belligerently antiunion. Many developed mutual insurance funds to pay indemnities to members fighting strikes. Some fined members who happened to hire union officials.

With the tradition of concerning itself with everything, the government often intervened in labor disputes. In 1892 it enacted the first conciliation and arbitration law, providing for government aid in the use of voluntary procedures. For the next decade, these procedures were invoked, however, in no more than 30 per cent of the recorded conflicts in any one year. As strikes increased in number and severity, the law's feeble procedures, adapted only to local conflicts, were used less and less. Without regard for the law, government officials intervened frequently on an *ad hoc* basis. With varying acceptance by the parties, mayors, subprefects and prefects, ministers and premiers, all attempted at various times to mediate or arbitrate disputes.

The government's earliest arbitral award arose out of the Carmaux miners' strike in 1892. It was first settled by a three-man board whose neutral third member was named by the Minister of Public Works. A second stoppage a few months later was settled by the award of the Minister of the Interior. The most famous arbitration was that of the premier himself, Waldeck-Rousseau, distinguished exponent of laissez-faire. In the Le Creusot steel strike of 1898, his award called for the establishment of an employee representation plan.

Often the public officials got better terms for the workers than their economic strength would have won; however, many settlements were soon upset. On other occasions the government stepped in to protect law and order, or order alone. Sometimes, with *agents provocateurs,* it seems to have stirred disorder. From time to time it jailed strike leaders or the leaders of anticipated strikes.

A continuous form of government intervention was the practice of subsidies, usually municipal, to the Bourses du Travail, in the form of rent-free buildings and small yearly cash budgets. The justification for this assistance was the placement work by the Bourses for unorganized as well as organized workingmen. The corollary of subsidy was supervision. This union leaders resented—almost to the point of ending the subsidy system.[25] Conflicts were frequent. Occasionally the authorities would cut off subsidies or close down an unruly Bourse, as they did for several years at Paris.

Government leaders were naturally disappointed that neither freedom of association nor subventions produced more moderate unionism. They

[25] See Chapter III.

observed that the provocations to extremism were great. The response of government in terms of social legislation was not impressive. It enacted an employers' liability law for work accidents in 1898; a women's and children's ten-hour-day law in 1900; an eight-hour-day law for underground miners in 1905; and a one-day's-rest-in-seven law in 1906. A weak first attempt at old age pensions (1910) was stillborn because of CGT opposition. French social insurance and labor legislation could not compare with those of Lloyd George's England—or Bismarck's Reich.

The workingmen of France had had full manhood suffrage early. This was a conquest of the 1848 revolution, revoked after the June Days, restored by the "Caesarian equality" of the Second Empire, and retained after sharp debate by the Third Republic.[26] Since they did not have to struggle for political rights, and since the political power within the Republic shifted gradually toward the left, especially after the Dreyfus case, workers were the more keenly aware of the paucity of social legislation. Of what use, they often asked, was the universal suffrage invoked in politicians' Sunday speeches?

The advent of the Socialists on the parliamentary scene produced little social reform. They first became a parliamentary force by the elections of 1893, which returned about 50 deputies of various shades of socialism. The Socialists began to win municipal office, too, settling down in the mayor's chairs of industrial cities such as Lille and Limoges.

In 1899 the socialist deputy Alexandre Millerand entered the government of Waldeck-Rousseau, the first European Socialist to sit in a "bourgeois cabinet." French and European Socialists were to argue for many years whether Millerand's action was that of an honest man helping to save the Republic shaken by the Dreyfus Affair, or that of a political climber betraying his principles for a ministerial portfolio. (Millerand's own continued progress to the right later strengthened the argument of those who cried betrayal.)

Jaurès, greatest of French Socialists, defended Millerand's action. But—in one of the few real manifestations of international socialist discipline—Jaurès and his followers bowed to the condemnation of "Millerandism" by the Socialist (or Second) International in 1904.

---

[26] The blessings of universal suffrage applied chiefly to the Chamber of Deputies. The Senate was elected by a complicated indirect suffrage designed, and succes fully, to make it a more conservative body. In the districting for the Chamber, as method of electing the Senate, workers and city dwellers of all classes w advantaged as compared with peasants and small townspeople. That was, to the common lot of city folk in most democracies. It has continued to be the the constitution of the Fourth Republic. Women received the franchise o

From then until 1936, except for several of the war years, the Socialists took no part in France's government coalitions. Individual leaders left the Socialist Party to take office, most conspicuously Briand, Viviani, and Laval. It was Briand, eloquent advocate of the general strike and of antimilitarism in 1892, who broke the national railway strike in 1910 by mobilizing the railroad workers into the army.

The first generation of the Third Republic had called for consolidating the republican form of government in the face of a series of major crises. Then had come the work of separating Church and State. But even after that, in the prewar decade, there was little social legislation. The most ambitious governmental program—labor legislation, social insurance, and income tax—was announced by Clemenceau when he formed his "great ministry" in 1906. As it turned out, his biggest achievement in labor affairs was his fight against the unionization of government employees. Pioneer in political democracy and in socialist thinking, France failed to move toward social democracy.[27] A broad social legislation program did not come until the Popular Front in 1936. That was "a generation later: a generation too late."[28]

---

[27] Among the analyses of the complex reasons for this failure, several of the most thoughtful and sympathetic are to be found in David Thomson, *Democracy in France: The Third Republic*, 2d ed. (Oxford, 1952); D. W. Brogan, *France Under the Republic: The Development of Modern France (1870-1939)*; a number of essays in *Modern France: Problems of the Third and Fourth Republics*, ed. by Edward M. Earle (Princeton, 1951); and François Goguel, *La Politique des partis sous la troisième république* (Paris, 1946).

[28] Thomson, *Democracy in France*, p. 176. (My citations to Thomson's book are to the first edition, 1946.)

CHAPTER III

THE FORCE OF SYNDICALISM

Among the union activists . . . there is a feeling of violent opposition
to the bourgeoisie . . . They want passionately to be led by workers. Some
people try to show the origins of the labor movement of today in the
principles of anarchism; others on the contrary try to find the origins in
socialist concepts . . . In my opinion, the workers' movement does not
come directly out of either of these two sources . . . It is the result of long
union action, created far more by events than by individuals. This action,
far from moving forward regularly, is characterized by incoherences and
studded with contradictions. And it is that way because it is the product
not of action as a consequence of principles alone, but of life renewed and
modified each day.

—Victor Griffuelhes, general secretary
of the CGT, *L'Action Syndicaliste,*
1908.

Our working class, scarcely freed of its swaddling clothes, suffers
cruelly from these two national vices: the spirit of system, and the spirit
of division.

—Daniel Halévy, *Essais sur le
mouvement ouvrier en France,*
1901.

The French unionists of the 1890's and the early 1900's developed
the body of practices and philosophy which we know as "revolutionary
syndicalism," or simply as "syndicalism." Syndicalism has been discussed by a number of able writers.[1] It is analyzed again here to point
up the elements which emerge from a later vantage point as those
which have had the most enduring influence on the unions.

This chapter discusses the syndicalist outlook on life, its emphasis on
the class struggle, antiparliamentarianism, direct action, and the general
strike, and the relationship of the intellectual theorists to syndicalism.
It then examines the reasons why syndicalism took hold in France.
Finally the balance between reformists and revolutionaries before the
war is considered. For, even while revolutionary syndicalism was the
official doctrine of the CGT, reformist currents were important. If the
first World War had not come, if the war had not been so long and

---

[1] See bibliographical Appendix.

costly, if the Russian Revolution had not intervened, the reformist currents might have become the unions' mainstream.

THE SYNDICALIST OUTLOOK

Out of the common fund of socialist and anarchist thought, the syndicalists took the idea of the class war as the dominant characteristic of economic life and social development, as a fact to reiterate rather than a theory to propose. "The class struggle places the workers in revolt against all forms of capitalist exploitation and oppression, material and moral," was the reaffirmation of the 1906 CGT convention in its famous Charter of Amiens.[2] "In its day-to-day demands, the union movement seeks . . . the increase of workers' well-being by the achievement of immediate gains, such as the shortening of hours, the raising of wages, and so forth. This effort, however, is only one side of the work of the union movement. It prepares for the complete emancipation which can be achieved only by expropriating the capitalist class."

The syndicalists, again like the Marxists and other socialists, saw the government as merely an agency of the ruling class, a tool of the employers. For the remedy—and here they parted company with the socialists—they looked not to conquest of the power of the state and collective ownership of industry, but to a clean sweep of the state, along with capitalist enterprise and the wage system. To replace them, the syndicalists, in terms reminiscent of Proudhon and Bakunin, envisioned a society of decentralized free workshops, coördinated through local unions, Bourses, and—in some loose ill-defined way—the national unions and the General Confederation of Labor. Said the Charter of Amiens: "The trade union, which is today a fighting organization, will in the future be an organization for production and distribution and the basis of social reorganization."

The last thing to look for in syndicalism, however, is a blueprint of the future; it was a fighting dogma and not a utopian construction. "It is pleasant to debate *ad infinitum* about the best future system," was the ironic reflection of Victor Griffuelhes, CGT general secretary. "I shall wait to make up my mind until I return from the voyage on which I can see it for myself."[3]

The syndicalists came to battle with the socialists over the role of the political party. All parties, they said, were a fraud; parliament was a sink of jobbery, corruption, and compromise. The socialists were no better than the rest; perhaps worse. Claiming to represent labor, they diverted the workers from the real issues, and dropped their cause

---

[2] See Appendix B for full text.
[3] *L'Action syndicaliste* (Paris, 1908), p. 4.

after they had arrived through their votes. Party politics did not represent true working class action. Parties were made up of men of all classes and conditions; the socialist parties were led by professors, doctors, lawyers, and journalists. Not the indirect and occasional act of voting, and then trusting to political intermediaries whom they could not control, but only the workers' own action, could emancipate them.[4]

Since many workers nevertheless had their individual political preferences and affiliations, the only protection for the union itself was political neutrality. The CGT's founding convention wrote into its statutes: "The affiliates composing the General Confederation of Labor must keep themselves separate from all schools of political thought."[5] The confederation, however, continued to debate the issue of relations with the parties. In 1906, in the Charter of Amiens, it adopted the statement which it long continued to cite as authority:

As far as the individual member is concerned, therefore, the convention affirms his complete liberty to take part, outside of his union, in whatever forms of action correspond to his philosophical or political views. It merely asks him not to bring up in the union the opinions he holds outside it.

As for affiliated organizations, the convention declares that, since economic action must be directed at the employers if the union movement is to attain its full results, the unions should not concern themselves with the parties and sects[6] which, outside and parallel with the unions, may in their own free way strive for social transformation.

DIRECT ACTION AND THE GENERAL STRIKE

Direct action was the way to achieve immediate gains as well as ultimate social revolution. Direct action usually meant economic pressure on the employers. It might also mean pressure on government— as distinct from parliamentary maneuvers—for example, the rioting against private employment agencies which was followed by legislation against the agencies. As Pouget said:

If the improvement they demand is a matter of government action, the unions pursue their aim by mass pressures on the public authorities, not by trying to get favorably minded deputies into parliament. If the improvement sought must be wrested directly from the capitalist . . . their means are varied, although always following the principle of direct action. Depending on the situation, they use the strike, sabotage, the boycott, the union label.[7]

---

[4] Here, as in other places in the text, I have tried to sum up the ideas of participants in their own phrases, in the hope that the account will be clearer if there is a minimum of reminder phrases like "they said" and "they declared."

[5] Maxime Leroy, *La Coutume ouvrière* (Paris, 1913), vol. 1, p. 333.

[6] "Sects" was a reference to the anarchists, who could not quite be called a "party."

[7] Emile Pouget, *Le Syndicat* (Paris, n.d., 1905?), pp. 18-19.

The ultimate form of direct action was the general strike. On the day that all the workers folded their arms, the syndicalists felt, neither the employer class nor the state would prevail against them. Even the troops—if they did not fraternize with the strikers—would be powerless against the entire proletariat on strike.[8] The general strike would be necessarily short and decisive, probably violent. It was impossible to predict when and how it might come. Perhaps it would grow out of some minor walkout; perhaps a railroad strike would give the signal for the "final struggle."

Pelloutier had distinguished the general strike from insurrection. "All the bloody revolutions have benefited only agitators and the bourgeoisie," he said.[9] Later, more was heard of the insurrectionary general strike. But unionists used the term "general strike" loosely, to mean sometimes a single day's demonstration for limited ends (such as the May Day 1906 national strike for the eight-hour day), sometimes an industrywide strike in a single trade or industry, or a local general strike of all trades, and sometimes to mean the revolutionary general strike which the term now evokes.

Georges Sorel, the chief theoretician *after* the fact of revolutionary syndicalism, saw the general strike as one of the "social myths" by which men are moved to heroic action, like the early Christian myth of the speedy return of Christ. Having none of the responsibilities of the union leaders, he did not have to argue, as did many of them, that the general strike would be the most practical form of struggle. He could wave aside objections to the realization of the general strike. "It is the myth in its entirety which is alone important . . . No useful purpose is served in arguing about the incidents which may occur in the course of a social war."[10]

Direct action did not necessarily involve violence, though it often would, and unionists could not shrink from violence. They often preached action for action's sake—"the gymnastic of action," Pouget called it.[11] Less often did they preach violence for the sake of violence.

---

[8] Some syndicalists calculated how many meters of railroad trackage would have to be guarded per soldier if the whole army was devoted to protecting only the railroad system. This calculation proved again that the general strike could not fail.

[9] Quoted by Jules Guesde in Guesde, Hubert Lagardelle, and Edouard Vaillant, *Le Parti socialiste et la confédération du travail* (discussion at 1907 Socialist Party convention) (Paris, 1908), p. 38.

[10] *Reflections on Violence*, p. 144. This is the only work of Sorel's translated into English. The T. E. Hulme translation of 1914 has been reprinted (Glencoe, Illinois, 1950), with a fine critical introduction by Edward A. Shils. Citations are to that edition.

[11] Emile Pouget, "Les Résultats moraux du mouvement du premier Mai," *Mouvement socialiste*, no. 176, July 1906, pp. 278-279.

Considering the class tensions in France, the CGT was party to surprisingly little violence: very much less, for example, than in the United States during the same period. The vocabulary of the syndicalists, however, was charged with verbal violence, with the words of irreconcilable conflict, often with military metaphor. That is one of the "dangerous contradictions which revolutionaries run into," as Georges Duveau said of an earlier radical. "Even when they are basically gentle, like Raspail, they employ words which have an odor of powder, they create disquiet and animosities, and despite themselves they prepare the bloody shocks of counter-revolution."[12]

It was the syndicalist intellectuals, not the trade unionists, who made a cult of violence. Hubert Lagardelle told a convention of the Socialist Party:

Indirect, parliamentary, and legalistic action puts the will to sleep. Direct action stimulates the latent forces of the individual . . . and brings to the foreground the faculties of enthusiasm, the need of combat, the thirst for conquest, which lift him to the sublime.[13]

Sorel carried the antipolitical implications of syndicalism to their logical antidemocratic conclusion. "The idea of the general strike (constantly rejuvenated by the feelings aroused by proletarian violence) produces an entirely epic state of mind," he declared. That was a state of mind conducive "to bringing about a continued progress in methods of production . . . It is to violence that socialism owes those high ethical values by means of which it brings salvation to the modern world."[14]

More basic and longer enduring than the famous "myth of the general strike," was the related myth of class, of the proletariat as a homogeneous and separable force. Political socialism also nourished a myth of the working class as an entity, and as the source of virtue, wisdom, and the coming social transformation. Among the syndicalists this belief was both an inner conviction and a weapon against the socialists. Pelloutier remarked that the class struggle interested him more "as a means of preservation of the unions against the invasion of the petty bourgeois socialists" than as a dogma. For "the unions don't give a hoot for theory, and their empiricism . . . is worth at least all the systems in the world, which last as long and are as accurate as predictions in the almanac."[15]

Despite Pelloutier's professed contempt for systems (he was thinking of the systems of others), the trade unionists more and more made

---

[12] *Raspail* (Paris, 1948), p. 36.
[13] Guesde, Lagardelle, and Vaillant, *Le Parti socialiste,* p. 31.
[14] *Reflections on Violence,* pp. 277-278.
[15] *Histoire des bourses,* p. 242.

a dogma of the class struggle. They tended, in the illuminating phrase which Professor Perlman has applied to the intellectuals, to see labor as "an abstract mass in the grip of an abstract force."[16] They could not help observing, often with bitterness, the denials of class solidarity —the difference between the organized minority and the unorganized mass, the gap between the active few and the passive "egotistical" union majority, the conflicts of interest among different trades. Yet class remained the firmest reality to them and to most French workers.

Industrialists and financiers were no more patriotic in their daily doings than unionists. But they did not make a creed and a display of antipatriotism, as did the syndicalists. For more than a century after the revolution, into the Commune and later, a Jacobin nationalism had been part of the tradition of the left. Now it gave way to a spectacular antipatriotism. Pouget found that nothing was more absurd than a patriot without a patrimony.[17] "The proletarian cannot have any father-land. He cannot be a patriot," was Griffuelhes' assertion of a syndicalist and socialist commonplace. "It is easy to philosophize on the idea of the fatherland when one has just clipped a few coupons or signed the purchase deed for a chateau."[18]

As one war scare after another passed over the continent, the CGT resolved that "to any declaration of war, the workers must immediately respond with the revolutionary general strike."[19] It was sharply critical of the German and other unions which refused to put the general strike against war on the agenda of international trade union conferences. Impatiently it rejected their contention that this was a matter not for the unions but for the socialist parties.

The CGT was noisily antimilitarist. The army was not only a seat of reaction and a menace to the peace, but in its use against strikers the CGT saw the worst marks of the class state. Unions and Bourses attempted to keep in touch with conscripts, some sending them small cash allowances. They fed them literature inciting to disobedience, at the least the refusal to fire on striking workmen.

The syndicalists liked to assert that they were apolitical. They insisted on the primacy of "the economic" and of the relations of pro-duction over "the political." Their doctrine was, to be sure, antipolitical party and antiparliamentarian. But, rejecting the action of political parties, they simply preached their own forms of political action, notably

---

[16] Selig Perlman, *A Theory of the Labor Movement* (New York, 1928), p. vii and *passim*.

[17] *Les Bases du syndicalisme*, p. 15, Leroy, *La Coutume ouvrière*, vol. 2, p. 824.

[18] *L'Action syndicaliste*, p. 42.

[19] Extraordinary conference of Bourses and national unions, *L'Humanité*, October 2, 1911, Leroy, vol. 2, p. 808.

the general strike, and their own political objectives: the fight against militarism and war, and the complete transformation of the social order.

The Socialist Party had to reconcile itself as best it could to these attitudes of the organization to which belonged many of its members, voters and potential voters. It swallowed the notion of the general strike.[20] Faced with the Charter of Amiens' declaration of political neutrality, the Socialist convention of the same year, after lengthy and somewhat resentful debate, could only conclude hopefully, but in the face of the facts: "The fundamental agreement between the political action and the economic action of the proletariat will necessarily lead to a free coöperation between the two organizations without confusion or suspicion."[21]

One may agree with Elie Halévy that revolutionary syndicalism was "a doctrine which really opens a new era in the history of socialism and which lacked only a prophet of the stature of Karl Marx to be appreciated as it deserved."[22] Or one may dismiss it with Schumpeter as a doctrine that, "unlike Marxism or Fabianism, cannot be espoused by anyone afflicted by any trace of economic or sociological training. There is no rationale for it."[23] In any event, it owed comparatively little to the intellectuals who are usually the theorizers and rationalizers. It was the product of working trade union organizers, many of them largely self-taught, skilled mechanics or artisans. Of those who made an essential contribution to its development the only one who may be branded an intellectual by origin was Pelloutier, who was a young journalist before becoming a full-time union official.

Most of the syndicalist intellectuals took no part at all in union activities, so they had time to write full-length books. But, as Sorel himself explicitly stated, without undue modesty, they simply took over the ideas of the workers' leaders.[24] Nor did Sorel and company exert

---

[20] Jaurès made some sensible and penetrating observations on the conditions of its possible use. "Grève Générale et Révolution," *Etudes socialistes* (Paris, 1902), pp. 97-121.

[21] Guesde, Lagardelle, and Vaillant, *Le Parti socialiste*, p. 5.

[22] *L'Ere des tyrannies: études sur le socialisme et la guerre* (Paris, 1938), p. 177. Elie Halévy did not endorse the doctrine to whose importance he pointed.

[23] *Capitalism, Socialism and Democracy*, 2d ed. (New York, 1947), p. 339.

[24] "We have invented nothing. . . We have limited ourselves to defining the historical bearing of the notion of the general strike. . . It would be impossible for us to exercise any direct influence on such a work of formation." *Reflections on Violence*, p. 61.

Sorel's "paternity" of syndicalist doctrine is put in its proper light by Lewis L. Lorwin, *Syndicalism in France*, 2d ed. (New York, 1914), pp. 155-158. See also Scott H. Lytle, "Georges Sorel: Apostle of Fanaticism," in *Modern France*, pp. 283-287. Cf. the personal reminiscences of Maxime Leroy about Griffuelhes: "He did not know Sorel, having only vaguely heard of him in conversations. 'I read Alexander Dumas,' he liked to say." "Griffuelhes et Merrheim," *L'Homme réel*, no. 40, April, 1937, p. 3.

much influence on the unions. It was not union leaders who would speak of the "myth" of the general strike. A myth announced as a myth loses its power to move.

Outside the trade unions, books circulate more easily than pamphlets; full expositions appeal more than scattered strike stories or convention proceedings; writers read other writers. It is by Sorel and his followers that the syndicalist idea became best known, especially abroad.

WHY SYNDICALISM TOOK HOLD IN FRANCE

One of the interesting problems of labor history is why the syndicalist philosophy took hold where it did. In attenuated form it had some vogue in England as Guild Socialism; it had some brief success in Norway; it was one of the strands in the American Industrial Workers of the World (IWW). But only in France, Italy, and Spain were there strong syndicalist movements, and only in France was it the prevailing doctrine of an important trade union movement. To be sure, the revolutionary syndicalist current was matched by a reformist current of more or less equal strength in the CGT before the war. But before considering the reformists, we should examine the reasons for the force of revolutionary syndicalism.

The explanation is not in any one factor. American employers were as anti-union as those of France and far more ready for violence. Homestead and Ludlow were bloodier than the massacres of Fourmies and Villeneuve, without turning unionism into syndicalist channels. The American courts put obstacles in the way of union activity and social legislation unknown to French workers. Lack of geographical and social mobility deepened class conflict in France, but in the United States the western IWW's were the most mobile type of frontier workers. British and American workers suffered from periodic crises of unemployment unmatched in France. The workers of Germany and Austria knew a worse social inferiority than the French, and it was compounded by political disabilities, yet few of them became syndicalists. It was the complex of economic development, social structure, employer attitudes, political factors, personalities, and union structure in France which produced syndicalism.

The slow rate of economic development, the continued prevalence of small workshops, the lack of entrepreneurial daring gave French workers the feeling that they had little to expect from gradual processes. Such were their employers and such workers' expectations from the state of the economy, that revolutionary change was easier for many to envisage than day-by-day gains in their conditions of life and work. A revolutionary solution held greater attractions and risked less than in countries where capitalism was more dynamic. Even as they expressed their alarm over the spread of the Taylor system and the speed-up in France, CGT leaders wished they could exchange their own unenterprising anti-union employers for the no less anti-union but more enterprising employers of the United States. With such employers,[25] they thought, French unionism would itself take on greater force.

Employer attitudes—harsh and arbitrary shop regulations (in the larger plants), social barriers but few manifestations of social responsibility—enforced the counsel of impatience among workers. They saw little chance of improvement through either collective negotiation or personal advancement in the industrial and social hierarchy. The only way out, to many socially conscious and articulate workers, lay in a new social order.

Social inequality was as provoking as economic injustice. Citizens of a country which has not passed through a feudal age cannot easily imagine how long its heritage conditions social attitudes. Working class leaders who had mastered both skilled trades and books through their own efforts found social inferiority particularly galling.

The quality of "ouvriérisme," an attitude of working class self-sufficiency, an "of, by and for the proletariat" spirit, is still strong in France. Defensive, imperialistic, romantic—call it what one will—this spirit led to, and found justification in, the syndicalist philosophy, in which the workers alone, through their unions, would remake the world. With this sort of workers' imperialism, however, the élite of the syndicalist movement felt a genuine sense of responsibility to develop the knowledge and skills with which the middle class had acquired its position. Some unionists might be content simply to "consult their biceps before speaking their minds," as a hatter complained.[26] But men like Pelloutier and Alphonse Merrheim stressed the importance of the workers' self-education and self-discipline.

A century of revolutions made the revolutionary promise and the "half-revolutionary"[27] method of syndicalism plausible. One did not take the regime for granted in a country which had had fifteen different regimes—and no peaceful constitutional revision—since 1789, which during the nineteenth century had lived under two empires, two monarchies, and two republics. A revolution seemed an almost normal way to effect political and social change. The June Days and the Commune were bloody enough to call for revenge—but not bloody enough to inhibit all thought of violent revolution.

---

[25] See for example, Emile Pouget, *L'Organisation du surmenage, le système Taylor* (Paris, 1914); also Victor Griffuelhes in *Le Mouvement socialiste*, 1910, cited by Dolléans, vol. 2, p. 128.

[26] Cited by Jean Vial, *La Coutume chapelière* (Paris, 1941), p. 164.

[27] The adjective is that of Clapham, *Economic Development of France and Germany, 1815-1914*, p. 275.

Revolution was the opium of the working people for whom religion had no appeal. The greatest of French socialists lamented "the quasi-mystic awaiting of a liberating catastrophe which allows people to avoid clarifying their thinking or determining their goal." [28]

Syndicalism reflected the failure to develop either organic or working relationships, a division of labor, between the socialist parties and the unions. After all the party fragmentation and the sectarian squabbles in the unions, the debates of "Millerandism," and the meager legislative results of socialist parliamentary activity, relations between unions and political socialism were worse than in any other European nation.

Perhaps if the national unity pact among the socialist parties in 1899, at the time the CGT was first building its organization, had endured, working relationships with the unions might yet have been developed. By the time the socialists achieved a united party in 1905, the CGT's attitude was hardened. In part because of that very hostility of the unions, the socialists, even after their unification, could not attract the CGT by strength in organization and in legislation. Nor were the socialist parties of the Third Republic endeared to the workers by government persecution, as they were in Italy and Germany.

The socialist leaders were conspicuously middle class intellectuals and professional people. "The most substantial difference between syndicalism and political socialism, apart from tactics," Robert Michels observed, "is to be found in a difference in the leaders of the respective tendencies. . . . The advocates of syndicalism infer, by a bold logical leap, that the policy of the leaders of working class origin must necessarily coincide with the policy of the proletariat." [29] A certain number of renegades from the ruling class could be a source of strength. But there was something wrong, workers felt, when more than a generation of socialist party activity produced only one national leader who was a worker. [30]

The coming of many anarchist workers into the unions in the 1890's threw an added weight in the balance against the socialists. In Czarist Russia anarchists might continue to rely on "propaganda of the deed" (bomb throwing), but in the French Republic they soon gave it up, after a few spectacular outrages and the inevitable repression. Overcoming their repugnance for organizations with regular officers and

[28] Jean Jaurès, *Etudes socialistes*, p. lii.
[29] *Political Parties*, trans. by E. & C. Paul, 1915 (reprinted Glencoe, Ill., 1949), p. 298.
[30] That one was the printer Jean Allemane, leader of the Allemanist Socialists. He was to be the only major Socialist Party leader in the Third Republic who was a working man. There were of course trade unionists active in socialist politics in lesser leadership capacities.

majority votes, the anarchists entered the new unions. They supplied a number of the leaders of the Federation of Bourses and the CGT. The anarchists carried with them their violent contempt for socialist politics. Often, Daniel Halévy observed, they joined with conservatively minded workers to ridicule socialist deputies: "Those jokers are just like all the rest. Let's run our own affairs."[31]

Anarchism as a conscious current of ideas could not have been so strong had it not fed into a stream of antigovernmental feeling. Frequent dependence on the government did not diminish this antigovernmental attitude, any more than it diminished distrust of the government by farmers or industrialists seeking tariffs or subsidies. The ambivalence of government attitudes helped fortify the antigovernmentalism of the syndicalists. The government, like any government, was not consistent. Now it was granting subsidies to the Bourses or trying to mitigate employer intransigence in a strike. Then it was cracking down on an unruly Bourse, or sending troops against strikers, refusing its own employees the right to organize, or pigeonholing social legislation. So the government's direct help to the unions left its beneficiaries resentful rather than grateful.

The unionists never quite resolved the question of government subventions to the Bourses. They were suspicious and defensive about the possibilities of "domestication." They might talk about their "principle of taking the money where it is;"[32] they might distinguish a subsidy voted by parliament as "more moral and surer than one obtained from the municipality or departmental council," since "the latter requires presenting requests and the signature of the Prefect and the Minister of the Interior."[33] But the Bourses were no longer the promising new idea they had been when a Paris municipal subsidy made possible the establishment of the first Bourse. They were now labor's own institutions, taking an active part in strikes and antimilitarist agitation.

Repeated convention resolutions evaded the issue with the characteristic solution of a "formula." In 1906, at Amiens, after having adopted the syndicalist charter of independence, the Bourses resolved to create reserve funds towards "the hour when the workers' class consciousness will be strong enough and will have decided to do without subsidies."[34] But in 1910, 103 Bourses were receiving 355,000

---

[31] *Essais sur le mouvement ouvrier en France* (Paris, 1901), p. 283.

[32] So the Bourse of Arles described its request to the municipal and departmental councils for a subsidy enabling it to hold an agricultural workers convention. J.-B. Séverac, "Le quatrième congrès de la Fédération des Travailleurs Agricoles du Midi," *Mouvement socialiste*, no. 184, March 1907, p. 267.

[33] Georges Yvetot, "La Deuxième conférence des bourses du travail," *Mouvement socialiste*, No. 186, May 1907, p. 443, quoting Briat.

[34] *Ibid.*, p. 446.

francs of municipal subventions and 52,000 francs from the departments, plus free rent and maintenance in many public buildings.[35]
Neither subtle formulas nor extremist doctrine relieved syndicalist
leaders of the consequences of dependance on the authorities they defied.

NATIONAL CHARACTER

National character we take not as meaning "race" or "blood" or
mysterious imperatives whispering from ancestral caves, but the combination of culture, habits, and expectations of behavior formed by
education and traditions. National or group psychology is, to be sure,
always a bundle of contradictions. Frenchmen are "emotional" and
"impulsive;" Frenchmen are "practical" and "logical." They are
"zealots;" they are "skeptics." And so on, with considerable truth and
even relevance. Regions, too, have their own spirit, as do certain trades
and crafts. The psychology of nations and groups, moreover, changes
with time and history and new environment. Ideally one would need
to make place in any discussion for these and other variables. The
subject of national character degenerates easily into vapid nonsense or
pernicious chauvinism and racism.[36] Historical differences, however,
do exist; they are reflected in something like national behavior patterns;
they influence social movements.

French unionists themselves lay the heaviest stress on national
characteristics. Griffuelhes wrote of the French working class:

It has all the defects which characterize the Latin: the lack of follow-
through and tenacity in its action, which is made up of passing waves of
wrath, which a little nothing arouses and a little nothing appeases. It has
little endurance, not that it is incapable of endurance, but because it attaches
more importance to the effort of an hour or a day. For that effort it gives
itself completely. Its action is like fireworks which explode in brilliant colored
clusters and leave traces only in memory and regrets. Then if the effort is
successful and brings results, everyone notes it, not dreaming that to maintain
it action is still necessary.[37]

Individualism and egalitarianism are characteristics of the nation's
democracy which were particularly strong in the prewar CGT mem-

[35] J.-B. Séverac, *Le Mouvement syndical*, vol. 7 of *Encyclopédie socialiste, syndicale
et coöpérative de l'internationale ouvrière*, ed. by Compère-Morel (Paris, 1913), pp.
150-154.

[36] It is of interest, even to those disturbed by explanations in ethnic terms, that
syndicalism acquired a real hold only in Latin countries, and that in France its hold
was weakest in several of the least Latin regions, the north and northeast. The success
of syndicalism in Norway was of the briefest duration. The syndicalist strength, it will
also be seen, was restricted to traditionally Catholic countries. It was slight in the
Protestant countries, almost all of which (Germany is the great exception) have had
functioning democratic institutions.

[37] Victor Griffuelhes, *Voyage révolutionnaire* (Paris, n.d.-1910?), p. 7.

bership. That membership was to a high degree made up of skilled workers in small and middle-sized shops rather than one of mass operatives in heavy industry. That was in particular the character of the Paris membership, which made up perhaps a third of the entire organization, and of the building trades, the largest national union of the CGT. The important metal trades union had its members chiefly in the smaller fabricating establishments rather than in the big metallurgical mills.[38] The workers subjected to a real factory discipline in the great iron and steel mills of Lorraine were hardly touched as yet by union organization. On the other hand, the organized miners and particularly the textile factory operatives of the north were not revolutionary syndicalist but reformist in orientation.

Individualism and egalitarianism have their negative sides. Since the struggles against the double absolutism of king and church, as André Siegfried says, Frenchmen are apt to consider all authority as tyrannical, so that "liberty is not a constructive concept."[39] Distrust of government was elevated to a principle of politics. In their behavior as unionists, Frenchmen reflected this civic attitude. Distrust of union government and union officialdom found its doctrinal base in syndicalism. In practice, decentralization went even beyond the rules of union constitutions. The unionists showed a continuing skepticism, often hostility, toward their own officials and central organs. "At Lyon we are paid to be suspicious of union leaders," said a delegate attacking Pelloutier at the 1900 convention of the Federation of Bourses.[40]

National character was invoked to explain the reluctance to pay dues. "Our impulsive and rebellious temperament does not lend itself to high dues," affirmed the committee of organization for the CGT convention of 1902.[41]

The fondness for general ideas is a national quality manifested in

---

[38] Cf. John Bowditch, "The Concept of Elan Vital: a Rationalization of Weakness," in *Modern France, Problems of the Third and Fourth Republics,* ed. by E. M. Earle (Princeton, 1951), pp. 36-37.

[39] "Approaches to an Understanding of Modern France," *Modern France,* p. 10.

[40] Maurice Pelloutier, *Fernand Pelloutier: Sa vie—son oeuvre, 1867-1901* (Paris, 1911), p. 115.

[41] Leroy, *La Coutume ouvrière,* vol. 1, p. 214. The committee went on to say, "If we are ready for painful sacrifices of another nature, we have not yet learned of the enormous advantages which would come from the power of union treasuries fed by higher dues."

Leroy finds that the low dues doctrine was first enunciated at the CGT convention of 1896. The system of high dues, it was there argued, was to be condemned "because it maintains in the minds of most of the union members a spirit of egoism which leads them to repulse if not to hate the comrade who for any reason does not pay his dues." *Ibid.,* vol. 1, p. 213. The convention, nevertheless, refused to follow one anarchist delegate who, carrying the doctrine to its ultimate conclusion, had organized a union without any dues; it refused to admit this union.

French unionism. To be sure, Griffuelhes could emphasize that working class action "has not been determined by any formulas or theoretical affirmations . . . It has consisted simply of a series of daily efforts, attached to the efforts of the day before not by rigorous continuity but only by the environment and the state of mind of the working class."[42] But that environment included, and that state of mind demanded a general verbalized framework, a system of belief such as syndicalism offered. "It is a strange taste, but real; no matter how miserable he may be, no matter how degraded by alcohol, the European worker remains sensitive to the seduction of an absolute formula," said one of the most acute and sympathetic observers of the period.[43] This "absolute formula" might be the vision of an ideal society; it might be merely the sonority of a revolutionary phrase. In any event the general idea itself becomes a force working in the same direction as the conditions which created it.

Most important, syndicalism was a philosophy which grew out of, and corresponded to the state of the unions themselves. The unions were essentially organized from the ground up rather than from the top down, by local action, by workers in the trade, or by the Bourse du Travail, rather than by national unions. Organizations loose in structure and discipline fostered a philosophy of "federalism" or decentralized administration. A minority unionism found it easy to stress the role of active devoted minorities rather than large, passive memberships. The keepers of meager treasuries found it congenial to despise the fat bank accounts and insurance reserves which would "paralyze the will to action." Pouget rejoiced that the French unionists were not interested in the "mirage of mutual benefit activities."[44] A small and fluctuating membership and the difficulties of many local strikes encouraged the vision of sudden victory through the general strike. That would depend less on organization and funds than on one vast "surge of class consciousness" led by a militant élite.

Jules Guesde might sneer at the revolutionary syndicalists: "Your unionism is very special. It is distinguished from unionism in other countries by the fact that it includes so few unionists."[45] No doubt he was bitter, because the syndicalists rejected his political tutelage. Griffuelhes serenely declared:

The French unions do not have any of those strong treasuries whose fullness is so proudly proclaimed by numerous foreign unions, especially

---

[42] *L'Action syndicaliste,* p. 8.

[43] Daniel Halévy, *Essais sur le mouvement ouvrier en France,* p. 109.

[44] Emile Pouget, *La Confédération générale du travail* (Paris, 1908), p. 9.

[45] Guesde, Lagardelle and Vaillant, *Le Parti socialiste et la confédération du travail,* p. 42.

those of Germany and England. To the millions of francs of the employers, the French unions do not oppose the painfully amassed sous of the proletariat, for they know that on this terrain the struggle is far too unequal. They make up for the lack of big treasuries by enthusiasm, energy, the sense of sacrifice, and the higher sense of struggle.[46]

The syndicalist rationalization of weakness was paralleled by the military theory developed at the other end of the French social scale. Aristocratic and conservative officers argued that in a war the disparities between French and German manpower and industrial strength would be more than compensated for by the French character, the will to fight, and the "spirit of the offensive."[47]

REFORMISTS AND REVOLUTIONARIES

The zealots, as Brogan says, are as characteristic of French politics as the ironically skeptical majority.[48] Two decades' acceptance of revolutionary syndicalism as official CGT philosophy and the heritage of syndicalist behavior in French unionism ever since should not hide the importance of other opinions. Revolutionary syndicalism was the belief of a small majority, if majority it was, among CGT members. The CGT itself was a minority of all organized French workers, who, according to government figures, numbered 1,026,000 in 1914. The CGT then claimed some 600,000, but had fewer.[49] The organized were a fraction of the six million industrial workers in France.

The reformists in the prewar CGT were certainly almost as numerous as the revolutionaries, perhaps even more numerous, and their outlook was spreading among syndicalists in responsible union positions. They believed in the possibilities of collective bargaining and legislation, in dealing with employers and government. Some believed in the unions' working directly with the Socialist Party. Many opposed the CGT's antimilitarism. Some opposed the notion of the general strike.

A number of the most solid affiliates of the CGT were predominantly reformist: printers, textile workers, railroad workers, miners. The

---

[46] Victor Griffuelhes, "Les Grèves et le Syndicalisme Français," *Le Mouvement socialiste*, No. 172, March 15, 1906, pp. 254-255. In concluding his article, however, Griffuelhes suddenly remarks that if the French unions had the financial resources of the German or English organizations, the strike results he has been discussing would have been even better.

[47] John Bowditch, "The Concept of Elan Vital: a Rationalization of Weakness," *Modern France*, pp. 32-43; Brogan, *France under the Republic*, p. 422, note 1, pp. 468-469.

[48] Brogan, p. 427.

[49] Three hundred thousand, said Georges Dumoulin, "Les Syndicalistes français et la guerre," (1918) reprinted as Annex XV to Alfred Rosmer, *Le Mouvement ouvrier pendant la guerre: de l'Union Sacrée à Zimmerwald* (Paris, 1936), p. 532. At the convention of 1920, Dumoulin gave 350,000 as the prewar membership, CGT, *XVᵉ congrès confédéral, Orléans, 1920*, p. 180.

printers and hatters had collective bargaining and benefit fund experience. The textile workers of the North had close relationships with the well-established Socialist Party organization in that region of Guesdist tradition. The railroad workers and miners looked to the government for legislation on safety and hours. It is not true, however, as is sometimes stated, that the revolutionary syndicalist strength lay only in the smaller and weaker unions. The building trades, biggest union in the CGT, the maritime workers, and the metal workers were among the predominantly revolutionary unions.

The structure of the CGT gave some added weight to the revolutionary syndicalists. In conventions, the voting system carried federalism to its ultimate. Each local union had one vote whether its membership was twenty or two hundred or two thousand. Not all the small locals, however, were revolutionary or vice versa.

Within each union, whatever its majority, there was a minority of a differing opinion. What is most important, and most difficult to know, is the depth to which the differing philosophies had penetrated, both among their nominal adherents and among the unorganized. (The events of August 1914 were to give some indication of this.) The reiterated resolutions calling for the general strike and other articles of syndicalist faith are not to be taken at face value. Certainly some of the men who voted for these resolutions were simply being as militant —in the French scene that meant revolutionary—as the next fellow. They were responding to expectation and bowing to a usage which called for "a revolutionary motion at the end of a labor convention, like a stretto and a forte at the end of a piece of Italian music."[50]

Why then was—and is—revolutionary syndicalism spoken of as synonomous with the old CGT? That was the official doctrine of the confederation, soon given the sanction of tradition. The revolutionaries controlled the national CGT offices for the most part. These were positions from which the affiliated unions' action could not be controlled, but from which doctrine could be enunciated.

Reformist unionism was to be seen, writ larger, in other lands; syndicalism was the doctrine original to France. It was the more forceful, ostensibly the more "complete" and self-sufficing doctrine. Its exponents, union leaders, and especially intellectuals, were more articulate, more vociferous than the reformists. The reformists were occupied more with union business than with union doctrine. They did not agree among themselves on all issues, notably on relations with the Socialist Party.

Extremism is by its nature shriller than reformism. Perhaps the

---

[50] Daniel Halévy, *Essais sur le mouvement ouvrier en France*, p. 81.

narrow majority of syndicalism within the CGT made it even shriller. Is there a Gresham's law of intellectual currency? The alarmed government and employers of France, the press and right-thinking citizens, gave prominence to the revolutionary doctrine rather than to the reformist (without doing much to encourage the latter). Rumors of impending war made the antimilitarist declarations of the syndicalists and the idea of a general strike tying up mobilization all the more dramatic.

Paris gave the revolutionaries added importance. There they had much of their strength. The typographers of Paris, for example, were the one section of that union that rejected reformism.

In the half dozen years before the war, the CGT went through an inner crisis, of which the conflict between reformists and revolutionaries was one element. The perennial question of government subsidies was another, which summed up the contradictions between speech and action. The lack of financial independence poisoned other relationships; government subsidies fed suspicions. A wealthy revolutionary sympathizer secretly furnished funds for a national CGT headquarters building. The personal squabble which caused Griffuelhes angrily to resign as general secretary (1909) was related to the mysteries of this financing operation.

The revolutionary syndicalist current was receding in the few years just before the war. The optimistic revolutionary expectancy characteristic of the growing European workers' movements, socialist and trade union, was high. But the notion of the imminence and success of the general strike could not be forever maintained. There was no unlimited or serious general strike in France in the period of revolutionary syndicalist ascendancy. The nearest approach, the railway strike of 1910, was easily smashed. May Day 1906 was a 24-hour strike for the 8-hour day, and a failure. Many of the trades were looking to the government for special protective laws. A union bureaucracy was developing with vested interests in the present, not in the social revolution.

The syndicalist leaders, while still unwilling to tie themselves to the parliamentary Socialist Party on their right, showed increasing impatience with the extremists on their left. Pierre Monatte declared:

I do not know which, politics or insurrectionalism, has done more harm not only to the labor movement but also to the true revolutionary spirit. Both turn people away from union action. There will be a true revolutionary situation only when we set up strong economic organizations in our own country and when we have reëstablished the old International in Europe.[51]

---

[51] "La C.G.T. a-t-elle rectifié son tir?" *Vie ouvrière*, vol. 5, no. 93, August 5, 1913, pp. 137-138.

In 1913 the conference of Bourses and national unions refused to call a general strike against longer military service. In the fight against the three-year military service bill, the CGT coöperated with the Socialist Party for the first time.

Stung by criticism of the anarchists, some of the leading syndicalists, including Léon Jouhaux, CGT general secretary from 1909 on, issued a declaration of principles in 1913 which presaged the change that might have come with another decade of peace:

We strongly reaffirm our right, in accord with the whole of organized labor, to modify our forms of recruitment and of propaganda in line with the modifications introduced in the domain of industry by our adversaries. In our opinion, a movement which failed to take account of the transformations going on about it and froze in a fixed attitude would be a movement without life, without influence, without future.[52]

The contradictions between theory and practice were sharpening. In July 1914 the CGT polled its constituent bodies to determine the agenda for the convention scheduled for that year. There were twice as many votes for discussion of the shorter work day and the "English weekend" as for antimilitarism.[53] In a matter of days the war turned both into academic questions.

---

[52] *La Bataille syndicaliste,* August 27, 1913, reprinted in *Le Mouvement socialiste,* vol. 34, No. 253-254, July-August, 1913, pp. 126-129.
[53] Paul Louis, *Histoire du mouvement syndical en France* (Paris, 1947-1948), vol. I, p. 281.

CHAPTER IV

WORLD WAR AND LABOR SCHISM (1914-1930)

The decisions of the CGT conventions on the attitude of the working class in case of war become effective from the moment when war is declared. . . . If it occurs, the declaration of war must be, for each worker, the signal for immediate cessation of work. . . . To any declaration of war, the workers must, without delay, respond with the revolutionary general strike.

—Resolution of special conference of Bourses du Travail and national unions of the CGT, October 1, 1911.

Women who weep at this moment, we have done all we could to spare you this sorrow. Alas, today we can only deplore the accomplished fact. Could we have asked a greater sacrifice of our comrades? Cost us what it may, we reply: No.

—Manifesto of the CGT, August 2, 1914.

The war shattered overnight the ideological structure the CGT had built up since the 1890's. In the first hours of mobilization, anti-militarism, internationalism, the class struggle, the defiance of government, and the disdain of political parties disappeared. The only demonstrations were not of resistance to mobilization but of grief at the assassination of the well-loved socialist tribune, Jean Jaurès.

In a deeply emotional speech at Jaurès' funeral, Léon Jouhaux, the young general secretary of the CGT, declared that in their ancestral memories Frenchmen would find the strength to meet the crisis. "In the name of those who are going off to war—and among whom I am one—I declare that it is not hate of the German people that moves us toward the field of battle, but hate of German imperialism." Amidst the applause and tears that followed Jouhaux's peroration, the voice of a senator, a bitter enemy of the CGT, was heard: "And these are the men whom we wished to throw into jail!"[1]

Could the CGT have done anything to stop the war? Certainly not, even had it been stronger, in France alone. Could the Socialist International? It was far too weak. But the feeling of responsibility was long to haunt them. By the end of July, when the French labor leaders and the international socialist leaders began making frantic but ineffectual moves, even the diplomats and rulers of the great powers were no longer in control of the chain reaction mounting since the Austrian ultimatum to Serbia.

The revolutionary syndicalist view of the world and the kindred international socialist concept were based upon self-deception as to the weaknesses of capitalism and of national patriotism. They were part of the optimism of the age. Labor leaders and socialists had nourished that optimism in many meetings of the like-minded. They had taken for granted their own slogans about the primacy of the class struggle and the international solidarity of labor. They had been deceived by the numbers of socialist votes in elections and socialist deputies in the parliaments of Germany and France.[2]

The Socialist International and the even looser trade union international had no plans for international action against mobilization or war, no central authority by which to carry out the warnings to government or the promises to humanity. French Socialists, led by Jaurès, had for years tried in vain to persuade the Socialist International to endorse the international general strike as one answer to the threat of war. On the agenda for the International Socialist Congress scheduled for August 1914 once again was the French proposal that: "Among all the means employed to forestall and prevent war . . . the Congress considers as particularly effective the workers' general strike simultaneously and internationally organized in the countries involved . . ." The chief opposition had come from the German Social Democrats, domi-

---

[1] *La Bataille syndicaliste,* August 5, 1914, quoted by Alfred Rosmer, *Le Mouvement ouvrier pendant la guerre: de l'Union Sacrée à Zimmerwald* (Paris, 1936), p. 118. For the CGT's great reversal, see also Dolléans, vol. 2, pp. 206-226; Montreuil, pp. 311-316; Brogan, pp. 527-530; David J. Saposs, *The Labor Movement in Post-War France* (New York, 1931), pp. 24-32, and Henry W. Ehrmann, *French Labor: from Popular Front to Liberation* (New York, 1947), pp. 77-80. For the European setting, Lewis L. Lorwin, *Labor and Internationalism,* pp. 89-96 and 134-146; and Merle Fainsod, *International Socialism and the World War* (Cambridge, 1935). The atmosphere of Paris and the French labor movement is faithfully reproduced in vivid detail in the novel of Roger Martin du Gard, *Summer 1914,* vol. 2 of *The Thibaults* (translated by Stuart Gilbert, New York, 1941).

[2] The French Socialists received 1,380,000 votes in May 1914 and elected 101 deputies out of 602.

nant party in the International. All that the International had agreed to enjoin upon its members, after twenty years of discussion of the threat of war in capitalist society, was:

If a war threatens to break out, it is the duty of the working class in the countries concerned and their parliamentary representatives . . . to do all in their power to prevent war by all the means which seem most appropriate to them, which will naturally vary according to the sharpness of the class struggle and the general political situation.[3]

The CGT leaders had no plans whatsoever for a general strike, even if they had been so reckless with their own and their followers' lives as to call one. Pierre Monatte, in his assault later on the CGT wartime leadership, said: "I shall not reproach the Executive Board for not having launched a general strike against the order of mobilization. No! We were all powerless, all of us. The wave passed over us, and it carried us with it."[4]

In the crisis, workers behaved like other Frenchmen. Socialists behaved like most socialists in other belligerent nations. Were they to leave democratic France defenseless before imperial Germany? (Were the Germans to leave their socially advanced fatherland defenseless before absolutist Russia?) National traditions, ancestral patriotism, and the habits of obedience to authority asserted themselves. "Events have submerged us . . . Today we can only deplore the accomplished fact," the CGT avowed in a manifesto to the workers of France.[5]

IMPACT OF WAR ON THE CGT

Soon Jouhaux was a "commissioner of the nation" and other CGT officials were serving on government boards and joint committees with employers. The Socialist Party sent Jules Guesde and two other top leaders into the Cabinet, the first Socialist ministers since Millerand. The CGT and the Socialist Party set up a joint action committee.

People knew that the government had ready a list of several thousand militant unionists, anarchists and extreme socialists[6] who were to be locked up on the day of mobilization for war—"Carnet B," it was called.

---

[3] Lewis L. Lorwin, *Labor and Internationalism,* pp. 91-92. These words are from the resolution of the Stuttgart Congress of the International in 1907, reaffirmed by the Copenhagen Congress of 1910. Added to it, and quite out of keeping with its mild vagueness, was an amendment of the left: "Should war break out nevertheless, it is their duty to coöperate to bring it promptly to a close and to utilize with all their power the economic and political crisis created by the war to arouse the masses of the people and precipitate the downfall of capitalist domination."

[4] Dolléans, vol. 2, p. 222.

[5] August 2, 1914, cited by Rosmer, pp. 114-115.

[6] Pierre Laval was one of the names on the list.

Fortunately for the country's unity, the Minister of the Interior convinced the government, over the opposition of the Minister of War, that there was no need to use "Carnet B." Some union activists were arrested by local prefects' decisions. But in general the labor leaders found themselves accepted by the government which they now accepted.

Later on, the antiwar minority in the CGT charged its leadership with having sold out, with having made a deal to save its own skin by supporting the war. It is true that the leaders of the CGT were swept off their feet in July and August, 1914. But no decision or indecision of the leadership explains the dramatic about-face of the labor movement in 1914. Some of the leaders, as they later said, had worries about their own safety from the police. But in August 1914 they more accurately reflected the feelings of the mass of workers than when they had passed the resolutions for a general strike against war.

The structure of the union movement felt the rude shock of war. This was in great part the result of the industrial disorder caused by the calling up of almost three million reservists in a few weeks, the shutdown of many plants, and the overrunning by the Germans of the nation's most industrialized areas. These cut membership of the CGT drastically, dislocated its cadres, and reduced its activities.

"No student of the French war effort between 1914 and 1918 can help being filled with admiration." [7] But the government was terribly slow to begin the industrial side of that war effort. Gradually it recognized the character of the struggle it faced. It recalled industrial workers from the front, drew women into the factories, recruited foreign laborers. It stimulated the development of a new heavy industry around Paris and in other unoccupied areas. For example, as soon as the war broke out, the Renault auto plant in the Paris suburbs, with 5,000 workers, came almost to a standstill. By the end of the war, it was employing 25,000 men and women, and had largely completed the process of replacing hand labor with mass production methods.

The government fixed hours and working conditions for the vastly increased numbers of women employees, determined minimum wages for the munitions plants, and, in the war industries, set up the first system of shop stewards. Only in 1917, when strikes became serious, did it establish conciliation and arbitration machinery and ban strikes in war production.[8] Of these innovations (most made by administrative regulation rather than by law), few were to survive the war.

---

[7] Thomson, *Democracy in France*, p. 179.

[8] The socialist Albert Thomas was Minister of Munitions until 1917, when left-wing pressure forced the socialists to leave the cabinet. Thomas was later to be the first Director General of the International Labor Organization.

With the settling down of industry and the boom in war production, CGT membership gradually recovered. In some industries, most notably among the metal workers and the railroad workers, it went far beyond prewar figures. While the local unions and departmental federations (the successors to the Bourses) had comparatively few functions, the confederation and the bigger national industrial unions strengthened their positions. They took the chief role in negotiations with the government, and supplied labor representatives for a host of agencies dealing with manpower, work safety, relief, family allowances, and social welfare.

Wages in war industry at first seemed fairly high, although workers resented the military type of discipline in many plants. However, with the mounting cost of living, there were strikes, but until 1917 all on economic grounds. Gradually the horrible losses in what seemed a hopelessly inconclusive struggle, the reports of scandalous profits, and the increasing weariness created a deep discontent with the war itself. The losses were almost more than any country could stand, especially a country of low birth rate. Eight million men were mobilized—one fifth of the total population. Of these, almost three out of four were casualties: 4,500,000 were wounded, over 1,300,000 were killed.[9] From the blood-letting of those fifty-one months, France has never quite recovered in numbers, in vigor, and in leadership.

The old sentiments against capitalism and against war slowly revived, as the stalemate in the trenches continued month after blood-soaked month. There were spontaneous mutinies on the Western front and strikes against the war itself—a big munitions strike in Paris early in 1918. Increasingly important was a left-wing minority in the CGT, with its strongest base among the Paris metal workers. The leadership was wrong to collaborate in the war effort, it argued. France must make peace at once, a peace without victors or vanquished.

The Russian Revolution, especially in its Bolshevik phase, gave a new tone to the strikes and new strength to the minority within the CGT. The great revolution which the workers of France had so long talked of, and failed to make, the Russians had apparently achieved. A generation later Gaston Monmousseau, anarchosyndicalist railway leader turned Communist, wrote with rare candor about the feelings he and others had after the October Revolution:

If someone had said to us at that moment, "You are blindly following Lenin," they would have been saying only the strict truth.

---

[9] A similar rate for the United States at its 1950 population (155,000,000) would mean 31,000,000 mobilized; more than 17,000,000 wounded; over 5,000,000 killed.

But if they had added, "You are merely adoring the Leninist deity," we would have responded in all simplicity, "We do not know exactly what Leninism is, but we love and we follow Lenin because he is the leader of the Socialist Revolution, and we are revolutionaries."[10]

The minority was not a static grouping. Some of the antiwar union leaders, after attacking the leadership of Jouhaux *et al.*, swung over to their support because of the threat to the CGT's unity and independence. Notable in this category was Alphonse Merrheim, a leader of the metal workers, one of the most honest, thoughtful, and devoted figures of the movement.

When the war ended, in all countries suddenly out of the long ordeal, the tide of unrest was rising, immense with vague expectation of change. In France that tide was swollen by the million and a half new CGT members without any experience in union life. They came into labor organizations lacking a philosophy or experience; they found no apparatus able to absorb them. A great number represented a new type of membership: unskilled and semiskilled machine operators, many of them foreigners, who met the needs of wartime industrial growth, accelerated mechanization, and larger factory units.

The new factory workers—products of a "second industrial revolution, violently carried through in the worst conditions"[11]—were most prominent in the Paris area, hitherto an area of small and middlesized enterprises. In this area, as important in the CGT as in the industrial and political life of the nation, a region of extremes in trade unionism and in politics, the Reformists have never since recovered leadership.

THE NEW PROGRAM OF THE CGT

The leadership insisted that it was still true to the revolutionary syndicalism of the Charter of Amiens. (No group took issue with another in the CGT without invoking the Charter of Amiens, as no self-respecting American political leader would fail to invoke the Constitution.) The new spirit of the majority appeared, however, not in such platonic declarations, but in the "Minimum Program" advanced by the CGT in 1918, just after the war ended.[12] Despite the vagueness of many of its formulas and the ritual intonation of revolutionary verbiage, the Minimum Program sounded the major themes of the reformist CGT of the interwar years: social reform within the existing system of society, nationalization of key industries, a progressively greater share of labor responsibility for economic decisions, and international coöperation.

---

[10] "Merci! Camarade Stalin," *Servir la France,* no. 54, December 1949, p. 5.

[11] Thomson, *Democracy in France*, p. 45.

[12] For the text of the Minimum Program, see Léon Jouhaux, *Le Syndicalisme et la C. G. T.* (Paris, 1920), pp. 205-213.

The Minimum Program demanded the determination of wages by collective bargaining, the extension of trade union rights to government employees, and a general eight-hour day. It demanded old age, sickness, disability, and unemployment insurance. Dropping the syndicalist slogans of "the mine to the miners" and "the factory to the workers," it launched the formula of "industrialized nationalization."[13] Nationalization was to be implemented not by the bureaucratic power of the state alone, but by mixed public corporations, "administered by the qualified representatives of producers and consumers."

The syndicalist idea of functional economic groups survived in the demand for union representation in the management of nationalized industry and for a national economic council. The council, bringing together the representatives of all national economic interest groups, would carry democracy and planning into production and distribution.

While emphasizing the economic causes of war inherent in capitalism, the Minimum Program for the first time identified the CGT with the avowed aims of national foreign policy. Endorsing Wilson's Fourteen Points, it asked a seat at the peace conference. Later the CGT was to support the League of Nations and the International Labor Organization.

So great was the unrest throughout France and Europe that even Clemenceau's government made considerable concessions. Some were symbolic: it appointed Jouhaux to the Peace Conference delegation. It supported the "labor clauses" of the Treaty of Versailles, which set up the International Labor Organization. More to the point at home, early in 1919 it put through a general eight-hour-day law, for which the CGT had long been agitating. This was really only an enabling act which enacted the principle and left the ways and means largely to agreement between unions and employers.[14] Specific eight-hour acts for miners and the merchant marine were also passed.

In the same year, 1919, it enacted the first law to give collective agreements legal standing and enforceability[15]. The political fight which boiled within the CGT prevented the unions from taking advantage of the concessions by government and employers. The number of collective agreements in industry grew rapidly at first: in 1919 (the peak year until 1936) 557 new agreements were registered with the Ministry of Labor, as compared with a prewar high of 252 in 1910 and a wartime

---

[13] The industries proposed for nationalization by the 1919 CGT convention were: railroads, shipping, mines, electric power, and banking. *Ibid.,* p. 238.

[14] For an analysis of the administrative unworkability of the law, see Marjorie R. Clark, *A History of the French Labor Movement, 1910-1928* (Berkeley, 1930), pp. 72-73.

[15] For a brief discussion of the law, see Laroque, pp. 294-295; Saposs, pp. 204-207; Georges Scelle, *Le Droit ouvrier,* 2d ed. (Paris, 1929), pp. 61-71, 99-102.

low of practically none in 1915 and 1916.[16] With economic activity on the upswing, a number of strikes for wage increases and shorter hours achieved success.

Not so with the two most spectacular strikes of the period. Both were complicated by the internal struggles within the CGT. The strike of two hundred thousand metal workers in the Paris region in 1919 began as a rank-and-file uprising against the terms of an agreement on the eight-hour day. This was the first agreement the national union had ever succeeded in writing with the national employers' association. First the local unions repudiated the national and regional leadership; then they themselves lost control of the strike to improvised "action committees." Wild and unrealistic, reviling and physically threatening the union leaders, the strikers put aside their economic demands and shouted for revolution. They got neither, and after four weeks they went back without any terms.

THE GENERAL STRIKE OF 1920

Even worse was the defeat of the railway strike and the general strike of 1920. An irregular but successful rail strike in February 1920 was settled by government intervention. The subsequent failure of either management or government to implement the settlement helped the extremists win control of the union at its national convention soon after. Late in April they called the men out again, demanding enforcement of the earlier settlement and immediate nationalization of the railroads. But the union had not prepared the men for another strike. Its own national committee, divided between revolutionaries and reformists, had voted the strike by the narrow majority of 28 to 22. The plans for nationalization had not been worked out yet; this key demand was hardly understood by the union members, let alone the general public. Half the men did not answer the strike call; many of these worked 15 to 16 hours a day. The alarmed bourgeoisie turned out technological school men to run trains and civic committees to help feed Paris. The government kept some traffic moving on all the roads. So ill-prepared were the advocates of revolutionary action that when the government threw the union's executive board into jail, they did not even have a substitute executive named and ready to take over.

The union had not consulted the confederation about calling the strike. But as the strike faltered, it persuaded or shamed the CGT leadership, against its own better judgment, to back it with a general strike, the first unlimited general strike in its history. Three successive "waves

[16] Saposs, pp. 191-192. The Ministry of Labor did not gather data on collective agreements prior to 1910.

of assault," a week apart, were to paralyze the nation's economic life. After the first (miners, dock workers, and seamen) and second waves (metal workers, road transport, and building trades) were launched, it was clear that the strike was a catastrophic failure; the third wave of unions was not called out. A month after the strike had begun, the last of the railway men went back to work, completely beaten.

The government and the railways cracked down on the strikers and the CGT. Twenty-thousand railwaymen were dismissed. The government (now headed by the ex-Socialist Millerand) prosecuted the CGT for violation of the law of 1884. A Paris court ordered the confederation dissolved for carrying on political activity not permitted a trade union body. However, when the CGT appealed, the government sensibly permitted the case to lapse; the decision was never enforced.

THE SPLIT IN THE LABOR MOVEMENT

The loss of the general strike and the mass dismissals on the railroads were followed by a catastrophic drop in CGT membership. From the peak of perhaps 2,000,000 at the beginning of 1920, membership was down to about 600,000 by the end of the year. Feeling in the shrunken organization was further embittered by recriminations over the strike disasters. The issues between right and left came to a head after the newly formed Communist International created the Red International of Labor Unions (RILU). The moderate and socialist national trade union centers had just revived an expanded International Federation of Trade Unions (IFTU), of which Jouhaux was one of the founders and vice presidents. The formation of the RILU and its attacks on the "yellow international" (the IFTU) were one more declaration of open war on trade unionists and Socialists everywhere who would not accept Moscow direction.

The violence of the fight within the CGT exceeded anything the French unions had ever known. The minority condemned both wartime support of the government and the postwar participation in the Versailles conference and the ILO as treason to the cause of syndicalism. It demanded a return to the revolutionary principles of the CGT and affiliation with the RILU.[17] In its growing strength appeared "the revenge of class consciousness . . . and of pacifism, with a definitely international and anti-patriotic sting,"[18] after the war's disillusionments. But

---

[17] The move to join the RILU was made conditional on acceptance of reservations formulated by the French leftists to safeguard the independence of affiliated national centers. Moscow showed no sympathy for these reservations, however.

[18] Robert Michels, *First Lectures in Political Sociology,* trans. by A. de Grazia (Minneapolis, 1949), p. 166.

the minority, composed of revolutionary syndicalists of the old stripe, anarchists, and adherents of the new Communist International, was united only in its attacks on the reformist leaders.

In the Socialist Party, as in the unions, the Russian revolution exerted tremendous attraction. There the divisions were even more complex than in the CGT. The anti-Communist leadership showed the effects of Jaurès' irreparable loss. Léon Blum and his party colleagues were weaker than Jouhaux, Dumoulin, Merrheim *et al.,* in the CGT. In 1920 the supporters of Moscow took over the apparatus of the party and affiliated it, renamed the Communist Party,[19] with the Comintern. The anti-Moscow minority, left with far fewer followers, but most of the leaders and parliamentary deputies, set about reorganizing the Socialist Party.

In an increasingly embittered atmosphere, the CGT debated and redebated the issues between the shrinking reformist majority and the growing revolutionary minority. Merrheim, the former revolutionary syndicalist, saw the issue with unusual clarity. Like most European unionists at the time, he sympathized with the beleaguered Russian Revolution and deplored Allied intervention in Russia. But he warned that "a regime established in the moral and material conditions of the Russia of today cannot maintain itself, at least for a generation, except by dictatorship." A generation's clear sight is as much as is given to most men.

"I do not claim the right to judge the acts of the dictatorship now existing in Russia," Merrheim said. "But I deny the right of Lenin to extend and impose that dictatorship on all parties, all nations." He had known Lenin and Trotsky; as he told the CGT convention of 1920, the Russian Bolsheviks had made clear their methods and doctrine even before the war. "It is this same doctrine, totally opposed to our own . . . which they want to impose on us under the surveillance of the Executive Committee of the Third International."[20]

Meanwhile the minority organization spread out through a network of "Revolutionary Syndicalist Committees" rather effectively boring from within at the local union level. The revolutionaries captured the Paris region organization and several national unions, including the building trades. The reformists, after getting large majorities at the 1919 and 1920 conventions, found themselves in 1921 with a hair's

---

[19] Moscow insisted upon the new name "Communist Party." The party was also called the French Section of the Communist International, although neither this term nor its initials SFIC ever acquired the currency of the initials SFIO for the Socialist Party ("Section Française de l'Internationale Ouvrière,"), French Section of the Labor and Socialist (Second) International.

[20] CGT, *XV⁰ Congrès Confédéral, Orléans . . . 1920, Compte Rendu . . ,* pp. 373, 363.

breadth edge. They had reason to fear that the convention majority represented only a minority among the membership. They summoned the leftists to dissolve their Revolutionary Syndicalist Committees, and, when they refused, began expelling them from the unions and departmental federations. The split was now formalized.

The CGT had been unified only since 1902, and the Socialist Party since 1905. The party split was not to be healed. The Socialist and Communist parties were to draw together and fall apart several times, but not to reunite. The CGT was to reunite, split again, reunite, and split a third time within the next generation; even in its years of formal unity it continued to reflect party cleavages. More closely than in any other country, schism and reunification in the CGT reflected turns in international politics.

DUAL UNIONISM : THE COMMUNIST CGTU

Expelled from the CGT, the Communists, anarchists and syndicalists continued with the business of setting up their own organization : the General Confederation of United Labor (*Confédération Générale du Travail Unitaire*), the CGTU. As a concession to the deep sentimental appeal of unity and to the syndicalists' hopes for reunification, the new CGT rejected the qualification "Révolutionnaire," which it was, in favor of "Unitaire," which it was not.

The syndicalists and anarchists were numerically more important than the communists at the time of the split. For two or three years, the communists drew into their movement many of the syndicalists, including some of the best, such as Rosmer and Monatte. It requires an effort at this date to see how syndicalists, enemies of the state and of political parties, could have embraced the Soviet Union. In its early years, the Bolshevik revolution had a strong syndicalist tinge and seemed to be realizing much of the syndicalist dream. Workers' soviets were playing a large role; the Bolshevik Party had not yet taken control of the state; the state and party had not yet domesticated the unions.[21] (That the syndicalists should have erred so is, at any rate, less surprising than that distinguished scholars and sophisticates, such as the lifelong Fabians, Sidney and Beatrice Webb, much later should have seen their revolution in Soviet communism.) In a few years most of the syndicalists were alienated by Moscow's interference with the French party and the purge of French Trotskyites. Meanwhile, they helped the communists take over control of the CGTU, which became the "guinea pig of Leninist-Stalinist tactics"[22] of trade union conquest by party.

---

[21] Cf. Franz Borkenau, *World Communism: A History of the Communist International* (New York, 1939), p. 168.

[22] Michel Collinet, *Esprit du syndicalisme* (Paris, 1952), p. 98.

By its second convention, in 1923, the communists, under the lead of Gaston Monmousseau, were able to affiliate the CGTU to the RILU. After 1924 the communists were in full control of the CGTU. Some of the syndicalists, finding the Communist Party politicians harder to work with than the reformist "politicians" whose hold over the CGT had moved them to scission, carried through another split. But the "third CGT" (the "Confédération Générale du Travail Syndicaliste-Révolutionnaire") which they set up was only a shadow organization. Some syndicalists remained within the CGTU, others went back into the CGT.

The CGTU became an adjunct of the Communist Party, although this relationship was never formalized in the statutes. Important officials were all Communists. Interlocking directorates and a subordination of confederation policies to those of the Communist Party achieved the purposes for which recognition in the statutes was not essential.

While the syndicalists were still potent in the CGTU, they wrote into its statutes one of their favorite ideas, which they had never succeeded in getting the old CGT to adopt—the ineligibility of union officials to reëlection. The Communists scrapped that provision. They tried to scrap too the extreme "federalism" or decentralization of the inherited CGT structure. They made voting strength at conventions proportionate to membership represented, to replace the old one-union-one-vote principle. They attempted to create regional federations to replace the departmental federations, and regional unions to replace local unions. In these the party functionary type of official would replace the elected official close to his local union base. The reorganization was unsuccessful, because of the general decline of the CGTU.

The CGTU had taken a majority of the CGT with it at the time of the split. Gradually its membership fell off, as a consequence of internal fights, hopeless and politically inspired strikes, and the weakness of the Communist Party itself.

The French Communist Party was one of the largest in any capitalist country. But it was torn by dissensions, splits, and purges. Among those who soon left it or were expelled were many of the syndicalists. The party's leadership was still that of its socialist origins, largely professional and middle-class rather than working class. In 1924 the party's organ *Cahiers du Bolchevisme,* found that the party was composed "20 per cent of Jaurèsism, 10 per cent of Marxism, 20 per cent of Leninism, 20 per cent of Trotskyism, and 30 per cent of confusionism." [23]

At the 1920 split the Communists had about 130,000 members to the

---

[23] Gérard Walter, *Histoire du parti communiste français* (Paris, 1948), p. 179. The solution recommended at that time was of course "100 per cent Leninism."

30,000 who followed the Socialist minority. Within a few years the Socialists were ahead in both membership and electoral strength. Communist Party membership fell below 40,000 by 1930. But the party obtained 11 per cent of the total vote in 1928—1,064,000 to the Socialists' 1,698,000.[24] In the 1932 national elections, they dropped to 775,000 votes, as compared with 1,943,000 for the Socialists.

Some of the causes of Communist weakness were vividly summed up by the party's long-time secretary general, Maurice Thorez. This was the situation he found in 1930:

The membership was falling off. Arbitrary decisions at the top, a passive discipline required at all levels, the snuffing out of all free discussion, suspicion, silence where acquiescence was lacking, tightly sewn lips, no fruitful criticism, the atmosphere of a barracks. . . It was the caricature of a party, a party reduced to impotence, vegetating, turned in upon itself, instead of being the conscious active vanguard of the working class.

That, said Thorez, was how the group in control of the party had misinterpreted the "democratic centralism" advocated by Lenin. And in its labor work it:

showed the greatest disdain for the realities of daily life . . . preferring the empty phrase to concrete analysis, and thereby dooming the workers' action to sterility and impotence. . . Work in the unions was looked down upon, socialist workers were insulted, the slightest strike was made a political issue.[25]

The Executive of the Communist International intervened frequently to set the French party on the right path. It rebuked it for failing to develop the factory cell structure essential to control the unions and influence the workers. The interventions of Moscow cost the party and the CGTU many of their undisciplined members and leaders. The party changed leadership several times before finding in Maurice Thorez a leader who combined working class origin ("honorary miner," said his enemies), energy, ability, and personal appeal with a proper respect for Moscow and Stalin.

The Soviet Union was weak, and so was the Comintern, after postwar revolt subsided in central and eastern Europe. Soviet Union, Com-

---

[24] A word on the reporting of votes in this book. (1) Votes are given for metropolitan France, not including the Algerian departments. (2) Votes given are those obtained on the first ballot of two-ballot elections, which alone indicates relative popular support. On the second, or run-off ballot, held if no candidate receives a majority on the first, a *plurality* is sufficient to elect. For the run-off, therefore, parties often make electoral deals, some withdrawing their candidates in favor of others more or less close to their own views, to defeat their worst enemies.

[25] Maurice Thorez, *Fils du peuple* (Paris, 1950 edition), pp. 70-71.

intern, and French Communist Party could not yet build a strong communist trade union movement in France. Their demands upon it weakened its position among workers and isolated it. Greater success was to come only in the mid-1930's, when they abandoned rigid sectarian policies in favor of the popular front appeal.

THE REFORMIST CGT

The CGT outstripped the CGTU in numbers and in influence. This was not a matter of new recruitment of industrial workers, but chiefly the result of the affiliation or reaffiliation of important national unions of civil servants. Some of those unions had joined the CGT at the war's end, but resumed their autonomy because of the split. In 1927 the federation of civil service unions, with 300,000 members, autonomous since 1922, rejoined the CGT. The civil servants became a decisive element within the confederation and reformist unionism. Despite the many antimilitarists and left wingers of various shades in their ranks, these unions had a fundamental stake in the orderly processes of society and politics, and in friendly relations between the CGT and the government. They were as a whole the best organized group of wage earners, with the steadiest employment and the best dues-paying habits. By the late 1920's, unions of government workers made up almost half of the CGT's membership; in the CGTU the proportion was smaller.[26]

In both confederations, another large bloc of membership was that of unions in public utility types of industry: railroads, local transport systems, mining, gas and electricity, shipping. In these government-regulated industries, workers were protected from the worst anti-union activity by employers. Railroads were an exception, because of the 1920 strike, but even there the unions could function to some extent. These too were industries protected from the winds of international competition by their monopoly character or by government subsidies. Their unions looked to the state for satisfaction of many of their demands for working conditions, pensions, and so on.

In the unregulated private sector of industry, neither confederation made much headway. The major unions of purely private employment, the building trades, metal working, and textiles, soon fell from their high membership just after the war to figures below those of the immediate prewar days. The CGT printing trades union was the outstanding exception, both in degree of organization of its industry and in collective bargaining relations. Maintaining its extensive system of bene-

---

[26] See membership tables in Saposs, pp. 137-138. After the Herriot government declarations of 1924, the civil service unions enjoyed a *de facto* government tolerance and recognition, although legislation to that effect was pigeonholed,

fits and a rather tight administration, it held members when many other unions saw theirs melt away. By the time of their reunification, early in 1936, the CGT and CGTU together counted only 650,000 members in private industry, including public utilities, trade and agriculture. That was only a little over 6 per cent of those employed by private enterprise.[27]

Not only the CGT but even most of the CGTU unions dropped their systematic hostility to bargaining within the capitalist framework, and sought to make agreements where they could. Under the conditions of low membership and dual unionism, however, there was little collective bargaining in most of private industry. Employer hostility to bargaining successfully reasserted itself. Only in mining and in shipping, among the basic industries, was bargaining widespread. The number of newly concluded agreements declined from 557 in 1919 to 345 in 1920, to an average of 160 per year in 1921-1925,[28] and to a mere 22 per year during 1930-1935. By 1933, only 1.4 per cent of the workers in the metallurgical industries and 2 per cent of those in textiles had their conditions regulated by collective agreement; for industry and commerce as a whole, the figure was 7.5 per cent.[29]

In philosophy and method—if not in verbal expression—the CGT took on much of the quality of the predominant type of western European unionism. It pursued programs of evolutionary change, and sought conciliation with other groups in the community. When the government failed to take up its idea of a national economic council, the CGT formed one of its own. Its Economic Council of Labor brought together representatives of the CGT, the autonomous civil service unions, the coöperatives, and for a time the new union of technicians. Its major contribution was a plan for the nationalization of the railroads. The council was an aspect both of the new constructive unionism and the impatience with a Parliament which failed to act on social problems. In 1924, the government created a National Economic Council. Although its powers were negligible, the CGT joined it.

Parliamentary lobbying became a major activity of the CGT. It worked with the two parties of the traditional "left," the Socialists and, for a time even more, the Radical Socialists.[30] The latter took part in most postwar cabinets; coöperation with them offered more practical advantages. The Socialists seemed a bit too theoretical and intransigent

---

[27] Ehrmann, p. 25.

[28] Saposs, p. 192.

[29] Ehrmann, p. 26.

[30] Radicals and Radical Socialists are misnomers for a party that had been on the left decades earlier, and was in this period a left center party. Radical Socialists moved more or less continuously rightward during the Third Republic, as the political axis itself less steadily moved leftward.

for trade unions anxious for legislative and administrative action. From 1917 to 1936 the Socialists refused all opportunities to take office in governmental coalitions, although they supported Radical Socialist premiers after the "left victories" of the 1924 and 1932 elections.

In contrast to its opposition to the 1910 pension law, the CGT helped put through a reluctant Parliament the nation's first comprehensive social security system. The law, effective in 1930, provided sickness, disability, death, maternity, and old age benefits, and some meager unemployment assistance (not insurance). The CGT then devoted a great deal of its efforts to setting up the autonomous social insurance funds provided for by the law. Employers generally opposed the social security law. What possibilities the law's passage offered for a better atmosphere of industrial relations were therefore lost.

Another element of social protection for workers was introduced by family allowances, sums paid to workers on the basis of their dependent children and the mother's remaining at home instead of going out to work. An increasing number of employers had been paying family allowances, under the influence of Catholic social doctrine, or general social-welfare-mindedness, or desire to attach workers to themselves and ward off unionization. Employers had voluntarily pooled contributions in private funds to spread the burdens. The CGT had attacked the allowances as employer paternalism; if they were to be paid, let the state assume the responsibility and cover all workers. In 1932 a law made family allowances compulsory, requiring employer membership in family allowance funds, which continued to be financed exclusively out of employer payroll taxes.[31] The amounts remained modest until the family allowance law of 1939. But they added a permanent segment to the wage structure, which was not a recompense for labor furnished but a partial payment of a social debt (or subsidy to larger families).

Part of the energy of the top CGT leadership went into international organization, both trade union and intergovernmental. Jouhaux was active in the International Federation of Trade Unions and the International Labor Organization, which was associated with (although not a part of) the League of Nations. "The mystique which in the years 1920-1934 sustained the CGT was the internationalist mystique of the building of the peace at Geneva and by Geneva," remarks the man who was the confederation's education director in this period.[32] This was one more case when the leadership was out of touch with the rank and file, for the League of Nations and the ILO, after the early hopes placed in

[31] Taxes were not based on the family responsibilities of the firm's own employees, since that would have penalized the hiring of the heads of large families.

[32] Georges Lefranc, writing under the nom de plume of Jean Montreuil, *Histoire du mouvement ouvrier,* p. 401.

them, never acquired the hold of a "mystique" over the French worker.

One major adaptation to new conditions was the strengthening of the bureaucracy in which the confederation and most of its unions had been so weak before the war. It was no longer fashionable to deprecate the treasuries, large memberships, and bureaucratic apparatus of unions in neighboring lands, such as Germany, Belgium, and the United Kingdom. Although the CGT was still a long way from achieving their solidity, its leaders sought these once despised advantages.

The confederation tightened its structure of government. It ended its historic system of division into two sections, the national unions and the Bourses du Travail (and later department federations). Representation of both the vertical and horizontal units was assured by the national committee ("comité confédéral national"). To this important organ each national union and each department federation sent one representative. Before the war, provincial bodies generally designated Paris unionists to represent them at the confederation level. Now they sent their own top officials. Larger funds were available for travel. Larger importance was attached to representation in top CGT councils. The CGT and most of its unions replaced the one-local-one-vote system in conventions by a modified form of proportional representation.[33] This "proportioned proportional" system still favored the smaller local, but far less than before.

The leadership made efforts to introduce the practices of higher dues, increased benefits, and strike funds, but here it made only slight headway. Both reformist and communist unions seemed for the most part powerless to combat the old low-dues philosophy. The leaders who for a generation had preached the virtues of low dues, in part because they were the practice, now found their members almost impervious to appeals for change.

CATHOLIC UNIONISM

The French working class had by the middle decades of the nineteenth century almost entirely turned its back on the church. Sensitive and astute churchmen were later to say that the church had turned its back on the workers. It gave them little comfort in the early stages of the industrial revolution. It seemed all too clearly allied with their masters in factory and—until the Third Republic—in government. The alliance of church and royalists in the first generation of the Third Republic sealed

---

[33] "Proportional representation" is here used to mean voting strength in conventions or committees in proportion to membership represented. The term is also used frequently in France to mean representation on union directing bodies for opposing wings or caucuses in proportion to relative strength, instead of election by majority decision.

its divorce from the industrial workers. When Leo XIII urged French Catholics to "rally" to the Republic, and when (in 1891) he promulgated the social doctrine of *De Rerum Novarum,* he spoke to a working class which was, except for a few devout areas, altogether "dechristianized."

There were Catholics who spoke out against social injustice. But the most influential of these appealed more to employers than to workers. They were men like Count Albert de Mun, highborn and highminded, who proclaimed "we are the counterrevolution on the march."[34] Fearing the trade unions as a device of class warfare, they argued for "mixed unions," including both employers and employees. Foreshadowing the modern corporatist idea, the "mixed unions" were based in part on the dubious analogy between the family and the industrial community, in part on a nostalgia for the hierarchic system of the Middle Ages.

The first Catholic unions, and still the strongest today, were among white collar employees. The pioneer was the Paris clerical workers' union founded in 1887. By 1909 it had 5,000 members. In 1913 it joined with locals in the provinces to set up the first national union of Catholic workers. Under the able leadership of Jules Zirnheld, it moved from its early timidity and church control to greater vigor and independence in trade union action. In 1891 the first textile workers' union was formed by Catholics in the north. In the early 1900's the Catholic unionists had to fight competition from two sides. The "pseudo-syndicalism" of the "yellow" or company unions exercised an attraction for many Catholics. Others went into the CGT, a few in a conscious but hopeless effort to change it.

The French Confederation of Catholic Workers, the CFTC (*Confédération Française des Travailleurs Chrétiens*), was formed in 1919. In the same year the International Confederation of Christian Trade Unions was founded in Paris.[35] The CFTC adopted a "federal" structure like that of the CGT. That it had problems in common with those of the CGT was clear from its president's statement that of the 140,000 claimed members in 1920 only 65,000 paid dues (very low dues at that) to the CFTC.[36]

In contrast to the two CGT's, the CFTC sought social justice and economic democracy not through the class struggle but through coöper-

---

[34] Paul Vignaux, *Traditionalisme et syndicalisme: Essai d'histoire sociale (1884-1941)* (New York, 1943), pp. 34-35.

[35] I have translated "Chrétiens" in the name of the French Confederation as "Catholic," which is more precise than "Christian." In the international, however, "Christian" is the only appropriate term since several affiliates are Protestant unions (from Holland and Switzerland), in addition to the more important Catholic trade union centers.

[36] Zirnheld, p. 83.

ation with employers and the state. Its initial statement of principles urged "the education and collaboration of the various elements in production, organized in different groups, and associated in joint organisms where the independence and rights of each will be respected."[37] It looked toward self-regulation by each industry through collective agreements and joint labor-management commissions at various levels: "the free trade union in the organized trade or industry." ("Organized" in this slogan referred, not to union organization, but to organization of all elements for industrial self-regulation.) In its pursuit of coöperation with employers, the CFTC did not abandon the right to strike. It was active in the wave of postwar economic strikes in clothing, in banking, and in some textile and metallurgical centers. But it opposed the 1920 general strike as a political strike.

The foundation of the Catholic Workers Youth (*Jeunesse Ouvrière Chrétienne*) in 1927 was another move to bridge the gap between Catholicism and the working class. The JOC in time became a nursery of labor leadership, which helped the CFTC unions get over their feelings of inferiority among industrial workers. The JOCists, as they were called, infused class consciousness and solidarity into the newer industrial unions of the CFTC. An anticlerical observer, the mystic Simone Weil, an intellectual who threw herself passionately into a factory worker's life, wrote: "The JOC alone has concerned itself with the misfortune of working class adolescence. The existence of such an organization is perhaps the only sure sign that Christianity is not dead among us."[38]

For all the Catholic unions' moderation, and for all the CGT and CGTU attacks upon them as company unions, they were not generally welcomed by employers. The most damaging attack on them came from the Catholic leadership of the powerful textile employers' association of Roubaix-Tourcoing, "strong in their virtue and their fortune, charitable and authoritarian . . . leaning on a system of company welfare work and a technique of anti-unionism."[39] They complained to the Vatican that the CFTC was slipping into Marxism and stirring up class hatred. Zirnheld's restrained autobiography hints at the anguish of the five years' wait before the Vatican, in 1929, signified its total rejection of the charges.[40]

---

[37] Quoted in Vignaux, pp. 43-44.
[38] Simone Weil, *L'Enracinement* (Paris, 1949), p. 61.
[39] Vignaux, *Traditionalisne et syndicalisme*, p. 41.
[40] Zirnheld, pp. 155-172. See also R. P. Stéphane-J. Piat, *Jules Zirnheld, Président de la CFTC* (Paris, 1948), pp. 181-203. Zirnheld remarks that Mathon, spokesman for the Roubaix-Tourcoing employers, was in Rome to visit Mussolini when he lodged his complaint with the Vatican, *Cinquante années de syndicalisme chrétien*, p. 159.

The years just before the depression were among the few periods of prosperity France has had in this century. To win the war, the economy had put on a burst of speed in the development of heavy industry and mass production methods. After the war, industrial activity was fortified by the return of Alsace with its textile and metal-fabricating industries and Lorraine with its iron and steel plants. Activity was spurred by the tasks of reconstruction. There was full employment and a call for workers from abroad. With America's doors closed by new immigration laws, France was the chief outlet for overcrowded European nations, notably Poland and other Slavic countries.[41] Between 1921 and 1931 there was a net influx of 1,340,000 people. In 1930 there were 3 million foreigners in France, about half of them employed, in addition to tens of thousands of French North Africans. Exercising the prerogative of a relatively prosperous civilized people, the French left more and more of their heavy and dirty labor to the foreigners and North Africans. Georges Navel recounts the amazement of an Italian working alongside him after the war on a road-mending gang: "You should be in an office, you're a Frenchman."[42]

The last half of the decade of the 1920's saw a considerable rationalization of industry. Industrial production reached a high point it was not to attain again for almost a generation. But the small and middle-sized establishment continued to dominate the industrial scene. In 1931, only 26 per cent of the workers in industry were employed in establishments of over 500 workers; over 41 per cent were still to be found in establishments of 1-50 workers (as compared with 19 per cent in the United States).[43] Smallness meant a certain social stability, as compared with the social risks of wider and more rapid proletarianization. It also meant a grave threat to that stability in the long run because of the association between smallness and slowness of technological and economic progress.

---

[41] Georges Mauco, Les étrangers en France (Paris, 1932).

[42] Georges Navel, Travaux (Paris, 1946),p. 147.

[43] Since these figures include mines as well as industry, they somewhat overstate the importance of the larger unit. Jean Fourastié and Henri Montet, L'Economie française dans le monde (Paris, 1950), p. 61. For more detailed figures on several industries, based on the 1936 census, see Pierre George, "Etude statistique des dimensions des établissements industriels (Rapport préliminaire)," in Gabriel Dessus and others, Matériaux pour une géographie volontaire de l'industrie française, Cahiers de la Fondation Nationale des Sciences Politiques, no. 7 (Paris, 1949), pp. 107-143.

CHAPTER V

THE RISE AND FALL OF THE POPULAR FRONT
(1930-1939)

> The social laws, which it is so easy to criticize after the event, were the
> price we paid to avoid civil war.
>
> —Léon Blum, *For All Mankind*
> (written in 1941), 1946.

> Who will deny that it is much more difficult to get discipline from
> industry for what is commonly called "constructive action" than when it
> tends simply to defend positions of fundamental resistance?
>
> —C.-J. Gignoux, president of the
> General Confederation of French
> Employers, *Patrons, Soyez des
> Patrons!* 1937.

The depression came later to France than to most industrial countries.
It reached its depth early in 1935, but it was not really to lift before the
war. The fall in industrial production in the two years 1931 and 1932
wiped out two decades' gain in the rate of creation of real income.[1]
Prices went down faster than wage rates, so that real wage rates moved
up. To workers, however, this characteristic phenomenon of depression
meant less than the fact or the fear of unemployment. At the worst period about 1,400,000 were unemployed; about 500,000 were receiving
the small unemployment assistance benefits. Perhaps half of the employed were on short time.[2] The figures were grim enough, although
mild compared to those of Germany, Britain, and the United States.

France averted the worst of mass unemployment by shifting the burden to the country's foreign workers. About half a million of them left
the country. The unions, although firmly internationalist in speech,
naturally enough encouraged the use of the "emigration valve." Ques-

---

[1] The index of industrial production, which had by 1930 reached 140 (with 1913 as
base), by 1932 fell back below the 1913 level. For convenient consultation of general
industrial production indexes, see André Piatier, "La production industrielle en
France de 1898 à 1950," *Revue économique*, vol. 1, no. 1, May 1950, pp. 121-128.

[2] Michel Collinet, "The Structure of the Employee Classes in France during the
Last Fifty Years," *International Labor Review*, vol. 67, no. 3, March 1953, p. 224.

tions of justice aside, the foreign workers' departure was "one of the most serious losses of the depression for a country in France's deplorable demographic position."[3]

Along with unemployment came falling farm prices and a decline in the position of the middle class, including the "new middle class" of technicians and civil servants. A series of cabinets, notably that of the ex-leftist, Pierre Laval, reduced government payrolls and spending and, keeping the franc overvalued, kept imports down by quantitative restrictions. But with economic activity constricted, tax receipts went down even more than government expenditures. These deflationary policies alarmed the unions without winning the much-wooed confidence of business.

Dissatisfaction with the parliamentary democracy of the Third Republic had been endemic since its foundation, flaring up in periodic crises with their highest fever in Paris. Now this sentiment, feeding on depression and the apparent impotence of the government, took the more modern forms of fascist leagues and reluctant admiration for fascist "achievements." The "order" of trains running on time and no unions running at all on the other side of the Italian frontier had seduced a few Frenchmen's thoughts. The far bigger and newer order of Hitler created a more dazzling example and a greater threat.

The Stavisky scandal, revealing deputies and government officials in widespread financial crookedness, seemed to give the fascist leagues their opportunity. On February 6, 1934, they summoned their followers to demonstrate against "the slut," Marianne. That day the Communists had their followers out in the streets with them. "One cannot fight against fascism without fighting against social democracy," said André Marty in *L'Humanité*, the party organ.[4] He called on the workers to demonstrate "against the fascist bands, against the government, and against the Social Democrats who weaken the working class by dividing it." Communists joined fascist veterans, the royalist lunatic fringe, and others in the confused rioting that threatened the parliamentary regime. Against the rioters streaming toward the Chamber of Deputies, the police finally held the bloody field. The Daladier government resigned, but the republic still stood.

The most vigorous counterattack came from the CGT, aided by the Socialist Party. The CGT called a one-day general strike for February twelfth as a "warning and a manifestation of strength and decision" to defend "the fundamental liberties without which life is not worth living." The Communists insisted first on calling their own demonstration

---

[3] D. W. Brogan, *France Under The Third Republic*, p. 649.
[4] February 6, 1934, cited by Walter, *Histoire du parti communiste français*, p. 251.

on February ninth. But Communist workers could not help seeing that February sixth had been a near-victory for the fascists, and February ninth a dubious sacrifice of working-class heads against police clubs. As late as the eleventh the Communist press was writing. "The working class will reject with disgust the socialist leaders who have the cynicism and the gall to try to drag the workers to the struggle against fascism to the chant of the *Marseillaise* and the *Internationale.*"[5] The same day, on the eve of the CGT-Socialist strike, it had to switch instructions and call upon workers to join the manifestation of the twelfth.[6] This they did with enthusiasm.

February twelfth remains one of the great days in the history of French labor. It saw its first successful general strike. Aims and method were far from what the old syndicalists or Sorel had dreamt of; they were limited, defensive, and orderly, not revolutionary. The aims were not those of a single class, but of all democratically-minded Frenchmen : the defense of the republic, but not of shady republican politicians. With the strength of deep purpose, with no appeal to violence, over a million men and women stopped work in the capital; in the provinces too there were impressive demonstrations. "Curious paradox : the economic strike is hardly possible, but the political strike succeeds."[7]

The success of the first great common action of the CGT and the CGTU seemed to confirm the rank-and-file belief in the virtues of labor unity. That unity was now to be effected, to differing degrees, in party and trade union action. The Communist parties of the world were moving toward the new united front policy. The Soviet Union and the Comintern had belatedly concluded that Hitler, instead of liquidating the German Social Democrats in their favor, was pointing a gun at the workers' fatherland. The Franco-Soviet alliance was the statement of the new Soviet policy in diplomatic terms. The united front was its statement in organizational strategy; this policy was to lift the Communist parties of many nations out of isolation into new and far greater influence in political and trade union life.

The French Communist and Socialist parties in July 1934 concluded a "unity of action pact," calling for common action against the fascist leagues, for the defense of democratic institutions, and against war preparations. Each party agreed not to attack the other, although otherwise keeping its freedom of action. The rapprochement, the basis for

[5] *L'Humanité,* February 11, 1934, cited by Walter, p. 263, note 23. Walter's book, it may be noted, is not unfriendly to the Communist Party.

[6] *Ibid.,* p. 256; Adolf Sturmthal, *The Tragedy of European Labor* (New York, 1943), p. 265.

[7] Michel Collinet, *Esprit du syndicalisme,* p. 73.

the later Popular Front, was imposed by what Léon Blum called "a spontaneous and irresistible instinct of the masses."[8]

REUNIFICATION OF THE CGT

The CGT and the CGTU had both talked unity at length and to no result during the years of the schism. To the Communists, for domestic reasons alone, unity was now most desirable. The CGTU was still losing members at a time when the Communist Party was picking up members. The CGTU put a double pressure on the none too willing CGT leaders. In negotiation at the top on methods of unification, it gave way on all disputed points, leaving the CGT with the responsibility of thwarting unity if it dared. In agitation at the base it fostered the creation of unified locals, in opposition to CGT discipline, to confront the CGT leadership with accomplished fact.

Reunification was agreed upon in 1935, between a CGT which then had about three-fourths of a million members and a CGTU with no more than one third as many. It was carried through in stages from local union amalgamation upward, as the CGT had insisted, to give weight to its numerical advantage over the CGTU. The first convention of the reunited CGT, at Toulouse in March 1936, debated the points of structure and policy still at issue. The ex-CGTU leaders attempted to introduce the Communist principle of "democratic centralism," but the majority kept the traditional "federalist" structure. The CGT maintained its membership in the International Federation of Trade Unions, although agreeing to try within the IFTU (as it did without success) to achieve unity with the Red International of Labor Unions.

On CGT relationships with political parties—the crux of the issue of communism in trade unions—the basic differences were obscured by liberal quotations on both sides from the Charter of Amiens. The 1906 declaration of independence from political parties was reaffirmed, but no longer interpreted in terms of aloofness. The workers had a greater stake in society than in 1906; the fascist threat made that vivid. The CGT reserved the right to make temporary common cause with political organizations: "Despite its neutrality toward political parties, it cannot remain indifferent to dangers that may threaten public liberties and social gains."[9] The Communists agreed they would not reconstitute their

---

[8] *A l'echelle humaine* (Paris, 1945) (translated as *For All Mankind*, New York, 1946), pp. 103-104. Writing in 1941, in the light of Pétain's Vichy regime, he concluded that without the "unity of action pact" and the later Popular Front, "one can scarcely doubt that France would have been reduced four or five years earlier to the condition of Franco's Spain."

[9] For CGT statutes as adopted at the Toulouse convention, and slightly modified by the 1938 convention, see *La documentation française, Notes et études documentaires,*

fractions or caucuses in the CGT, after obtaining a special dispensation to that purpose from the Comintern.[10] They kept their factory cells, however, and these became more active than ever. Their official abandonment of the party fractions was "only a parade gesture covering the work in depth of the cells."[11]

It was easy later to see that the platonic declarations in favor of "trade union independence" offered little guidance to the CGT either in coöperating with the Popular Front government which took office in 1936, or in coping with the Communist drive for power within the unions. Reformist leaders were later to say they were fully aware of the dangers from the Communist position inside the new CGT.[12] Perhaps at the time they put too much hope in the Communists' professions of fair play in a common fight against fascism. Perhaps they felt too secure in their agreed 6:2 majority on the Executive Board. Perhaps, in the euphoria of the Popular Front, no one could possibly foresee the tremendous Communist gains ahead.

Another CGT reaction to the depression and the fascist threat at home was its "Plan." The 1918 Minimum Program had first shown the CGT's capacity to speak in terms of the general interest as well as labor's special concerns and its bent for economic planning within a modified capitalist society. The Plan of 1934-1936 called for immediate measures of unemployment insurance, the forty-hour week, paid vacations, and large-scale public works to fight unemployment. It demanded the nationalization of key industries along the lines of the Minimum Program and national economic planning, using credit as a major lever, and for that purpose nationalizing the Bank of France.[13] The reformist leaders hoped that the plan might take on symbolic and emotional significance, to generate a new drive and the "mystique" conspicuously

---

no. 1239 (Paris, December 2, 1949), "L'évolution intérieure de la CGT," pp. 15-18. For English text of the preamble, see Ehrmann, appendix I.

[10] Michel Collinet, "La Bureaucratie et la crise actuelle du syndicalisme ouvrier français," *Revue d'histoire economique et sociale,* vol. 29, no. 1, 1951, p. 71.

[11] Collinet, *Esprit du syndicalisme,* p. 99.

[12] Cf., for example, Raoul Lenoir in 1948: "When we carried out the reunification at the Toulouse convention of 1936, we were 750,000. The CGTU, which had started with 550,000 to 600,000, had been reduced to 145,000. We wanted them to carry out a real unity. I was the one responsible for discussing with Frachon the conditions of unity; no one could fool me on the value of the conditions which we imposed on the CGTU. When we spoke of complete independence toward the Socialist Party, toward the Communist Party, toward all parties, toward all governments, when they signed that, we knew full well that it had no value for them. For, as far as honesty goes, there is no morality among them." Force Ouvrière, *Congrès constitutif, compte rendu . . . 1948,* p. 8.

[13] For the Plan, see Jouhaux, *La C.G.T., ce qu'elle est, ce qu'elle veut* (Paris, 1937), chapters IV-V.

lacking in the postwar CGT. But whatever its appeal to the union bureaucracy and to intellectuals, the plan failed to enthuse the masses.

THE POPULAR FRONT

The times which brought an entente between the Socialist and Communist parties and reunited the CGT produced another wider political reconciliation. This was the Popular Front, constituted by the Socialist, Communist, and Radical Socialist parties, the CGT, and several minor organizations. It was a temporary and defensive electoral alliance of the representatives of farmers, lower middle class, and workers, brought together by the deepening of the depression, the government's deflationary policy, and the attacks on republican institutions.

Socialists and Radical Socialists had made second-ballot alliances in many previous elections. Now the Communists returned to the electoral "solidarity of the left,"[14] which the Comintern had told them to abandon before the 1928 elections. In the two years since the 1934 riots, the Communist Party had altered its course almost 180 degrees. The first Communist Party to make the popular front turn, it swung around from the sectarian, antinational, antimilitarist, "class against class" line to a broad antifascist, ultrapatriotic appeal. It held out its hands to Catholics, Socialists, and middle class elements. In line with the Franco-Soviet alliance, it voted for larger military credits and a longer term of military service.

The national elections of May 1936 were a victory for the Popular Front. Most significant was the shift to the left among the Popular Front parties, the result in part of a leftward trend of the voters, in part of the second-ballot combinations which for the first time gave the Communists seats in parliament comparable to their voting strength. The Radicals—a center party, it will be recalled, not radical—lost somewhat. The Socialists, with about the same number of votes (almost 2,000,000) as in the 1932 election, became the largest party in the Chamber for the first time. The Communists almost doubled their 1932 vote to poll a million and a half votes; in the Paris region they polled more than the Socialists and Radicals combined. They had 72 deputies instead of their 10 in the previous Chamber.

The election returns following the CGT reunification released a flood of hope and pent-up energy in the working class which in May and June swept through factories across the country. Almost 2,000,000

---

[14] In the 1936 elections, the Popular Front parties agreed that on the second ballot the others would withdraw in favor of the one in each district receiving the highest vote on the first ballot. On the two-ballot system of elections see Note 24, Chapter IV, *supra*.

workers struck in June; three-fourths of the strikes were sit-downs. The demands were for the right to organize and bargain collectively, which employers had been successfully resisting, for wage increases and better working conditions. The strikers behaved all in all with amazing moderation and good humor, and with friendly respect for the machines around which they sat, sang, ate, and slept.

The CGT had neither the organization nor the interest to launch the sit-down strikes. When the strikes entered into the realm of legend, as they soon did, the Communists were quite as willing to take the credit as their enemies to give them the blame. Actually, the strikes were almost entirely spontaneous: the doing of Communists, Trotskyites, anarchists, and pure syndicalists, organized and unorganized. As at other moments of labor upsurge, the workers' hopes from trade union and party action were so inextricably combined as to be almost undifferentiated one from the other.

In the midst of the sit-down strikes, a Popular Front cabinet took office. Léon Blum became the first Socialist premier in French history, at the head of a government of Socialists and Radicals. He invited the CGT to take a place in the cabinet. This offer the CGT directing bodies unanimously refused. The old apolitical tradition was strong among most, and the Communists had their own reasons. The Communist Party itself declined any place in the cabinet. Although promising support, it kept its freedom of action.

Before anything else, Blum had to do something about the sit-down strikes. The Popular Front government could not be expected to clear the factories by force. As Blum reminded Parliament, even the employers in their hour of fear did not ask him to do that. And he could later say with justifiable pride that in the greatest social upheaval of the Third Republic not a single drop of blood had been shed.[15]

Summoning the representatives of employers and workers, Blum rapidly negotiated with them the vastest general collective agreement in the nation's history, the Matignon Agreement.[16] To represent the workers he called in the CGT. To represent the employers he called upon the CGPF, the General Confederation of French Production (*Confédération Générale de la Production Française*). An organization founded with government stimulus in 1919, the CGPF was a loose federation representing chiefly the large employers and those in industry

[15] Chamber of Deputies, June 26, 1936, p. 1607.
[16] For text of the agreement, see René-P. Duchemin, *Organisation syndicale patronale en France* (Paris, 1940), pp. 310-312. For English text see Appendix C. The name commonly given the agreement is that of the Premier's office building, the Hôtel Matignon.

rather than commerce. It had not taken a great role hitherto in labor relations, nor did it have a mandate from its membership to do so. The sit-down strikes and government pressure forced the CGPF to agree to a complete reversal of the labor relations of most private industry. Jouhaux properly called it the greatest victory in the history of French labor. Employers were to regard it as a humiliating defeat.

The employers assented in principle to "the immediate conclusion" of collective bargaining agreements. Agreements were to include provisions for workers' rights to organize, for an end to anti-union discrimination in hiring and firing, and for the election of shop stewards. Wages were to be increased between 15 per cent for the lowest paid and 7 per cent for the highest paid, an average of 12 per cent—figures arrived at by the arbitration of Blum himself. The employers promised not to take any sanctions for strike actions. The CGT promised—what proved more difficult—to end the strikes.

The agreement was followed by a group of laws which constituted the "French New Deal." These were passed with unheard-of rapidity by the Chamber of Deputies and the always more conservative and slower Senate. In fact, all the important labor legislation of the Popular Front, except for compulsory arbitration, was passed within a few days in June 1936. The collective bargaining law implemented the Matignon principles. Another law instituted vacations with pay (two weeks after one year's employment). A third law provided for a 40-hour week, to be introduced, without reduction of earnings, by government decrees for each industry after consultation with labor and employer organizations.

GROWTH OF THE UNIONS

The CGT grew faster than any free trade union movement had ever grown, from the one million it claimed at reunification to a claimed 5,300,000 members a year later. Although the claimed figures were somewhat inflated, the real growth was phenomenal. In a number of industries, CGT membership went up ten to twenty times.[17] This largely spontaneous rush into the unions occurred chiefly among mass production workers, but also among white collar employees and technicians, hitherto almost impervious to organization. The CGT was at last genuinely representative of the mass of wage earners.

Sudden growth strained the fabric of the CGT unions, and brought a shift in control within many of them. It was 1919 again, on a far larger scale. The new members, most of them unskilled or semiskilled workers, were practically all without any notions of union activity or

---

[17] See figures for individual CGT unions in Appendix G.

union responsibility. While absorbing the flood of members, the unions had to take up all the new tasks thrust on them by the Matignon Agreement and the accompanying legislation. Most unions had only a few officials and those badly paid. The former CGTU elements were much better off than the old CGT elements, for they could utilize the Communist Party cadres.

The Communist Party, momentarily surprised and even annoyed by the swamping of the unions by the inrush of members, quickly threw itself into the work of organizing the new recruits and the swollen unions. It now profited richly by its achievement (in France alone of all countries) of a working class base and structure.[18] With the CGT's shortage of organizers and officials, Communist Party activists moved into positions of leadership of this "new horde who knew nothing of traditional unionism." They were most effective in the Paris region, where the traditional unionism "was practically dissolved in a bath of sulphuric acid." [19] By 1938 the Communists had moved from a minority position at reunification into control of the national metal, chemical, food, agriculture, leather, electric power, and building trades unions.

The CFTC too grew greatly in that "divine poetry of numbers" which the Pope had extolled to a group of CFTC pilgrims.[20] It was not engulfed by the tide of the Popular Front, in which it refused to join, or the expansion of the CGT. It supported most of the CGT's strictly trade union demands but opposed sit-down strikes. From less than 150,000 members early in 1936, its ranks were swelled to perhaps 500,000 a year later. Discounting the CGT's claimed membership figures, the CFTC argued that its numbers relative to those of the CGT were 1:6 or 1:7.[21] It had to wage a continuing fight to maintain the concept of union pluralism—in short, its right to exist and to represent its members. For the suddenly powerful CGT made attempts to establish a near-closed shop in some industries, or at the very least exclusive rights in over-all national representation and in single-industry bargaining.

To meet the new industrial relations situation, employers reorganized their national association. The CGPF showed its new emphasis by taking the name of General Confederation of French Employers (*Confédération Générale du Patronat Français*), instead of General Con-

[18] Borkenau, *World Communism: a History of the Communist International* (New York, 1939), p. 390.
[19] Michel Collinet, "Masses et militants: la bureaucratie et la crise actuelle du syndicalisme ouvrier français," *Revue d'histoire economique et sociale*, vol. 29, no. 1 (1951), pp. 71-72.
[20] R. P. Piat, *Jules Zirnheld*, p. 262.
[21] Vignaux, p. 61.

federation of French Production. It made a real effort to bring in commercial establishments as well as industrial, and small and middle-sized establishments, along with the large concerns which had dominated the organization. Recovered from its fright, it blamed its president, Duchemin, for having signed the Matignon Agreement and eased him out of office. His successor, the vigorous C.-J. Gignoux, called for an end to concessions and urged, "Employers, act like employers!"[22]

COLLECTIVE BARGAINING

For the first time collective bargaining spread through French industry and trade. The 1936 law brought to bear new compulsory mediation machinery and the influence of the Ministry of Labor on the conclusion of agreements. Agreements had to include the freedom to organize and the right of workers to elect shop stewards.

The law stressed two important concepts new in French industrial relations: that of the "extension" of agreements, and that of agreements by the "most representative organizations" of workers and employers. Blum had first spoken of worker representation through exclusive bargaining agents, the concept introduced into American law by the Wagner Act in this period. When it came to official interpretation of the law, however, the government decided that more than one union organization might be "most representative" in any given bargaining unit or area—plant, locality, district, or industry. Numbers in the bargaining unit as a whole were the chief but not the only test of an organization's right to be designated "most representative."[23] The CGT, although hardly any longer denying the independence and *bona fides* of the CFTC, effectively shut the minority unions out of the signing of most agreements. The CFTC was restricted chiefly to white-collar employment and in industry to a few areas of traditional Catholic strength, notably Alsace. The government had the power to "extend" the provisions of an agreement concluded by the most representative organizations, to cover those employers and employees, in the same industry and area, who were not represented by the signers of the original agreement. (The practice of "extension" is discussed in chapter XI.)

In the second half of 1936, over 2,300 agreements were registered. By the outbreak of war, some 8,000 agreements had been concluded. Signers on the employer side were almost all employer associations, rather than individual employers. Some of the agreements were local,

---

[22] This was the title of an energetic, hortatory little book he published. *Patrons, soyez des patrons!* (Paris, 1937).

[23] For a clear brief description of this complex doctrine, see Ehrmann, pp. 43-45. Current issues of representativity are analyzed in Chapter XI.

others districtwide or regional. Only 18 were nationwide, none covering a major industry; the most important was banking. Of the 693 agreements extended, most were departmental or local; 196 covered the Paris region.[24]

The spread of agreements was not enough to ease the tension in industrial relations. As Pierre Laroque, one of the chief architects of the new system of labor relations and its historian, wrote in 1938, "The majority of employers suffer social reforms rather than accept them."[25] The law required the election of shop stewards, but gave them little protection against employer reprisals. Workers often struck against discrimination in the hiring and firing of stewards and union activists. The unions complained of employer refusals to carry out arbitration awards. Meanwhile price rises were eating up wage gains.[26] The workers had their shorter work week and their paid vacations. But since real weekly earnings were no higher than during the depression, they felt cheated.

Employers naturally resented the concessions forced from them. The government had dictated their terms of defeat; "henceforth let the government assume all the responsibility of the new situation," said one member of the employer delegation at the Matignon conference.[27] Employers complained of the sit-downs which still took place and of quickie strikes, arising out of lack of discipline or Communist agitation, of CGT workers' pressure on unorganized fellow workers, and of CGT unions' attempts to control hiring, especially in the building trades. They were aroused by the invasions of what they had long taken for granted as management prerogatives. "We have to decide whether an employer is master in his own house in France—whether there are still employers left," said the head of the electrical industry association.[28]

The atmosphere was one of uncertainty and of gnawing conflict. Symbolic was the unhappy state of the biggest job in Paris, the construction of the 1937 International Exposition. When the fair grounds opened, after both builders' slow downs and workers' strikes, the only three pavilions completed were those of Fascist Italy, Nazi Germany, and the Soviet Union.

---

[24] O. Raffalovich, "La Conclusion des conventions collectives de travail," *Revue française du travail*, vol. 4, no. 1-2, January-February 1949, p. 18.

[25] *Les Rapports entre patrons et ouvriers*, p. 357.

[26] See for example, tables of cost of living indexes and retail price indexes, Paris and 300 cities, January 1935-August 1939, in Joel Colton, *Compulsory Labor Arbitration in France, 1936-1939* (New York, 1951), pp. 30-31.

[27] Quoted by Gignoux, p. 7.

[28] Jules Verger, *Le Temps*, October 24, 1936, cited by Colton, p. 28. As for himself, he added, "I prefer death to surrender." Later he was to take a prominent part in the Vichy régime.

The Blum government was aware that the spirit of labor relations counted more than the letter of the new laws. With prices rising and expected to rise further after the devaluation of the franc, it tried to get the CGPF and the CGT to agree on procedures for arbitration of disputes. After months of negotiation, when the CGPF and the CGT had apparently agreed upon a text, the employers suddenly quit the talks. "The traditional opponents of state intervention in industrial relations shifted responsibility to the state."[29] Failing to get agreement of the parties, the government acted by legislative fiat. In December 1936 the first compulsory labor arbitration law was passed. This act (amended in 1938) was the final labor legislation of the Popular Front.

The CGT had asked for compulsory arbitration. In the face of the difficulties with employers, and the restlessness of its own members, compulsory arbitration seemed the only way to prevent widespread strikes, which the CGT leadership feared would completely alienate public opinion. The CGT suddenly accepted, under a friendly government, what it had always opposed as an intolerable restraint.

The law was one of the few compulsory arbitration measures ever adopted by a democratic industrial nation in peacetime. Its operation was then, and has continued to be, a subject of warm debate. It limited but did not abolish strikes. Its mandatory conciliation procedures had considerable success, particularly in smaller disputes. Its mandatory arbitration procedures provided an orderly though not always satisfactory method of wage adjustments in a time of rapid price rise and social ferment. Weighing its contribution in the light of the hostility between labor and management in France, Joel Colton concludes his detailed study: "Despite its theoretically compulsory nature, the French arbitration system represented no more than a large-scale social service —the establishment of governmental machinery to assist in the settlement of industrial disputes."[30] How well did this machinery ("social service" is perhaps misleading) foster or inhibit collective bargaining? The habits of collective bargaining mature slowly, though the requirements may come in with a rush of legislation and organization.

Contract negotiation too often degenerated into a mere reliance on the decision of the government-appointed "super-arbitrator," with little attempt by the parties themselves, or the two arbitrators they named, to bargain out agreements.[31] Repeatedly the government had to prolong

---

[29] Colton, p. 43. See also Laroque, p. 360.

[30] *Compulsory Labor Arbitration,* p. 155.

[31] Of the 2471 arbitration awards in the year March 1938-February 1939, only 4 per cent were arrived at by the arbitrators named by the parties; 96 per cent were made by the "super-arbitrators" named by the state. Ehrmann, p. 48.

the duration of collective agreements by law, because of the failure of the parties to agree on terms. In a touchy social and political situation, it feared the consequences of widespread expiration of contracts all at about the same time. Ehrmann holds that "on the whole the system weakened rather than strengthened the active participation of business and labor in the normalization of industrial relations." [32]

On this absorbing question, final judgment is impossible because of the shortness of the experiment, the political tensions of the day, and the choking off of collective bargaining at the outbreak of war. But great weight must be given the warning sounded by the CFTC in 1939:

The collective agreements tend to be reduced to the uniform repetition of the legal obligatory clauses; conciliation and simple arbitration are too often treated as pure formalities, with solutions expected only from the "super-arbitrators." The sources of these trends are clear: in conflicts the representatives of the parties themselves prefer not to accept their responsibilities; they unload them on the third party. . . . One cannot remain free except by accepting responsibility.[33]

FAILURE OF THE POPULAR FRONT

"The success of the Popular Front experiment depends on the success of its economic policy," wrote Jouhaux.[34] By the time his words were in print, in 1937, that policy was manifestly failing. The cornerstone of the policy was the idea that wage increases and the 40-hour week would generate increased purchasing power, absorb the unemployed, and revive industrial output. Higher sales volume would allow the absorption of higher total labor costs with no increase in unit costs. The purchasing power theory had its affinities with the American New Deal in its early years. Unlike the New Deal, however, the Popular Front did not lean on deficit financing. In its absence, wage increases and the 40-hour law turned out to be feeble economic stimulants. Price rises rapidly negated the increases in wages. Urban workers' added income, moreover, went largely to buy more food rather than the manufactured goods whose turnover the government wanted to quicken.

Employers generally applied the 40-hour week, contrary to the intent of the law's authors, not as a basic employee work week, but as a plant week, working their machines only a single shift. The CGT was willing to see plants restricted to the "five eights" (five days of eight hours) so as to make enforcement of the law easier. This excessively rigid application of the 40-hour week held back the output of skill categories

---

[32] *French Labor*, p. 49.
[33] Quoted by Vignaux, p. 72.
[34] *La C. G. T., ce qu'elle est, ce qu'elle veut*, p. 7.

and industries needed to fill industrial pipelines and create other jobs. "The reduction of the work week lowered the ceiling on production instead of raising that on employment."[35] Unemployment hardly decreased.

Smaller employers, pinched for credit, were hit hard. But the profits of larger employers, many working on the expanded arms program, held up well. Management responded to its steeply increased labor costs,[36] not by the increases in efficiency which the reform-plus-recovery theory anticipated, but by price increases. "The creative spirit and the willingness to take risks have been weakened," the conservative Finance Minister, Paul Reynaud, reported in 1938. "This—let us not fear to say it—is the root of the evil, for it adds a sort of moral abdication to the material difficulties."[37]

If in the disturbed political and industrial climate, management was unwilling to invest in modernization, labor was largely indifferent to the need of higher productivity under its shorter work week. Total output hardly improved; building activity actually declined sharply. By 1938, industrial production was only 5 per cent higher than 1935, the worst year of the depression; it was still 25 per cent below 1929. Alone among major European countries, France was not producing significantly more.

Blum was too conscious of the precarious foundations of his cabinet to attempt to translate the slogans of the Popular Front into fundamental reforms in the structure of the French economy or French political life. In addition to its labor laws, the chief Popular Front reforms of the government were to bring under a measure of public control the powerful Bank of France, and to give the nation a majority control of the railroads (whose deficits it had long been meeting) and aircraft production. But even Blum's early promise of a "pause" in

[35] François Goguel, *La Politique des partis sous la troisième republique* (Paris, 1946), p. 354. Much of the legislation and administrative regulation is conveniently summarized in U. S. Department of Labor, Wage and Hour Division, *Maximum Hour Legislation in France, 1936-1940* (Mimeographed, Washington, 1941). On the much-debated relation between the 40-hour week and the fall of France, see, in addition to books already cited, Henry W. Ehrmann, "The Blum Experiment and the Fall of France," *Foreign Affairs*, vol. 20, no. 1, October 1941, pp. 152-164, friendly to the experiment. See also Premier Daladier and Finance Minister Paul Reynaud's important "General Report to the President of the Republic on the Decrees Issued in Execution of the Law of October 5, 1938," November 12, 1938, which is translated in full in *The Economist* (London), November 19, 1938, pp. 363-368.

[36] In the year April 1936-1937 manual labor wage rates increased about 60 per cent. M. Kalecki, "The Lesson of the Blum Experiment," *Economic Journal*, vol. 48, no. 189, March 1938, p. 26.

[37] Reynaud and Daladier, "General Report to the President . . . ," cited in note 35, above, p. 365.

reform could not check the flight of capital out of France. The government waited too long before carrying out an inevitable devaluation of the franc. But shrinking from exchange control, it could not check the "hemorrhage of gold" which was further weakening an anemic economy.

The active reform phase of the Blum government lasted only a few months; the government itself a year. In the next year the Popular Front coalition disintegrated completely. A second Blum government in 1938 was only a few weeks' interlude in the drift to the right. By mid-1938 the Radical Socialist Edouard Daladier was heading a government without socialist participation or the pretense of a Popular Front program.

The Popular Front did not cave in only, or even chiefly, because of the weakness of its economic program. The social groups and political parties whose needs had seemed to coincide at one moment drifted apart. The farmers were appeased by the higher prices created by the Blum government's new Wheat Board, a poor harvest, and workers' increased spending for food. With domestic fascism seemingly arrested, farmers and middle class voters worried instead about growing Communist strength and continuing industrial unrest. The Communists and Socialists fell out over foreign policy, Communist sniping at the government they refused to enter, and the Communists' outbidding of their rivals in appeals to workers.

What remained after the Popular Front, the vast brief experiment which sought to bring France up to date in social legislation and to end the alienation between the working class and the rest of the nation? A vital experience in the negotiation of collective agreements by strengthened unions and employer associations, and the mediation and arbitration of disputes. A breach in employer authority and paternalism in the plant. The myths on both sides about the 40-hour week. A gain in workers' living standards which was chiefly that of leisure: the shorter work week and the paid vacations. Nostalgic memories among workers for the easy triumph of the sit-downs. Bitter memories among employers at forced concessions and shop turmoil.

It is easy to say now that almost none of the conditions for the success of the Popular Front experiment existed: a strong, responsible labor movement; a measure of employer acceptance of the limitations on employer authority; the revival of industrial production; a continuity of government policy in favor of collective bargaining; a minimum of international security for France. The CGT was a prey to factional dissension and increasing manipulation by the Communists. Employers made none of that adjustment to a new relationship with labor which

American employers made, rather amazingly, after the validation of the Wagner Act. In part for the same reasons there was little economic recovery under Blum, and no continuity of government social policy after Blum. Hitler deprived France of the freedom to make social experiments that could not be absorbed without social turmoil.

The Popular Front was perhaps doomed, even before it took office, by the pressure of international fascism. France was stagnating industrially, while Nazi Germany was arming, expanding its industry, training its men. In March 1936 Hitler marched into the Rhineland, gambling on the incapacity of France and Britain to use their strength to defend the peace of Versailles and Locarno. But France remained absorbed in her domestic concerns and domestic quarrels.

The bitterness generated by the issues of the Popular Front and Nazi aggression reversed the historic foreign policy roles of right and communist left. Following what they took to be their class interests, many on the right moved toward appeasement: "Rather Hitler than Blum." The Communists meanwhile combined their own vigorous "neo-chauvinism" with international collective security and the defense of Spain and Czechoslovakia. They were the only party to vote in Parliament against the Munich agreement. The Socialists were divided and paralyzed. Blum as premier had promoted the nation's rearmament, but soon it was impossible for the party to maintain a nominal unity except by a stultifying avoidance of the basic issues of foreign policy.

The labor movement as a whole, except for its active Communists, was more aware of the problems of the 40-hour week and unemployment than of the threat to its own and the nation's survival. The drift to war and the fear of war, finally coming to dominate the French political scene, increased the tensions within the CGT. Munich brought close to a head the bitterness among the three major groups: the Communists, the Jouhaux group in the center, the *Syndicats* group[38] on the right. The Jouhaux group placed more reliance on the League of Nations than on the Franco-Soviet Pact, but it was anti-Munich. On international grounds, therefore, it joined with the Communists to constitute a majority at the 1938 CGT convention soon after Munich. The *Syndicats* group, which included the most strenuous anti-Communists, was pacifist and pro-Munich.

THE GENERAL STRIKE OF 1938

International issues and divisions were behind the catastrophic general strike of November 30, 1938. Daladier, given the "full powers"

---

[38] It derived its name from that of its weekly paper, founded in 1937. The Communists continued to publish their own weekly *Vie ouvrière,* which had been the CGTU organ, after the unification of 1936.

which Parliament had refused to Blum, immediately used them to issue decree laws modifying the 40-hour week.[39] Despite the symbolic importance of the 40-hour week, the Communists would not have made an issue of the decree laws alone. They hoped to use the force of the CGT to attack, perhaps to overthrow, the government of Daladier, "the man of Munich." They induced the CGT to threaten a one-day general strike if the decree-laws were not revoked.

Jouhaux and the moderates in the CGT soon saw that a general strike could not possibly succeed. Few workers cared to risk their jobs to protest the complex new regulations, which they could not yet understand, on the 40-hour week. Many welcomed the chance to make some more money by working overtime. As for striking against Munich, they were even more divided. Most important, workers were dissatisfied but apathetic, after all the strikes, alarms, and excursions since the hopeful days of 1936.[40]

Daladier, eager for the showdown, refused to negotiate with Jouhaux and his associates or offer them any face-saving formula by which to call off the strike. He "requisitioned" the workers on the railroads and other essential industries, under the terms of the National Service Law. The law, recently passed with CGT approval, required government consultation with the unions and management on manpower requisitions, but the government brushed aside this requirement. The requisitions were in most cases obeyed. Few workers struck—the miners' union, disciplined though anticommunist, was the chief exception—and the public services operated. The strike was a calamity for the CGT.

The aftermath was a great wave of dismissals of strikers and union activists, in both government and private employment. Despite employer association pleas for moderation, many employers could not resist the occasion to retaliate for the sit-downs and Matignon. Within the CGT, recriminations over the miscarriage of the strike further embittered the factional fight. Millions of members dropped out of the CGT; when the war came, the shattered organization had no more than 2,000,000 members.

In the nine months between the general strike and the general mobilization, there were practically no strikes. CGT representatives were dismissed or resigned from most of the tripartite advisory or regulatory

---

[39] The decree laws did not require parliamentary approval. They were the standard device by which a parliament impotent to act repeatedly turned over its responsibilities to the cabinet, each time a right wing cabinet, in the period between the wars. See Otto Kirchheimer, "Decree Powers and Constitutional Law in France," *American Political Science Review*, vol. 34, no. 6, December 1940, pp. 1104-1123.

[40] For a brilliant description of this state of mind, see Goguel, *La Politique des partis*, pp. 396-397.

agencies set up in recent years. There was an end to active government-labor and labor-management collaboration. But it was more than that. "The scope of the democratic process was being continuously narrowed and the representative organizations of the working class were almost totally excluded from national life."[41] This was the atmosphere in which the union movement and the whole nation, pessimistic and divided, entered the inevitable war.

---

[41] Ehrmann, p. 125.

CHAPTER VI

WAR, OCCUPATION AND RESISTANCE (1939-1944)

It is false to claim today that the defeat of our country is due to the exercise of the liberty of its citizens, when the domestic causes of defeat are the incompetence of our general staff, the weakness of our administration, and the disorder of industry.

—Manifesto of the Twelve CGT and CFTC leaders, November, 1940.

The general run of organized labor never got it into their heads that the only thing that counted was as complete and rapid a victory as possible for their country, and the defeat, not only of Nazism, but of all those elements of its philosophy which its imitators, in the event of success, would inevitably borrow. They had not been taught, as they should have been by leaders worthy of the name, to look above, beyond, and around the petty problems of every day. By concentrating attention on matters concerned with the earning of their daily bread, they ran the risk of discovering that there might be no daily bread to earn.

—Marc Bloch, *Strange Defeat: A Statement of Evidence Written in 1940*, 1949.

Like the clash of arms a generation earlier, the war brought a tremendous shock to the CGT. Union life was disrupted by the mobilization and by an inner crisis which this time came at the beginning of the war, with the Nazi-Soviet pact. When it was clear that the "workers' fatherland" had made a disguised alliance with the national enemy, the factional hatreds seething within the CGT exploded.

Some of the department federations and industrial unions in which anticommunist sentiments were strongest immediately began to oust leading Communists. The central executive bodies of the CGT expelled those of their members who were "unwilling or unable" to condemn the Nazi-Soviet pact, a few days after the Russian invasion of Poland in September 1939. "There will be no split," said Belin, leader of the *Syndicats* group. "In every union we will force the communist leaders, as distinguished from their followers, to leave."[1] Actually the anticommunists did not restrict the purge to the top, but threw out members all down the line who would not specifically disavow the pact. Organizations in Communist hands, notably the Paris region federation, they had to dissolve and reconstitute.

The government dissolved the Communist Party and its subsidiary organizations and banned its publications. It might have done better, after banning the organizations, to tolerate the daily *L'Humanité* and other publications for a time, permitting them to discredit the party by their defense of the pact, the Soviet invasion of Poland, and the war against Finland.[2]

In the first three weeks after the declaration of war, the Communist Party and union leaders still claimed to support their country against Hitler, although they defended the Nazi-Soviet pact. This was the ambiguous line by which they first sought to absorb the shock of the pact and the war. Then, called to order by the Kremlin, they moved into complete opposition to the war. They ridiculed the "legend of the so-called anti-fascist character of the war," assigning responsibilities with Bolshevik impartiality between Hitler and the "Anglo-French-American imperialists and capitalists."

THE CGT AND THE WAR ECONOMY

Had the war been prosecuted differently, the clandestine defeatist communist propaganda might have had little effect on workers. But the "utter moral disarray"[3] of the Daladier government was apparent. It never made its war aims clear to the people. It tolerated defeatists and profascists in high places. Civil liberties suffered needless violence. Many noncommunist union activists were dismissed from government or thrown into internment camps. The economy was managed with inefficiency and obvious inequity.

The CGT was practically shut out of that management, despite the willingness of its reformist leaders to coöperate. The position it received compared painfully with that of 1914-1918. The Daladier government made little attempt to get voluntary understanding among government, labor, and management. It found bureaucratic regulation of the labor market, wages, hours, and working conditions easier. Wages were strictly controlled, while price control was utterly inadequate. The government suspended hours legislation and decreed changes in work-

---

[1] *Le Journal*, September 29, 1939, cited by Ehrmann, p. 146.
[2] Cf. Rossi, *Les Communistes français pendant la drôle de guerre* (Paris, 1951), pp. 37-38.
[3] Albert Guérard, *France: A Short History* (New York, 1946), p. 234.

ing conditions without proper consultation of management or labor. It not only withdrew overtime pay bonuses, but reduced pay for overtime to 40 per cent below base rates. France alone of belligerent nations penalized overtime work.[4]

By decree the government suspended not only collective bargaining on new wage agreements but even the compulsory arbitration law. It froze the provisions of existing agreements and arbitration awards, except as modified by new government regulations. In defense plants a change might be negotiated, not between management and labor, but between the Ministry of Labor and the ministry responsible for the procurement in question. The government "requisitioned" many workers, but in most cases not the plants of their employers. Resentments were enhanced by the differences in pay scales and in discipline among men laboring side by side, who included army conscripts assigned to factories. Protesting unionists might find themselves not only dismissed but simultaneously drafted for the front lines.

There were no real strikes during the war. Sporadic individual walkouts brought military trial and prison terms for the strikers. Industrial relations remained tense, especially in the bigger plants. A possibility for better relations was offered by the government's decree substituting for the election of shop stewards by all workers in a plant the method of designation by the "most representative" labor organizations, that is, in most cases, the CGT. This measure, designed to bar Communist stewards, gave the CGT the control over the stewards which it had earlier sought in order to avoid friction between union representatives and stewards. Labor-management relations were not eased by the new system, however, because in many plants employers prevented the designation of any stewards; in others they dismissed stewards, who no longer had what protection the compulsory arbitration law had given them.

CGT membership sagged under the impact of the expulsions, the mobilization of five and a half million men, and the lack of trade union functions. Workers were bewildered and discouraged by the ambiguous attitude toward the war of many of their leaders in the CGT and the nation and by communist propaganda in the name of the class struggle and proletarian internationalism. Early in 1940 the confederation itself claimed only 800,000 members.

---

[4] Ehrmann, p. 180. U. S. Department of Labor, *Maximum Hour Legislation in France, 1936-1940*, pp. 59-62. The 40 per cent differential between regular and overtime rates did not benefit the employer, but was collected by the government. The government justified the measure as an anti-inflation device and as a device to equalize conditions between mobilized and nonmobilized workers.

The CFTC was spared any political split. Generally it showed a realization of the stake of France and of labor in the war's outcome. Its membership declined comparatively little, and it received greater recognition than before by the government as one of the "most representative organizations." In their coöperation with Jouhaux and other prowar leaders of the CGT, the CFTC leaders drew closer to the older confederation. These working relationships were to take on greater importance in the dark years ahead.

Not until the Nazi armies drove into France did the CGPF consent even in principle to an agreement with the labor organizations. "To the hour of the greatest dangers, must correspond the hour of greatest duties," declared a joint CGPF-CGT-CFTC statement May 29, 1940. "In the struggle for independence which republican France must sustain, there is no room for selfish interests or for class actions or doctrines. Employers and workers become partners, inspired by the same desire for unity and social peace, indispensable for victory."[5] But it was too late to assume the "greatest duties" in what was all too literally the "hour of the greatest dangers." National unity might not have saved republican France from Nazi Panzers and Stukas. Disunity and defeatism helped make defeat inevitable.

VICHY AND OCCUPATION

To the strange shabby regime that came into power at Vichy, free labor organizations and free political parties were alike abhorrent. Yet Vichy was a reluctant satellite and its "National Revolution" a partial, halting, and uncertain dictatorship. It quickly dissolved the national labor confederations, the CGT and the CFTC, the CGPF, and the steel and coal trade associations. But it never succeeded in setting up a labor front like the German or a corporative state like the Italian. Nor did it even come close to creating the single party of fanaticism and terror which is the basis of a modern totalitarian state.

To the extent that Vichy had a philosophy, it was that of a corporative organization for business and labor. But for years it debated how such an organization should be applied to labor, in debates stirred as much by personal intrigues as by conflicts of doctrine. We need not go into these sterile, confused, sordid, and often unreal debates among various shades of corporatists, between corporatists and more ardent collaborators, between unoccupied Vichy and occupied Paris.

A number of labor leaders collaborated in greater or lesser degree with the Vichy government. Their motives were complex and mixed.

---

[5] *Le Peuple,* June 6, 1940, cited by Ehrmann, p. 231.

Like most Frenchmen, they thought the war was all but over in June 1940. They took for granted the defeat of Britain and therefore, for all the visible future, German domination of Europe. There seemed no other government possible for the overwhelmed nation than that of Pétain; if they did not welcome it, they resigned themselves to it. Anticommunism or pacifism or both falsified the judgment of many. Some, hugging old socialist hopes for the unification of Europe, thought Europe's unification would last and Hitlerism would pass.[6] Some of course acted for reasons of personal advancement, with whatever rationale other reasons could supply. Some Catholic unionists who coöperated with the Vichy regime argued that their action was "to save what could be saved." "Your jobs," replied other Catholic unionists.[7] Georges Lefranc argues for René Belin, assistant general secretary of the CGT until its dissolution, Pétain's first Minister of Labor, that he and his friends tried to use "what remained of the French government" to build barriers against the double menace of social reaction and communism.[8]

For a year after the dissolution of the national trade union and employer confederations, Vichy worked and wrangled to produce a Labor Charter ("Charte du Travail"), which was to be the cornerstone of the new corporate edifice. Promulgated in October 1941, the Charter was to do away with the unionism France had known—voluntary, militant, and pluralist. It set up the principle of compulsory membership for all except civil service, maritime and railroad workers, in single unions ("syndicats uniques") for each branch of economic activity in each locality. The unions were to have no more political or religious concerns. The doctrine of class struggle was officially banned, as were its manifestations in strikes and lockouts.

The major organs of labor relations were to be the "social committees" ("comités sociaux"), composed of representatives of employers, workers, and—as a third separate group—technicians and supervisory personnel. One type of the social committees was to rise in a pyramid from the local to the national level in each "occupational family" or industry. Another type of the social committees was to function at the plant level. They were, however, to keep out of economic

---

[6] Louis R. Franck, "In Defeated France: The Forces of Collaboration," *Foreign Affairs*, vol. 21, no. 1, October 1942, pp. 44-58.

[7] Gérard Dehove, "Le Mouvement ouvrier et la politique syndicale," *La France economique de 1939 à 1946* (Paris, 1948), p. 767.

[8] *Les Expériences syndicales en France de 1939 à 1950* (Paris, 1950), p. 36, and *passim*. In any event, in 1949 the French judiciary released Belin without trying him for acts of collaboration. (If he had been apprehended soon after liberation, his fate would certainly have been different.)

questions and deal only with social welfare questions. The Charter stated the leadership principle: "Employers will enjoy the authority which corresponds to the social, technical, and financial responsibilities which they carry."[9] The running of the business was to be the exclusive concern of the boss, commented a Catholic unionist, but the lives of the workers a joint concern.[10]

The unions would be supervised both by social committees and the state. According to the ministerial report on the Charter, the unions would "live and function under the authority of the social committees, and take their inspiration from their doctrines, which could only be those of the state."[11]

The Pétain government reorganized industrial production more effectively than labor relations. All-employer committees called "comités d'organisation" (which may be translated as "industry committees") were set up for all industries. They had power to allocate materials, control prices, and rationalize production and distribution. These could be powers of life and death over enterprises. In many cases they were exercised by representatives of big business in behalf of the bigger concerns. The committees were probably as ably run as the resources of the pinched economy permitted. They drew some of the best administrative brains of the nation, many of whom had long been impatient with parliamentary democracy.

The "corporations" were supposed to emerge from the meshing, in each trade and industry, of social committees (with their labor functions) and industry committees (with their production and price functions). But the industry committees went their way from 1940 on, playing a dominant role in economic life, even fixing the rules for the employment of labor, while the social committees were not even fully set up except at the plant level. Most of the elaborate structure of the Labor Charter never got beyond the stage of blueprints, or bickering over blueprints. As of December 1943, only 130 out of a planned 15-20,000 "syndicats uniques" were in existence.[12]

Belin resigned as Minister of Labor in 1942. Pétain then called in Hubert Lagardelle, ardent pre-World War I theorist of revolutionary syndicalism, and more recently, as an embassy official in Rome, friend

---

[9] Quoted in Emile James, *Les Comités d'entreprise* (Paris, 1945), p. 29.

[10] Vignaux, p. 166.

[11] Cited by Louis Baudin, *Esquisse de l'économie française sous l'occupation allemande* (Paris, 1945), p. 43. On Vichy labor legislation, see also *Revue française du travail,* no. 13, April 1947, "Le droit transitoire des conventions collectives," pp. 340-351.

[12] André Rouast and Paul Durand, *Précis de législation industrielle (Droit du travail),* 4th ed. (Paris, 1953), p. 81, n. 1.

and counselor of Mussolini. He roused no more labor support than had Belin for the Charter or the corporations. After Lagardelle's resignation in 1943, Vichy abandoned the attempt to show direct labor coöperation. By 1944 the rabidly pro-German forces were in full control at Vichy, displacing the more "traditional" authoritarians around the old Marshal. Pétain's last labor minister was Marcel Déat, onetime Socialist deputy, violent pro-Nazi, and unsuccessful leader of one of the sleazy little fascist parties. The chief business of the Minister of Labor by then had become the German demands for forced labor.

LABOR RESISTANCE

Despite the dissolution of the confederations, much local, department federation, and even national union activity of the CGT and CFTC continued, in a curious twilight area between the legal and the clandestine which characterized the ambiguity that was Vichy. Dissolution hit essentially the central organs of the confederations. In the northern zone, occupied by the Germans from the armistice on, conditions for the unionists were more difficult than in the southern zone, which was not occupied until the Allied invasion of North Africa in November 1942.

Labor leaders were naturally as unprepared as the rest of the nation for life after June 1940. For the collapse had been not only one of armies in the field, but of political institutions and of intellectual values —what Pétain called "the lies which have done us so much harm." Slowly, however, the numbing effect of the defeat began to wear off. National spirit and democratic traditions raised their heads again. The enduring elements of the labor union heritage were reaffirmed as early as November 1940, in a mimeographed circular which came to be known as the "Manifesto of the Twelve." In the long line of manifestos and resolutions which mark the epochs of French labor history, this is one of the clearest, despite the confusion of the times. In it nine reformist CGT leaders and three CFTC leaders spoke out against the dissolving of the two confederations, and for the rights of workers to belong or not to belong to whatever union organizations they chose and to be represented by delegates of their own election. From occupied Paris they stoutly declared that "in no case, under no pretext, and in no form could the French union movement admit anti-Semitism, religious persecution, the punishment of opinion, the privileges of wealth."

Groping for new slogans to replace the old ones, the Manifesto proposed "the free union, in the organized industry, under the sovereign state." This was the nebulous prewar Catholic formula of "the free union in the organized industry," with the new concluding phrase as a sign of the times. Hopefully the Manifesto affirmed, "It is not necessary

to choose between unionism and corporatism. Both are equally necessary."[13]

Labor opposition became clearer and more overt when the Labor
Charter was promulgated and the government attempted to set up the
"syndicats uniques," the official obligatory unions. Members of the
Syndicats wing of the CGT, led by Belin, furnished most of whatever
active support there was for the new order of labor relations symbolized
by the Labor Charter. The Jouhaux wing was generally in opposition to
the Charter, and increasingly so after Jouhaux's arrest and deportation
to Germany as a hostage. "As long as the Germans are not at London,"
he had said, "the war is not lost and we need not behave as if it were."
In a sense this continued the debate over Munich between the Belin
and Jouhaux followers a few years earlier. Catholic opposition to Vichy
was not embarrassed by Pétain's vigorous overtures to the church and
the rallying of many of the clergy to his regime of "work, family, and
fatherland."[14] CFTC leaders had been debating the issues of corporatism for some years. But, even had they not been so concerned with the
freedom of the individual, CFTC leaders could hardly be expected to
give up the right to their separate unions (in a country where they were
a small minority) in favor of the "syndicats uniques."

The developing resistance gained the powerful addition of the Communist Party. After the capitulation, the party's first instructions to its
cadres, in June 1940, had said "the enemy, which in any imperialist war
is within one's own country, is overthrown. The working class of
France and of the world must see this event as a victory and understand
it means one enemy less."[15] General de Gaulle was a reactionary and
"an agent of English financiers who would make the French fight for
the City of London."[16] It reminded French workers, "Get it straight
that it is not in the victory of one imperialism over another that our
salvation lies."[17] Upon the German invasion of Russia, it threw itself
into the struggle against the Germans (it had been anti-Vichy), praised

---

[13] CFTC, *Unité syndicale ou unité d'action: Recueil des textes et des documents . . .*
(Paris, no date, 1945?) pp. 5-11. The full text of the Manifesto is given in Appendix D.
For a later, somewhat more equivocal text by the same group (the Committee of
Trade Union and Economic Studies), see Lefranc, *Les Expériences syndicales*, pp.
98-101.

[14] For an eloquent French Catholic comment, see (in addition to Vignaux), Jacques
Maritain, "Religion and Politics in France," *Foreign Affairs,* vol. 20, no. 2, January
1942, pp. 266-281.

[15] Cited by A. Rossi, *La Physiologie du parti communiste français* (Paris, 1948),
appendix, note A, pp. 395-396.

[16] For example, citations, *Ibid.,* pp. 44, 86.

[17] *Ibid.,* appendix, note C, p. 413, citing *L'Humanité* of June 20, 1941, two days
before Hitler's invasion of Russia.

De Gaulle, and put aside the proletarian revolution in favor of a redis-covered patriotism and appeals for national unity with all groups.

It was easier for the Communists to switch in mid-1941 to a "national front" line than it had been in 1939 to switch in the opposite direction. They were now moving in the direction of popular feeling. Like the similar turn from sectarianism to the united front in 1934, similarly dic-tated by the needs of Soviet foreign policy, the 1941 turn was to bring the party a larger following and new power. To the resistance it brought the one experienced clandestine party organization, with its hardened cadres, its dedicated energy, its considerable working class influence.

When the Germans imposed forced labor on France in 1942, they gave a new and impelling basis to the resistance. The reluctance of French workingmen to leave for German factories was intensified by reports of Allied bombings of Germany, just beginning in force. Many able-bodied young workers fled to the "Maquis,"[18] the difficult country of hill and bush. They were the foundation of much of the organized armed resistance to Vichy and the Germans. To Gauleiter Sauckel, mobilizing French manpower for German industry, Vichy Premier Pierre Laval once suggested, "You are the envoy of General de Gaulle." Sauckel barked, "No, of Chancellor Hitler." "Ah," said Laval, "I thought you were the envoy of General de Gaulle—for the organization of the Maquis."[19]

SECOND REUNIFICATION OF THE CGT

The new international alignment, coöperation in the resistance, and postwar hopes, led to the reunification of the CGT. Representatives of the Jouhaux wing of the reformists and of the Communists agreed to reunite the organization underground, at Le Perreux in April 1943. The reunified organization was at all levels to reëstablish the "physi-ognomy"—that is the balance of forces in leadership—of the CGT of September 1939, just before the split. The confederation Executive Board was reconstituted with five Reformists of the Jouhaux wing and three Communists.[20]

The CGT and the CFTC early rallied to De Gaulle as the symbol and

---

[18] The name, originally applied to wild and bushy land, was soon applied also to those who took refuge and joined the resistance in such terrain.

[19] J. Baraduc, *Dans la cellule de Pierre Laval*, p. 82, cited by David Thomson, in *Two Frenchmen: Pierre Laval and Charles de Gaulle* (London, 1951), p. 93. Thomson summarizes the problem of the labor draft, pp. 92-97. See two articles in the *International Labour Review* (ILO), vol. 47, 1943, pp. 312-343, and vol. 49, 1944, pp. 38-51, on the mobilization of French workers for Germany.

[20] The text of the agreement is in *Notes et études documentaires*, No. 1239, *L'Evolution intérieure de la CGT, op. cit.*, pp. 19-20.

head of the resistance. They sent delegates to London and to Algiers to work with the Free French movement. Their delegates took prominent places in De Gaulle's Consultative Assembly at Algiers; the Assembly elected as its president a CGT leader, the reformist Georges Buisson. Inside France, the CGT and CFTC representatives sat in the local and departmental committees of liberation and the National Council of Resistance, along with representatives of the resistance groups and political parties from extreme right to the Socialists and Communists. (De Gaulle invited two Communists into the Free French government. They became the first Communists to sit in any French cabinet.) Workers of all shades of opinion were active in the resistance: in the fight against forced labor, in propaganda, intelligence networks, in sabotage, especially on the railroads, in the Maquis, and in preparations for wider action after the long-awaited Allied landings.[21]

The resistance, said one of its Catholic right-wing leaders later, "was far more than the 'men of the left,' who too often loved the International more than they loved France. The resistance was far more than the 'men of the Right,' who in other days were too often deaf to the needs of social reform."[22] The resistance, in the sense of active organized military, paramilitary, or intelligence formations, was necessarily a comparatively small number; the majority of people are not heroes. "Those who were with the resistance from the start . . . know how few and solitary they were at the beginning as at the end."[23] From the Allied military point of view General Eisenhower paid his tribute to the resistance.[24] Harder to measure, but vital too, was what the resistance contributed to restoring the self-respect of a great but lacerated nation.

The story of the occupation and the resistance has yet to be written. One history puts the number of forced laborers sent to Germany at 600,000; political deportees at 115,000, of whom only 40,000 survived; and those shot by the Germans and Vichy as at least 30,000.[25] The CGT estimated its martyrs at 7,000 activists shot and 8,000 deported.[26] For most people—neither heroes nor collaborators—life somehow went on under the occupation. Economic life was sharply reduced by the short-

[21] For the Communist-led CGT's account of "The Working Class and the CGT in the Resistance," see *La Voix du peuple*, 5 série, no. 1, January 1946, *Rapports confédéraux* (to the 1946 convention), pp. 11-34, 42. For a less rosy view, see Lefranc, *Les Expériences syndicales, passim.*

[22] Guillain de Bénouville, *The Unknown Warriers: a Personal Account of the Resistance* (New York, 1949), p. 343.

[23] *Ibid.*, p. 342.

[24] "Without their great assistance the liberation of France and the defeat of the enemy in Western Europe would have consumed a much longer time and meant greater losses to ourselves." *Crusade in Europe* (New York, 1948), p. 296.

[25] Henri Michel, *Histoire de la résistance* (Paris, 1950), p. 124.

[26] *Le Peuple,* March 31, 1945.

age of materials and fuel and the German policy (except in concerns working on German orders) of creating unemployment as an inducement to workers to volunteer for work in Germany. The index of industrial production (with 1938 as 100) fell to 62 at the beginning of 1941 and 52 two years later. Price controls broke down in the face of old weaknesses of administration plus new patriotic and price incentives to sell in black markets. Wage controls were far more effective, in part because of German policy to induce Frenchmen to volunteer for work in Germany. Real wage rates for skilled workers (with 1938 as 100), estimated at 71.7 in 1940, fell to 61.3 in 1941 and 58.7 by October 1943.[27]

Many employers did what they could, by legal means and illegal, to give higher wages and get more food to their employees. Food supplies were tragically short, but thanks to continuing personal ties between city and country, workers' families often subsisted on packages of butter and meat, paid or gift, from relatives and friends on farms. When Allied bombings became massive, it was workers who were frequently the victims, in factories or in homes near the railroad marshalling yards. The political repression of Vichy and the Nazis struck down many workers and union officials.

Even under Vichy and the occupation there were strikes. The biggest was a coal strike in northern France in the spring of 1941, which, the Communists later pointed out, came before the German invasion of Russia. As the war went on, the demonstrations and stoppages for immediate demands—higher wages, safer working conditions, better food supplies—took on increasingly political overtones. In August 1944, with the Allied armies sweeping forward from Normandy, the railroad workers and the police of Paris struck, and the capital rose against the occupants. A joint committee of the CGT and the CFTC called a "general strike for liberation," effective chiefly in Paris.[28] The strike and the uprising in Paris aimed to show France and the world that Paris was liberating itself, rather than waiting for the Allied armies.[29] Some of the leaders also sought to put the resistance organizations in the

---

[27] *Etudes et conjoncture: union française,* no. 5-6, December 1946-January 1947, p. 314.

[28] On the Paris events, see Adrien Dansette, *Histoire de la libération de Paris* (Paris, revised ed., 1946). For a good description of life in the capital during the strike and the insurrection, see Jean Galtier-Boissière, *Mon journal pendant l'occupation* (Garas, 1944), pp. 250-285.

[29] The insurrection and strike forced SHAEF to change its plans and to dispatch two divisions to liberate Paris, to avoid the possibility of another tragedy like that of Warsaw. It had been felt that Paris was then of no military value. General Bradley worried about the logistical problem, seeing Paris in terms of "4,000,000 hungry Frenchmen," *A Soldier's Story* (New York, 1951), p. 384. But, as Eisenhower said, *Crusade,* p. 302, the liberation of Paris "had a great impact on people everywhere."

strongest position vis-à-vis De Gaulle's Provisional Government. Many people thought that a social revolution was at hand.

"Paris fights today so that France may speak the day after. The people is in arms tonight because it hopes for justice tomorrow," wrote the sensitive patriot, Albert Camus, in his resistance paper on the eve of liberation. "A liberty conquered by these convulsions will not have the tame and tranquil visage which some people dream of. This terrible birth is that of a revolution."[30] How much of a revolution and whose revolution were questions before France and the labor movement.

---

[30] *Combat*, August 24, 1944, in Albert Camus, *Actuelles, chroniques 1944-1948* (Paris, 1950), p. 20.

PART TWO

THE UNIONS SINCE LIBERATION (1944-1953)

CHAPTER VII

COMMUNIST COÖPERATION AND UNION CONQUEST
(1944-1947)

> If we were capable only of shedding our blood each time it was neces-
> sary to defend the soil of our country as in 1793, or liberty as in 1830 and
> 1871, and not of taking the power we earned, we would be failing in our
> mission.
>
> —Louis Saillant, to convention of
> the CGT federation of the Marne
> department, August 1945, *Le Peuple,*
> September 1, 1945.

> The emancipation of the working class is inseparable from the inde-
> pendence of the country, itself inseparable from its economic recovery. The
> battle of production is really a class struggle, in which the workers' in-
> terests come up against the special interests of the trusts, the two hundred
> families, and the financial oligarchy.
>
> —Executive Board Report to the
> 1946 CGT Convention.

As Paris was liberated and the German armies were swept from all
but a few pockets of French territory, Frenchmen expected—many with
fear, more with hope and confidence—that a new France was to arise
out of the defeat and the self-questioning, out of the resistance and the
victory. In this new France, the "social problem" would at last be on
its way toward solution.

Liberation and the Fourth Republic beckoned the unions to a new and
great role. Labor had played a large part in the organization of the resistance and the liberation. Its representatives had refused to accept Hitler's New Order and Pétain's National Revolution. Workers had been
in the vanguard of organized resistance. Their contribution was ac-
claimed by those of good conscience and some of uneasy conscience. In
this acclaim there was some element of an emerging myth—a myth of
the nation's quasi-total resistance and its self-liberation—which grew
naturally out of the nation's effort to regain its wounded self-esteem.[1]

---

[1] Later the Communists, in the process of rewriting history, suppressed references
to the contribution of the Western Allies to liberation, except for bombing destruction.

For its record, this myth had to rely considerably upon the workers' real contribution in the Maquis, in strikes and sabotage.

Most of the nation's élites stood discredited: the military, the higher levels of the civil administration, the press, financial and industrial leaders. They were held responsible for failing to prepare the nation's defense, for preferring Hitler to the Popular Front, for supporting Vichy and profiting from the occupation. They themselves had lost confidence in their ability to run the country, and the nation shared their lack of confidence. Labor, on the other hand, was then hardly blamed for the national catastrophe, for it had been virtually excluded from national decision after 1938. It was only later that people suggested that all elements of the community were responsible, in greater or lesser degree, for the fall of France.[2]

"France tomorrow will be what its working class is," the resistance paper, *Combat,* declared in its first postclandestine issue.[3] Few would have disagreed, and none openly, with General de Gaulle's tribute to the "importance of the role which the patriotism of the working class, its wisdom, its courage played in the resistance of the nation to the enemy, which they play now in its reconstruction, which they will play tomorrow in its regeneration."[4]

The programs of the resistance groups[5] and the government of Algiers drew largely upon reforms advanced by the CGT and the CFTC between the wars. In the generous moments of the liberation, almost everyone was talking in vaguely socialistic, or at least social, terms. It seemed as if Léon Blum had been right when, in his prison cell, in the darkest moments of the defeat and abdication of the Third Republic, he had written, "The Fourth Republic will be one of social welfare or it will not be at all."[6]

Things went farther than social reform in some areas of the country. Parts of the South and Center, notably those liberated by resistance forces, were for a time out of reach of the effective rule of the Provi-

---

[2] Among the few earlier suggestions that there had been a failing of all classes was the profound and moving analysis of Marc Bloch, perhaps the most important single book on the reasons for the fall of France, *L'Etrange défaite: témoignage écrit en 1940* (Paris, 1946), translated as *Strange Defeat* (London, 1949), pp. 134-143. See also Léon Blum, *A l'echelle humaine,* written in 1941, p. 118.

[3] Cited in *Combat,* April 9, 1946.

[4] Speech to the Consultative Assembly, March 2, 1945, *L'Année politique, 1944-1945* (Paris, 1946), p. 448.

[5] For the program of "Measures to Apply upon the Liberation of the National Territory," of the National Council of the Resistance, see *L'Année politique, 1944-1945,* pp. 429-431; for English text, David Thomson, *Democracy in France* (2d ed.), pp. 276-278.

[6] *A l'echelle humaine,* p. 131. Blum was reversing the prophecy of Thiers when the Third Republic was being born: "The Republic will be conservative, or it will not be."

sional Government. Here and there liberation brought a semirevolution-
ary situation, with summary executions of collaborators and alleged collaborators, seizures of factories and their operation by employee committees. Paris buzzed with rumors about the wild doings of areas from
which it was cut off. But the central government soon asserted its control. With the French Communist Party supporting the government and
the war, matters soon calmed down—to the regret of some of the party's
more enthusiastic followers, old and new.

In the heady atmosphere of liberation, the unions rapidly rebuilt their
organizations. Once again, as in 1936, members rushed in on the tide of
great political events and hopes. Trade union liberty had been restored,
and the Labor Charter abolished, by the Provisional Government at
Algiers.[7] The CGT received the vast majority of new union members.
By September 1945, it claimed 5,454,000 members in 15,040 local
unions,[8] and over a million in the Paris region alone.[9] The CFTC, also
strengthened by its role in the resistance, grew rapidly to new heights;
at its first convention, a year after liberation, it claimed about three-
quarters of a million members in 2,400 local unions.[10]

Immediately after liberation, in September 1944, and again insist-
ently on several occasions during the following year, the CGT urged the
smaller confederation to amalgamate with it. It offered the Catholic
unions proportional representation in the leadership of a combined
movement. These offers the CFTC executive bodies refused politely,
although with increasing firmness and even visible annoyance as the
CGT made efforts in some areas to establish a *de facto* closed shop. Although in the enthusiasm immediately following liberation some of its
local bodies had urged unification, the CFTC never seriously considered
giving up its separate existence. But the Catholic leaders did not yet consider it good form to mention their well-grounded apprehension that the
CGT would soon be under full Communist control. They offered to continue unity of action, as in the underground. This would be preferable,
they said, to "a fusion which risks being only confusion." ("Unity of
action" is a standard form for refusing organic unity.) This offer the
CGT brushed aside in favor of renewed invitations to amalgamate.

The first postwar convention of the CFTC in September 1945 gave
the definitive and unanimous answer. It cited current disagreements on
political action, women's work, and parochial schools as illustrating the

---

[7] Ordinance of July 27, 1944, *Journal officiel*, August 30, 1944. The confiscated
property of the CGT and CFTC was returned to them. The dissolved CGPF was not
mentioned in the ordinance.

[8] *Le Peuple*, September 28, 1945, p. 1.

[9] *Vie ouvrière*, April 4, 1946.

[10] Dehove in *La France Économique et sociale de 1939 à 1946*, p. 776.

"grave divergences of principles and programs" between the two organizations which made fusion hopeless. Reiterating its offers to coöperate with the CGT at the local, departmental, and national levels, it once again affirmed its traditional belief in union pluralism as "one of the highest expressions of the exercise of liberty and democracy."[11]

Even the noncommunist leaders of the old confederation berated the CFTC for "disappointing the CGT's hopes of trade union unity. The CGT gives unity a value in itself."[12] The communist leadership, muttering about the church hierarchy's blocking trade union unity, restated its purposes more menacingly: "There remains to us now only one way, for we continue determined partisans of unity within a single CGT. That is to work tooth and nail to liquidate disunity at the workplace itself."[13] In short, to establish a *de facto* or *de jure* closed shop, by all the pressure it could command at the shop level and through the government. In this it was to be largely unsuccessful.

SOCIAL AND ECONOMIC REFORMS

A considerable part of the reform program of the resistance was enacted in the first two years after liberation. At the time little objection was offered to the principle of any of these reforms. Thus only a small minority of extreme right-wing deputies (on no bill more than 11 per cent of those voting) voted against the 1946 nationalization laws. After 1946, there was almost no further social reform.

The coal mines, gas and electric production and distribution, the Bank of France, the four largest deposit banks, and the thirty-four largest insurance companies were nationalized, with compensation to the former owners.[14] The large Renault automobile company was nationalized, without compensation, after Louis Renault died awaiting trial for collaboration. In line with the old CGT formula of "industrial

---

[11] Decisions of CFTC Executive Bureau, September 26, 1944; National Committee, April 15-16, 1945; and convention, September 17, 1945, *Syndicalisme*, September 22, 1945, pp. 2, 4. The texts of the most important resolutions of the two confederations and correspondence between them are collected in the CFTC brochure already cited, *Unité syndicale ou unité d'action.*

[12] Robert Bothereau, *Nouvelles économiques,* January 18, 1946.

[13] Frachon at CGT convention, *Congrès national . . , 8-12 April, 1946, Compte rendu . . ,* p. 29.

[14] On the problems of nationalization, see René Gendarme, *L'Expérience française de la nationalisation industrielle et ses enseignements économiques* (Paris, 1950); Marcel Ventenat, *L'Expérience de nationalisation: Premier Bilan* (Paris, 1947); International Labor Office, *Labor-Management Coöperation in France* (Geneva, 1950), pp. 97-139; two articles by David Pinkney, "The French Experiment in Nationalization, 1944-1950," *Modern France,* pp. 354-367; and "Nationalization in France," *Yale Review,* September 1950; two articles by Adolf Sturmthal, "The Structure of Nationalized Enterprises in France," *Political Science Quarterly,* vol. 67, no. 3, September 1952, pp. 357-377, and "Nationalization and Workers' Control in Britain and France," *Journal of Political Economy,* vol. 61, no. 1, February 1953, pp. 43-79.

nationalization," complete state control was avoided, in favor of tripartite boards of directors representing labor, consumers, and government.
Union representatives, a large majority named by the CGT and a minority by the CFTC, were placed on the boards of directors of nationalized industries. In some industries, not only did CGT leaders represent
labor, but other CGT officials were named as consumer industry representatives. CGT officials were appointed also to high positions in the
bureaucracy of the nationalized industries.

The social security system was overhauled and its benefits substan-
tially extended. Family allowances, greatly enlarged in 1939, were
raised to much higher levels. Health, maternity, invalidity, and old age
insurance benefits were increased. Workmen's compensation was taken
out of private insurance company hands and made part of the public
system. No provision was made for unemployment compensation; the
old system of unemployment assistance (or relief), with its small benefits, continued. Social security was to cover not only wage earners but
the entire population; this policy proved impossible to implement except
for family allowance benefits.

The complex structure of social insurance administration was considerably unified, though not centralized. The various friendly society
types of separate funds were amalgamated (over Catholic protests) on
a geographic basis. Workmen's compensation, health, and old age insurance were brought under one administration, with family allowances
left under another. These measures of unification applied only to the
"general" social insurance system. Despite the proclaimed unification,
vested interests succeeded in maintaining a large number of separate
systems, notably those for civil servants, railroad workers, maritime
workers, miners, gas and electricity workers, agricultural workers, and
innumerable smaller groups.

The changes marked an advance in the state's recognition of social
responsibility and a declared purpose to redistribute the national income.
It was no doubt only pardonable exaggeration for the Director of Social
Security in the Ministry of Labor to speak of the advance "from social
insurance to social security."[15]

---

[15] Pierre Laroque, "From Social Insurance to Social Security: Evolution in
France," *International Labour Review,* vol. 57, no. 6, June 1948, pp. 565-590. See also
J. Lajugie, *La Sécurite sociale* (Paris, 1948), pp. 88-124; F. Netter, *Notions essentielles
de sécurité sociale* (Paris, 1951). For a brief English description, see La Documentation française illustrée, *Social Security in France,* (Paris, no date: 1949?), text by
the Ministry of Labor. For perhaps the first extensive critical review of operations, see
Cour de Comptes, *La Securité sociale, années 1950-1951,* a report to the President of
the Republic, in *Journal officiel, annexe administrative,* March 18, 1952, pp. 135-296.
The report is discussed in three unsigned articles in *Droit social,* vol. 15, nos. 8, 9, and
10, September-October, November, and December 1952, pp. 553-564, 627-644, 701-709.

In the administration of social security, the workers' representatives were given a preponderant place, on the theory of keeping the largest possible measure of policy control in the hands of the insured. One set of quasi-autonomous boards of administration was established, under state supervision, to run the social insurances, and another set of public boards to run the family allowance system. Elected representatives of workers received three-fourths of the seats on the social insurance boards. On the family allowance boards, since employers were also recipients of family allowances, employer and worker representatives were equal in number.

Another reform was to realize the old trade union demand for a voice in management, by the establishment of labor-management plant committees ("comités d'entreprise"). Made up of elected representatives of employees, presided over by the employer or plant manager, the committees were given control of plant social welfare work and consultative powers in production and economic decisions. The law required the election of committees in all enterprises employing fifty or more workers. (The committees are discussed in detail in Chapter XIV).

The institution of shop stewards was revived by law, and their election required in all establishments employing more than ten workers. Like the other forms of workers' representation just noted—social security board administrators and plant committee members—they were elected from slates put up by the unions. To remedy a defect made clear under the Popular Front, the law tried to give the stewards meaningful protection against arbitrary discharge. The stewards' right to handle grievances was independent of any collective agreements. In fact, collective bargaining was still not permitted at the time of passage of the shop steward law in mid-1946. (For discussion of the shop stewards, see Chapter XIV.)

Labor took a place on public economic planning and policy agencies. The new constitution provided for a National Economic Council, representing the major national economic groups of the country, to advise on economic and social legislation. It elected as its president Léon Jouhaux, whose CGT had sponsored such a council for a generation. CGT and CFTC union heads sat on the Council of the Monnet Planning Commission for the nation's economic modernization and reëquipment.[16] In preparing its first general investment program, the commis-

---

[16] See series of reports (some available in English) by the Commissariat Général du Plan de Modernisation et d'Equipement (more generally known by the name of Jean Monnet, its director from its foundation in 1946 to 1952). Also Jacques Dumontier, *Budget économique et capital national* (Paris, 1951); Pierre Uri, "France: Reconstruction and Development," in Howard Ellis, ed., *The Economics of Freedom* (New York, 1950), pp. 239-298; Harold Lubell, *The French Investment Program: a Defense*

sion sought the ideas and the "grass roots" participation of interested economic groups; several CGT leaders headed industry "modernization committees." Labor spokesmen sat on a host of other regulatory and advisory bodies required by the system of wage, price, materials, credit, and other economic controls.[17]

The strength of labor and the concern for social welfare showed in the Constitution of the Fourth Republic, finally adopted in October 1946. Specified in its preamble were "the duty to work and the right to obtain employment" and the right to "health protection, material security, rest and leisure" and "the means to lead a decent existence" when unable to work. It assured everyone the right to join the union of his choice, to strike, and "through his representatives, to take part in collective bargaining to determine working conditions and in the management of enterprises."[18]

RECONSTRUCTION AND LIVING STANDARDS

The workers gave unstinted coöperation in the rebuilding of the nation's economic life. By great efforts with meager and worn equipment, they made it possible to break the two critical bottlenecks of rail transport and coal. The index of industrial production (1938 = 100) had reached the low point of 21 at liberation and 32 in the hard winter of 1944-45. It climbed back to 62 by the end of 1945. By the end of the following year it stood at 88, with coal production and rail traffic above the 1938 levels.[19] Although the destruction had been greater than in the first war, the industrial economy recovered its prewar levels more rapidly.

Workers' claims to higher living standards were deferred not only until the end of the war, but well beyond it. The CGT called on them to

---

of the Monnet Plan (Paris, 1951, photo-offset) ; Richard Ruggles, "The French Investment Program and Its Relation to Resource Allocation," in Modern France, pp. 368-381 ; and R. V. Rosa, "The Problem of French Recovery," Economic Journal, vol. 59, June 1949, pp. 154-170.

[17] These bodies are described, as of early 1948, in the International Labor Office study, Labor-Management Coöperation in France.

[18] For text of the constitution in English and debates and referenda preceding its adoption, see Foundation for Foreign Affairs, Foundation Pamphlet No. 2, A Constitution for the Fourth Republic [unsigned, Otto Kirchheimer] (Washington, 1947), and Gordon Wright, The Reshaping of French Democracy (New York, 1948).

[19] Etudes et conjoncture: union française, vol. 1, no. 5-6, December 1946-January 1947, p. 280; vol. 2, no. 8-9, March-April 1947, p. 10.

References to prewar levels of economic activity, unless otherwise stated, are to 1938, the usual and obvious base for comparisons. But it must be recalled that 1938 was a year of stagnation, with industrial production 25 per cent below 1929.

Industrial production index numbers cited throughout include building, unless otherwise noted, although the building figure is one of the least reliable components of the index.

"roll up their sleeves" in the interest of the nation's recovery, to produce now, and make demands later.[20] "To produce is to win the battle of democracy," said a large banner across the 1946 convention hall. "The highest form of our class duty is to develop production to the maximum," the head of the miners' union told the delegates in words repeated over and over again. "That is why winning the battle of production is winning a class battle against the trusts." Only the trusts and reactionaries wanted to put the brakes on production, "to hamper economic recovery, aggravate the suffering of the people, increase discontent, and replace our democratic government by a reactionary government."[21] And the CGT's convention manifesto asserted: "The first duty is to raise production . . . In the present state of the country, the effort of production by labor must be considered the indisputable right of workers to participate in the renaissance of France."[22] The CGT helped develop and promote the ambitious Monnet Plan, with its stress on capital investment at the expense of consumer goods.

"Yesterday we were in the opposition, and we could permit ourselves some vagaries," Gaston Monmousseau told the CGT's Paris region convention in 1946. "Today it is the trusts who are in opposition, and we who bear the responsibilities."[23]

Coöperation in reconstruction was also the watchword of the Communist Party, which rapidly affirmed its position as the strongest of the three parties (Socialist, Catholic MRP, and Communist) which governed France until mid-1947. Maurice Thorez, its outstanding figure, condemned as an army deserter in 1939, was amnestied by De Gaulle in late 1944 so that he might return to France from Russia. Immediately and on numerous public occasions he sounded a line both patriotic and governmental: coöperation with the authorities, a powerful national army, and economic recovery. The nation's most famous ex-miner, he harangued the miners in his home area of the North with the message of production.

"We are a government party," Thorez told the 1945 Communist convention. "We must be equal everywhere to our responsibilities before the party and before the nation."[24] More significant than any general discourse was his support of the government in De Gaulle's decisive conflict with the communist-led resistance agencies. Thorez backed the

---

[20] See for example the 1944-1945 speeches and reports of Benoît Frachon, co-general secretary of the CGT, collected in *La Bataille de la production* (Paris, 1946).

[21] CGT, *Congrès, 1946, Compte rendu . .* , p. 52.

[22] *Ibid.*, p. 373.

[23] *Vie ouvrière*, March 28, 1946.

[24] Thorez, *Une Politique française: renaissance, démocratie, unité,* Report to Tenth National Convention of the Communist Party, June 26-30, 1945, p. 59.

government's dissolution of the "patriot militia," (more or less armed irregulars in cities and factories), its absorption of the fighting partisan formations by the regular army, and its subordination of obstreperous committees of liberation to the regularly constituted local and departmental authorities. For the time being this action set at rest fears that the Communist Party would try to maintain a framework of independent and parallel state power within the state, through private armies and the network of committees of liberation.

From their posts in the government and in the CGT the Communists sternly repressed any rank-and-file inclination to slacken or to strike. Thus Frachon even lectured a young miner reported to him as staying away from work one Monday because of a heavy bout of dancing over the weekend.[25] To derisive suggestions of "Stakhanovism" from embittered anti-Communists, Frachon and other Communist CGT leaders replied, "We have never let ourselves be impressed by partisan criticisms against our campaign for production, even when these criticisms claimed to be for the protection of the workers."[26]

When the Paris typographical workers struck for higher wages, the Communist Minister of Labor, Ambroise Croizat, leader of the metal workers' union, denounced them on the radio. And Monmousseau pointed out, "It is not by accident that the typical fascist organ L'Epoque (a Paris·rightist daily) today defends the workers' right to strike, at a moment when the essential problem is to produce ever more. Trotskyite elements, opposing the effort of production, and pushing for ill-considered strikes, meet on the same ground as the reaction."[27] The old reformist, Capocci, whose white-collar workers union had launched a few strikes, declared his astonishment that for the first time at a CGT convention the strike was treated as a maneuver of the employer class, and comrades were hissed for strike talk.[28]

For almost two years after liberation, there were no serious strikes.[29] The immediate postwar strikes characteristic of most capitalistic countries did not occur—or, rather, were postponed until 1947.

COMMUNIST CONTROL OF THE CGT

The Communist Party was no prisoner of its own slogans of unity and coöperation. It sought the realities of power, and nowhere with

---

[25] La Bataille de la production, pp. 158-159.
[26] Ibid., p. 216.
[27] Introduction to Frachon, La Bataille de la production, p. 10.
[28] CGT, Congrès, 1946, Compte rendu . . , p. 128.
[29] Man days lost through strikes in 1946 totaled only 312,000. Revue française du travail, vol. 1, no. 11, February 1947, p. 200. No strike loss data have been published for 1945; the number would be negligible.

greater effectiveness than in the trade union movement. It made the CGT the chief mass base of its power. The party had its men ready to move into the unions as soon as they could be openly reconstituted. With vigor and self-assurance, sometimes with fraud and force, they installed themselves in key positions in local unions, department federations, and national organizations. The methods ranged from regular election to character or physical assassination.[30] In some cases they formed strike committees just before liberation, predominantly Communist in makeup, which turned themselves on liberation into union executives to the exclusion of non-Communist leaders. In at least a few cases, they arranged for extralegal arrests of opponents by the patriot militia, and held elections in their rivals' absence. They had means, which their competitors lacked, to obtain black market paper supplies for organization and propaganda. In their factory cells and union fractions they had the best means for keeping in touch with rank-and-file sentiment and controlling union activity from the base up.

All parties and groups, from right to left, and in the unions reformists and Communists both, had had their heroes and their traitors. The Communists managed a magnificent show of speaking and acting as if there had been no treason or weakness in their own ranks; for almost two years few people took it upon themselves to remind them there had been any. Many of the most zealous and articulate anti-Communists had been prewar pacifists, hence "pro-Munich"; Belin and other *Syndicats* leaders had served under Vichy. The Communists succeeded in identifying anti-Communist with antinational and antiworking-class behavior. They used the trade union purge commissions to purge the union movement not only of collaborationists but also of potential opposition leaders.

By March 1945, at the first CGT National Committee meeting since liberation, the Communists were strong enough to change the distribution of seats on the Executive Board, to acquire nominal parity with the reformists, instead of the three-to-five ratio of the 1943 reunification.[31] In September they were in clear control of the confederation. They named their top trade union leader, the very able Benoît Frachon, to the

[30] Rossi, *La Physiologie du parti communiste français*, pp. 443-445, describes assassinations and attempted assassinations, shortly after liberation, of trade union leaders who had quit the Communist Party after the Nazi-Soviet Pact.

[31] Actually, they obtained a majority: Pierre Le Brun, nominally neutral, and at that time calling himself a Radical Socialist, voted steadily with them. Louis Saillant, originally named to the Board as a reformist, more and more openly sided with the Communists. Both were to remain with the CGT when the non-Communists seceded late in 1947.

newly created post of co-general secretary, alongside Léon Jouhaux, general secretary since 1909. Jouhaux was largely occupied with international activities and functions of public representation. Frachon, with a growing majority back of him, exercized far greater control over internal organization and policy.

By April 1946, at the first convention since 1938, the Communists showed a majority of at least four to one. The highest vote the minority could muster was 4,872 against the 21,238 which supported the Communist proposals to change the CGT system of voting.[32] The votes reflected majority and minority strength in the CGT fairly accurately. It was greatly to the interest of the Communists to maintain the appearance of a nonpolitical CGT. They gave the reformists, therefore, a far larger representation than their numbers required on the elected executive organs.[33] To the disgust of the more militant non-Communists, the reformist leaders accepted.

For the first time since its foundation in 1895, a political party was in command of the General Confederation of Labor. The Communist Party had acquired this position partly through better and more ruthless organization, tactics and leadership; partly through its resistance activities; partly as a result of the revival of old dissatisfactions among French workers.

In the confused and critical months of 1944 and 1945 when the political party and trade union structure was revived, a well-organized party interested in power had an incalculable advantage over loosely organized rivals interested in ideas, talk, and petty politicking. Alone of the resistance bodies, political parties, and union groups, the Communists knew what they wanted and moved firmly to get it.

The Communists had the only political organization fully equipped to operate as a party. They had maintained their organization, despite heavy losses, throughout the underground period. The Socialists had dispersed their resistance activity in a number of different organizations. The MRP (the Mouvement Républicain Populaire), the only other party whose program might make any appeal to workers, was new and loosely organized. As a Catholic party, it could not hope to reach more than a small minority of labor.

The Socialists, lulled by the general talk of socialism in the air, alternated between illusions of "Socialism master of the hour" and acute

---

[32] CGT, *Congrès 1946, Compte rendu . . ,* pp. 336-337. (Abstentions and contested votes amounted to another 430 votes.) For another test vote, on accepting the executive report, the minority was even smaller. *Ibid.,* p. 289.

[33] A continuation of nominal parity on the Executive Board; fifteen out of thirty-five seats on the Administrative Commission. *Le Peuple,* April 13, 1946, p. 1.

feelings of inferiority toward the tougher Communist Party. They made their traditional public display of division and hesitation. Some of their debates were over unreal issues of "la doctrine," over such fine verbal questions as whether to revise the party preamble to read "class action" instead of "class struggle." For six years, from mid-1945 on, they rehashed the issue of whether to stay in the government or leave it. Actually their cabinet positions and municipal offices hid an increasing weakness in the real sources of power. They failed to coördinate party action with trade union action. Some of the ablest Socialists in the CGT, notably Albert Gazier, Robert Lacoste, and Christian Pineau, gave up the trade union movement for parliamentary and ministerial life. The CGT's non-Communist wing could not afford their departure.

The Communists had a leadership tested by years in clandestine operations, or in jail. It was strong in men with manual workers' backgrounds, in which the other parties were conspicuously lacking. It was more vigorous and more disciplined, yet more flexible than its rivals. Publicly the Communists from 1944 until mid-1952 showed neither uncertainty nor disagreement. Trade union and party action supported each other with no overt conflicts, whatever the underlying divergences.

The resistance and the Soviet entry into the war had given the Communists a chance to cover up memories of the Nazi-Soviet Pact, and they did a thorough job of it. They made the most effective parade of their rediscovered patriotism, of their great role in the resistance, and of their martyrs. No other party had suffered such losses. Others were reluctant, either out of respect for the martyrs or out of uneasy consciences about past anti-Communism, to question publicly the Communists' attempted monopoly of the resistance and its martyrs and their publicity as the "party of the 75,000 firing squad victims." The party profited now from the Nazi and Vichy practice of blaming all sorts of patriotic opposition on "Communists." It profited too from the revived aura of the Soviet Union, its wartime prestige and postwar power.

Many people, including young men and women with leadership qualities, had had their first taste of political activity in the resistance. Many were attracted to the Communists by their ability and sacrifices, by personal contacts in hours of fraternity and common danger. Many responded to the possibilities the Communists offered after liberation to place party recruits in positions they controlled in the CGT, in government ministries, and in nationalized enterprises. Recollections of the ineffectiveness of the Third Republic gave a special appeal to the Communists' form of "effectiveness." It was common to hear people say, "The Communists are the only people who get things done, who mean business." The nature of the "business" might be examined later. For the moment the Communist Party seemed the best bet to many normally desirous of making a career or anxious to see a renovation in France.

The Communists devoted far more money and attention to press and publications than their rivals.[34] They built up a vast network of front organizations, reaching almost every possible interest group—women (hitherto little organized), farmers, youth, tenants, sports lovers, tradesmen, writers and artists, war prisoners and deportees, veterans of the resistance. To every group, they offered special interest appeals. They were the first, for example, to come out for higher prices for farm products (while demanding more food at lower prices for city dwellers).

The Communists made it easy to join the party. As after every period of mass influx, there would probably have to be a perod of weeding and discarding later. But for the moment, one might even apply by signing an application blank in a party paper.[35] The party membership soared to three times its Popular Front peak, to a million members. Its vote in the elections of 1945 and 1946 topped the five million mark.[36]

Resistance action and Soviet prestige, leadership and organization, manipulation and purge could not alone explain the Communist Party's tremendous success in gaining workers' support. Other older and deeper tides were running in its favor. For workers were soon convinced that they were again bearing a disproportionate share of the nation's economic burdens, through food shortages, price inflation, and tax inequities. Their sense of injustice aroused, they turned in what was almost a conditioned reflex of protest to the party which was supposed to be "farthest left."

WAGE AND PRICE PROBLEMS

The De Gaulle government kept the system of wage controls it inherited from Vichy, adding union and employer representatives to the wage boards. Even though "black wages," up-grading, and various nonwage perquisites increased earnings beyond those shown in any statistics, wages were far better controlled than prices. The Provisional Government gave large wage and family allowance increases immediately

---

[34] Jean Mottin, *Histoire politique de la presse* (Paris, 1949), gives the number of Communist dailies in 1944 as 31, with a press run of 2,816,000 or 26.8 per cent of the restricted total daily press printing at the time. (Cited in *Encyclopédie politique de la france et du monde* (Paris, 1950), vol. 2, p. 392. In June 1945, the party spoke of 17 dailies and 58 weeklies, in its central committee report to the Tenth Party Convention. This total would exclude papers not officially controlled by the party but dependably following its line. There are no figures on the quantities of brochures, throwaways, factory bulletins, posters, etc., in which the Communists excelled.

[35] Gordon Wright, *The Reshaping of French Democracy*, p. 67.

[36] In comparing votes with prewar figures, note that women first obtained the suffrage after liberation.

after liberation.[37] These helped to make up for the long period of real wage compression by the Germans, and incorporated in official wages some of the illicit increases given by employers during the occupation. After March 1945, further wage increases came only after price increases. But the problem was essentially one of food supplies, not of nominal wages. Wage increases were immediately translated into demand for food items, which simply encouraged producers to hold out (successfully) for higher prices.[38]

Black markets continued to flourish in all the essential food items—butter, meat, coffee, bread. As in poorer lands, the cigarette was a medium of exchange. The common barometer of real prices was the black market quotation for butter. Workers received just enough to buy some necessities at black market prices. As a doctor in a Paris children's hospital remarked, "There are two sorts of children, those whose parents buy on the black market, and those whose parents bring them into my clinic."

In a practice which the public authorities had repeated since long before the French revolution, food prices were fixed, but supplies were not assured. The government held out neither price incentives, although legal farm prices were too low, nor sanctions, for it dared not collect food quotas by force or punish black marketeers. Farmers, who during the occupation had found it patriotic to sell on the black market, now simply found it natural. The failure to organize the food supply was the greatest single cause of the continuing inflation and the growing urban discontent. "The nation is now asking in its prayers for its daily bread," said the Paris radio.[39] "It no longer asks for grandeur, a large army, or good institutions."

It was not only that workers had to spend well over half and often two-thirds or more of their wages on food.[40] Worse, the flagrant black market operations and black market restaurants symbolized an inequality and a corruption that withered the promise of liberation. Despite the shortages of everything, retail and wholesale outlets multiplied as soon

[37] By October 1944, skilled workers' hourly wages were 45 per cent higher than in April 1944 in the provinces, and 31 per cent higher in Paris. Unskilled rates were 52 per cent higher in both the provinces and Paris. *Etudes et conjoncture: union française,* vol. 2, no. 5-6, December 1946-January 1947, p. 122.

[38] *Ibid.,* devoted to an inventory and review of the economic situation since liberation. See especially summary by F. Louis Closon, director of the Institut National de la Statistique et des Etudes Economiques (INSEE), "Depuis la libération: Réflexions sur un bilan," pp. 5-11.

[39] "Voix de Paris," February 10, 1946.

[40] See Henri Brousse, *Le Niveau de vie en France* (Paris, 1949), pp. 36-40, for summary of studies of consumer expenditures; *Etudes et conjoncture: union française,* vol. 2, no. 10-11, May-June 1947, p. 78, for figures of food costs in relation to wages.

as the government lifted the wartime prohibition on the establishment of new businesses. Anyone who had any goods to sell could make a profit in black, gray, or perfectly legal dealings. By 1947 over 100,000 new commercial establishments had been set up since liberation in Paris alone.[41]

The wage-price picture of this period cannot be reproduced with any exactitude. The government published no cost of living figures; the importance of the black market nullifies the value of such retail price data, chiefly for food items, as were issued. Wage figures were incomplete and untrustworthy. Nevertheless the best "guesstimates" may indicate the order of magnitude of the fall in workers' purchasing power as compared with prewar, and its failure to rise as national output rose.

The official National Institute of Statistics and Economic Studies (INSEE) estimated hourly wage rates in October 1946 as giving unskilled workers 60 per cent of 1938 purchasing power; semiskilled workers, 62½ per cent; and miners, 90 per cent.[42] Hourly wage rates, however, ignore the postwar increases in family allowance benefits. Table 1 compares money and real monthly earnings (direct wages plus family allowances) for Paris workers in 1946 and 1947 with 1938, in each case those of a family head with dependent wife and two children.

TABLE 1

MONTHLY EARNINGS (INCLUDING FAMILY ALLOWANCES) AND PURCHASING
POWER OF PARIS WORKER WITH DEPENDENT WIFE AND TWO CHILDREN, 1946–1947.
(Indexes, 1938 = 100)

Money Earnings	October 1938	October 1946	April 1947	October 1947
Unskilled	100	620	685	902
Skilled	100	578	633	778

Purchasing Power	Year 1938	October 1946	April 1947	October 1947
Unskilled	100	71	80	69
Skilled	100	65	73	59

Source: Institut National de la Statistique et des Etudes economiques, *Etudes et Conjoncture: Union française*, vol. 3, no. 2, February 1948, p. 11.

[41] Robert Buron, moderate MRP deputy, later Secretary of State for Economic Affairs, Assemblée Nationale, *Débats,* December 22, 1947, p. 6060. See also Jean Romeuf, *L'Entreprise dans la vie économique* (Paris, 1951), pp. 9-10.

[42] *Etudes et conjoncture: union française,* No. 5-6, December 1946—January 1947, p. 314. The INSEE found retail price data so unsatisfactory that it used wholesale prices to calculate real wages.

Because of the significant part of family allowances in total earnings, unmarried workers and small family heads were disadvantaged as compared with the smaller number who were heads of large families. So were skilled workers and technicians, as compared with the less skilled, since family allowances bore no relationship to wage differentials. Paris workers lost some of their traditional differentials above those in the provinces. Unskilled workers narrowed the rate differentials between themselves and the skilled; women the differentials between their wage rates and men's. In the baroque wage structure of the period, the many payments in kind, flat-sum bonuses, and allowances further compressed the occupational wage hierarchy. Old relationships in the structure of wages were upset, to the discontent of many and, given the general wage-price distortion, the satisfaction of few.

Most workers were too dominated by the struggle of daily living to get any satisfaction from the institutional reforms, even had these worked more smoothly than they did. The plant committees made little change in workers' relations to their foremen or employers. Union power was exercised in national councils, but not where workers could see its benefits in real wages. The gains in social security for some were obscured by the lower direct wages for all. The politicization of nationalized enterprises[43] helped spread disillusionment with this reform.

Politics no longer reflected the hopes of a national rebirth. "The parties . . . have not been worthy of their martyrs," the journalist Rémy Roure, himself a resistance hero and Buchenwald prisoner, wrote less than two years after the liberation. "We have not achieved that great reconciliation we dreamed of in the time of our common struggles. The spirit of party, the spirit of class and of caste have killed the spirit of the resistance."[44]

For a time the Communists made the best of both governmentalism and the gathering social discontent. From the one they drew power and patronage; from the other they could still profit because of their traditional position on the far left. There was little discipline in the government coalition. Each party claimed for its own ministers credit for any popular move and blamed the more frequent unpopular developments

---

[43] To take an example, of 18 members of the board of directors of the national coal mines, 12 were CGT members, of whom at least 10 were known as Communist Party members. The board elected Victorien Duguet, Communist head of the national miners union, chairman. The chairman of the regional coal mining board of the major mining basin was also a Communist Party member and CGT official. Ventenat, *L'Expérience de nationalisation*, pp. 139-140; Sturmthal, "The Structure of Nationalized Enterprises in France," *Political Science Quarterly*, September 1952, p. 370; *Révolution Prolétarienne*, n.s. no. 8, November 1947, "La Politicisation des Houillères Nationales," pp. 36-42.

[44] *Le Monde*, May 26-27, 1946, in his *La Quatrième république: Naissance ou avortement d'un régime, 1945-1946* (Paris, 1948), p. 257.

on the other parties. At this game the Communists were less inhibited than the Socialists or the MRP.

But this equivocal position became increasingly difficult even for the Communists to maintain. Workers could forgive the Communists a good deal which they would not pardon in other parties, because only the Communists seemed to them a working class party. They could give the party the benefit cf doubt and assume it was really more attached to social change than to governmental office. But as production recovered and workers still felt the pinch of rising prices and food shortages, their resentments accumulated and they chafed at the restraints imposed by communist policy.

Despite Communist control of the union apparatus, both protest and apathy began to show. In 1946 several breakaway movements took place. The first was a minor affair. Some anarcho-syndicalists withdrew from the CGT to set up their own confederation, the Confédération Nationale du Travail (National Confederation of Labor). Bravely the CNT asserted the eternal validity of the principles of the 1906 Charter of Amiens. Despite the anachronism of its doctrine, this protest against political domination of the CGT warned of events to come. Important groups of railwaymen and Paris subway operators broke off to form independent unions.

In mid-summer of 1946 the first major strike since liberation took place. It was an outlaw strike by communications workers for wage increases, led by Socialists, Trotskyites, and pure syndicalists. The strike succeeded over the opposition of the Communist-dominated national executive of the union. The insurgent strike committee then set up an autonomous union. The Ministry of Posts, Telegraphs and Telephones happened to be headed by non-Communists. The new union was recognized by its employer.

Within the CGT, the chief opposition to the Communists centered in the group known as Force Ouvrière (Workers' Force), FO. It included many of socialist persuasion, and others who were pure or apolitical syndicalists. Of the latter, most were of evolutionary outlook; some still breathed the old revolutionary syndicalist fire.[45] The caucus was informally organized and loosely bound together by the publication and local distribution of the weekly paper, *Force Ouvrière,* which in 1945 had succeeded the reformists' clandestine *Résistance Ouvrière.* Its national leaders were the reformists around Léon Jouhaux, the remnants of those who in the 1920's and the 1930's had run the CGT.

---

[45] For the sake of convenience, and to avoid the negative term "non-Communists," we may call the FO group as a whole "reformists," although the term does not accurately characterize all of its members.

Until late 1946 or 1947, the Communists may have expected to take power by parliamentary means, and within a near future. Soviet expansion, the formation of the "people's democracies" in Eastern Europe, the vacuum of power in the West, their own party and trade union power, and the flabby resistance of their rivals in France, might have made their hopes look realistic. Work discipline and atrophy of the strike habit may have seemed to them essential for a Communist-run France. But whatever their hopes, they saw by the spring of 1947 that they were in real danger of being "outflanked on the left" by a growing though ill-organized opposition of many elements ranging from Trotskyites to reformists. The Communists' opposition to sliding wage scale demands and their attempt to persuade the workers of the virtues of incentive pay systems had failed.[46] Wildcat strikes were breaking out in many places.

The election of employee representatives to the administrative boards of the general social security system in April 1947 gave another warning.[47] The CGT naturally described its 59 per cent of the total vote as a victory. The 26 per cent of the vote received by the CFTC slates, however, indicated both unexpected CFTC strength and disaffection among CGT members. Out of a total of 7,750,000 men and women eligible to vote (employees of industries which had special social security systems did not vote), 5,790,000 cast their ballots. The CGT received 3,280,000 votes—at a time when it claimed 6,000,000 members. The CFTC, claiming 800,000 members, received 1,458,000 votes. For every 100 members it claimed the CGT received only 55 votes, while the CFTC got 182.

In April 1947 an independent local union, under Trotskyite leadership, called a stoppage in one department of the nationalized Renault works at Boulogne-Billancourt. This plant in the Paris suburbs is the nation's largest and, from every psychological and political criterion, its most important single plant. In it the Communist Party and the CGT had invested considerable effort. The CGT denounced the stoppage publicly, and privately urged the management to dismiss the

---

[46] They preached incentive pay systems as a means of increasing wage income while pushing production. See for example, resolution of the CGT convention, *Congrès, 1946*, p. 353.

[47] Ambroise Croizat, "Dans la sécurité sociale—Bilan et enseignement d'une élection," *Cahiers du communisme*, vol. 24, no. 6, June 1947, pp. 497-508, with annex giving results department by department, pp. 554-570. Croizat admits that anti-Communism played a considerable part in the results. He reports the "slaughter" of 38 secretaries of CGT departmental federations, many of them "esteemed" members of the Communist Party, who failed of reëlection (p. 503).

Results of the 1947 and 1950 social security elections are given in Table 2, Chapter X, *infra*.

instigators. Despite its efforts, the strike spread through the plant like wildfire. CGT leaders reminding the Renault workers of the need for production and the danger of strikes had the new experience of being hooted down.

THE ROAD OF OPPOSITION

At this moment, the Communist leaders of the CGT made a major turn. Briskly reversing their field, they took over leadership of the strike they could not smash, then came out for general wage increases. When the Communist deputies and ministers voted in Parliament against the cabinet's wage policy, early in May, they in effect read themselves out of the cabinet. The next day the Socialist Premier, Ramadier, forced them out of the government.

The Communists were able to leave the government on two issues popular among their threatened labor following: primarily, wage demands; secondarily, their opposition to the Indo-Chinese War, on which the cabinet had nearly broken up two months earlier. That war was distant, ill-known, and unpopular among most Frenchmen. Workers were traditionally anticolonialist, although more concerned at this time with the high cost of living than the high cost of empire.

For domestic reasons alone, the Communists might have had to break with the government. Foreign and colonial policy reasons had been accumulating. The presence of Communist ministers in the government had not paid off in French attitudes toward Soviet foreign policy objectives.[48] The international breach had widened with the Truman Doctrine announcement and the Big Four Council of Foreign Ministers deadlock at Moscow in March 1947. It was to become irreparable after Molotov walked out of the Paris Marshall Plan talks in July. These events in the history of the Communist Party we note because they were to determine the action of the CGT.

The government coalitions since De Gaulle's resignation early in 1946 had been "tripartite"—Socialist, Communist, and MRP. The cabinets which held office from the Communist departure to the 1951 elections were made up essentially of the MRP, the Socialists, the Radical Socialists, and some smaller center groups. They had to fight on two fronts: against the Communists and (less certainly) against the newly formed Gaullist movement, the Rally of the French People (Rassemblement du Peuple Français). The RPF, despite General de Gaulle's assertion of a nobler destiny for it, took on the characteristics

---

[48] François Goguel, *France under the Fourth Republic* (Ithaca, 1952), pp. 23-25. Note that the Communists were tossed out of the Italian government at almost the same time.

of a political party. Between these two obstreperous extremes, both pushing for a liberating catastrophe, the middle-of-the-road parliamentary and government coalition called itself the "Third Force."

In June 1947, the month after the Communists left the government, a widespread epidemic of strikes caused a loss of 6,416,000 man-days,[49] twenty times the figure for the whole of 1946. As yet the strikes were all for economic demands. The Communists and the CGT were making up for lost time, but they did not rush to the brink of insurrection. Until the foundation of the Cominform in September, the party apparently failed to realize the depth of Soviet opposition to the Marshall Plan. For several months it behaved as if a "constructive opposition" might bring it back to the government from which it protested its unjust "exclusion." The September 1947 *Cahiers du Communisme* still declared: "Of course, France like England must not refuse American aid but, as our comrade Thorez made clear, its independence must be jealously maintained."[50] Out of the cabinet, the Communist Party readily mended cracks in its solidity caused by its governmentalism.[51] But trade union harmony was not to be restored, since the conflict within France, as between East and West internationally, was not to be appeased but, in the years ahead, to deepen. For the unions, the first chapter of postliberation history—the chapter of social reform, of union power in the nation, and of uncontested Communist leadership of labor—was over.

---

[49] *Revue française du travail,* vol. 2, no. 18, September 1947, p. 818. See Table 12, Chapter XIII, *infra,* for 1947-1952 strike figures.

[50] Léon Mauvais, "Après le congrès socialiste de Lyon," *Cahiers du communisme,* vol. 24, no. 9, September 1947, p. 839. See also in same issue, pp. 819-828, Jacques Duclos, "Notre politique."

[51] Aron, *Le grand schisme,* pp. 192-193.

CHAPTER VIII

COMMUNIST OPPOSITION AND CGT SCHISM
(1947-1953)

In the strikes, we must dissociate what is aggression against the institutions and doctrines of the Republic from what is the legitimate or at least the natural manifestation of want and suffering.

—Léon Blum, to the National
Assembly, November 20, 1947.

The Republic, ah comrades, we must feel what that means. Not the capitalistic Republic . . . we do not want that! The Republic we demand, which you demand, I am sure, is that which our comrades of the people's democracies, present here, have already fully realized; it is also the total liberation which has been achieved in the USSR.

—Julien Racamond, CGT secretary,
at the CGT convention of 1948.

The second phase of postliberation union history, opening with the Communist turn from coöperation to opposition, reached a climax in the 1947 general strike and the resultant civil war in labor ranks. The creation of the Force Ouvrière confederation and another great CGT strike movement were followed by a third phase, one of comparative stabilization of the relative positions of the rival union movements. The unions were reduced to a declining role in the national community and a feeling of frustration, despite the considerable economic recovery of France and the restoration in 1950 of free collective bargaining.

The June 1947 strikes were followed by the usual summer vacation lull. By September the international rift was fully proclaimed by the foundation of the Cominform and its attacks on the Marshall Plan and right-wing "Socialist traitors." In October Maurice Thorez admitted that the French party had been slow to recognize the threat to French independence and peace in the Marshall Plan, the "attempt by war-

mongering American capitalists to enslave Europe."[1] A month later
the CGT launched what amounted in all but name to a general strike,
directed at the convalescent economy and the shaky Third Force
government of France. The strikes brought to a head the crisis in relations between the CGT and the government and the crisis within the
CGT.

THE GENERAL STRIKE

The background of the strikes was a series of national and international political events which appeared then to portend decisions of the
first importance. On the national scene, the new party of General de
Gaulle made its first electoral appearance, and scored a sensational success in the nation-wide municipal elections. On the international scene,
significant moves were expected from the London meeting in November of the Big Four's Council of Foreign Ministers. In the United
States the Marshall Plan was about to come up before Congress for
the first time. How much each of these factors influenced international
and French Communist strategy, and hence the CGT in its strike timing
and goals, it is hard to say. Perhaps the CGT leaders themselves did not
know how far they wanted to carry the strikes until they saw how they
developed.

It is unlikely that the Soviet Union wanted the French Communist
Party to make a full bid for power, which would have risked civil and
hence international war, for which the Soviet Union was hardly ready.
Probably the major purpose was to disrupt the growing Western
Alliance centering, on the continent, around a restored France. Whether
or not the Communists wanted to bring their enemy De Gaulle to
power, by causing a breakdown of the Third Force government, they
were at least willing to take that risk. A De Gaulle government might
have produced, within the country, a concentration of anti-Gaullist
forces of the left around the Communists. It would have made France
a balky partner in Western European coöperation and in dealing with
the United States.

International communist strategy does not of itself create strike
potentialities. The strikes were made possible by the increasing discontent of workers during the summer and fall of 1947. This discontent
was not something the Communists called into being; when they went
into the opposition, they simply released a powerful brake. Food shortages were still acute. The index of purchasing power of hourly wage
rates—taking January 1946 as base (itself about one-third lower than

---

[1] To Communist Party Central Committee, October 30, 1947. Mario Einaudi and
others, *Communism in Western Europe* (Ithaca, 1951), p. 78.

prewar)—had fallen to 93 in July 1946, and to 80 at the beginning of 1947; it had risen to 84 by April 1947, then fallen to 78 by July and 68 by October 1947.[2]

In November the CGT National Committee voted to "consult" all workers in the plants, members or not, on whether to call a general strike for wage increases and a guaranteed sliding scale.[3] The government did not deny the justice of workers' claims, but it offered a smaller immediate increase, and refused to guarantee automatic quarterly adjustment of wages to price increases.

Back of the CGT's ostensible demands, however, were the Communists' increasingly virulent attack on the Marshall Plan and a demand for their return (on their own terms) to a "government of democratic union," which they suggested was the only way of achieving social peace. At the November CGT National Committee meeting, they carried a resolution which denounced the Marshall Plan as "part of a plan of subjugation of the world by the capitalist American trusts and preparation of a new world war," and likened French participation in it to Munich.[4]

The Force Ouvrière leaders now fought back publicly. At the National Committee, they defended the Marshall Plan, mustering 127 votes against 857.[5] They opposed the "general consultation" of all workers, arguing that the CGT could be bound only by the vote of its own members, not by that of members of other unions or the unorganized. When the resolution carried, Jouhaux publicly dissociated himself and the minority from the decision.[6] The Communist majority called a special meeting of the National Committee for December 19 to examine the results of the "general consultation" and decide whether to call a general strike. Before that date, the strike wave had broken on the nation.

Asking parliament for investiture as Premier in the midst of the strikes, Léon Blum reminded the nation that "In the strikes we must dissociate what is aggression against the institutions and doctrines of the Republic from what is the legitimate or at least the natural mani-

[2] "Evolution des salaires et des traitements en 1947," *Etudes et conjoncture: union française,* vol. 3, no. 2, February 1948, pp. 3-23; above data from table, p. 8. Due to differences in methods of calculation, it is not possible to relate these post-January 1946 index numbers to prewar. But the earlier index showed October 1946 wage rates at about 62 per cent of 1938. For monthly earnings comparison, see Table I, Chapter VII, *supra.*

[3] For demands, see *Le Peuple,* November 15, 1947.

[4] *Ibid.,* p. 5; *Force ouvrière,* November 20, 1947, pp. 6-7.

[5] *Ibid.* Both publications give the text of the reformist resolution in support of the Marshall Plan.

[6] *Le Peuple,* November 15, 1947, p. 4.

festation of want and suffering."[7] It was just this separation of economic protest from political enterprise which circumstances made so difficult.

The strikes began with a series of walkouts in three widely separated nerve centers. In Marseille, a turbulent port and a center of Communist power, there were riots after the municipal elections and a stoppage to protest streetcar fare increases. In Paris, metal industries workers struck for cost of living wage adjustments. In the coal mines of the North, the strike began as a protest against the dismissal of a Communist union leader from his post as official of the nationalized mines and as a demand for a down payment on wage increases. These and other strikes were woven into a nation-wide pattern in which the major ostensible demand was for a cost of living increase and a sliding wage scale.

The CGT did not call a general strike, although it came to refer to the wave of stoppages as a "generalized strike." Some of the big national unions called all their men out, though not on a single date: the miners, railroad workers, dock workers, building trades. Other unions permitted or encouraged local and regional walkouts, but issued no national strike calls. A number of departmental federations called area-wide general strikes. The regular CGT executive did not take general direction of the movement. Because of the developing opposition by the reformist leaders, the Communists set up a special National Strike Committee, composed of the majority members of the confederation's Executive Board, several Paris region CGT Communist leaders, and Communist heads of 20 national unions. Thus they by-passed the minority members of the CGT Executive Board and of the national union executive bodies. Some of the reformist officials were practically isolated during the strikes, with even their mail and telephone calls cut off.[8]

Even in less class-conscious countries than France, labor leaders seldom care to come out publicly against strikers. Gradually, however, the FO leaders made clear their opposition. They and the CFTC demanded secret ballots on whether to strike or, in the case of strikes already launched, whether to stay out. The CGT majority leaders tried to conduct votes by show of hands in open meetings, an old Communist tactic. The FO leaders quietly dropped their earlier objection to con-

---

[7] *Le Monde,* November 22, 1947, p. 1. Blum failed to get from the National Assembly the absolute majority necessary for investiture. Robert Schuman, MRP, then became Premier.

[8] See L. Fréour, one of the national secretaries of the building trades and wood workers union, *Force ouvrière,* December 18, 1947, p. 3, and G. Ouradou, a national secretary of the railway workers union, *Force ouvrière,* December 11, 1947, and December 18, 1947, p. 5.

sultation of nonmembers of the CGT, since the wider the electorate, the less likely was it to approve the strike. In many plants government labor officials conducted the strike referenda by secret ballot.

Jouhaux and his group meanwhile negotiated with the government, in particular the socialist Minister of Labor, Daniel Mayer, to keep a face-saving settlement open to both sides. By the time the strikes had reached their maximum intensity, however, the FO group was issuing daily communiqués, rivaling those of the National Strike Committee. The battle of the communiqués conveyed the atmosphere of near civil war.

Much of the brunt of the fight against the strike was borne by the autonomous unions of the railroad, communications, and Paris subway workers. They and FO and CFTC activists in the provinces, especially on the railroads and in the mines, faced threats, violence, and sabotage on the part of CGT and Communist Party militants and strong-arm squads. The most spectacular and tragic episode was the derailing of the Paris-Tourcoing express, manned by strikebreakers, with the loss of 20 lives.[9] The CGT promptly denounced the wreck as an act of provocation, for which the strikers could not possibly be responsible.

The CFTC publicly warned that without protection the nonstrikers could not hold out much longer. "Unless the government guarantees freedom to work other than by fine words and speeches," the head of the Catholic railway union wrote, "we shall be left looking like suckers who believe in Santa Claus."[10] The government moved slowly to a position of firmness and force against the strikers. Ramadier, who resigned as the strike wave began, for reasons largely unconnected with the strikes, was succeeded as Premier by Robert Schuman, one of the most respected of the MRP leaders. As on many other occasions in Europe when troops have had to be used, it was a Socialist who was Minister of the Interior—the energetic Jules Moch.

The government made several compromise pay offers, which were rejected by the CGT, before it acted to protect those willing to work. It also placed before Parliament emergency legislation to make a show of force by calling up 80,000 reservists; this may have been necessary to reassure the country and warn the Communist strategists. It also proposed to stiffen the legal penalties for sabotage and interference with

---

[9] *Le Monde,* December 4, 1947. A list of sabotage attempts was read to the National Assembly by the Minister of the Interior, Jules Moch. Assemblée Nationale, *Débats,* November 29, 1947, pp. 5256-5257, and another December 3, 1947, *Débats,* p. 5467.

Incidentally, during this period, thanks to nonstriking railwaymen, Thorez was able to return to Paris by train from a Moscow visit.

[10] André Pailleux, *Syndicalisme,* November 27, 1947. p. 2.

the "right to work," by special penalties to expire at the end of February 1948; these provisions were of doubtful necessity. In the National Assembly, however, only one deputy (of the right-center) pointed out that existing law was quite adequate and that the government was making a fight for powers which, basically, it already had.[11] Jouhaux and the FO group opposed the penal code amendments.[12] The CFTC seemed divided in its opinions, but offered no objection.[13] The Communist deputies staged a raucous five-day filibuster. The measures were enacted at 4:15 a.m. December 4, with only the Communists in opposition, after some of the most violent scenes in the parliamentary annals of the Fourth Republic.[14]

The strikes were moving toward a showdown. At their height, they closed down the mines and the ports completely, most of the building and metal working industries of Paris and a number of other cities, many gas, chemical and textile plants, and part of the postal and communications services; they slowed or halted a large part of the railways. The CGT declared that 3,000,000 strikers took part in the movement, that 2,500,000 were out at its height, and 1,500,000 were still out when it was called off.[15] No exact figures can be offered.[16]

When the rail strike had broken down almost everywhere except in the southeast, and when the Paris subway workers refused to follow a strike call, it looked as if the wave was spent. The political objectives of the strike had been underlined by Communist violence and sabotage. Workers were hungry, and they were finally realizing the futility of a political strike against economic recovery. Moreover, for the first time

---

[11] Emmanuel Temple, Independent, Assemblée Nationale, *Débats,* December 3, 1947, p. 5485.

[12] Jouhaux, radio speech, December 2, 1947, *Le Monde,* December 4, 1947, p. 2.; *Le Peuple,* December 6, 1947, p. 1.

[13] The president of the CFTC found the government's proposal, as amended in parliamentary debate, "acceptable." Gaston Tessier, *Syndicalisme,* December 4, 1947, p. 1. Maurice Bouladoux, general secretary of the CFTC, however, writing on the same page of the same issue, washed his hands of responsibility for the legislation: "We have asked the government to protect those, who responding to our appeal, want to work; let us leave it the responsibility for the means it uses." He thought "a government willing to bear down on the saboteurs and seditious could find in the penal code arsenal all the arms it needed."

[14] Assemblée Nationale, *Débats,* November 29-December 4, 1947.

[15] *Le Peuple,* December 13, 1947, p. 4.

[16] Ministry of Labor figures, which do not separate the "generalized strike" losses, show a total of 7,546,000 man-days lost in November and 6,967,000 in December. *Revue française du travail,* Vol. 3, No. 1-2-3, January-February-March 1948, p. 95. A hostile observer, Georges Lefranc, cites a figure of "over 2,000,000" strikers. *Les Expériences syndicales en France de 1939 à 1950,* p. 187, note 17. *Force ouvrière* declared that "80 percent of the French working class had rejected the political strike," December 25, 1947, p. 6.

since liberation, the government insisted that it was not going to pay strikers for lost time.

On December 9, the National Strike Committee called off the strikes, "to regroup and reassemble our forces for future combats, which will be hard." Dissolving itself, the Committee paid its respects to the "government of reaction and of hunger," subservient to the "American reactionaries who act among us as in a conquered country and would smash or domesticate our unions."[17] However, it took proper credit for getting a better settlement than the government had at first offered.

Benoît Frachon analyzed the lessons of the strikes in the party organ, *Cahiers du Communisme*.[18] He dwelt on the "positive side." The strikes had widened the breach between government and workers, and between Socialist Party and workers. Or, as he put it, "The brutality of the government's response, the reactionary attitude of the Socialist leaders . . . greatly contributed to the clarification of a number of political problems in the minds of workers." The strikes had dealt a blow to recovery. Looking forward, Frachon predicted that the working class "would not accord its enthusiastic participation in production to men and a government who have shown themselves its determined adversaries." The strikes had apparently served as useful training; they had brought forth "new leadership elements (cadres) capable of taking responsibilities in periods of combat."

Frachon was sufficiently worried to warn that the adversaries of the working class should not consider the strikes a "remarkable success" for them. Anyway, he said, "nothing would have been more injurious than to let the working class sink into greater misery without a fight. It would have turned away from its trade unions." When Frachon published these lines he could not yet know to what extent the working class was going to "turn away" from the CGT. As the strikes showed the political side of CGT control more clearly, a great number dropped all union membership; many turned to a new trade union center, that of Force Ouvrière.

THE CGT SPLITS AGAIN

The strikes made the schism in the CGT inevitable. Until the last, however, both the majority and the minority protested their devotion to the revered concept of unity. Early in November, Jouhaux, returning from a visit to the United States, wrote, "At last they are beginning

[17] *Le Peuple*, December 13, 1947, p. 4.
[18] "Une étape de la lutte des classes en France: Les grandes grèves de novembre-décembre 1947," vol. 25, no. 1, January 1948, pp. 5-33. The passages quoted here are all from pages 28-29.

to recognize in America that the split in their trade union movement is the cause of the weakness of labor."[19] Meeting in its first national conference, just before the strikes, the Force Ouvrière caucus declared that "unity is more than ever necessary."[20] As late as November 20, with the strikes approaching their height, Jouhaux wrote: "Never, as far as we are concerned, will we take the responsibility of dividing the workers when national and international circumstances offer such dangers to the public liberties and the peace."[21]

Experience, sentiment, temperament all made the FO national leaders hesitate about splitting from the CGT. Most of them had already lived through two splits in the movement. They knew how weak the divided unions were in the face of employers and government. They—Jouhaux as much as any—shared workers' sentiment for unity. They were no longer young; they had matured from organizers and agitators to administrators and public figures, representatives of labor on the national or—like Jouhaux—on the international scene. They were hardly the rough and tumble fighters and sleepless organizers needed to build a new movement in the teeth of Communist energy, money, and ruthlessness backed by the resources of the best organized party in France. They would have to leave the Communists in control of the apparatus and the name of the CGT. In 1921 and 1939 the reformists had tossed out their opponents and retained the organization. Now, Jouhaux observed, they would have to go out into the rain without an umbrella.

The local activists of FO, smarting from Communist violence, forced the decision. At a meeting a week after the strikes ended, they faced their national leaders, in their more comfortable Paris offices, with a harsh alternative. Either they set up a new organization, or their following would melt away: continuing to struggle within the CGT in order to gain a majority, or even to secure respect for the rights of the minority, was out of the question. Following the FO caucus vote, "as disciplined trade unionists" Jouhaux and the other four minority members resigned, on December 19, 1947, from the CGT Executive Board.[22]

---

[19] "Retour des Etats-Unis," Le Peuple, November 8, 1947, p. 1. See also his article in Force ouvrière, November 6, 1947, p. 1.

[20] Force ouvrière, November 13, 1947, p. 12. One of the few open warnings of a willingness to split had been given by the blunt and embattled head of the white collar workers: "The maintenance of unity, whether one likes it or not, is subordinated to the independence of the trade union movement." Oreste Capocci, "Propos d'un sauvage," Force ouvrière, October 2, 1947, p. 2.

[21] Force ouvrière, November 20, 1947, p. 1. The reference to national circumstances is not to the Communist strike wave, but to the threat of De Gaulle.

[22] Force ouvrière, December 25, 1947, p. 1. Frachon ridiculed Jouhaux's statement that he was "following discipline in resigning," Le Peuple, December 20, 1947, p. 1. and December 27, 1947, p. 1. Robert Bothereau, who was to be FO general secretary,

In the split FO took with it a majority of the civil service workers unions, the large white collar workers national union, a few minor industrial unions, and some of the smaller department federations. In fields in which FO had been a minority, that minority set about creating national unions. In addition several autonomous organizations which had left the CGT earlier, notably the railway workers and the communications workers, affiliated with FO. At its constituent convention in April 1948, the new organization claimed over a million members.[23] It formally named itself the *Confédération Générale du Travail-Force Ouvrière*. The first half of the name was to show that "it continued the old CGT." For this was the name which over half a century had signified "trade union movement" to most French workers.

The CGT majority could no longer speak with plausibility in the name of French organized labor. The CGT was left largely as the trade union arm of the Communist Party. Many non-Communist workers remained in it, although among the important leaders only a few non-Communists did not secede. One of these, Alain Le Léap, a civil service union official, was made co-general secretary, to replace Jouhaux with a nominal non-Communist. In fields in which the national union had gone with FO, the CGT reconstituted a new national organization, based upon a significant minority who had not seceded. The large teachers' union voted to secede from the CGT, but against joining FO; it remained independent. The one important national union of non-Communist leadership to stay in the CGT was that of the printers. For reasons having nothing to do with ideology or principle, it remained in the CGT—only to see the Communists soon take control of its executive.

Another national center had been formed shortly after the war. This was the Confédération Générale des Cadres (General Confederation of Technicians and Supervisory Employees), the CGC. Technicians, engineers and supervisory employees, generally dubious about trade unionism, had joined the CGT in some numbers on the morrow of the Popular

---

explained that the minority members of the CGT Executive Board had "bowed" to the vote of the FO conference, because they were "disciplined toward those (the minority) whom they morally represented" on the Executive Board, *Force ouvrière,* December 25, 1947, p. 1.

Several documents relating to the CGT internal conflict in November and December 1947 are brought together in *La Documentation française, notes et etudes documentaires,* no. 1239, December 2, 1949, "L'Evolution intérieure de la CGT," pp. 20-28. For summary of CGT position, see its brochure *Les Responsables de la scission démasqués* (Paris, no date [1948]).

[23] FO, *Congrès constitutif, 1948, compte rendu* . . . , p. 18, Bothereau, general secretary, even speaks of moving close to 1½ million. New organizations usually inflate their membership claims.

Front victory. After liberation, again on the crest of a political wave, many had joined the CGT. A large number of these drifted out, as it became clear that the CGT was neither the wave of the future nor the best defender of their interests in a period of inflation.

Both the CGT and the CFTC tried at first to shut out the CGC from government wage commissions, contesting its patriotic *bona fides*.[24] They failed in this attempt. The CGC showed it could be at least occasionally militant, by staging a one-day national demonstration strike in 1946 to assert its representative character. It became the leading organization of technicians and supervisory personnel in industry; in the civil service it was weaker. It organized many workers who were not cadres, notably traveling salesmen and foremen; the latter came to comprise about half of its membership.

The CGC joined the CFTC and FO in the attempt to hold back inflation. The three confederations formed a "price reduction bloc" ("Cartel de la baisse"), which asked price control and anti-inflationary measures by the government, rather than money wage increases. This was not an easy position to take. For the new FO organization it was especially difficult, because it seemed to lend a certain credence to the CGT accusation that FO was a creature of the Socialist Party and of the government in which the Socialist Party sat.

The Socialist Party greeted with joy the formation of FO, as did the parties farther to the right, delighted to be able to say on such good authority that the CGT was a tool of the Communist Party. This public rejoicing went, indeed, too far for the comfort of FO or the success of its recruitment. If the CGT was dominated by an antigovernmental political party, many workers thought, it was hardly worth leaving it to join a rival union dominated by a governmental party.

"Governmentalism" would have been a minor handicap if the government had been able to stem the tide of inflation. In the midst of the strike wave, Premier Schuman had said of his own wage offers, "The measures taken by the government to give immediate and effective relief to the workers are still inadequate. They can be completed only within a general program; otherwise there will be inflation. The government will devote itself to the development of all those measures . . ."[25] Actually, although Schuman and his Minister of Finance, René Mayer, did more than many other cabinets to fight inflation, they never developed their "general program." After a few months of price stability early in 1948, the inflation resumed, knocking the bottom out of the

[24] The criteria of "representativity" included that of "patriotic attitude during the occupation."
[25] *Le Monde,* November 30-December 1, 1947, p. 4.

wage policy of the CFTC-FO-CGC bloc. It broke up the bloc itself and the chances for responsible continuing coöperation among the three non-Communist confederations. Pressed by their rank and file, they added their voices to the demands for wage raises.

As a Force Ouvrière leader remarked, after a stormy meeting with delegates from the provinces, "We are right, but our followers are hungry." Unless some tangible sign of improvement could be shown, the leaders were likely to cease being either right or leaders. Despite the rise in production,[26] workers did not see the improvement in their conditions which they had been told would accompany a higher national output. By September 1948, food prices in Paris had risen 32 per cent since the end of 1947, while wage rates among semiskilled Paris metal workers had risen only 21 per cent.[27]

THE COAL STRIKE OF 1948

A year after the generalized strikes, the CGT found the occasion for another assault on the still precarious French economy. The coal mines were the chief target. The CGT spread the strike to the ports, and tried to spread it to the railroads and other critical areas, but only in the mines was the stoppage effective. The immediate issue was a government order attempting to tighten discipline, reduce absenteeism in the mines, and cut down the aboveground work force. The CGT soon added wage demands. FO and the CFTC hesitated briefly, called 48-hour mine strikes, then denounced the CGT strike as a political move.

Although less widespread than the 1947 strikes, the coal strike bit deeper. For the CGT miners union called out the safety and maintenance men, in a move unprecedented even in the strikes under the occupation, when the mines were privately owned and coal was going to the Nazis. The move forced the government to use troops and police in protecting the mines from flooding, gas, and irreparable damage. To the Communists' added profit, it was again the Socialist Jules Moch who, as Minister of the Interior, brought in the troops. There were widespread clashes between troops and strikers; three strikers were killed, hundreds on both sides were wounded. As in 1947, the CGT used large numbers of foreign workers as shock troops in the clashes. Sabotage of the mines was too much even for old-style revolutionary syndicalists. The honest *Révolution prolétarienne* declared: "How, if it was only a matter of

---

[26] The index (on a 1938 base) averaged 110 for the first nine months of 1948, as compared with a 1947 average of 99.

[27] *Etudes et conjoncture . .* , vol. 4, no. 6, November-December 1949, pp. 54, 64. For unskilled (male) labor in the Paris metal industries, the rise during this period was 18 per cent.

winning their demands, could they (the CGT) have launched that senseless order to call out the men on the safety services? This incredible idea could not have arisen in the mind of a French trade unionist attached above all to the cause of the working class. It is alien to our movement, contrary to its practices and its traditions."[28]

Léon Blum, who in 1936 had refused to summon the police to clear the factories of sit-down strikers, reminded the miners that they were among the best paid workers in the country; he compared the stoppage with the epic strikes he recalled from his youth:

The mines are under collective management, in which the working class and the unions participate to the greatest extent. The political, social and even religious terrorism which used to prevail, and for which the employers were responsible, is nothing but an old memory . . . The miners are free . . . Or, at least, if they are still oppressed, it is not by the employers but by a group of fanatics . . . to whom too large a proportion of our working class submits because of the persistence of habits of discipline and class solidarity.[29]

The coal strike, launched October 4, did not come to a complete end until November 29. Like the 1947 strikes, it was a failure in trade union terms. Once more, in terms of international Communist strategy, it was at least a partial success. An immediate result was the loss of 5½ million tons of coal,[30] which had to be replaced with more expensive coal from the United States, at the sacrifice of industrial equipment purchases. Indirect losses, impossible to calculate exactly, may have been the equivalent of one-eighth of all of France's ERP aid for the year.[31] The fissure between government and workers was deepened by the intervention of troops and police and the battles around the mines.

In the 1947 strike wave, the CGT had taken the risk of splitting its organization; in 1948 it risked further defections by leading a great losing strike. The CGT survived the two crises, shaken, yet with its apparatus intact. It lost members, in the mines and elsewhere. But FO was unable to capitalize fully either on the disaffection of those who left the CGT or on the dissatisfaction of many who remained within the organization. The CGT remained beyond challenge the largest and strongest trade union center.

---

[28] Editorial by M.C. (Maurice Chambelland?), *La Révolution prolétarienne*, n.s., no. 20, November 1948, p. 1.

[29] *Le Populaire*, October 28, 1948.

[30] ECA: *European Recovery Program, France: Country Study* (Washington, February 1949), p. 18.

[31] C. L. Sulzberger, *New York Times*, December 23, 1948, quoted American experts in Paris, who set the loss at $156,000,000, or 12 per cent of ERP aid to France for the United States fiscal year 1948-1949.

In 1949 another national trade union center was formally established. First called the Independent Labor Confederation (CTI), it later took the name of the General Confederation of Independent Unions ("Confédération Générale des Syndicats Indépendants"). The CGSI was made up of three elements. One was the Gaullists, who for some time had been flirting with the idea of setting up their own specifically Gaullist unions; they already had factory groups, which recalled the factory cells of their arch-opponents, the Communist Party. A second element was made up of ex-Communists, many of whom had left the party at the time of the Nazi-Soviet Pact ("graduates of the class of 1939"), and had been excluded from the CGT after liberation. The third element was composed of labor leaders who had held office in the Vichy labor structure, and had likewise been purged out of the CGT in 1944-1946. The organization's most conspicuous quality was its willingness to fight back against communist pressure in factories. But the CGSI showed only local strength here and there; it suffered from being identified in workers' minds as Gaullist.

RETURN TO COLLECTIVE BARGAINING

Industrywide and area employer organizations had generally survived through the Vichy years, some overlapping with the official industry committees. At the liberation they moved with caution and deliberation until they discovered that their fears of wholesale purges[32] and bloody revolution[33] were unfounded. The De Gaulle government itself named an employer "Committee of Fourteen" to give a form of representation to employer interests in national economic councils. But in the hostile atmosphere after liberation, employers did not revive a general national organization until the end of 1945. Only in June 1946 did they formally create an association to replace the prewar CGPF: the National Council of French Employers, CNPF (*Conseil National du Patronat Français*). Warding off charges of wartime collaboration with Vichy and the Germans, it named as its president Georges Villiers, an industrialist who had been a deportee in Germany. The CNPF rapidly acquired a cohesion and authority greater than that of its prewar predecessor, the CGPF.

Collective bargaining was postponed until the economy was on its

---

[32] The Commission for the Reconstitution of Employer Associations, set up to purge those guilty of collaboration, did not exercise the same rigors as the parallel trade union commission.

[33] For a brilliant description of the atmosphere of a factory town soon after liberation, see the novel of Marcel Aymé, *Uranus* (Paris, 1948), translated as *The Barkeep of Blémont* (New York, 1950).

feet. In December 1946, however, the government introduced, and Parliament unanimously passed, a law restoring bargaining on all issues but wages.[34] An early return to free wage bargaining was promised, but it was not to come for over three years.

The 1946 law envisaged an elaborate system of collective bargaining. Within each industry national agreements were to be negotiated first. Only after such agreements had been signed could regional and local agreements be made. Agreements had to cover a list of specified issues. No agreement was valid without government approval. With that approval, the agreement was automatically extended to the whole of the industry and geographic area of the original contract. The system was, on the one hand, too rigid and controlled; and on the other hand, with wages excluded, it was devoid of major substance. It turned out to be stillborn; under it only a handful of agreements was reached. In some negotiations interminable wrangles took place over the criteria of "representativity" and the right of various unions to take part in negotiations. The CGT metal workers spent over 2,000 hours in national negotiation without reaching agreement on most of the clauses at issue.[35] The only two national contracts for any large number of workers were those covering bank employees and streetcar workers.

Explaining the refusal to decontrol wages in the 1946 law, the Minister of Labor had said that the state must keep control over the "essential factors" in the economy.[36] Within the next two years, however, the government lifted most controls on food and clothing prices. The demand for the decontrol of wages grew steadily. In November 1949, FO staged a nationwide demonstration strike for a full return to freedom of bargaining, in which the CGT and CFTC unions joined. To the great relief of the FO leaders, the CGT did not manage to take over the strike or prolong it beyond the original twenty-four hours. Soon after the strike was called, the government introduced the bill which, after extensive parliamentary debate, became the collective bargaining law of February 11, 1950.[37]

---

[34] For text of the law, No. 46-2924 of December 23, 1946, see *Journal Officiel*, December 25, 1946, with rectifications, December 29, 1946 and January 5, 1947.

[35] Marius Patinaud, Communist deputy, former Under Secretary of Labor, Assemblée Nationale, *Débats*, December 15, 1949, p. 6906.

[36] Daniel Mayer, Minister of Labor (Socialist), *Revue française du travail*, vol. 2, no. 10, January 1947, p. 3.

[37] For debates on the law, see *Assemblée nationale*, Débats, December 15, 16, 20, 21, 23, 31, 1949; January 3, 4; February 2, 3, 8, 1950; Conseil de la République, *Debats*, January 26, 27, 28, 1950.

For text of the law, no. 50-205 of February 11, 1950, see *Journal officiel*, February 12, 1950, with rectifications February 22 and March 14, 1950, or *Droit social*, vol. 13,

The 1950 law abandoned some of the 1946 controls which had hampered bargaining: the requirement of government approval for agreements and the priority of national over regional and local agreements. The National Assembly rejected the government's proposal of compulsory arbitration, which was opposed by both employers and unions. Likewise it rejected the attempt of the Council of the Republic, the less important upper house of the legislature, to require arbitration for conflicts that might endanger "services and activities essential to the national existence." Instead the law prescribed compulsory conciliation and voluntary arbitration for all disputes. Otherwise it did not regulate the right to strike, in either private or government employment. For what it defined as full-fledged collective agreements, subject to extension, the law set forth a long list of issues to be covered. It permitted simple wage agreements, however, on the assumption that these would merely bridge the gap until the full collective agreements were concluded. Except for those government-owned industries which were regulated by separate statutes and for the civil service, all employment (including agriculture) was covered by the law. Finally, the law provided for the setting by the government of a national guaranteed minimum wage.

The first round of bargaining under the new law showed dramatically how the positions of labor and employers had altered since the war's end. Workers, naturally if too optimistically, in their anticipations had equated a return to wage bargaining with a large increase in wages. Bargaining began at a moment of financial stability and industrial stagnation. Prices had shown the greatest stability in a decade; at the end of 1949, they were only 4 per cent higher than at the beginning of the year. Wages had also been stable, having advanced an estimated 2 per cent during the year.[38] Industrial production, however, had failed to gain during almost the entire year, for the first time since liberation. A series of strikes for wage rises, the most important in the Paris region metallurgical industries, were almost all dismal failures for the unions. The

---

no. 3, March 1950, pp. 104-109. The text, with commentary, is also in *France: documents,* n.s., no. 41, March 1950, "Législation du travail."

For commentary on the debates and the law, see the series of articles by the distinguished professor of law, Paul Durand, in *Droit social,* vol. 13, no. 3, 4, and 5, March, April and May 1950, pp. 93-101, 155-162, and 186-193; Jean Rivero, "Conciliation et arbitration dans la loi du 11 février, 1950," *Droit social,* vol. 13, no. 4, April 1950, pp. 145-151; Adolf Sturmthal, "Collective Bargaining in France," *Industrial and Labor Relations Review,* Vol. 4, No. 2, January 1951, pp. 236-248; and Joel Colton, "The Rejection of Compulsory Arbitration in France: the New Law on the Settlement of Labor Disputes," *Arbitration Journal,* n. s., vol. 6, no. 1, 1951, pp. 42-49.

[38] *Etudes et conjoncture: . . ,* vol. 6, no. 3, May-June 1951, pp. 135, 78.

workers generally went back to work on the terms—increases of 5 to 8 per cent—laid down by the CNPF before the strikes began.[39] Or they accepted the employers' terms without striking.

The process of writing collective agreements turned out to be far slower, and the agreements less inclusive in their provisions, than the lawmakers or the unions had expected. By the end of a year's operation of the law the Minister of Labor announced that some 816 contracts had been concluded, of which 77 met the definition of full collective agreements.[40] Most contracts were simple wage settlements. A great number of issues—paid vacations, plant committees, shop stewards—were regulated by law. For employers to meet union demands on these issues even part way would have meant concessions beyond what the law required. Such concessions they were generally strong enough to refuse.

The obvious inequality of the bargaining partners alarmed the genuinely conservative in church, press, and government. The cardinals and archbishops of France issued calls for social justice and a living wage, which some employers denounced as "clerical meddling."[41] The conservative Paris daily, *Figaro,* warned:

If the workers' demands come up against a spirit of intransigence, then the entire working class will again turn toward revolutionary hopes. And those hopes, the Communist Party is there to mobilize. . . There are strikes —those of pure political agitation—whose failure weakens the Communist Party. There are other strikes whose failure may strengthen it.[42]

To the non-Communist unionists, this first economic contest seemed to confirm fears that the employers were still the old hereditary enemies, "avid of gain . . . and utterly lacking in comprehension," the FO Executive Board observed gloomily.[43] A Catholic writer commented:

I do not believe there is an employer offensive, in the sense at least of an organization deliberately tending to crush the working class. But I believe— how could one fail to, in the light of the evidence—there is an employer

---

[39] *Le Monde,* February 21 and March 14, 1950; Marcel Tardy, "L'Economique et le Social," *Le Monde,* March 17, 1950; *Figaro,* March 16 and 17, 1950; *Bulletin du CNPF,* March 5, and March 20, 1950.

[40] *Revue française du travail,* vol. 6, no. 3-4, March-April 1951, p. 140, and Assemblée Nationale, *Debats,* March 16, 1951, p. 2081. In neither of these two statements do the figures add up. The figure of 816 is the aggregate of the Minister's subtotals rather than the "almost 900 agreements" he refers to in the article cited.

[41] *Le Monde,* March 17, 1950; *New York Herald Tribune, Paris edition,* March 17, 1950. See also *Figaro,* March 3, 1950, and *Le Monde,* March 21, 1950.

[42] *Figaro,* May 9, 1950, p. 1.

[43] CGT-FO, *2ᵉ Congrès Confédéral, 25-28 octobre, 1950, Rapports confédéraux,* pp. 16, 28.

blindness. From this conflict . . . only one victor emerges crowned with the laurels of real victory, and that is the class struggle.[44]

Nor was the very moderate CGC much more optimistic. Privately one of its leaders, himself a responsible company official, compared the attitude of employers, now back in the saddle, with that of royalist emigrés on their return in 1815 from exile by the Revolution and Napoleon.

THE PRESSURES OF INTERNATIONAL POLITICS

The CGT had for a time moderated its political agitation to make possible joint action with other unions in negotiation and strikes. After the early 1950 strikes, the Communists intensified the political exploitation of the labor confederation. The Stockholm petition for the "outlawing" of the atomic bomb, launched by the worldwide Communist front of the Partisans of Peace, became major business at union meetings and in the CGT press. The campaign against the European Recovery Program continued with renewed force as it was tied in with the North Atlantic Treaty and the slowly developing rearmament program. The CGT proposed to prevent "the manufacture, handling or shipment" of goods of war.[45] It was unable to prevent American ships from landing military aid supplies, but it was able for a time to restrict their unloading to Brest alone of all French metropolitan ports. It kept up an agitation which occasionally boiled over in incidents of sabotage and violence. One of the most spectacular was a sort of Boston Tea Party in which a crowd in Nice threw into the Mediterranean an artillery launching ramp destined for Indo-China.[46] It denounced the Schuman Plan as soon as it was broached.[47]

The CGT was active in the World Federation of Trade Unions (WFTU). All the major national trade union centers of the world except the AF of L had joined to set up this organization in 1945. Louis Saillant, CGT secretary, was its general secretary from its inception; he had been chosen as not too committed to either the Communists or the Socialists. Jouhaux was one of the original vice presidents of the WFTU. Its headquarters were in Paris. When FO was formed, the majority at its constituent convention insisted on attempting to affiliate it with the WFTU, although a minority pointed out how completely the Communists had come to control it. FO's gesture of sentiment for inter-

---

[44] Jean Baboulène, "La Fin des grèves ne liquide pas le conflit social," *Témoignage chrétien,* April 7, 1950.

[45] See for example, resolutions of special meeting of Administrative Commission and national union executives, *Le Peuple,* January 4, 1950.

[46] *Servir la France,* no. 57, April 1950, p. 12 and photograph, p. 9.

[47] CGT Executive Board communique, *L'Humanité,* May 11, 1950.

national "labor unity" was rebuffed by the WFTU, itself by then a prey to disunity.

The WFTU, unlike the old labor internationals, merely reproduced world power alignments. The Marshall Plan conflict brought to a head the growing dissension in the WFTU. Early in 1949, the American CIO, the British Trades Union Congress, and the Netherlands Federation of Labor withdrew, followed in due course by all the non-Communist affiliates of the WFTU. These national centers with the AF of L then set up the International Confederation of Free Trade Unions (ICFTU). In the founding of the ICFTU, FO representatives, led by the veteran internationalist, Jouhaux, were active. By 1950 the international situation had so far deteriorated that the French government tossed the WFTU out of its lavish rent-free headquarters in a government requisitioned mansion in Paris. The WFTU then moved its headquarters to the Soviet sector of Vienna.

In the freely developed international labor movement before the first World War, the "international trade secretariats" of metal workers, transport workers, printers and so on, had preceded federation among the national centers and retained an autonomous position. The WFTU set up a number of subordinate "trade departments," to coördinate internationally the activities of Communist-led unions in specific industries. CGT unions were conspicuous in a number of the trade departments. A CGT leader headed the maritime department. Its opponents suspected that its major purpose was the sabotage of transport and communications, especially in the event of overt hostilities between East and West. (To counter its activities in the Mediterranean area, the International Transportworkers Federation, allied with the ICFTU, and strongest of the democratic international trade secretariats, created a Mediterranean department, headed by the dynamic Marseille FO dock workers' leader, Ferri-Pisani.)

Together with the Soviet zone German unions, the CGT launched a number of propaganda efforts in support of Soviet foreign policy. The Confederation and the East German Free Trade Union Federation, various CGT national unions and their Soviet Zone opposite numbers, joined in a stream of bellicose antiwar declarations against western German rearmament, against the Schuman Plan, and against the production and transport of war materials.[48] The first joint declaration for the defense of peace was issued a few days before the Korean invasion.[49]

---

[48] See, e.g., L'Humanité, June 20, August 15, August 18, September 21 and October 16, 1950. Cf. Verdier, in Le Populaire, June 21, 1950; Figaro, August 18, 1950.
[49] Le Peuple, June 21, 1950.

The CGT executive did not lose a day in condemning the "aggression" against North Korea.[50]

For the free unionists, the Korean War and the rearmament meant new and indefinite delays in the meeting of social claims, and more difficult choices at home and abroad, than for the CGT. As with most Frenchmen, the first response was one of wholehearted support of United Nations and United States action. The passage of the months diluted this feeling. Concern rose lest the conflict spread, perhaps to envelop and destroy France. There was a resurgence of the feeling of France's helplessness between "the two blocs." With one bloc there could, except among Communists, be little sympathy; but identification with the other was qualified and resented.

What workers and the free unions saw ahead at home increased their insecurity and pessimism. Korea immediately ended the respite from chronic inflation. Even before the rearmament program was launched, French prices started climbing steeply. Between mid-1950 and the end of 1951 retail prices in Paris rose 32.8 per cent. The precarious balance of the economy produced a greater price rise than in any other country of the Western alliance except occupied Austria.[51]

The most insistent union demand was for a sliding scale of wages. The 1950 collective bargaining law had called for a government-fixed minimum wage, which had been first set in August 1950. So rapidly did prices rise that the government had to raise the minimum twice during 1951, after strikes and union agitation. The legal minimum made itself felt not only at the bottom of the occupational hierarchy, but all the way up the wage structure. Actually, therefore, a tacit form of sliding pay scale was in widespread operation.

Wage increases might periodically overtake, or even occasionally anticipate, price increases. But rearmament seemed bound to hit workers hard. As taxpayers, they were least able to avoid the hand of the fisc in a tax system which one authority had called, with understandable hyperbole, "more iniquitous than that which provoked the French Revolution."[52] There were untapped sources of tax revenue in the business, farming and professional communities. But none of the coalition governments had either the internal cohesion or the courage to try raising taxes except by increasing the taxes which were easiest to levy and to collect, of which the indirect taxes were an increasing part. The most

---

[50] *Le Peuple,* June 28, 1950.

[51] As compared with the 1949 average, retail prices at the end of 1951 had risen 11.8 per cent in the United States, 17.6 per cent in Great Britain, 6.9 per cent in western Germany, and 42.9 per cent in France. R. Dumas, "L'évolution des prix en 1951," *Revue d'économie politique,* vol. 62, no. 3-4, May-August 1952, p. 292.

[52] Maurice Duverger, *Le Monde,* December 21-22, 1947.

broadly accepted claims of labor—a modest, steady increase in purchasing power, an expanded housing program, a less sordid allowance for the aged—would probably have to wait until the Greek Kalends. To millions of French workers and even to the free unions inequity in distributing the rearmament load obscured the very need for rearming.

The rightward trend of politics since 1947 further alarmed the unions. Inevitable in part as a reaction to the Communist departure from the government, this was a trend paralleled in other democracies, even in those where the Communists had not built up a popular following. The June 1951 national elections, the first since late 1946, confirmed the trend.[53] A new form of the ever-changing electoral law was designed (successfully) to reduce the Communist representation and favor the center parties, ranging from Socialists to Independents, who were willing to join in electoral alliances. The popular vote was more meaningful than the assignment of seats in the National Assembly. The Communists lost only slightly—9 per cent of their 1946 vote—although dropping 88 seats. Despite the loss of half a million ballots, they still led all other parties, with almost 5,000,000 votes.[54] The Socialists lost a fifth of their 1946 votes; the MRP a half. The Gaullists, who had not been in the field in 1946, lost popular support as compared with their phenomenal showing in the 1947 municipal elections.

The new Assembly showed little disposition to tackle the problems of economic progress or France's international position. In vain did chronic budgetary deficits focus the need for fundamental reforms. The Pleven government fell because the Assembly would not give it the authority to lessen expenditures, the Faure government fell because the Assembly would not let it raise more money in taxes. With the Socialists settled in the opposition, the only change possible was to move somewhat farther right in making up a cabinet.

Antoine Pinay, Premier during most of 1952, was an independent who had served unobtrusively in several preceding center governments. His term of office illustrated the problems of economic development and social reform which were critical in the long run to French workers. He was able to get Parliament to vote an amnesty for tax frauds, but not a reform of tax assessments and tax collection. He avoided any new taxes, but only by cuts in government capital investment in such fields

---

[53] For good brief analyses of this election, see *Le Monde,* June 19, 20, 21, 1951, with detailed district returns; François Goguel, *France under the Fourth Republic* (Ithaca, 1952), pp. 79-120; Raymond Aron, "France, Still the Third Republic," *Foreign Affairs,* vol. 30, no. 1, October 1951, pp. 145-151; and Mario Einaudi, "The Crisis of Politics and Government in France," *World Politics,* vol. 4, no. 1, October 1951, pp. 64-84.

[54] If the 1946 electoral law had been in force in 1951, the Communists would have obtained 180 seats instead of the 101 they received; the Gaullists 144 instead of 120, out of a total of 622. Goguel, *France under the Fourth Republic,* p. 118.

as electric power, which narrowed the base for future expansion of real national wealth. Mendès-France, Radical Socialist deputy, was one of the few who tried to bring his colleagues to face the unpleasant choices with which history and the cold war had saddled them. "Four years ago," he said early in 1953, "investment expenditures were double military expenditures. Now military expenditures are twice as much as invest- ments . . . In 1952 we started less construction than in 1951 . . . We are the only country in all Europe to do so."[55] With the aid of a fall in world raw material prices, Pinay achieved the first price stability since 1949, and even reduced prices slightly. But the seemingly inevitable accompaniment in the rigid French economy was an interruption of the rise in industrial production, an increase in unemployment, and fears of greater economic stagnation.

With the upward price spiral checked during his first months in office, Pinay was ready to put through his own version of the pending sliding pay scale bill. He had already given investors a "sliding scale" by float- ing a government loan with repayment guaranteed (by a tie-in with the price of gold) against depreciation of the franc. The unions attacked the bill's reference point for wage-price "parity." (Five per cent increases above that point in the index of Paris retail prices would call for man- datory increases in the government-fixed minimum wage.) The govern- ment naturally chose its parity point as far as possible above the point at which the price index stood when the law was under debate. The Socialists and Communists, who earlier had been calling for a sliding scale, voted against the Pinay bill. The MRP split its vote; the Gaullists, equally torn, chose to abstain. The bill passed with most of the deputies of the traditional right, defenders of employer interests and laissez-faire, voting in its favor.[56]

POLITICAL STRIKES

The year 1952 found the Communists making their frankest political use of the CGT. The relationship was symbolized by the decision of the National Committee to demote the dull official CGT weekly, *Le Peuple*, to bimonthly status, and make the Communist Party's union weekly, the livelier, scurrilous *Vie Ouvrière*, the official organ of the confedera- tion. As the director of *Le Peuple* said, "This is the end of an equivocal situation."[57] Gaston Monmousseau, director of the *Vie Ouvrière*, de- clared: "The mission of *La Vie Ouvrière* . . . is accomplished! *La Vie*

[55] *Le Monde*, March 26, 1953.

[56] Law No. 52-834 of July 18, 1952, *Journal officiel*, July 19, 1952. For summary of its legislative history, see A. Philbert, "Le Problème de l'échelle mobile des salaires," *Droit social*, vol. 15, no. 9, November 1952, pp. 592-599.

[57] *Le Peuple*, April 10, 1952, p. 2.

Ouvrière no longer has any reason to exist as the organ of a revolutionary wing within the CGT."[58]

The evolution of the *Vie Ouvrière*, started in 1909 as a critical, candid, revolutionary syndicalist journal, later taken over by the Communists, and now a sheet of shrill, reckless polemic, summed up many of the changes in the labor movement. The old syndicalist and anarchist journals had had a salty quality, independence, and, for all the violence of their argument, a concern with moral issues and the dignity and responsibility of the individual. Their Communist successors retained only the violence. The expansion of Soviet power had debased the coinage of radical abuse.

A series of undisguised political strikes moved from failure to greater failure. Trying to exploit the memories of February 12, 1934, the Paris Region CGT called a protest strike when the government forbade manifestations to commemorate the 1934 anniversary. The day after, one of the party leaders declared: "The great significance of yesterday's strike is that it is by far the most important political strike in France since the War."[59] But a few weeks later Lecoeur, party organization secretary, admitted, "a certain section of the working class remains unaware that the strike is as much the weapon of the worker for political as for economic struggles."[60] And: "The economic demands were not sufficently tied in with the strike, or were tied in only formally."[61]

In May General Ridgway succeeded General Eisenhower at SHAPE (Supreme Headquarters of the Allied Powers in Europe). The Communist Party called for demonstrations against the American general, in which the CGT invited "all organizations, all workers to join with all patriots, with all partisans of peace, with all honest folk."[62] Riots in many sections of the country (with one death) showed the party and the CGT able to mobilize thousands of their cadres, but no veritable mass strike. Among the hundreds arrested was Jacques Duclos, the party's parliamentary leader and one of its ruling quadrumvirate during the long absence of the ailing Maurice Thorez in Russia.[63] Seized near the scene of the Paris demonstration, which had been banned by the police, Duclos was accused of plotting against the security of the state.

Despite the failure of the Ridgway demonstrations, the CGT immediately called for strikes to free Duclos. "Manifest, stop work, strike for the defense of peace, of bread, and of our liberties. Demand the freeing

---

58 *Ibid.*
59 Etienne Fajon, *L'Humanité,* February 13, 1952 .
60 *L'Humanité,* February 27, 1952.
61 *L'Humanité,* March 1, 1952.
62 Communiqué of Executive Board, *Le Peuple,* June 1, 1952, p. 16.
63 In 1950 Thorez had gone to the Soviet Union, ostensibly for medical treatment, after a paralytic stroke. He did not return until 1953.

of Duclos," said the Executive Board.[64] As one CGT leader vaguely explained later, it called for "immediate not ephemeral action," for "general action but not a general strike."[65] The Paris region federations and several national unions, notably the mine and rail workers, issued strike calls. In the crucial areas, the response was slight. The Paris public services functioned. CGT squads forcibly occupied the Renault plant, but they were chased out the next day by non-Communist workers.[66] Only two per cent of the workers of France struck, the government claimed.[67] However, the government had not left everything to the good sense of the rank and file. The night before the strike the police had taken several score CGT and party activists into custody, releasing them only after the day's test of strength was over.[68]

The Duclos strike was a hopeless adventure for the CGT; party and union leaders must have known it would be. A big strike, political or economic, could be a success only if it drew wider support than the party or the CGT faithful. Apparently the party felt it would lose more, either in French or Russian eyes, if it tolerated the jailing of a top-flight leader without somehow fighting back. Duclos remained in jail. For the moment the party's only consolation was the verdict of the official experts that the two dead pigeons found in Duclos' car when he was arrested were of a type fit only for eating and not, as the state contended, for sending messages, subversive or otherwise. When Duclos was released a month later, it was by judicial finding and not by mass pressure.[69]

After the Duclos strike a number of Communist and CGT offices were raided, documents said to be treasonable were seized, and a number of Communist union officials, including Molino, CGT secretary, were thrown into jail. In October Alain Le Léap, co-general secretary of the CGT, was arrested for "attempted demoralization of the army." In 1953 a warrant was issued for the arrest of Frachon, who went into hiding. Despite all these "provocations," the CGT's protest remained almost entirely verbal. It kept up a stream of indignant resolutions, but attempted no such strike as it had called for Duclos.

The patent blunders of the Ridgway and Duclos strikes did not signal the collapse of the CGT, however. Again the confederation survived a

---

[64] Executive Board communiqué, May 29, *Le Peuple*, June 1, 1952, p. 16.

[65] Pierre Lebrun, "Premier Bilan," *Le Peuple*, June 15, 1952, p. 1.

[66] For an interesting account from an FO point of view, see Maurice Vassil, "Chez Renault: des rodomontades au fiasco," *Cahiers Fernand Pelloutier*, no. 25, June 1952, pp. 25-28.

[67] Minister of the Interior, *Le Monde*, June 5, 1952.

[68] *Le Monde*, June 5, 1952, gave the number thus detained as "about 60."

[69] As a deputy, Duclos could be held only if "seized in the act." The magistrates found this condition was not fulfilled.

series of disastrous strikes. The same apathy among workers which made even Communists reluctant to strike prevented any real revolt or breakaway movement in the CGT or the Communist Party. Not even the first open rift in the party since 1940, the party's well-publicized disciplining of André Marty and Charles Tillon, outstanding national leaders,[70] shook workers' support. Once more the rival unions and political parties were unable to capitalize on the vulnerability of the Communist Party and the CGT. The nationwide municipal elections of 1953 found the Communists losing only slightly, and the Socialists gaining slightly. The forces of the CFTC and FO remained roughly stabilized in their weakness vis-à-vis the CGT.

The increasing discontent and frustration of the free unions with employers and government was manifest at the FO convention of November 1952. Over the opposition of its executive Board, the convention voted to withdraw from the Inter-Union Center for Productivity Studies.[71] The action was notable less for its practical consequences than for its symbolic value, a gesture of impatience and impotence. The CFTC warned: "The head of the government [Pinay] repeats cheerfully that while the union leaders protest against his policies, the workers do not demonstrate, and concludes that they approve. The reasoning is perhaps too simple, for the apparent weariness of labor has many causes . . . It is in the general interest to show that one should not count too much on apathy: the awakening may be painful."[72]

In repeated tests since 1947, the workers of France had refused to follow the partisans of violence and catastrophe to the verge of insurrection. But in most of the expectations so high at liberation, they had been disappointed. By 1953 they held no great hopes in their government, their employers,—or their own organizations. They had a profound skepticism as to what they could do through the unions or the political parties. Their pessimism was reinforced by a feeling of helplessness in the drift of international events. The resentments they felt were sterile, not creative of sustained action or solidarity. "Hope deferred maketh the heart sick." This state of mind weakened the Communist potential for action. Even more it inhibited the assertion of democratic political and trade union forces.

---

[70] Marty had been for a generation the party's "hero of the Black Sea mutiny," an episode in the French intervention against the Bolshevik revolution. Tillon had headed the party's armed forces in the resistance, the Franc-Tireurs et Partisans. Party faithfuls for over 30 years, both were among the 10 members of the Politburo. Marty was expelled, Tillon demoted to the ranks.

[71] *F.O. Informations, compte rendu . . . du 3ᵉ Congrès Confédéral*, pp. 244-260. The resolution was voted by 5,193 votes against 4,327, with 1,422 abstaining; p. 403.

[72] Georges Levard, executive board report, *Syndicalisme*, October 23, 1952, p. 2.

PART THREE

UNION STRUCTURE, INDUSTRIAL RELATIONS,
AND POLITICS

CHAPTER IX

THE STRUCTURE AND FUNCTIONING
OF THE UNIONS

A Frenchman likes to take a minority position, even within his
minority.

—FO local union leader.

Our unionism was doomed to decrepitude. It was steadily losing the
confidence of the mass of workers because the workers made it live from
hand to mouth.

—Victor Vanlerenberghe,
L'Echo des Mines, CFTC
national miners' union,
February 1, 1952.

With the Bolshevik party as its model, molded out of the raw material
of its national character, the French labor movement acquired its personality. And the hand of Maurice Thorez, like that of the artist, molded
all its aspects.

—Auguste Lecoeur, "Parti et
syndicats," *Servir la France,*
June 1950.

The weakness of structure, so closely related to the functioning and
ideology of the syndicalist unions, helps to explain the CGT's vulnerability to political party envelopment and seizure. The continued weakness of the union movement's structure underlies much of the unions'
weakness in bargaining and their reliance on government action. This
chapter shows the broad outlines of French union structure in terms as
far as possible common to the three main workers' confederations, paus-
ing from time to time to note significant differences among them. First
it must note the contrast between appearance and reality, between the
traditional façade and the present working interiors of the house of
French labor. It then takes up the major units of union structure: the
local union, the national union, the horizontal organizations (chiefly the
departmental federation), the confederation. It observes some of the

problems of centralization and relationships between leadership and rank and file. It looks at effects of party control of the CGT, and listens for a moment to the battles of the caucuses within the free unions. Finally it considers the perennially critical question of union dues.

APPEARANCE AND REALITY

Formally the confederations' structure is logical, decentralized, under close membership control, and independent of political parties. Most unions have similar organs of government at each echelon, and similar rules. Industrial unionism predominates. There is a fairly small number of national unions in each confederation: the CGT had 40 in 1950, the CFTC had several more, FO several fewer. (The AF of L then had 107.) Within the confederation, jurisdictional conflicts are few. As compared with the sprawling and overlapping jurisdictions with which history has endowed other union movements—the British, for example— the French structure, within each confederation, is neat and logical.

In form, power is decentralized. The confederation has few powers of compulsion or discipline over the national union. Within the national union, locals and regional bodies have great autonomy. Officials are elected for short terms, subject to recall. Further membership control is exercised through regular local assemblies, frequent conventions, and other representative bodies of national unions and confederations. Independence of outside organizations—employers, Church, political parties, and government—is an article of faith.

This is the form. The reality is vastly different. In the major segment of organized labor, communist controls have ended political independence, and vitiated both membership control of officials and the autonomy of union bodies close to the base. The logic of national union structure within each confederation is less important than the practice of competing unions of the three major workers' confederations, several splinter confederations, and many unaffiliated unions.

The formal structure is still largely that inherited from syndicalist days. That structure was the product of an economy of small-scale production and comparatively decentralized product markets. It was the creation of organized workers who were a small minority of the wage earners of the nation, largely an *élite* of skilled workmen. The local components—local unions and Bourses du Travail—were initially the most vital elements of the structure; unions were organized from the ground up rather than by national unions or confederation. Voting systems favored the small organizations against the large. Union government realized the formula of "the free individual in the local; the free local union in the national; the free national union in the confederation."

Finances were even more limited, and bureaucracy more rudimentary than in the formative periods of many other Western trade union movements. Discipline at every stage was loose and voluntary. Syndicalist doctrine, which stemmed from these attitudes and practices, helped perpetuate them.

There were of course exceptions. The printers, more like printers in other countries than like their countrymen in other unions, had a strong centralized national union. The textile workers, composed of the largest group of unskilled machine tenders—followers of the disciplined Guesdist Socialist Party—developed a centralized and bureaucratized union.

The first World War gave union officialdom a new importance, in the government sponsored agencies of production, economic regulation, relief, and disputes settlement. Its role was enlarged, as in the United States, beyond any share it had been able to win for itself in the industrial process during peacetime. After the war, despite the split, CGT officialdom retained a measure of this gain. The CGT not only accepted the need of working within the capitalist economy, but it turned to government to direct that economy. The development of national economic plans, participation in the administration of social security, lobbying for the civil servants, and representation abroad in the ILO and international trade union bodies, all helped to strengthen the central office of the CGT. In the CGTU, the Communist bureaucracy wielded power over an emaciated body, after it had driven all opposition out of the confederation. The CGTU had naturally begun with a structure paralleling that of the original confederation. Attempts to tighten the structure to suit party requirements achieved little because of the weakness of both CGTU and party. When the CGTU reunited with the CGT, it was on the basis of the old structure.

The CFTC, from its formation, had a loose "federal" structure similar to that of the CGT. It did not adopt the centralized structure characteristic of Catholic trade union movements in other countries.

At the liberation, the two confederations resumed by and large the forms of organization they had had before the war. The CGT carried through some mergers and altered its voting system in favor of the national industrial unions and the big department federations which the Communists controlled. In general, however, it retained most of the old forms. After the split, FO kept to the same structure, going back to some forms of "federalism" which its leaders had vainly sought to preserve in the postliberation CGT.

Trade unions almost everywhere are organized along the two axes of basic interest: the vertical axis of trade or industry and the horizontal one of community and region. Figure 1 sums up the major

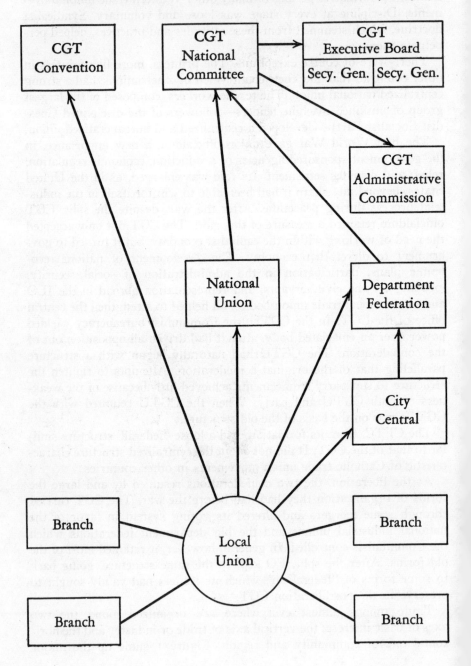

Figure 1
STRUCTURE OF THE LABOR CONFEDERATION:
CONFEDERATION GENERALE DU TRAVAIL (CGT)

organs of the confederation structure as seen in the CGT; they are in general those of the CFTC and FO as well.

THE LOCAL UNION

The basic unit of the movement is the local union ("syndicat"). It is the delegates of the local unions, not the national unions, who represent the membership at conventions of the confederation. The local union sets its own level of dues; it is required only to give the national union and the confederation the prescribed per capita payments.

There are infinite variations in the size and coverage of locals. The local's jurisdiction may be plantwide or, much more frequently, area-wide: a city or even a whole department. If it covers more than one plant, it usually has sublocals or branches ("sections syndicales") for each employer unit or for separate crafts or branches of its industry.[1] The railroad workers' locals have "technical sections" for the various important operating and nonoperating rail services; these sections have more autonomy than ordinary sublocals in the formulation of union demands.

The local union may embrace a membership of anywhere from less than a dozen to several thousand. In large plants it may be broken down by departments or among production, clerical, and technical and supervisory employees. The CGT has urged that every large plant have a local, rather than a sublocal, of its own. Its policy is to have no more than a single local in a single plant. The CFTC may have several, one for clerical workers, and another for engineers and technicians, in addition to the industrial union local for production workers.

The sovereign body of the local is the general meeting ("assemblée générale") which convenes at intervals varying from a month to a year. In some locals the general meeting elects the local executive body. In others the executive is composed of the dues collectors or other representatives of the sublocals. The egalitarian workers who founded the CGT unions had little use for the term president. It is ordinarily reserved for the chairman of the meeting, newly designated each time by those in attendance. The chief official of the local, as of almost every form of union executive, is a general secretary, or sometimes simply a secretary. He is selected, usually for a year's term, by the local's general meeting or by the executive committee from among its own membership. Whether the general secretary is a paid full-time official or a man still working at the bench depends on the union's size and treasury.

---

[1] Unlike the local union, which under the law must be registered, the branches have no juridical existence.

Very frequently the full-time officer is an employee of a government enterprise or large private firm who has been allowed full time for union business. A general secretary has most of the functions we would expect to find in a president, business agent, and corresponding secretary. At all levels the treasurer's functions are kept separate from those of the secretary.

Intermediate between the local and national levels, the locals of one union within a department or region may form a council or joint board to coördinate action and often bargaining. Thus the metal workers of the CGT in and around Paris, which are organized in areawide locals by industry, form the powerful Metal Workers Council of the Paris Region.[2] The CGT clerical employees in the same area coördinate the work of their six locals (banking, insurance, social security administration, commerce, publishing, and miscellaneous office workers) through a Paris region council. The CGT railway workers union has a network of district organizations based on the once independent companies which now make up the national railway system. The district organizations had great autonomy until 1945; since then the district conventions no longer elect the railway union's national council.

The intermediate union bodies often parallel the jurisdiction of area employer organizations for labor relations. Given the system of areawide industry bargaining, it is natural that they have great latitude in negotiation and strike action.

THE NATIONAL UNION

The national union ("fédération") remains to a considerable extent what the word historically and literally signified: a rather loose federation of locals or regional bodies.[3] Its supreme authority is the convention, meeting every year or two years; the three-year interval of the CGT printers is exceptional. The convention usually elects (directly or indirectly) the executive board ("bureau fédéral"), a body of six, eight, or twelve secretaries headed as a rule by a general secretary. Some secretaries may continue to work at their trade; others are full-time officials. In principle the powers of the executive board and the general secretary are closely circumscribed. Policymaking authority between con-

---

[2] The "Région parisienne" generally denotes the department of the Seine, of which Paris is a part, and the surrounding department of the Seine-et-Oise. In these two departments are concentrated almost a fourth of the nation's industrial population. Some Paris region bodies also include the neighboring department of the Seine-et-Marne.

[3] A few national unions are "syndicats nationaux." These are simply national unions with a structure tighter than that of the ordinary national union or "fédération." Most "syndicats nationaux" are unions of government administrative employees.

ventions is in the hands of a national committee, chosen as a rule on the basis of regional or industrial groups within the union. Lesser powers are entrusted to an executive commission elected by the convention. Smaller and meeting more frequently than the national committee, and less representative, it is charged with administrative rather than policy decisions. The locals may be consulted directly by referendum on major decisions, but less commonly than they were in earlier years.

CRAFT AND INDUSTRIAL UNIONS

The debate of craft versus industrial organization went on for years inside the CGT. The issue was only partially settled by the decision of the Amiens convention of 1906 to accept no further craft union affiliates and to promote the fusion of existing craft organizations. Fusion took years to achieve and was not accepted by all. For example, only 5 out of 37 machinists' locals went into the metal workers union in the large-scale fusion of 1909, and the national machinists organization seceded from the CGT in protest.[4] The gradual encroachments of technology on the crafts reinforced the CGT's policy. The number of member national unions was reduced from 70 before the Amiens convention to 53 before the first World War, and 44 before the 1921 split. The process of national industrial union formation was largely completed with the mergers during the first war of practically all the railroad unions, and immediately after the war of a number of regional agricultural unions and of several electrical workers' organizations.

Extensive jurisdictions have thus been created. Within each confederation there are: a single rail workers' union, a single metal workers' union extending from basic iron and steel to all the diverse metal end products from pots and pans to shipbuilding and automobiles; a printing trades' union covering the range of mechanical production workers in printing and publishing; a chemical workers' union including rubber products and oil refineries; a food workers' union including food processing, bakery, hotel, restaurant, and café workers; a single building trades union. Among the few national craft unions remaining are the barbers, jewelers, and the ancient and honorable corporation of the coopers.

Within industrial unions, local unions may still follow craft lines, for example, in the building trades. Other unions, of a multi-industry character, may have locals for single industries. Craft or occupational category unions abound in a few local situations, notably the Paris public transportation system.

---

[4] Michel Collinet, *Esprit du syndicalisme,* esp. pp. 23-36.

At the national level, special industry departments or divisions reflect the varied interests of the different industrial branches within the union's jurisdiction. The industry divisions have service functions, such as research and technical coördination; they do not ordinarily have the same measure of autonomy as the intermediate regional bodies. They are regarded as administrative divisions of the national union, rather than as emanations of the locals below.

The rail workers have "national technical sections" corresponding to the major rail service operations. The CFTC national metal workers union has nine industry divisions: basic steel, aviation, farm machinery, railroad equipment, orthopedic appliances, office machinery, electrical equipment, shipbuilding, and—the most active—automobiles. But in bargaining and strikes, it is not the industry divisions but the union's regional organizations, cutting across industry lines, which "have the direct responsibility for action."[5]

The chief exceptions to industrial unionism occur in the organization of clerical, technical, and supervisory employees. White collar workers in Europe are set off from production laborers not only by their work but also by social status. The CFTC and FO each has a separate union of clerical employees and another union of technicians, engineers, and supervisory employees. The CFTC has a separate union too for white collar employees in mining.

There has been a running battle since the war over industrial unionism in the CFTC. The issue has not been that of craft unions in industry but of jurisdiction over the office workers of industrial concerns. So far the confederation has supported the powerful office workers' union against the vigorous claims of the younger industrial unions. The issue has not been entirely settled, however. After the breakdown of talks with the union of clerical employees and the union of technicians and supervisory personnel in 1950, the metal workers announced flatly that they would admit any local unions of clerks or technicians which might apply.[6] The CFTC office employees of the chemical companies switched from the clerical workers union to the chemical workers: "their wishes must be respected," remarked the head of the industrial union which took them in. These jurisdictional rows also represent a conflict between different philosophies of union action.

In government administration (as distinguished from nationalized industry), there are a number of national unions, some for a single ministry's employees, others covering a group of ministries. Within

---

[5] CFTC Fédération de la Métallurgie, 25ᵉ congrès, *Rapport moral, présenté par le bureau fédéral,* September 1950, p. 33.

[6] *Ibid.,* p. 69.

each confederation there is a national coördinating council of the government workers' unions.

The teachers, who are well organized, have traditionally had a sense of solidarity with manual labor. But the national union has remained autonomous since leaving the CGT in 1948. It has repeatedly voted against joining FO and against returning to the CGT. A minority of its members also carry cards in the separate teachers union of either the CGT or FO. The CFTC has one union of teachers in church schools and another, stronger union of teachers in state institutions.

In organizing the "cadres"—technicians, engineers, and managerial staff—the confederations have followed different methods. The CGT after the war dissolved its separate technicians union, always suspect to the Communists as "Trotskyite." Instead it sought to enroll the cadres in the appropriate industrial unions. In recognition of their special problems of recruitment and representation, it created an interunion council to look after their interests, and named an engineer as member of the CGT executive board. The CFTC and FO each has a separate national union of technicians and supervisory personnel (which in the CFTC includes foremen).

The largest number of cadres have chosen the autonomous Confédération Générale des Cadres. Operating in both private and public employment, the CGC takes as its jurisdiction all but top managerial personnel, which it defines as those named directly by boards of directors. Following the rule of organizational expansion, it has organized all those it could. These include large numbers of foremen, also traveling salesmen and white collar employees, who are not, strictly speaking, "cadres."

HORIZONTAL ORGANIZATION

The chief form of horizontal organization is the departmental federation ("union départementale"), made up of all local unions of the confederation within a department. Much less important is the parallel body at the city level, the city central ("union locale"). The two correspond roughly to AF of L federations and city centrals or CIO state and city industrial union councils. Affiliation of local unions with the department federation is a condition of membership in the confederation; affiliation with the city central is optional.

Department federations and city centrals are delegate bodies, electing their officers at annual conventions. Between them they carry on many of the functions of the old Bourse du Travail. Unlike the Bourses, they are not independent centers of power or of trade union philosophy. Especially in the CGT, they have become essentially administrative units of the confederation. In FO and the CFTC some of the department heads retain a measure of independent authority.

The name Bourse du Travail persists as that of the structure housing the city central. It is financed by the municipality but administered— subject to municipal government regulations—by the unions. After the 1947 split, except in the comparatively rare cases where the majority of the local CGT went over to FO, the old organization retained control of the Bourse quarters. In some cities FO shares Bourse space, alongside the CGT, by informal arrangement or pending the outcome of litigation. The CFTC bodies generally continue to maintain their headquarters apart from the Bourses. The Grenoble city administration solved the problem of union rivalry by adding another story to the Bourse, retained by the CGT, to house FO and the CFTC. Where the FO and CFTC are kept out of the Bourse by the CGT, the municipality may give them small subventions in lieu of Bourse quarters.

The city central in most localities has little power, although it may help to administer weak local unions. Its own officials are apparently none too sure of their role; Frachon had to remind those of the CGT: "Our city centrals have a lot more importance than some of their leaders think."[7]

The department federation officials have far more responsibility for industrial relations, and far less concern with legislation, than American state federation or industrial union council officers. Significant legislation is all national. But its administration at the department level involves the federation officials. So does representation on the numerous government regulatory, advisory, or mediation agencies convoked on a department basis to deal with labor relations, manpower, public contracts, and so on. Much of labor-management relations is on a departmentwide or district basis. Since few of the national unions, even in the CGT, can do an adequate job of servicing their local unions, the department federation officials must often help in organizing, negotiations, or strikes.[8]

In the Paris region, city central and department federation are combined. The CGT also maintains neighborhood "interunion centers" in each of the 20 Paris boroughs and in 70 suburban localities, which correspond to city centrals. A secretary of the Paris region federation suggested that these neighborhood interunion centers might help the activi-

[7] Speaking to CGT convention, *Le Peuple,* May 28, 1951.

[8] For an interesting brief description of the work of a secretary general of an FO department federation, see Pierre Richou, head of the Gironde (Bordeaux) federation, "Un Secrétaire d'union départementale sur le tas," *Cahiers Fernand Pelloutier* (FO workers education center), n.s., no. 2, November 1950, pp. 1-2.

ties of the shop branches more than a centralized local union. But, he added, "of course the locals alone remain responsible for their branches. The interunion centers only aid and coördinate the union work at the local level."[9]

There is a strong suggestion here of the way in which various mechanisms of coördination may get in each other's way. Local unions, city centrals, and department federations have clashed even in the coördinated CGT. The department federations, embracing locals of all unions, felt that the departmentwide councils of a single national union encroached upon their functions and their income. So they condemned them unreservedly, "sometimes a little frivolously, sometimes even bureaucratically," complained the CGT leadership.[10] In the capital cities of the departments, where city centrals and department federations must live side by side, they trod on each other's toes so that one local leader asked whether "coexistence" was possible.[11]

Periodically the confederations have turned to regional organization to supplement or replace the departmental. The 90 departments of France are relatively small areas, many with small populations and that chiefly rural. In half the departments the urban population is under 200,000.[12] In only 17 of the departments is the industrial proletariat more than one-fifth of the active population.[13] Many departments therefore are unable to support even the most rudimentary services of a department federation. One purpose of regional organization is to spread personnel and services more economically, over a more viable unit than that of the department. Another purpose is to give the confederation a closer contact with department activities and a closer check.

Under the occupation and Vichy both the Communists and the reformists organized clandestine operations regionally. So did the reunited CGT as a temporary measure as French territory was liberated, paralleling the Provisional Government's emergency administration through regional commissioners. It named a pair of delegates, one reformist and one Communist, for each region. Regional organization

---

[9] L. Monjauvis, "Le Problème des centres inter-syndicaux," *L'Humanité,* June 9, 1950.

[10] R. Arrachard, "Pour une structure syndicale plus efficace," *Servir la France,* No. 41-42, November-December, 1948, pp. 44-45.

[11] Louis Duchesne, secretary of Toulon city central, "La Cohabitation de l'union locale et de l'union départementale, est-elle possible?" *Le Peuple,* January 27, 1949.

[12] INSEE, *L'Espace économique français* (Paris, 1951), pp. 17, 23. This figure overemphasizes urbanization, because it is based on a century-old definition of "urban population," i.e., agglomerations of over 2,000 inhabitants. The figures are from the 1946 census.

[13] Goguel, *France under the Fourth Republic,* p. 113. His figures are based on the 1936 census, but there has been comparatively little change since then.

lapsed after the war. But a few years later it was revived by both the
CFTC and FO, with varying success. The CFTC encourages weaker
department federations to unite in regional federations. It carries on
certain activities, notably education, largely on a regional basis; the
north has a regional strike fund. The CFTC names regional delegates
responsible for representing the confederation in each region. In FO
the confederation decision to name regional delegates has been only
partially implemented, after meeting with opposition from some of the
department organizations fearing a loss of autonomy.

The confederation puts forth the lines of general national policy for
its affiliates. Its officers represent them in dealings with government or
join the unions directly concerned on important delegations to the authorities. It sends representatives to national consultative and quasi-
regulatory bodies. It deals with the National Council of French Employers on general wage and economic policy. It represents its wing of
the trade union movement in the major international affiliations and
relationships. Nominally its powers of compulsion over its national
union affiliates are negligible.

Final authority in the confederation is divided between the convention ("congrès"), supreme when it meets, and the national committee.
Only the convention may alter the constitution of the confederation.
The biennial convention (until 1949 annual in the CFTC) is made up
of elected delegates of the local unions. Since there are thousands of
locals in each confederation, a single delegate may represent a number
of small locals.

In FO and CFTC conventions and national committees, the principles of federalism and autonomy survive in voting systems weighted in
favor of smaller units (in FO), in open debate and divided votes. FO
conventions continue to be "meetings of people of the same mind who
get together to disagree among themselves." Some of the disagreements
arise from basic policy differences. Others represent the release of steam
by local delegates, manifesting the traditional desire to keep leaders in
their place, and the current dissatisfactions of the rank and file. Some
delegates come instructed by their locals to vote against the executive
reports. In FO it is still true, as Jouhaux wrote long ago, that "a 'fine
convention,' as they say, is one which debates opposing lines of general
policy at full length."[14]

Like Moliere's famous doctor, the CGT can say, "We have changed
all that." Since 1946, voting in convention and national committee has

[14] *Le Syndicalisme et la C. G. T.,* p. 131.

been based entirely on numbers represented. The rule of enthusiastic unanimity has replaced the clash of opinions and caususes. Its conventions since the postliberation split have given its top leadership the unqualified approval and the generous applause characteristic of public meetings of the Communist Party and the organizations it fully controls. At the 1948 convention a delegate speaking for a tiny minority reminded the audience and the chairman, impatient with his attack on the leadership, that Frachon himself had just called for more criticism and self-criticism. "Yes," shouted a delegate, "constructive criticism. This is calumny."[15]

The national committee ("comité confédéral national") of the confederation is an institution for which American union government has no analogy. It is composed of a representative of each national union and of each department federation, with two representatives for the Paris region federation. Thus it gives a large place to the horizontal organizations, which are more than twice as numerous as the national unions. The national offices tend to be more powerful in the committee, however. Some of the department federation secretaries are on the payrolls of their own national unions or detailed from jobs in nationalized industry. In the CGT, many of the department secretaries are in effect appointees of the confederation.

Meeting ordinarily twice a year, the national committee is the supreme authority of the confederation between conventions, although no longer the sort of council of ambassadors of semisovereign powers which it was in the old CGT. In some respects its power is greater than that of the convention. In the CGT and FO it elects, and may recall, the executive board members. Only the national committee may call a nationwide general strike. To be sure, the CGT in 1947 showed that such a strike can dispense with the name and formal national call.

The CFTC has a structure somewhat different, giving the place which the national committee has in the CGT and FO to a national council ("conseil confédéral") meeting every two months. It is composed of 44 members, half elected by the convention and half named by the 22 largest national unions and department or regional federations. The CFTC has a less important national committee, whose chief power is budgetary, which meets twice a year, with a representative of each national union and each departmental or regional federation, as in the CGT and FO, plus enough national union representatives (in proportion to their membership) to equal the number of departmental and regional representatives.

Between conventions and national committee meetings of the CGT

[15] CGT, *XXVIIe Congrès . . . 1948, compte rendu*, p. 52.

and FO, an administrative commission ("commission administrative" or "commission exécutive"), elected by the national committee, has the responsibility indicated by its title. It meets monthly. Its 35 members, chosen from all major unions and areas, form a compressed edition of the national committee (of which its members are ex-officio nonvoting members). Between administrative responsibility for agreed policies and the formulation of new policies, the line is hard to draw; the administrative commission in practice may decide policy as well as supervise its operation.

The full-time executive organ of the CGT and FO is an executive board ("bureau confédéral"), of 12 members in the CGT; 7 in FO; 10 (not all full-time) in the CFTC, with an inner board of 5 officers. The board members or secretaries, as they are called ("secrétaires confédéraux"), normally give up their national union or department federation leadership positions upon election. Thus they retain no independent bases of power with which to reinforce their positions within the confederation. The chief executive responsibility in the CGT still rests with two general secretaries, although the historic reason for this anomaly disappeared in 1947, two years after the creation of the second general secretary's post. The heads of the CFTC and FO have the title of president.

The CFTC is the only confederation which normally has a president in its executive bodies, at all echelons, an honorific office related to the doctrinal and white collar origins of the movement. Until the sweeping change in its statutes in 1953, the CFTC's president had the mandate to "assure the maintenance of the doctrine and the discipline of the confederation."[16] Gaston Tessier's successor as president, Maurice Bouladoux, was expected to be less paternal and more of a conciliator, charged with the external relations of the confederation, while the new general secretary, Georges Levard, carried on its administration. In Force Ouvrière, the office of president was created especially for the personality of Léon Jouhaux, to put his national and international name at the head of the new organization, while a younger man, Robert Bothereau, handled the administration as general secretary.

In the CFTC national unions the general secretary has more important functions than the president. In most cases, moreover, he is a full-time official in Paris, while the president generally is either not a full-time official of the union or is stationed out of Paris in some other CFTC post. In the other confederations the office of president may be

<hr>

[16] Chapter XII, Article 26, of pre-1953 Internal Regulations of the CFTC. For old and new statutes see *27e congrès confédéral, La C.F.T.C. réforme ses structures, Projet de modification des statuts et du règlement intérieur, 1953.*

created for special personal reasons, as it was in FO's gas and electricity workers' union to provide a place for the retiring general secretary, or in the Haute-Garonne department federation originally to offer a spot for the CGT general secretary should he switch to FO.

CENTRALIZATION AND DECENTRALIZATION

Centralization has overtaken the unions in two ways. The more dramatic and far more effective centralization is that imposed on the CGT from without by party control. The other is the slow, halting response of the unions themselves to economic and political change and their own growth.

Mass production workers who have come into the unions in the last generation have been prepared to accept more centralization of union functions (and to take less interest in union operations) than the more independent workingmen of the CGT's syndicalist years. The unions have faced larger employer units, producing for wider markets, organized in more potent employer associations. The unions have dealt with the national government, no longer as a matter of occasional pressure or bursts of violence but on constant, vital business. After 1944, government wage fixing and other economic controls of the scarcity period, social reforms, nationalization, national economic planning and government investment multiplied the unions' need to deal with the national government and in national policies. So did the ostensible closeness to labor of the cabinets and legislatures of the several years after 1944. It looked then as if collective bargaining, when it resumed, would be on a national industrywide basis.

Union structures reflect such changes only gradually. In the CGT, the official structure has changed, but not as much as the locus of power. A survivor of the old CGT can easily recognize the forms of the national unions and of the confederation whose statutes still declare: "The General Confederation of Labor, based on the principle of federalism and liberty, guarantees and respects the autonomy of the organizations which conform to these statutes." (Article 2.) When the CGT executive board discussed the constitutional amendments to put before the 1946 convention, the Communists proposed outright suppression of this article. In the face of the reformists' indignation, they dropped the proposal.[17]

The deepest changes in the locus of power in the postliberation CGT —those flowing from party control—were naturally given no constitutional sanction. But the Communist union leaders did carry through im-

---

[17] Robert Bothereau, *CGT, XXVIe Congrès, 1946, compte rendu*, p. 297.

portant overt changes. Their enthusiasm for amalgamation and centralization was based in part on the pragmatic concern with union direction and discipline from the top. In part it also reflected Marxist ideas of the industrial concentration expected to follow the war. "It is evident," said the 1946 CGT convention resolution on structure, "that in each industry production is in fact oriented and regulated almost entirely by the great employers, the cartels and trusts."[18]

The Communist leaders merged a number of national unions. They amalgamated the furniture and wood workers' union with the larger building trades' union. The venerable union of hatworkers merged with the clothing workers, who cover both men's and women's garments. Six unions of merchant marine officers combined into one. Looking ahead, the leadership foresaw a possible fusion of the textile and clothing unions and a colossal merger of the five unions of railroad, general transport, dock workers, sailors, and merchant marine officers.

On the other hand, the Communists stripped the General Federation of Civil Service Unions, a holding company of seven national unions,[19] of its power. They made it simply a supercommittee of autonomous unions, each of which was henceforth affiliated directly with the confederation instead of through the General Federation. This was a simpler and more logical structure. The Communist interest in logic and autonomy here arose from the fact of reformist control of the central office of the old General Federation.

On the local level, the leadership set to joining "all the specks of little locals almost barren of any capabilities for practical action."[20] Many of these were craft locals, survivors of half a century's debate over the forms of local organization within national industrial unions. They were merged into departmentwide locals called "industrial" locals but often multi-industry rather than single-industry units.

The leadership had to call a halt, however. By the 1948 CGT convention, it rebuked excessive centralization and the wrong kind of mergers, "made in a mechanical fashion." It spoke a good word for the craft local, "a tradition which remains dear to the spirit of many workers." Within industrial locals, "the internal structure should permit the different categories to meet to discuss their own particular demands. Local

---

[18] *Ibid.*, p. 362.

[19] Ministry of Finance; Ministry of National Economy; Air, War, and Navy; National Education; Public Works; general administration (including several ministries) ; and the newly formed police union.

[20] *Voix du peuple,* 5th series, no. 1, January 1946. *XXVIᵉ Congrès, rapports confédéraux,* p. 108. The report of the commission on trade union jurisdiction and organization, pp. 105-109, is a capital document. See also "La Vie des fédérations Nationales," pp. 115-140.

executive bodies should be so constituted as to represent all categories of membership." These principles, declared the convention, should govern not only the locals and sublocals, but also the national unions.[21]

"Most of our organizations are too centralized, in industrial as well as in territorial coverage," Arrachard, general secretary of the building trades union and high Communist Party official, pointed out. Such organizations were "unnatural," like "the obese who become infirm and impotent." He gave his own union as an example. "In the abstract, setting up a so-called industrial local, as against the old craft locals, had a seductive appearance." But the departmentwide unit was too large for the handling of workers' demands. The technological changes that were supposed to accompany postwar reconstruction had not materialized. (The building trades would seem to be a poor field for Marxist prediction.) Craft skills and little single-craft employer units continued to dominate the industry. But decentralization, like centralization, could be justified out of the Communist book: "Activists who doubt the utility and the necessity of still taking account of crafts and occupations . . . would understand much better if they studied the structure of the Soviet unions, which . . . are much more decentralized industrially than ours."[22] Soon all members were invited to contribute to the discussion in *Le Peuple* of "excessive centralization" and "methods of bringing workers closer to unions."[23]

The geographic base was obviously insufficient for local union life. Organization had to be strengthened at the shop level. Arrachard put it bluntly, "Let us reinforce the foundation, so that the roof does not fall on the heads of those below."[24] In an executive board report to the national committee, Raynaud, CGT secretary, said, "The problems of organization are dominated by the necessity of making the shop more than ever the essential base of the movement." The CGT's principal weakness was "our weakness of organization in the shops. We do not have union branches in all the places we should have them. When they exist, most of the time they are not effectively organized and their functioning is up to a single comrade."

It was not so much participation at the base as control over the base which worried the leaders. The result of the weakness in the shops, said Raynaud, was that "the unions, even the department federations,

---

[21] Resolution on structure, *CGT, XXVIIe Congrès, 1948, compte rendu*, p. 255.

[22] R. Arrachard, "Pour une structure syndicale plus efficace," *Servir la France*, no. 41-42, November-December, 1948, pp. 33-45.

[23] Jacques Marion, "Il faut ouvrir largement la discussion," *Le Peuple*, January 27, 1949.

[24] *Le Peuple*, March 3, 1949.

are sometimes cut off from the shops. The union organization thus finds itself little by little incapable of playing its role of direction."[25]

The CGT needed firmer organization at the shop level to capitalize on its "unity" appeals to other unions and other workers. "Unity" has been for many years the chief tactical weapon of the Communists' arsenal.[26] The revived unity campaign aimed to overcome the isolation with which the Communists' "hard line" after 1947 threatened them; to foster agitation and strikes which the CGT alone could not carry off; to push the long "peace offensive" of the Soviet Union; and to dislocate, atomize, and absorb competing union organizations. The old tactic of the Comintern was again in order: "United front from above only, never; from above and below, sometimes; from below, always."[27] At the shop and local level, especially if they utilized economic grievances and soft-pedaled political demands, the CGT unity drives stood their best chance. Their success depended on strong shop branches and locals.

Finally, the internal strength of the unions at the factory level was of vital concern in any planning for possible clandestine operations of the CGT or the Communist Party. This may have been in Arrachard's mind when he spoke at a national committee meeting in November 1949 of making each shop unit a "citadel" of the union. "The class struggle unfolds in the enterprise," the CGT told its activists. "It is the shop which is the main scene of the battle."[28]

In their period of governmental coöperation, the Communist Party and the CGT, with the expectation of taking power by envelopment or seizure at the top, had stressed the importance of industrial concentration to the unions. In opposition now, they laid stress on their work at the base.

Centralized control of a trade union movement cannot be mechanical or complete where there is political democracy. In a few years communist control riddled the compartmentalization of the CGT, nullified the autonomy of locals and national unions, and turned representative control of elected officials into mere ratification.[29] It reduced opposition within the confederation to individual mutterings or apathy. Yet conflicts among different trades or occupations are not exorcised. Orders are not always carried out fully and promptly, sometimes not at all.

---

[25] H. Raynaud, "Les Problèmes d'organisation à la lumière de la critique et de l'autocritique," *Servir la France,* no. 54, December 1949, pp. 16-18.

[26] This matter is discussed in its industrial relations context in Chapter XI, *infra.*

[27] Cited in "Comment réaliser le front unique," *Cahiers du communisme,* vol. 29, No. 2, February 1952, p. 198.

[28] CGT, *Cours de militants,* no. II, "Qu'est-ce que la C. G. T.?" no date (1949?) p. 19.

[29] The mechanics of that control are further discussed in Chapter XV, *infra.*

Strike calls may bring partial or perfunctory response, especially if political aims are transparent. There remains a skepticism of leadership and of political party ties which Communists qualify as "the musty old smells of anarchosyndicalism and petty bourgeois individualism."[30]

There are none of the compulsive devices of closed shop, check off, or union hiring hall, nor the positive attractions of exclusive bargaining rights and contract administration to hold members in line. Participation by members in their locals and by local bodies in higher CGT organs has sagged. In 1950 the CGT expressed its disappointment with the results of an intensive national checkup of the department organizations. In the Oise, for example, the department federation convention met with a mere 63 of 200 local unions represented, and with only 10 candidates for an administrative commission of 30.[31] In the Vaucluse, half of the locals sent no delegates to the department convention; only 5 candidates offered themselves for the administrative commission.[32] The Eure-et-Loir department convention rallied delegates from a scant 30 out of 188 local unions and 3 out of 10 city centrals.[33]

Control may be so extensive as to defeat its own purposes. Before the 1951 convention, the CGT carried on a campaign for "union democracy." Said one official: "Discussion is the weak point of too many of our meetings. We have not known how to establish broad exchanges of opinions, to give the time necessary for them, and where necessary to oblige comrades to make known their point of view."[34] The CGT press carried article after scolding article on the manifestations of loss of workers' interest in their unions. It had to criticize the laxness of union officers and activists, the disappearance of small locals, the failure of locals to collect dues and transmit payments to department and national union treasuries, and the failure of the latter to pay their per capita to the confederation.[35] Naturally it laid the blame on officials' failings and mechanical causes, not on politicization of the movement or other fundamental reasons for workers' disaffection.

---

[30] Gaston Monmousseau, "Merci, Camarade Stalin," *Servir la France*, no. 54, December 1949, p. 4.

[31] Marcel Dufriche, "La Campagne pour l'appel de Stockholm comme moyen de revoir nos méthodes d'organisation," *Servir la France*, no. 59, June 1950, p. 17.

[32] *Le Populaire*, May 27, 1950.

[33] L. H. Revardeau, *Le Peuple*, June 21, 1950.

[34] A. Furst, *La Tribune des fonctionnaires*, quoted in *Le Peuple*, May 9, 1951.

[35] See report of Marcel Dufriche to the national committee, *Le Peuple*, April 12, 1950; articles on the Gironde department federation and the Creil city central, *Le Peuple*, May 10, 1950; Maurice, national general secretary of the leather workers union, *Le Peuple*, May 31, 1950; articles on the department federations of the Eure, the Ardèche, and the highly industrialized Nord, *Le Peuple*, especially issues immediately preceding May 1951 convention.

Not only the CGT unions felt the decline of workers' interest after 1948 and the sagging of administrative performance. In FO and CFTC it has been commonplace for years to speak of "the crisis of unionism." "Even within our organization," wrote an FO member in the provinces, "we still find this apathy which makes out of any movement a thing of little life and little value. The comrades do not want to take responsibilities and take only slight interest in the work of their officers."[36] At the first general meeting which marked the elevation of FO's branch at the great Renault plant in Boulogne-Billancourt to the status of a local, there were about 24 members present: one of their duties was to elect an executive committee—of 21.

The CFTC, in the long run more stable than the other workers' confederations, complained of "paper" locals, the fluctuation of membership, locals' utilization of funds without regard to the needs of per capita payments to higher echelons, inadequate administration at the departmental and national union levels, and habits of executive committees of shifting their own responsibilities to full-time officials.[37]

CGT LEADERSHIP AND RANK AND FILE

There are no one-man unions in France. There are unions run by small cliques; there are unions run essentially by a political party. But there is no important union identified as that of a single leader, controlling it through a personal machine. No one speaks of "Dupont's union" or "Durand's union." Nor do workers seem to get a vicarious satisfaction out of the display of power or wealth by their leaders. Government, whether of state or trade unions, still inspires distrust. Whatever their real power or way of living, union officials receive modest pay and need frequent mandates from their membership.

Statutory checks on the leadership are numerous. Officials must stand for reëlection at the appointed time, each year or two. In the executive boards at all echelons, the general secretary may be only the first among perhaps half a dozen secretaries almost equal in status. Major policies must be laid down by the representative bodies, conventions or national committees; their meetings are seldom long postponed.

Party domination, which has given the CGT unions a more solid bureaucracy and more capable administration than it has ever had, has taken most of the meaning out of the forms of membership control.

---

[36] Aristide Garcia, "FO face à la métallurgie de l'Allier," *Cahiers Fernand Pelloutier*, No. 25, June 1952, p. 13. For another illustration, see Richou, secretary of Gironde department federation, at FO 1950 convention, *Compte rendu*, pp. 71-75.

[37] CFTC, *25ᵉ Congrès . . . 1949, Etat des travaux de la commission confédérale des réformes de structure*, pp. 4-5.

That is not to say that the membership has no influence upon choice of leadership. Local CGT leaders are very often the most militant or most respected of their fellows. Dissatisfaction at the base can call forth a change in leadership. The Communist Party has little more use for the orthodox who fail than for the heterodox who succeed. But significant changes can be made only as party or higher CGT authority is willing. That authority can secure the election of the officials it chooses, or displace those in office with others it prefers to see elected.

The top Communist trade union leaders have been, by and large, far stronger individuals than those in the non-Communist unions. Frachon is outstanding in all the qualities of leadership required by the French trade union scene. Others, like Arrachard and Hénaff, head of the Paris region CGT, have shown Frachon's toughness and intelligence without his suppleness. Such men as Duguet of the miners, Tournemaine of the railroad workers, the late Croizat of the metal workers, Raca- mond[38] and Raynaud of the CGT executive board, have provided ex- perienced leadership of greater ability than that of most of their opposite numbers in the other confederations. Saillant, general secretary of the WFTU, for a time one of the CGT secretaries, one of the few important converts from reformist ranks, had an excellent record in the resistance, although perhaps his chief asset was opportunism and a nominal non- Communist political record. Lebrun, nominally non-Communist engineer member of the CGT executive board, is a man whose professional ability is recognized by his enemies. Men like these could have built a far more powerful movement if Soviet foreign policy imperatives had not made their task so difficult.

Party control has had an interesting two-fold consequence. In one way it has protected the leader; in another reduced his stature. It pro- tects the approved leader against the dangers of displacement, against organized caucuses or spontaneous rebellion. "The union movement includes only wage earners, so no divergence of interests exists within it," explains the CGT in a training leaflet. To this presumably self- evident truth it admits a seeming exception: there may be "different evaluations of common aspirations." These differences, however, are easily explained away: "the capitalists influence the thoughts of workers through their agents, their press, their radio."[39]

Party control, on the other hand, reduces the importance of the union leader by the threat of discipline or removal by an authority above that of his constituents. It subordinates his position to party and higher

---

[38] In 1953, Racamond, with a long trade union record (but, notably during the occupation, an uncertain party record), was dropped from the executive board in favor of Léon Mauvais, a top party representative, a "commissar" type.

[39] *Cours de militants*, no. 2, "Qu'est-ce que la C. G. T.?" no date (1949?) p. 11.

echelon CGT demands. The party has required criticism and self-criticism of union leaders hardly designed to increase their stature. At its 1950 convention the party flayed the sin of "economism," which Lenin early in the century had attacked in the Russian labor movement. Not only middle rank leaders, like those of the Paris subway and bus union, but so potent a figure as Marcel Paul, head of the national gas and electric workers' union and former Minister of Industrial Production, took blame for the "economism" which "blurs the necessity of the political struggle in the factories." [40]

A year later the heads of some of the most important unions were cut off or cut down to size. One was Arrachard, the aggressive general secretary of the building trades union, member of the CGT administrative commission, member of the Communist Party central committee, and for some years one of the foremost in expounding the party's trade union position. Confessing his personal failings in running his organization, he asked to be relieved of his post, to go back to work at his trade after twenty years in union office. [41] Within the space of a few weeks, new leadership was promoted in the food, railroad, metal, textile, communications, clothing, and gas and electric workers' unions, and in several important department federations.

Changes at lower levels have been numerous. The general secretary of the Indre-et-Loire federation was forced to admit that many of the CGT leaders in his department "do not have much weight with the union members and the workers themselves. This lack of confidence . . . is the result of nonrespect of trade union democracy in the designation of certain comrades to leadership posts." [42] The head of the department federation of the Jura was replaced by another comrade who showed "firmness in organization and a proper orientation." The former's too human reaction to his replacement astounded an official of the CGT's national commission on organization, who complained that the old general secretary was not "participating with enthusiasm in the collective effort," but instead "did not hesitate to say that his successor too would 'break his neck.' " [43]

[40] Auguste Lecoeur, *L'Humanité,* April 5, 1950. Further on "economism," see Chapter XV, *infra.*

[41] *Le Bâtisseur,* June 1951, report of meeting of national committee of the union, May 26, 1951. For the errors of the outgoing management, see also the speech of Le Querré, the new general secretary of the union, at the CGT convention, *Le Peuple,* June 7, 1951, p. 4. Cf. executive board report of CFTC national building trades union to 1952 convention.

[42] Jacques Chauveau, "Pour une liaison plus vivante de la direction de l'Union Départementale avec les syndiqués," *Le Peuple,* August 16, 1950.

[43] Gouzien, "Dans le Jura le redressement sera l'oeuvre de tous," *Le Peuple,* May 17, 1950.

Of such changes it is hard to say which may be due to the normal causes of official turnover and which to political requirements. Some of the changes may even be intended to show more non-Communists in the CGT leadership. Most are replacements of Communists by other Communists. Such a shakeup took place, for example, among mine union officials of the north a few months after the 1948 coal strike. Cynical observers suggested that some of those apparently purged were actually being relieved to go on "detached service" to be available for clandestine operations should repression or war drive the party and the CGT underground.

AUTHORITY IN THE FREE UNIONS: FO

Zirnheld, first president of the CFTC, pointed to the centralization of power in the German, Austrian, and Italian labor movements as one reason for their sudden disappearance when fascism decapitated their leadership. In contrast, he stressed the healthier basis of the autonomous local union as the cell of the CFTC organism.[44] In the CFTC and FO, traditional hostility to centralization and bureaucratization has not lost all its force. To be sure, Paris bureaucracies have been built up in the confederations and national unions. National officials may pronounce commitments which are beyond recall by the time the representative organs meet. But the bureaucracies are small in comparison with those of employer groups, weak in comparison with those of the CGT. They are modest too in comparison with the needs of representation and service. There is a striving for central controls; bureaucratization of the spirit has set in, but the flesh is starved for funds and staff.

In the free unions the inherited structure has persisted in fact as well as in form. The confederations have little weight with the national unions in specific bargaining goals or strike decisions. In many of the unions, moreover, these questions are decided at the regional or local, rather than the national level. Employers' rejection of industrywide bargaining has encouraged the continued decentralization of union functions.

In FO, weak leadership in many national union and confederation posts comes up against habits of autonomy and indiscipline below. Leadership is challenged both by the individualism of members and by minority caucuses. This is an old pattern, going back to the struggles within the unions among the adherents of various socialist parties and to the early controversies between reformists and revolutionaries. National character, some unionists like to say by way of explanation. Per-

---

[44] *Cinquante années de syndicalisme chrétien,* pp. 118-119.

haps, as a young FO leader from Montluçon remarked, "A Frenchman likes to take a minority position, even within his minority."[45]

Itself born of protest against ruthless majority domination, FO has seen the jealous assertion of minority rights and antibureaucratic feelings. "The unionists want the directors of the various organisms of the confederation to be not leaders but representatives; not guides but instructed delegates."[46] The debate over the new organization's statutes even brought up old syndicalist demands to limit the reëlection of officials and to give minority caucuses proportional representation on elected bodies. These demands were voted down.[47]

The lines of cleavage have been numerous and confusing, deriving more from attitudes and personalities than from specific issues. There have been conflicts over FO's relations with the government and with the Socialist Party; over FO's international policies and its identification with the anti-Soviet bloc. There have been conflicts over the receipt and distribution of outside financial aid. There have been constant debates over FO's lack of greater aggressiveness. The very failure of the organization to grow, which stirs recriminations, at the same time limits the opportunity for recognition and absorption of dissident spokesmen. There is no single or homogeneous opposition group; there have been no opposition candidacies for president or general secretary. Several minority groups, however, have at least loose organization and issue journals or bulletins.

A basic difference has come from the clash of reformist and revolutionary temperaments. Without entering into the detail of what Gérard Dehove has well called the "old guard" and the "new guard" of revolutionary syndicalism,[48] one should note that the "revolutionary" minorities do not dream of barricades or general strikes. But against the diversion of the CGT's tradition into Communist channels, they assert their own revolutionary mission. They cling to a view of the sufficiency of workers' economic action. In place of political lobbying or the con-

---

[45] "Etre minoritaire dans sa minorité." The English language has no single word for the common French concept "minoritaire."

[46] "Les Centrales ouvrières," *Revue de l'action populaire,* no. 37, February 1950, p. 103. The author of this unsigned article was then an official of a national union and member of the administrative commission of FO.

[47] The forms of constitutional change proposed by minorities depend not on theory but on the mechanics of the system under which they feel they suffer. An FO minority in 1950 proposed that the convention instead of the national committee elect the executive board. The CFTC minority, in 1947, likewise in the name of greater democracy, had proposed the reverse: that the national committee instead of the convention elect the executive board.

[48] In his excellent annual summary article, "Le Mouvement ouvrier et la législation sociale en 1952," for the *Revue d'économie politique,* 1953, which the author kindly permitted me to see in manuscript.

quest of political power, they affirm the old idea of "the conquest of the shop"; against "invading statism" and top-level arrangements, they stress "the workers' direct action."[49]

On the problem of relations with the other unions there are several points of view among the minority groups: that of joint action with all organizations, including the CGT; that of unity, up to and including organic unity, with all organizations except the CGT. One view not only refuses joint action with the CGT, but proposes that the government deprive the CGT of its legal recognition as a bona fide and "representative" labor organization. The various minorities of FO were able to defeat the divided and almost leaderless executive board at the 1952 convention by carrying a resolution against the confederation's participation in "productivity programs," on the ground that the leadership had obtained nothing worthwhile from employers or government in return for its participation. They forced the executive to end the acceptance of the disguised subsidies—allegedly from employer sources—to the provincial FO press.[50] Members of minority and majority prevented Léon Jouhaux from bringing before the organization his suggestion that FO join his "Fighting Democracy" organization, which they attacked as "neutralist" and a Communist front. The minorities continued, however, to have few members on the elected executive organs of the confederation.

THE CFTC: MAJORITY AND MINORITY

In the CFTC, majority and minority positions have been clearer, in terms of the composition of groups, industrially and regionally, and the issues involved. The majority leadership has been based on the white collar elements and several of the older industrial unions, textile

---

[49] U. Thevenon, secretary of the FO federation of the Loire department, "L'Union départementale de la Loire et l'orientation du mouvement syndicale libre," *Les Cahiers Fernand Pelloutier,* n. s. no. 1, October 1950, p. 4. See also "Proposition d'orientation de l'action économique et sociale de la C.G.T.F.O.," *Force ouvrière,* October 19, 1950, p. 5.

Some of the "old guard" of syndicalists in FO and outside who publish the monthly journal, *La Révolution prolétarienne,* have faced the anachronism of their position. With rare intellectual courage, they published contributions by both readers and writers —with all possible answers—on the question: "Is Our Title Absurd?" n. s., nos. 38, 39, 40, May, June, and July 1950.

[50] There was no indication that the subsidies were accompanied by any attempts to dictate policy. For attacks on subsidies to FO press through "BEDES," see, for example, Thorel and Walusinski at 1952 convention, *FO Informations, compte rendu . . . du 3ᵉ Congrès Confédéral,* pp. 69-70; 113-114; for formal assurances that the FO press would henceforth subsist only on union contributions, see Bothereau, *Ibid.,* p. 272. For a voluminous documentation on this question, see the forthcoming article by Gérard Dehove, cited in note 48.

workers, and miners, whose strength is largely in the north. The minority is composed of members of the newer unions in basic industry —the metal trades, chemicals, building trades, gas, and electric power— and intellectuals of the union of teachers in state schools and universities. A gap of generations divides the groups, with the minority led almost entirely by younger men, many with experience in the JOC and the resistance. The minority constitutes a left wing, which, except for a few erratic extremists, has been vigorously anti-Communist. Unlike the FO minorities, the CFTC minority has a number of executive posts in the confederation as well as control of national unions. It has been not only more coherent than the FO minorities, but more specific in its objectives, concentrating on one phase after another of its program—with varying degrees of success. It has been against any confessional quality to Catholic unionism, for industrial unionism, for neutrality toward the MRP, and for reforms of the CFTC structure. It has tried in vain to get the CFTC to abandon the International Confederation of Christian Trade Unions and affiliate with the broader anti-Communist International Confederation of Free Trade Unions. In its fight for ICFTU affiliation, it hoped to bring the CFTC and FO closer together inside France.

The minority has attacked "bureaucratization" within the CFTC. At the 1947 convention, it sponsored a resolution, defeated by a vote of only 2017 to 2610, which urged: "An effort at democratization appears indispensable to us to fight the peril which threatens every union movement in every country: bureaucratization. That is the control of the organization by a limited number of people who tend to constitute a closed circle, closed to the currents which stir opinion and rouse the base of the movement."[51]

In the face of continuing disagreements, the CFTC convention of 1948 instructed a special committee of 21 to consider the "uneasiness" within the confederation. Agreeing that it had "the duty of defining once and for all what should be the role of majority and minority in the union organization," the committee came to this unanimous conclusion:

Free discussions must permit all currents of opinion to explain their positions fully. Once the vote is taken, discipline applies to the entire membership. Nevertheless, those who hold a minority position, while fully respecting discipline, have the right to continue to fight by all regular and open means to explain their point of view and try to have adopted the solutions they consider best.[52]

---

[51] Syndicat général de l'education nationale, Commission de formation sociale, note no. 2, January 15, 1951, "Documents et remarques sur l'histoire du syndicalisme français d'inspiration chrétienne," p. 12.

[52] *Syndicalisme,* May 20, 1948.

Differences over relations with other unions and with the church suddenly boiled over in 1952—in part perhaps because of the temporary absence from the country of the minority's most experienced leader. The executive board majority voted a resolution criticizing the minority for "too close contact with groups animated by a different spirit," in this case FO unions and the International Metal Workers Federation with which the FO metal workers are affiliated. The minority members resigned from the executive board and moved to formalize an organization hitherto existing loosely around the *Reconstruction* bulletin. The convention of the CFTC half a year later saw the quarrel patched up by conciliation on both sides, aided by a center group. Changes in statutes satisfied the left wing by closer control of the executive board through the newly created national council, on which the left had sizable representation.

The possible participation of CFTC left wing unions along with FO unions in leadership training and organizing activities financed by the ICFTU, the International Metal Workers Federation, and the CIO, had precipitated the clash which for a moment threatened to disrupt the Catholic confederation. "The CFTC," said its general secretary, "asks rich foreign unionists not to meddle in our internal affairs."[53] For, as in FO, although much less acutely, the organization's internal relationships were complicated by its financial weakness.

THE DUES PROBLEM

The French syndicalists used to argue that the German unions had lost the will to fight because of the financial hostages they had given to capitalist fortune. In the light of later German history, these strictures may have been well taken. But low dues and all they connote have not strengthened the French unions' ability to fight or to serve the membership. They have been a source of confusion and self-questioning to French unionists.

Except for a few types of employment, notably the printers and some of the government workers, the unions have always charged low dues and collected them irregularly. The unions' normal difficulties have been increased by inflation. *Force Ouvrière* made these comparisons to show the decline in the purchasing power of the average member's monthly dues:

1935—dues at 6 francs a month bought 3.5 kilograms of bread;
1938—dues at 8 francs a month bought 2.6 kilograms of bread;
1950—dues at 50 francs a month bought 1.25 kilograms of bread.[54]

---

[53] Maurice Bouladoux, "La C.F.T.C., organisation majeure, détermine son action en toute indépendance," *Syndicalisme,* November 1952, p. 1.
[54] *Force ouvrière,* October 26, 1950.

In 1951 one CFTC union report showed that in the past year and a half, while its members had rejected the leaders' proposal to raise dues, union expenses had gone up in these proportions: union journal, 42 per cent; staff wages, 36 per cent; rent, 41 per cent; office expenses, 25 per cent; representation and other expenses by officials, 92 per cent.[55] (The 92 per cent increase in representation expenses was due in part to increased activity on joint commissions in the schools.)

All wings of the movement recognize the need for higher levels of dues and more systematic collection. The goal has been generally set since the war as an hour's wage per month. This is extremely low as compared with dues in most other countries.[56] It is all the lower since workers think of an hour's wages in terms of base pay rates, which do not include family allowances. Even this modest goal is far from fully realized in the dues scales of all unions.

Of the dues collected, about one fourth goes to the national union, almost as much to the department federation, and a very small percentage to the confederation. About half remains with the locals. (The city central usually gets no regular share of the dues.) In mid-1950, the metal workers, in many ways the élite of the CGT, charged each member about 60 francs (then about 16 cents) a month, less than an hour's wage. Of this amount they paid 12 or 13 francs to the department federations, 15 francs to the national union, and to the confederation 1.5 francs per month plus 25 francs a year for the dues card. The CGT printers' locals paid 50 francs a month to their national union, the merchant marine officers 70 francs; but the locals of the clerical workers union paid only 12 francs per capita, the dock workers 11 francs.[57] The building trades' union adopted a sliding scale for locals' per capita to the national union, which it set at a monthly figure of 30 per cent of the hourly minimum wage.

In the Paris area, in late 1951, CFTC dues, graduated according to individuals' rates of pay, were from 100 to 230 francs per month for metal workers; 100 to 150 francs for building trades workers. In the poorly paid clothing industry, they ranged from 70 francs to 150 francs.[58] The minimum wage in the Paris area then was 100 francs an hour.

[55] CFTC union of teachers in state institutions, *Ecole et éducation,* n. s., no. 83, February 23, 1951.

[56] See, for example, the figures on levels of dues and distribution of dues income in various foreign countries presented by Pierre Neumeyer, treasurer, to the 1950 FO convention, *IIᵉ Congrès confédéral, rapports confédéraux,* pp. 70-72, and a table of the same related to purchasing power of wages, *Force ouvrière,* June 14, 1951, p. 8.

[57] CGT, *Bulletin confédéral,* March 25, 1950, p. 11. The value of the franc at the official rate of exchange was then 0.28 cents.

[58] CFTC, Union Régional Parisienne, *Paris syndical et social,* December 1951, pp. 13-15.

All the figures set forth above represent theoretical levels, dues assessed but not necessarily paid. For the collection of dues is even more of a problem than the level of dues scales. Dues are paid to collectors of the local union or branch. Any system of dues checkoff is barred by the union pluralism which prevails at the plant as at the national level. Union philosophy would hardly permit a checkoff, nor would employers accept it.[59]

Initiation fees are nominal, equivalent to dues for a month or two. The member buys a card annually, for the price of less than half a month's dues. He is then supposed to buy dues stamps every month, which are pasted on his card. In most unions, however, he will be considered in good standing if he buys his annual card and half a dozen or fewer dues stamps a year. So relatively well-paid and proud a group as the Paris region council of the CGT metal workers, in determining the basis of representation for its constituent locals, calculated the number of individual members as one for each eight monthly dues stamps sold per year. Actually many unions, notably in the CGT, give away many cards and dues stamps. "At the beginning of the year," pointed out Racamond, CGT secretary, "one is in the euphoria of the purchase of the annual dues card and the payment of the first monthly dues. Then, about November, one perceives that a large number of members have not paid their dues for the past six months. Debts to the department federation and the national union are mounting. Those bodies cannot pay their per capita to the CGT."[60] Some CGT locals were so poor that the confederation permitted them to pay the 1951 convention fee, the trifling sum of 500 francs, in installments.[61]

A fragmented and retreating union movement is in a poor position to remedy the evils of "cut-rate unionism." There are no measures of compulsion which can solve the problems of dues income. Dropping a member for nonpayment subjects him, in most trades, to no practical disadvantages.

The possibilities of more adequate dues despite low wage scales are occasionally discussed by the unions in terms of workers' other expenditures. One union remarked that its dues, even after a recent increase, amounted only to the cost of one cigarette per day. The CFTC miners

---

[59] The only checkoff reported as of 1952 was that permitted, by individual authorization, in the agreement of the artists in film postsynchronization. Even this, a Ministry of Labor authority hinted, might violate freedom of association. Renée Petit, "Le Contenu des conventions collectives du travail," *Droit social,* vol. 15, no. 7, July-August 1952, p. 458.

[60] Julien Racamond, "Recruter de nouveaux syndiqués et les conserver par une bonne gestion financière," *Le Peuple,* November 8, 1950.

[61] Marcel Dufriche, *Le Peuple,* April 25, 1951, p. 3. Five hundred francs was less than $1.50.

union, after voting a drastic dues increase, risked further unpopularity by publishing a picture of two men lifting their customary glasses of conviviality, with the caption : "Two rounds will pay a month's dues."[62]

Low dues income, lack of tangible union services, dependence on government action, create a spiral of ineffectiveness and frustration from which the free unions are slowly trying to release themselves. They have been undergoing a "crisis of conscience" in the matter of dues. "The low level of dues payments is one of the elements responsible for the instability of our membership. One holds on only to that for which one pays something," said the CFTC.[63] It has voted considerable dues increases in the last few years, going well beyond price rises, and recommended sliding dues scales geared to members' wages. It has centralized the machinery of its dues accounting and distribution (but not the authority for setting dues levels) in confederation headquarters.[64] The confederation has also voted a modest monthly assessment for a central strike and organizing fund ; some of the national unions have earmarked some of their receipts for strike funds.

In Force Ouvrière, the examination of conscience has been linked to the need for independence from foreign union contributions and—in a different realm of discourse—from various forms of disguised subsidies. FO could hardly have launched its new organization against the entrenched CGT, backed by the Communist Party, on dues income alone.[65] But almost three years after its founding, its treasurer Pierre Neumeyer, one of the most respected men in French labor, reminded the national convention: "The hour has come for all our organizations to live only by means of their dues. And we must work to overcome this all too familiar tendency among Frenchmen to hate to pay dues as well as taxes."[66] On this need a minority leader was equally insistent: "Until this day the French trade union movement has never been able to introduce into the *mores* a policy of high dues, perhaps for the same reasons for which it has not succeeded in introducing a policy of high

---

[62] *L'Echo des mines,* January 16, 1952, p. 1.

[63] CFTC, Institut confédéral d'études et de formation syndicales, *Formation,* vol. 5, no. 32, February 1951, item 8, no pagination.

[64] For detailed discussion of confederation bookkeeping and distribution of dues income, see Jean Allidières, assistant general secretary of the CFTC, "L'Organisation Financière du mouvement," *Formation,* vol. 5, no. 34, April 1951, item 6.

[65] Early in 1948 FO received 40,000,000 francs (about $114,000) from the government out of funds built up by dues collected from workers under the Vichy Labor Charter. Although this grant was the subject of repeated outcry by the CGT, both the CGT and the CFTC had received money from the same funds. See FO, *Congrès constitutif, 1948, compte rendu,* pp. 16-17, 126-127.

[66] CGT-FO, *II° Congrès confédéral, 1950, rapports confédéraux,* p. 70.

levels of consumption and a high standard of living in the working class." [67]

The revolutionary syndicalist Monatte used to recall the story of Judas objecting to the wasteful expense of oil to bathe the feet of Jesus, drawing from it the moral that the administrator had killed the apostle in him.[68] Apostolate and bureaucracy seldom go together. Yet the free unions need more of both. They sometimes show excessive bureaucratization without the advantages of smooth-running administration. But some workers continue to suspect all organization as dangerous—particularly if it involves discipline or dues. In the refusal to face the necessities of adequate funds, staff, central services, and of delegation of authority to officials, there is a refusal to accept the necessities of operation in an age of industrial organization and the welfare state.

The refusal of class conscious workers to pay dues to maintain the institutions of group defense is one form of that lack of civic discipline ("incivisme") which so many thoughtful Frenchmen lament.[69] André Gide's famous observation is relevant to union behavior: "Everything proves to me, alas, that of all the peoples I know the French are the ones who most lack that civic sense and that solidarity without which a republic turns out worst for everyone." [70]

---

[67] Richou, *Ibid.*, p. 70.

[68] Dolléans, *Histoire du mouvement ouvrier,* vol. 2, p. 317.

[69] Thus François Goguel, *La Politique des parties sous la troisième république,* p. 551.

[70] *Journal* (Edition de la Pléiade, Paris, 1939), p. 668.

CHAPTER X

THE RELATIVE STRENGTH OF THE CONFEDERATIONS

The French wage earner is not very union-minded. He does not realize that the union does not have a force of itself, but only the force which its members give it: the force of numbers, of service, of possibilities.

—Metal workers' national union, CFTC, Executive Board report, September 1950.

The division in the trade union movement . . . would be a minor evil if it were not aggravated by the unimaginable indifference of a large number of wage earners toward trade union organization and action.

—Transport workers' national union, FO, Executive Board report, November 1950.

I have often asked my fellow-workers: "Why do you vote for the CGT?" Their answers come down to this: "But I've always voted for the CGT. You don't suppose I am going to change now." . . . To choose another party (than the Communist Party), another union, is practically to isolate oneself.

—*Esprit*, July-August 1951.

For a few years after liberation, it looked as if workers were breaking with the habits of rapidly inflated and deflated "balloon unionism" and developing the habits of passive mass membership, in which dues would be paid as a matter of course, few would attend meetings when things went well, but most would continue after waves of enthusiasm died down. The participation of the unions in the organs of public administration, their attitude toward production, the pressures on workers to show a union card (CGT or at least CFTC), all seemed to be turning union membership into a "formality made obligatory," as one reformist complained; "a man joins a union now more or less as he pays his social insurance tax." Beginning in 1947, however, events were once again to contradict those who predicted, as had good observers in the late 1920's, that the CGT was moving toward the unionism typical of most western European nations.

MEMBERSHIP FIGURES AND CONCEPTS

Interunion competition and union weakness in relation to employers make it unreasonable to expect reliable statistics. A minor matter, except that it is symptomatic, is the quality of bookkeeping. While excellent at the confederation level, it drops as one goes down to lower levels, and in many of the local unions (where dues are collected) it is feeble. More fundamental, the whole concept of membership is so blurred that, even were they interested in accuracy, the unions could hardly furnish accurate membership figures. The uncertainty of membership concepts shows in dues-paying habits and in union toleration of irregular payment and nonpayment. Few unions can speak quantitatively of "dues-paying members," nor is the phrase current. The system of collective bargaining makes it impossible for any union to speak of "numbers covered by contract."

Informed guesses of membership vary over a range of a million and more for the CGT alone. The unions' inflated claims need not detain us; the unions themselves do not take them seriously. At the other end of the scale, in early 1953 Michel Collinet suggested the following estimates: CGT, 1,500,000 members; CFTC, 600,000; FO 500,000; CGC, splinter confederations, and autonomous unions, 300,000: the total was "certainly below 3,000,000."[1] The head of the CFTC building trades workers estimated in the union's internal bulletin that the total of unionists was no more than 2,000,000.[2] (The number of wage earners is almost 12,000,000, of whom about 6,000,000 are in industry, mining, and transport.) Whatever the approximate numbers, the essential facts were that union membership had declined vastly since the 1946 peak, that the CGT had lost more than half of its members, that most of those who had left it had not gone into other unions, but had simply dropped out of the union movement. The great majority of the workers in private industry, remaining aloof from any organization, constituted what French unionists ruefully termed "the biggest union of all, the union of the unorganized."

---

[1] *Lettre aux militants*, 2d series, no. 10, March 1953, p. 2. Collinet, a reputable scholar, is militantly anti-Communist, it may be noted. For an earlier attempt to deduce "real" membership figures from published financial reports, and a sharp criticism of union claims, see "Quels sont les effectifs réels des syndicats ouvriers," *L'Economie*, September 2, 1949.

[2] Albert Detraz, "Elites syndicales et mentalité ouvrière," *Bulletin: Vie fédérale*, December 10, 1952, pp. 1-4.

Given the lack of membership figures and the irregular and tenuous dues allegiance of many classed as members, it is possible by several other tests to evaluate workers' support for the various unions. One test is strike behavior, in which the unorganized are to a certain extent represented by the organized. For some years the CGT, although stronger than all its rivals together, has not commanded enough support to wage important strikes on its own. It requires the participation of the CFTC or FO or both. Otherwise it fails to sway enough of the "gray mass of the unorganized" who, in many industries, hold the power of decision.

SOCIAL SECURITY AND SHOP ELECTIONS

There is a series of concentric rings of union influence, broadening out from steady membership and dues payment, to occasional dues payment by those nevertheless considered members, and finally to the purely electoral support manifested in the recurrent social security and shop elections. These elections provide tests of union influence almost as valid, in the French setting, as membership figures. They arise out of forms of employee representation in which all employees, unorganized as well as organized, must choose largely among union slates. There are no compilations of the plant-by-plant figures on the annual elections of shop stewards (compulsory in establishments of over ten employees) or of those of plant committeemen (compulsory in establishments of 50 or more employees). The figures for key plants and key industries, however, have shown the CGT almost everywhere holding its ground or losing slightly, after a stabilization at a lower level following the FO schism. It has generally obtained between 50 and 75 per cent of the votes of the production workers, considerably less among the clerical workers, and very much less among the cadres.

The closest approximation to an over-all view is provided by the triennial elections of the worker representatives on the boards of administration for the general social security system.[3] Table 2 shows the results of these elections in 1947 and 1950.

The social security elections, like French political elections, show a multiplicity of parties competing on platforms which combine special interest appeals with ideological overtones. In keeping with its general line, the CGT has been the least inhibited in appeals to pocketbook or class feeling. In the 1950 elections it called for larger benefits, abolition of the partial medical fees charged to the insured, and an end to employer representation on the boards. Not unlike national political elections, the

---

[3] There are also elections to the family allowance system boards, but, as only beneficiaries vote, the number of ballots cast is smaller and less representative.

votes expressed preferences among competing organizations based on a complex of reasons rather than among specific platforms or individual candidates. In its 1952 report on the social security system, the Cour de Comptes (High Court of Accounts) said of the elections: "Political or trade union considerations are most often determining. The great majority of the candidates and voters seem to forget the precise purpose of the election in which they are taking part. It is true that those covered by any given fund, paying contributions that do not vary from one fund to another, and receiving their benefits whether management is good or bad, can hardly judge the performance of their representatives on the fund's board of directors."[4]

TABLE 2

SOCIAL SECURITY ELECTION RESULTS, JUNE 1950 AND APRIL 1947

Slate	Number of votes[a]		Percentage of total vote		Percentage of major union vote	
	1950	1947	1950	1947	1950	1947
CGT	2,392,000	3,280,000	43.5	59.3	54.4	69.2
CFTC	1,173,000	1,458,000	21.3	26.3	26.6	30.8
FO	833,000		15.2		19.0	
Mutual insurance societies	610,000	508,000	11.1	9.2		
Family associations	290,000	288,000	5.3	5.2		
Miscellaneous[b]	206,000		3.6			
Total	5,504,000	5,534,000	100.0	100.0	100.0	100.0

Sources: Based on *Le Monde*, June 16, 1950; *L'Année Politique, 1950*, ed. by André Siegfried and others (Paris: 1951), p. 287; *Reconstruction*, June-July 1950 and August-September 1950.
  [a]Rounded off to nearest thousand.
  [b]Includes CGSI and other minor union slates in 1950.

Campaigning conditions reflect the general conditions of interunion competition. The CGT's wider organization and greater resources have enabled it to do more electioneering than its rivals. In the elections on a shop basis it can put up more slates. The social security elections, however, are on a geographical basis; in 1950 all three workers' confederations put up slates in all districts. The CFTC and FO campaigns were less extensive than those of the CGT. The CFTC undoubtedly benefited from a certain amount of ecclesiastical support. FO was least well equipped for the contest; some of its potential support, moreover, went to the mutual insurance societies, a number of which ran FO activists as their candidates.

  [4] Cour de comptes, "La Sécurité sociale, 1950-1951. Rapport au Président de la République," *Journal officiel, annexe administrative*, March 18, 1952, p. 231.

Despite the declining prestige of unionism and attacks on the unions by the family associations[5] and mutual insurance societies, the three major union lists obtained four-fifths of all the votes cast in the 1950 general social security election. In 1947 CFTC slates benefited from dissatisfaction with the CGT, which had no other outlet. In the whole of France there were only a few dissident lists put up by FO groups; the elections preceded the split by half a year. Upon its 1950 showing, the CFTC based its claim to be regarded as the second most important of the national centers and first of the non-Communist centers.

Among those not covered by the general social security system are the railroad, maritime, and mine workers, among whom the CGT's margin of superiority is even greater than in the general system. Results of elections during 1949-1952 from a few other fields are given in Tables 3, 4, 5, and 6: those for administrators of the miners' social

TABLE 3

VOTES RECEIVED BY UNION SLATES IN ELECTION OF
MINE SOCIAL INSURANCE FUND ADMINISTRATORS, 1951

Slates	Number of votes[a]	Percentage of votes cast
CGT	166,000	60.6
FO	59,000	21.4
CFTC	45,000	16.5
Autonomous	4,000	1.5
Total	274,000	100.0

Source: Based on *Le Monde*, July 8, 1951.
[a]Rounded off to nearest thousand.

TABLE 4

NUMBERS OF MINERS' DELEGATES ELECTED BY UNIONS, 1949 AND 1952[a]

Slates	Underground workers 1949	1952	Surface workers 1949	1952
CGT	148	127	66	57
FO	31	33	29	24
CFTC	13	18	18	16
Total	192	178	113	97

Source: *Le Monde*, April 20–21, April 22, 1952.
[a]The total number of delegates was reduced between 1949 and 1952 by the closing of some pits.

[5] These associations are welfare and propaganda organizations concerned with the interests of families, especially large families.

TABLE 5

VOTES RECEIVED BY UNION SLATES IN RAILROAD STEWARD ELECTIONS, 1949 AND 1951

Slates	1949		1951	
	Number of votes[a]	Percentage of votes cast	Number of votes[a]	Percentage of votes cast
CGT	240,000	63.3	221,000	63.1
CFTC	67,000	17.6	69,000	19.7
FO	56,000	14.9	41,000	11.7
Autonomous Cadres Union	14,000	3.7	14,000	4.0
Others	2,000	0.5	5,000	1.4
Total	379,000	100.0	350,000	99.9

Source: Based on *Le Monde*, April 20, 1951.
[a]Rounded off to nearest thousand.

insurance funds; miners' delegates; railroad stewards; shop stewards and plant committeemen at the Renault plant.

The support indicated by an occasional ballot is, to be sure, more conditional and less costly than union membership or willingness to follow a strike call. The vote is secret, the action anonymous. It costs nothing in personal risk or financial sacrifice. With this major reservation as to the intensity of support manifested, the social security and shop elections are the best periodic assessments of the various unions' relative influence.

TABLE 6

VOTES RECEIVED BY UNION SLATES IN SHOP ELECTIONS,
RENAULT PLANT (BOULOGNE-BILLANCOURT), 1950 AND 1952

	A. Shop Steward Elections, 1950			
	Production and lower-grade clerical workers		Cadres, technicians, and supervisory employees	
Slate	Number of votes	Percentage of votes cast	Number of votes	Percentage of votes cast
CGT	18,498	74.6	1,437	33.0
CFTC	2,127	8.6	932	21.4
FO	1,425	5.7	414	9.5
CGSI	2,270	9.1	—	—
Unaffiliated (Renault Democratic Union)	492	2.0	—	—
CGC	—	—	1,576	36.1
Total	24,812	100.0	4,359	100.0

Source: Based on *L'Humanité*, June 21, 1950; *Le Monde*, June 12, June 19, 1952.

TABLE 6 (*Continued*)

Slate	B. Plant Committee Elections, 1952			
	Production and lower-grade clerical workers		Cadres, technicians, and supervisory employees	
	Number of votes	Percentage of votes cast	Number of votes	Percentage of votes cast
CGT	17,074	63.0	1,022	22.6
CFTC	4,168	15.3	1,350	29.8
FO-CGSI joint slate	5,871	21.7	—	—
FO-CGC joint slate	—	—	2,158	47.6
Total	27,113	100.0	4,530	100.0

Source: *Le Monde*, June 12, June 19, 1952

THE APPEAL OF THE CGT

The political inspiration and tone of so much of the CGT's activity does not mean that all or even most of its rank and file are Communists. For most, membership in a CGT union does not represent a conscious option for the party line of the confederation, still less any wish to turn France into a satellite of the "workers' fatherland." Reasons for joining a CGT union or remaining in it after the schism may be those of union militancy, the personal prestige of local CGT leaders, obligation to the union, the comparative ubiquity of its organization, or sentimental attachment to "the old CGT." As in any split, there were at the FO split not two but three groups: those who chose to leave, those who chose to remain, and those who remained not out of deliberate choice but out of habit, or inertia, or fear of reprisal.

Class conformity is strong; it is reinforced by the weight of organization. The CGT and the Communist Party are almost everywhere; the other parties and unions are not. "To choose another party, another union, is practically to isolate oneself," remarked a miner, himself an anti-Communist.[6] In the CGT's claim that it includes more Catholics than the CFTC and more Socialists than FO,[7] there is enough truth to pain the leaders of those organizations.

For a Communist worker, membership in another union, if there is a CGT union accessible, would call for special party dispensation. The Socialist Party has not seriously attempted to forbid its members to

---

[6] "Conscience prolétarienne," *Esprit*, vol. 19, No. 7-8, July-August 1951, p. 155.

[7] Frachon at the 1951 CGT convention, *Le Peuple*, May 28, 1951. It is of course difficult to say who is really a Catholic, given the occasional and nominal conformity of many people in France.

join the CGT nor required them to join FO. The party "expressly asks that socialist activists still in CGT ranks quit that organization," declared the party's convention in 1952.[8] But no sanctions were proposed, even for those party activists or officeholders who were still in the CGT. The MRP, with much looser discipline, could not maintain any positive or negative requirements of union affiliation. For either the MRP or the Socialist Party to enforce such formal requirements would be out of character.

More to the point for Catholics than the attitude of the MRP is that of the church. The hierarchy has not forbidden membership in the CGT, although it has stated its preference for the CFTC unions:

The Assembly of cardinals and archbishops warmly exhorts Catholics to organize themselves more and more in the Christian unions. The teachings of the Sovereign Pontiffs have made that a duty for them, and those teachings have lost none of their authority at the present hour. For its part, the Assembly of cardinals and archbishops assures the CFTC of all its confidence. It is convinced that the Christian unions have not ceased to constitute for Catholics the normal means of assuring a just defense of their interests and their rights as workers, while at the same time infusing all occupational activity with the social morality of Christianity.

More liberal than the church in some lands where separate Catholic unions are organized, the French church has not excluded membership in other unions. The assembly of cardinals and archbishops merely declared:

If Catholics are sometimes constrained by circumstances to join other union organizations, we recall to them that it is a right for them, as well as a duty, to abandon nothing of the exigencies of their faith and to preserve themselves from irreligious influences.[9]

Some members of the hierarchy and of the local priesthood have been even more tolerant of membership in the CGT. "The Church respects the personal liberty of the worker in his choice of union, and leaves that responsibility to him," said the Bishop of Fréjus. "The Church does not forbid Christians to join FO or the CGT. But it has the right to say to them, 'Open your eyes and be careful never to fall into a spirit of party contrary to Christian principles.' "[10] Thus the church has distinguished between the CGT and the Communist Party.

Workers may see another manifestation, albeit confusing, of the

[8] *Le Populaire,* May 27, 1952.
[9] Declaration of the Assembly of Cardinals and Archbishops, March 4, 1948, cited in *Revue de l'action populaire,* no. 37, February 1950, p. 86.
[10] Msgr. Gaudel, in the *Semaine religieuse* of the diocese of Fréjus and Toulon, cited by *Le Monde,* April 15, 1952.

attitude of the church in the experiment, launched in the last decade, of worker-priests. These are members of the regular or secular clergy who doff their robes for work clothes and factory employment, usually take heavy unskilled jobs, and share the everyday life of workers as testimony to the church's concern with proletarian life.[11] They have been referred to as "the commandos of the church," although results from the daring experiment are not expected to be realized (if at all) before generations: they represent a "fifty-year gamble." Most are in the Paris region, although they are to be found in other areas.

Sharing workers' lives, and encouraging workers to take greater responsibility in society, the worker-priests have joined unions. Presumably on the theory that they should go "where the workers are," they have generally joined the CGT, not CFTC or FO. A number have taken office in CGT unions, been elected to plant committees on CGT slates, and even echoed CGT polemics against rival unions. This may be regarded as giving a certain ecclesiastical sanction to Catholic membership in CGT unions. CFTC unionists express the gravest doubts about this experiment, which they fear results in Communism penetrating Catholic circles more than Christianity penetrating Communist circles. The left-wing members of the CFTC are the most openly hostile. They compare the priests' arguments for going into the CGT to the arguments for participation in the Vichy government because it was the government of that period. "The Paris industrial suburbs are not the whole world. Because of the Communist preponderance in certain milieux where the worker-priests labor, they do not have the right to jump to the identification of Communism with the labor movement."[12]

A large percentage of the non-Communists in the CGT are trade unionists who have a sentimental attachment to "unity," which they translate as affiliation with the movement which groups the largest number of workers, or—to the same effect—as fidelity to the "old CGT." The attitude of many rank and file members may be illustrated by the decision of one of the most respected "pure syndicalist" leaders, Julien Forgues of Toulouse, not to leave the CGT at the FO split. (He had not left the CGT in two previous splits, nor had he left it under the occupation.) To people like Forgues—or rather of views like his, since there are few who possess his qualities—the CGT is unionism, the union, a religion to some who have no other religion. It is proof of the conservatism with which French workers cling to radical allegiances that

[11] For origins of the movement, see Abbé Henri Godin and Y. Daniel, *La France, pays de mission?* (Lyon, 1943). For a very sympathetic treatment of the worker-priest, including his relations with the Communists, see the moving novel of Gilbert Cesbron, *Les Saints vont en enfer* (Paris, 1952).

[12] "A propos de trois manifestes," *Reconstruction,* August-September 1950, p. A-4.

so many, even those who pay no union dues, should look upon the CGT as synonymous with unionism. Distrust of all political parties leads, curiously enough, to an underestimation of the importance of union control by the Communist Party. Since every party is out for its own interest, and since every party tries to influence the unions, one is no worse than the others. This is the fallacy to which the anarchist distaste for all political party action leads, the failure to make the vital distinctions among party aims and methods.[13] Paradoxically, too, the old anti-authoritarian feeling keeps some people inside unions they disagree with. Accustomed to being in disaccord with authority, they do not find it strange to remain in the CGT. The remark of a mechanic in Mulhouse illuminates this feeling. A Socialist and outspokenly anti-Communist, he said: "I stay in the CGT just to make things harder for them." Except in crises, this attitude has no way of making itself felt in union decisions. A few anti-Communists are in the CGT out of political policy, for example the sprinkling of Trotskyites strangely insisting on what they call "unity."[14]

The greatest center of CGT influence, as of the Communist Party, is found in the working class districts of Paris, and still more important, in the so-called "red belt" around Paris: the suburbs of working class tenements, of the automobile, machinery, gas, electric, chemical, and other industries. Another concentration is in the coal, metallurgical and textile areas of the north. A third is in the Eastern Mediterranean coast, with the ports of Marseille and Toulon, shipbuilding and navy yards, miscellaneous manufacturing, and the tourist industry of the Riviera. There are many smaller areas where CGT and Communist strength also go hand in hand; the coast of Brittany with its fishing, canneries, and arsenals, the Grenoble district with its light manufacturing industries, and islands of power here and there in most regions.

The CGT appeals to more of the production workers than does FO or the CFTC.[15] Its following, however, also includes a significant proportion of white collar workers. In every basic industry, with the exception perhaps of textiles, the CGT is not only the strongest union, but

---

[13] Cf. Georges Duveau, speaking of Proudhon's "caressing" of Napoleon III: "That is the danger of any fundamentally anarchist position. When one is disgusted by any and all government, whatever it is, one finishes by losing sight of certain elementary political realities." Introduction to Proudhon, *Les Contradictions politiques* (Paris, 1952), pp. 12-13.

[14] Deep are the mysteries of left-wing sectarianism. The French Trotskyites, divided into two splinters of a splinter party, have urged Socialist-Communist unity.

[15] The 1948 CGT convention reported the following breakdown of its 1,147 delegates: production workers, 731; white collar workers, 184; government administrative employees, 124; technicians, 83; engineers and cadres, 25. *Compte rendu, 1948*, p. 276. No comparable figures are available for FO or CFTC; the percentage of production workers would be far lower.

stronger than both the CFTC and FO together. The metal-working industries continue, as always, to supply a number of the élite of the CGT and of the Communist Party. In those industries, in the mines and on the railways, among the gas and electric power workers, the CGT (and Communist Party) following includes some of the best paid workers in France.

Miners' class consciousness is a familiar phenomenon. The Vichyism of some of their reformist leaders helped the Communists in the CGT take over the miners' union and coöperative organizations at liberation. Railwaymen are a particularistic group everywhere. Their concern with security and their better-than-average retirement conditions should hardly incline them to extremism. As with the miners, however, these conditions are associated with Communist union and party action after liberation. Nor does the CGT, the majority organization and one of those recognized by the government, necessarily spell extremism to them. Physically dispersed throughout the country, the railwaymen are sensitive to the farflung organization of the CGT and the Communist Party. The divisions among the non-Communist unions make the alternatives to the CGT none too attractive.

Large numbers of civil servants are CGT members. As in the nationalized industries, the comparatively sheltered conditions of employment make it safe to belong to the CGT, even to belong to the Communist Party. The government has purged Communists from some of the most sensitive jobs. It has been regarded as unthinkable so far, even if it were possible, to purge from ordinary clerical, administrative, or teaching jobs the rank-and-file members of a party polling one out of every four votes cast in national elections.

The CGT has made special national appeals, with language programs and language sections, to immigrant workers. It has more strength than the other centers among the Polish miners and steel workers of the north and east, among Italian mill hands, among Algerians and other North Africans in metropolitan France. These workers are somewhat cut off from the French communities around them by social, economic, or legal discrimination. The worst off are the North Africans, although most of them (the Algerians) are French citizens. Leaving their families in North Africa, these men do some of the least desirable and worst-paid work, live in the most wretched housing, and even in normal times face police crackdowns and social prejudice.

THE FORCE OUVRIÈRE CONSTITUENCY

Despite its apolitical platform, FO makes its greatest appeal to those who are socialist in party attachment or in temperament and to pure trade unionists. Some of its members might be called unaffiliated left socialists in outlook, who dropped out of the Socialist Party for reasons which are in large part the reasons for the party's decline in membership and influence since the war. They have not gone into the Communist Party's satellite, the tiny Socialist Unity Party.

FO's largest bloc of constituents is among the civil servants, where the Socialist Party is also strongest. Although it has significant minorities among the railroad, communications, textile, dock, and metal trades workers, its industrial following is nowhere dominant. It is most important in a few areas of traditional socialist strength, in the north, (where it is, however, far weaker than the Socialist Party), Limoges, and the Toulouse region.

In the greatest industrial center, the Paris region, FO is lacking in both numbers and discipline. It suffers from the same weakness which has characterized the Paris Socialist Party organization, which has repeatedly foundered on the reefs of irresponsible leftism, perhaps dazzled by the strong light of Communism in the area. Even in the clerical workers' union, whose national organization was a leading founder of FO, the bulk of the Paris region organization remained with the CGT. In the 1950 social security elections, FO obtained only 101,000 votes in the Paris region, as against the CFTC's 230,000 and the CGT's 688,000.

The old weakness of reformist unionism in the interwar years, its limitation to a largely white collar and civil servant constituency, has deepened since the war. There is no denying the large contribution to the history of French unionism made by the civil servants and white collar unions, far greater than in that of many other nations' labor movements. Nevertheless, its weakness among production workers makes the role of FO a secondary and often only a peripheral one in economic life, as it makes the Socialist Party role secondary in political life.

THE CFTC FOLLOWING

The CFTC remains strongest among the traditionally Catholic populations of Alsace, with its metal-working and textile industries; the north, with its cotton and wool textiles; parts of Brittany and Savoy; and the industrial concentrations of the southeast—Lyon, with its silk industry, Grenoble, and St. Etienne, the old "Pittsburgh of France." In Paris and in other cities, its chief support is among banking, insurance, department store, and other white collar employees in commerce and industry. Thus in the 1951 election of railroad stewards, it received only one fifth of the total vote, but a majority in the central administrative services in Paris. In many areas, notably in textiles and in white collar employment, a high percentage of its following is among women, more devout or at least conforming Catholics than their menfolk.

The CFTC, as we have seen, is not the only trade union home of Catholics. Unionized production workers not in the CFTC are much more likely to be members of the CGT than of FO. Among technicians, engineers, and managerial personnel, many are members of the CGC. Nor is the CFTC composed exclusively of Catholics. In the postwar years the CFTC unions have broadened the basis of their recruitment. They point to Moslem members, among other non-Catholic adherents, as evidence of their ability to gain support on strictly trade union grounds. Primarily under the impetus of the industrial unions of its left wing, the CFTC has diluted its religious color. In the first revision of its 1920 declaration of principles, the CFTC in 1947 replaced its opening reference to "the social doctrine defined in the Encyclical *De Rerum Novarum*" with the broader reference to "the principles of Christian morality." It also asserted its full independence of "all outside groups, political or religious."[16]

Most Catholic unionists before the war had a modest view of the possibilities of recruitment among the anticlerical workingmen of France. Zirnheld himself had written: "The future of the CFTC, as far as one may judge it now, will be that of a third party between the two great clashing forces of materialist inspiration, employer and labor, bringing home to them the truths and principles they need to arrive at practical and enduring solutions." To be sure, he looked forward to the CFTC's becoming not only a "third party," but an arbitrator.[17] But there was hardly any idea of its becoming a genuine mass organization. This possibility opened up before Catholic unionists with their wider contacts and the acceptance they won in the resistance and liberation, the surge of membership at liberation, and the penetration almost for the first time of typically industrial milieux. Catholic unionism was coming out of its "ghetto."

The needs of recruitment seemed to coincide with a more self-assured concept of industrial and political citizenship. Sharply distinguishing the temporal action of unionism from the realm of faith, the confederation's left wingers would like to take the friendly hand of the church entirely from the organization's shoulder. Obvious Church backing, they fear, keeps alive the old reputation of the CFTC as "a bunch of choir boys," and discourages recruitment among industrial workers.[18]

---

[16] Statutes, ch. I, art. 1, *Syndicalisme*, May 29, 1947.

[17] *Cinquante années de syndicalisme chrétien*, pp. 239-240.

[18] Mathevet of the Loire department (St. Etienne), at the 1948 CFTC convention, *Syndicalisme*, May 20, 1948.

Their argument holds that: "We should not introduce directives of the spiritual domain to make membership in our movement look like a sort of duty of conscience. It is up to us to win members by the influence and the effectiveness of the Christian trade union movement."[19]

The CFTC majority has insisted that the reference to "Christian morality" in its statutes offers a broad orientation from which it has not departed. It assures its members, "including Protestants, Moslems, and agnostics," that it is and will continue to be nonconfessional: "The CFTC has no keeper of its conscience or moral councilor outside of its own statutory organs based on the confidence of its conventions. If it were to be otherwise, the unity of the CFTC would not last a minute longer."[20] CFTC leaders occasionally remark that, though one cannot now repudiate the old name, if the confederation were being formed to-day it would take a name which did not include the adjective "Chrétien."

The CFTC is the least confessional of any of the national Catholic labor movements. It has avoided attachment to the Catholic political party, the MRP. Despite its independence and its showing of militancy, it is uncertain how much farther it can push the limits of recruitment in a land where the church is still associated with the middle and upper classes and where, in most regions, workers' attitudes to the church shade off from occasional nominal conformity or indifference to hostility.[21]

It is a familiar phenomenon in union history that the leadership may prefer internal tranquillity to larger membership. Gérard Dehove suggests that the majority leadership of the CFTC would rather restrict its recruitment to the customary Catholic sources so as to have a more easily manageable, if smaller, membership. "Le mouvement ouvrier et la législation sociale," *Revue d'économie politique,* vol. 61, March-June, 1951, p. 554.

[19] François Henry, at CFTC national committee, January 1948, cited by Syndicat général de l'éducation nationale, Commission de formation sociale, note no. 2. January 15, 1951. "Documents et remarques . . ," p. 10.

[20] Maurice Bouladoux, "La CFTC, organisation majeure, détermine son action en toute indépendance," *Syndicalisme,* November 1952, p. 1.

[21] See the French Institute of Public Opinion survey, *Sondages,* vol. 14, no. 4, 1952, "Le Catholicisme en France," especially table p. 36. Among wage earners, about 60 per cent of the men and 30 per cent of women maintain no religious practice. Less than one fifth of the men and somewhat over one third of the women are "devout," defined as going to confession and communion more than once a year. These figures cover only people baptized as Catholic.

Despite the Catholic political, intellectual, and union revival after the war, workers are detaching themselves from the church even in the old Catholic areas of Brittany, Lorraine, and Alsace. A Jesuit periodical writes: "Under the influence of general causes of which we are not the masters, the slipping into paganism seems to continue, perhaps accentuated." E. Rideau, "Après vingt-cinq ans de travail: les résultats de l'action catholique ouvrière," *Revue de l'action populaire,* no. 36, January 1950, p. 67.

CHAPTER XI

THE PARTIES TO COLLECTIVE BARGAINING

The nature and the character which we attribute to our adversaries helps shape our own methods of action.

—Maxime Leroy, *La Coutume Ouvrière*, 1913.

The freedom of bargaining is not the freedom not to bargain.

—Premier Georges Bidault, April 16, 1950.

In most of French private industry, genuine collective relations have scarcely been tried. One reason is that relations between employers and unions have seldom been those of the comparable power which might inspire respect, but usually those of victor and vanquished. The first large-scale experiment in bargaining was hardly launched in 1919 when the unions were torn apart by political strikes and schism. There was neither inducement nor pressure on employers to adjust to a new relationship. The Popular Front experience was broader and deeper. But employer resistance was stiffened by humiliation over the sit-down strikes and the Matignon settlement. Again the chance for the acceptance of new institutions was tragically short. In a little over two years the Popular Front was broken up, and the CGT was cut down by the 1938 general strike. From then on, and increasingly during the occupation and Vichy years, labor was the defeated party. Another brusque reversal came with the liberation. Employers, practically taking to their cellars for safety, were absent from the great economic and social decisions of 1944-1946. After 1947 the balance of power was more than redressed. By 1950, when the parties were free to resume the contractual relations halted in 1939, the relationship of forces was again one of patent inequality, with the stronger still gaining and the weaker, labor, still declining.

EMPLOYER ASSOCIATIONS

Almost all bargaining is on a multi-employer and multi-union basis. Typically, two or three or more unions deal with a single employer association, covering a locality or region, often a department. There is comparatively little negotiation on a single-plant basis, and far less on a companywide basis by multiplant companies.

The structure of employer organization is exceedingly complex, so complex that, as a leading association told its members, "obscurities and even errors concerning the structure and functioning of their trade associations persist in the minds of many employers."[1] Yet, as this association hastened to add, it is a logical structure. Figure 2 gives a simplified picture of the essential elements in the structure.[2]

The structure capped by the National Council of French Employers, the CNPF, is a pyramid based on regional and national organizations of three types. The "social" organizations (using the term in its French sense) deal with labor relations, wages, social insurance; they follow very broad industry lines. The economic organizations deal with production, technology, price, and marketing problems; they follow narrower industry or subindustry lines, specialized by process or product. A third type of association is the horizontal: the grouping of employers of all industries within a single region for the promotion of general employer interests. The regional associations, social and economic, are affiliated with corresponding national groups, which are in turn federated in the CNPF. Small and medium-sized establishments may join the General Confederation of Small and Medium-Sized Establishments, for a time an influential pressure group, which at the national level is affiliated with the CNPF.[3]

To visualize the structure of employer organization, let us take the example of the hypothetical Dumont Company in the Paris suburb of Vitry, assuming for simplicity's sake that it has only one plant, making one type of product. It employs 500 workers in the manufacture of automobile bodies. For collective bargaining purposes, Dumont belongs to

---

[1] Groupe des Industries Métallurgiques, Mécaniques, et Connexes de la Région Parisienne (Association of Metallurgical, Mechanical and Allied Industries of the Paris Region), *Notes documentaires*, June 30, 1949, p. 1. This document will be cited as Paris Region Metal Trades Association, *Notes*.

[2] Although the basic structure lends itself to schematic presentation, there is no uniformity in geographic coverage, industrial scope, or nomenclature. The names of employer organizations performing similar functions are varied: "syndicat," "chambre syndicale," "groupe" or "groupement," "union," and "fédération."

[3] One more form of organization may be noted: the associations of individuals, firms, or employer groups on an interest basis apart from that of trade or industry. There are, for example, a Young Employers Center, a Catholic Employers Center, an Association of Women Employers, a French National Committee of the International Chamber of Commerce, etc. These groups are loosely associated, but not integrated, with the CNPF. They do not carry on collective bargaining, but some, notably the Young Employers Center, have concerned themselves actively with such problems as wage systems and human relations in industry.

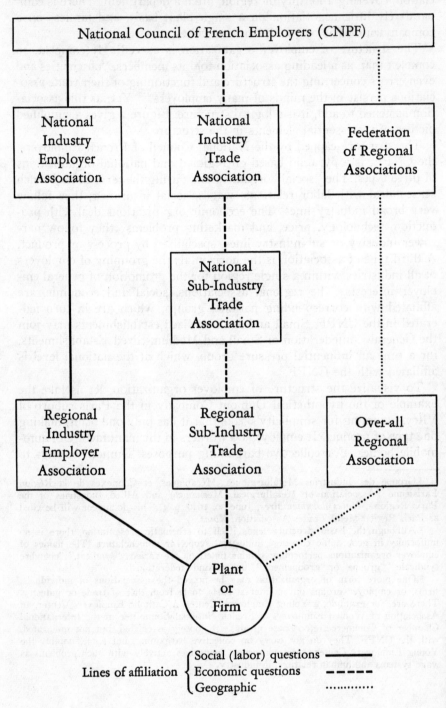

Figure 2
EMPLOYER ORGANIZATION: STRUCTURE OF THE CNPF

National Council of French Employers (CNPF)

National Industry Employer Association

National Industry Trade Association

Federation of Regional Associations

National Sub-Industry Trade Association

Regional Industry Employer Association

Regional Sub-Industry Trade Association

Over-all Regional Association

Plant or Firm

Lines of affiliation
Social (labor) questions ——————
Economic questions ―――――
Geographic ··············

the Paris Region Metal Trades Association, a member of the National Union of Metallurgical Industries. For economic purposes it belongs to the regional auto body builders association, a member of the National Auto Body and Wheel Manufacturers Association, affiliated with the broader National Federation of Automobile, Bicycle, Motorcycle, and Allied Manufacturers. It also belongs to the interindustry Southeast Paris Regional Association, which is one of the Federation of Regional Associations. Through all three channels, Dumont is represented in the CNPF. There is no individual plant or firm membership in the CNPF.

The National Council of French Employers is governed by a semi-annual representative assembly of 500, whose membership is allocated so as to "achieve an exact synthesis of the whole body of employers: industry and commerce, Paris and provinces; small, middle-sized and large firms."[4] The CNPF executive committee, which is the Council, is also a large body, with 90 members meeting about once a month. It elects the real CNPF executive, a board of 28, and its officers.

By the statutes of the CNPF, affiliated organizations retain full autonomy. Each group is bound by a policy decision "only to the extent that its representatives have not previously taken objection to that policy."[5] The weight of the National Council of French Employers, however, is far greater than the statutes indicate. Its scope and authority in public representation and labor relations, and its comprehensive membership, preclude any close analogy with the United States Chamber of Commerce or the National Association of Manufacturers.

The CNPF did a successful job of steering employer organization and the very function of the employer in society back to strength and respectability from their low estate at liberation. The fact that it has been criticized from one direction as too "soft" and from another as too static and rigid merely underlines its maintenance of delicate balance. Along with its authority in public affairs as a spokesman for employer interests, the CNPF exerts great weight in the practice of its affiliates and their members. Labor relations and general wage policy have been among the fields in which it has formulated policies and maintained employer cohesion.

GEOGRAPHIC SCOPE OF BARGAINING

The parties are free to negotiate on whatever geographic basis they choose. The 1946 law had required a national agreement in an industry

---

[4] Paris Region Metal Trades Association, *Notes*, p. 16. The Assembly is made up of 275 members for industry, 75 for commerce, 75 for the small and medium-sized enterprises, and 75 for the regional interindustry groups.

[5] *Ibid.*

before regional or local agreements could be concluded. This rigidity was not carried over into the present law.[6]

When bargaining resumed in 1950, the CFTC and FO made vain attempts to launch industrywide negotiations on a national basis, to offset their weaknesses in local and regional organization, and—they hoped—to level conditions upward. It very much wanted, said the CFTC building trades and wood workers union, "to avoid too brusque a transition between the system of government-fixed wages and a return to highly decentralized contractual discussions." It recognized that a national agreement "would perhaps be considered a minimum by the most favored regions, but it would have the advantage of bringing more substantial advantages to the workers of the least favored regions."[7] The CGT unions, stronger, more widely organized, and better led below the national level, could better afford regional or local bargaining. The CNPF took a general position in opposition to nationwide bargaining, and in favor of areawide industry bargaining, which then became the pattern (to the extent that there was bargaining) in most industries. It declared that:

An excessive centralization concentrating the discussion of collective agreements on the national level could result only in a triumph of political considerations to the detriment of a healthy appreciation of the real situation of enterprises on the regional or local level.[8]

The employer associations, not the unions, determine the bargaining units. In most cases the unit has been that of the primary employer organization, local, departmental, or regional.

After a year of rather frustrated efforts to write any collective agreements at all, the general secretary of FO complained: "The error of the lawmakers in 1950 was to permit the fragmentation of the system of collective agreements by not maintaining the priority of national agreements by industry. Each can therefore build his own shanty as he pleases without regard for the general interest. It is like trying to build a city without a central plan."[9] But there had been no living "system"

---

[6] References to the collective bargaining law are to the 1950 act, unless otherwise specified.

[7] Fédération Française des Syndicats du Batiment, etc., CFTC, *IX° Congrès fédéral,* March 1952, "Rapport sur les industries de Bois et de l'Ameublement," p. 5. "Rapport sur les industries du batiment et travaux publics," p. 36. .

[8] Report to general assembly of CNPF, *Bulletin du CNPF,* vol. 5, no. 62, February 5, 1951, p. 26.

[9] Robert Bothereau, "Le Régime des conventions collectives," *Revue economique,* vol. 2, no. 1, February 1951, p. 43. For a more nuanced expression of disappointment by another FO secretary, see G. D. Delamarre, "Réflexions sur les accords de salaires," *Force ouvrière,* November 16, 1950, p. 1.

to be fragmented, only a hope. Even the "system" of the 1936-1939 agreements had been essentially local or regional, not national. Nor had it covered all workers, even with the extension of agreements. The problem was less the lack of city planning than the lack of building, planned or unplanned.

In the first three and a half years of bargaining, as employers assured themselves that they would not have to grant great concessions, a handful of national agreements were negotiated: textiles, job printing, road transport, freight handling, chemicals, oil, rubber. The contents of most were minimal; many did not even include wages. (On the content of agreements, see Chapter XII, *infra.*) The important nationalized industries also practiced what was essentially national bargaining: coal, railroads, gas, and electricity. Most of these national agreements were expected to be (but often were not) complemented by regional or local agreements or annexes. From the standpoint of the unions, "A national collective agreement is like a skeleton which must be surrounded by flesh by local or regional settlements."[10] Most often little flesh was added.

The CNPF and its constituent area and industry associations are far superior to the unions in organization, discipline, resources, and self-confidence. Their coverage is extensive, and there are no really competing organizations. Group and class solidarity is keener than the spirit of competition. It can be reinforced if necessary by the threat of economic or social sanctions. The staffs of employer associations greatly outweigh those of all the comparable unions together. The national metal trades association, for example, had thirty-five professional people in its labor relations and social insurance department. In addition, its Paris region affiliate was largely and ably staffed; many district affiliates had sizable staffs, not to mention the considerable resources of individual employers.

The disparities are greatest at the regional and local levels. The unions suffer from lack of the trained negotiators and the detailed knowledge of industry that come with stable membership, adequate treasuries, and experience in collective bargaining and contract administration. The disparity was summed up by a CFTC national union head: "Our men usually begin by arguing that the employers can afford to grant a considerable raise, because productivity has gone up. After the employers have flooded them with figures which they are unable either to evaluate or contradict, they wind up saying, 'Well, the cost of living has gone up, so we need a raise.' " In all but major industries, the burden of the union's side may be carried by a harassed department fed-

---

[10] FO, Fédération des Transports (road and local transport), Reports to the 1952 convention, "Conventions collectives: Routiers," p. 3.

eration secretary negotiating with specialized employer association executives.

Regional employer groups can count on help from the national associations to an extent beyond the means of the unions. National employer associations recognize the importance of helping out in a local negotiation, if only to safeguard the interests of the industry in other areas. As the CNPF observed in 1950 when Parliament was debating the merits of national as opposed to regional and local bargaining: "Whatever system is adopted, one point seems definite. That is the necessity for a strict employer discipline within each industry, as well as a tight coördination among the associations which will be called upon to negotiate within the framework of the new law."[11] At the same meeting, several employers called attention to the dangers of regional discussion: the decision of regions poorly organized [in employer associations] would threaten grave repercussions for the others." The president promised that the CNPF together with the various industry associations would indicate clearly "the limits within which the discussions would take place." Qualified persons would be ready to go to any region which called for "aid in discussions."[12] The metal trades association national headquarters had four high level representatives assigned exclusively to liaison on labor questions with regional affiliates. In negotiations in a major food-canning region, the Breton canners association instruction was: "At the joint meeting with the unions, let the specialists delegated by the Paris office lead the discussion."

The CNPF itself publicly stated what it considered the permissible limits of wage increases when wage bargaining was first resumed. It also indicated the limits of concessions on the nonwage issues, the institutional clauses of collective agreements. For, the CNPF reminded its members, "Any yielding on these issues beyond what we have defined with the appropriate trade associations would have consequences for our firms just as serious as giving way on wage issues."[13]

The centralization of decision-making in the CNPF is enhanced by the role, important in any industrial country, of the metallurgical and metal fabricating industries. Ever since its rebirth, the CNPF has filled such top posts as its presidency and vice-presidency-for-labor-questions with metal trades officials, and (like the CGPF) used national metal trades staff on labor matters. Metal trades associations (which negotiate

---

[11] Labor relations and social welfare committee, report on wages and collective bargaining, January 7, 1950, *Bulletin du CNPF*, vol. 5, no. 44, February 5, 1950, p. 18.

[12] *Ibid.*, p. 16.

[13] Report to CNPF general assembly, *Bulletin du CNPF*, vol. 5, no. 62, February 5, 1951, p. 27.

regionally for the whole range of basic metals and end products) are pattern setters for much of the bargaining in private employment. Within the industry, there is further concentration of decision making. The key bargain (or unilateral decision) is that made by the Paris region association, whose members employ 400,000 workers—over one third of those in the nation.

THE GOVERNMENT AS BARGAINING PARTY

Another element of centralized decision in the formally decentralized collective bargaining system is provided by the government as an employer, through its own payrolls and the indirect influence of its wage policies on private employment. The government has on its various civilian payrolls over one fourth of the nonagricultural wage earners of France; their unions, civil service and industrial, include many of the strongest sections of the trade union movement.

The government's industrial employment (as distinct from the civil service) falls into two categories. (1) The nationalized enterprises in competitive fields (auto and aircraft manufacture, air transport, banking, insurance) and the semi-autonomous social security boards carry on full collective bargaining. (2) The larger group of government operated enterprises, of a monopoly character (which are enumerated in Appendix E) are specifically excluded from the application of the collective bargaining law. In the latter group of industries, notably the coal and potash mines, railroads, Paris transport, gas and electricity, general conditions of employment are regulated by "personnel statutes" and government decrees. Most of the postwar decrees and statutes were written in the days of greatest Communist Party and CGT power. Communist union leaders held the Ministry of Labor and, more strategic, that of Industrial Production. Drafted in consultation with the unions, the personnel statutes provided for broad union rights within the establishments, liberal safeguards in disciplinary measures, and large powers for shop delegates.[14] Wage rates in these industries, although nominally promulgated by the government, usually represent the culmination of a long process of economic and political bargaining, embodied in some form of agreement or "protocol," rather than simple ministerial fiat.

The temper of labor relations does not depend much on whether a government enterprise carries on full collective bargaining within the

---

[14] See for example the miners' statute, Decree No. 46, 1433 of June 14, 1946, and the gas and electricity personnel statute, Decree No. 46, 1541 of June 22, 1946, both modified by various subsequent decrees. For a good brief discussion, see Adolf Sturmthal, "Nationalization and Workers' Control in Britain and France," *Journal of Political Economy,* vol. 61, no. 1, February 1953, pp. 43-79.

law's definition. In both types of enterprise, full-time managerial heads do most of the negotiating. Agreements go through a board of directors made up of government, consumer, and union representatives. The tripartite boards were to have avoided the dangers of complete state control and excessive bureaucratization. But in collective bargaining, the union representatives on the boards are in an awkward position of conflicting loyalties—or would be if their union loyalties did not override their other board responsibilities. The weaknesses of the boards in bargaining have thrown that power more and more to the professional managers of state industries.

The diffusion of responsibility among government agencies is enhanced by the pulls of party competition within coalition governments. Wage settlements in government enterprise must be approved by the ministry directly responsible: e.g., the Ministry of Industrial Production for the mines or the Ministry of Transport for the railroads. A central power, at least that of final veto, is exercised by the Ministry of Finance. Older and better established than the other economic ministries, its power over wages is sharpened by the chronic deficits of the government budget as a whole and of many government enterprises. The most potent in the laborious process of government decision, it is usually the ministry least sensitive to social policy considerations. But, subject to political pressures, even a conservative French government is likely to give its employees better conditions than most private employers. Acquired advantages are hard to take away. This Premier Pleven found in early 1952, when a Parliament oriented to the right center nevertheless defeated his government on the issue of economy proposals which threatened to reduce railroad employees' retirement and welfare benefits.

Union rights are far greater in government industries and remuneration often better than in most of private industry. Union representatives sit not only on boards of directors but on promotion and discipline committees with powers unheard of in most private employment. Grievance handling is more of a joint process, with more protection to employees and to union delegates.

Workers enjoy greater security of employment than in private industry. If straight money wage rates are about the same, there seems to have been considerable upgrading. Nonwage perquisites are much higher: more generous medical care and pension rights, free housing or housing allowances, free railroad transportation, coal, gas, and electricity in these respective industries. Many of these perquisites existed, at least in part, under private ownership of the railroads, mines, and public utilities; most have been expanded under public ownership.

Neither material advantage nor public ownership, with union partici- pation in management, has been able to create a wholesome temper of labor relations. The CGT, strongest in all the key government indus- tries, has multiplied the difficulties; its animus toward the state is much deeper than its quarrel with private management. "The state is more rapacious than the private employers. With the state, the only arbitra- tion is that of combat," said the Communist leader Auguste Lecoeur, speaking as head of the CGT miners union of the north.[15]

Among most non-Communist workers and unions, attitudes are al- most as hostile, although the unions' policies are not those of the CGT's systematic obstruction. "We have a boss today as yesterday; he has changed his name, that's all," declared the head of the FO miners' union.[16] After the breakoff of long wage negotiations with the govern- ment, he wrote:

Mr. Minister, you offer the workers the equivalent of their miserable purchasing power of two years ago. It is appropriate that they . . . offer you the 950 kilograms of coal per day they produced two years ago, instead of the 1,250 they now average. . . The government has been cheating too long. It is up to us to play our cards now, and any card that wins is good enough to play.[17]

Few workers feel any real indentification with the nationalized indus- tries in which they work, as few citizens feel any great identification with their government. If the issue becomes dramatic in labor relations, it is only one aspect of the broader problem of the decay of civic author- ity in France.

MULTI-UNION BARGAINING

On the other side of the bargaining table, opposite well-knit employer associations or the government, the unions are divided and short of means. The free unions are loosely structured and poorly disciplined. Workers are tired and distracted by the political gymnastics of the CGT. The leadership can never be sure it will be followed by its own member- ship, let alone the unorganized. Even if the unions pooled their strength, they would represent a minority of the wage earners of private industry, although a majority of those in public employment. But no real or con- sistent pooling of strength is possible, given the unions' differences in basic interests. Multi-union bargaining is bound, on the union side, to be competitive, irresponsible, and uneasy.

---

[15] At national miners' union convention, *L'Humanité*, October 26, 1950.
[16] FO, *Congrès, 1950, Compte rendu* . . , p. 239.
[17] Noel Sinot, "A nous de jouer maintenant," *Force ouvrière*, November 9, 1950, p. 1.

"Unity of action" has been the CGT's foremost tactic for years. The forms and immediate aims of its unity tactic change with the hardenings and softenings of the party line. Its chief interest is in united action at the base, at the local and shop levels, where it may drive a wedge between rank and file and leadership of the other unions. Although united action through leadership agreement does not adequately serve the purpose of atomizing competing unions, the CGT is often prepared to agree on joint action at whatever echelon it can get it. When the unity line is strongest, the CGT is willing to withdraw intransigent demands to get agreement with CFTC and FO leaders.

The CGT's unity at the base tactic includes the absurd element of "participation" of the unorganized and their "representatives." The unorganized, by definition, can hardly participate as a group or delegate authority to their "representatives." The CGT's use of the unorganized requires skillful use of reliable "nonparty" and "unorganized" workers.[18]

The device for bringing in the unorganized is usually the "unity of action committee" composed of representatives of existing unions and the nonunionized. A standard directive when negotiations are impending or going forward is: "Carry the discussion into the plants themselves. Set up or reinforce the unity of action committees grouping *all* the workers belonging to *any* of the organizations *or to none.*"[19]

"Our collective agreement will not be won around the green table; it will be won in the plants," said a Paris CGT metal trades leader. The industry's other unions having negotiated an agreement without the CGT, he declared, "It is not possible for honest union leaders to decide themselves on propositions from the employers without getting instructions from the workers themselves."[20] The prescription was the usual formula: "Set up a unity of action committee in each shop, with the participation of the metal workers of *all opinions and the unorganized.*"[21]

The CGT generally defines unity of action in terms of the winning of unimpeachable economic demands. Occasionally, however, it lapses into the explanations which can come only from the special universe of Communist reasoning, in the language removed from all other reality. When Frachon in the midst of joint strikes attacked the leaders of other unions,

---

18 Cf. the excellent brief discussion, "Création du 'Sans-Parti,'" in Collinet, *Esprit du syndicalisme,* pp. 94-97. For a scolding of bungling CGT officials who pushed forward the wrong "representatives" of the unorganized, see Marcel Dufriche, "Les Luttes ouvrières en France," *Servir la France,* no. 41-42, November-December 1948, p. 31.

19 CGT executive board communiqué, October 4, 1950, *L'Humanité,* October 5, 1950. Underlining supplied.

20 André Lunet, general secretary of the CGT metal workers council of the Seine, *L'Humanité,* October 31, 1950.

21 *L'Humanité,* November 1, 1950. Underlining supplied.

"serving the antilabor policies of their parties," he conceded that "some comrades will say, 'Don't you think you will disturb the present unity of action?'" His reply was simply to ask, "Why should the denunciation of real traitors disturb honest men who are achieving unity of action?"[22]

The CGT may be even franker about the ultimate meaning of unity. Ordinarily losing no opportunity to strike, the CGT watched the FO miners late in 1952 go out on a hopeless strike, refused to join the walkout, and ridiculed its weak rival. Joint action with other unions was only a beginning, said Lecoeur. Real unity meant the disappearance of other unions in favor of the CGT: "Unity of action committees are all very well, we must set them up. But that is still not unity, it is only the preparation for unity. That is why we must set them up with this directive: 'for a single union, and down with disunity.'"[23]

The other unions are of course aware of the CGT's purposes. Nevertheless, in the state of weakness in which one union alone is almost certain not to win its demands, they find it hard to ignore the strongest union organization. "They can't do anything without us, and we can't do anything without them," remarked a CFTC leader in Brittany. Still less do their members understand how the CGT can be ignored. After all, the government recognizes the CGT, and employers deal with the CGT.[24] "When workers are feeble, it costs nothing to think they will be strong if they unite," explained a Lyon FO official.

Force Ouvrière at the confederation level rejects any collaboration with the CGT. This attitude was so strong that one of the CFTC executive board complained to his opposite number in FO, "You see the main danger in the CGT; we see it in the employers." The fact that FO issues from a split with the CGT adds a special risk to joint action. It raises the question: if FO is to practice joint action with the CGT, what was the use of splitting from it? But while the confederation has repeatedly denounced "unity of action," many of its locals and even national unions have found joint action with the CGT desirable or unavoidable. The situation was typified by the preoccupations of an FO leader in the

---

[22] "Défendez l'unité contre les traîtres," *L'Humanité*, March 11, 1950.

[23] "Pour un seul syndicat: à bas la division," *L'Humanité*, December 19, 1952. Cf. "Chronique de l'Unité d'Action," *Reconstruction*, no. 60, January 15, 1953, p. B-2.

[24] In other countries, too, relationships of employers and other unions to Communist unions seem to be governed by circumstance rather than moral or political principle. In 1953, great American corporations still found it necessary or desirable to deal with Communist-dominated unions. In the Netherlands, where the Communist trade union center is the smallest of four major centers, it is possible for the other unions, employers and the government to freeze it out of the regular processes of industrial relations. In Italy, on the other hand, where the Communist unions have a predominant position like that of the CGT, the employers' confederation has insisted on dealing with them, maintaining that bargaining without them would be meaningless.

southwest, one of the most energetic, and no left-winger. He called together the executive committee of his department federation to discuss the dangers of unity of action because "once again some of the locals seemed to be getting out of line." At the same time he was following the national railroad negotiations as an officer of that union. To a question as to whether the negotiating unions included the CGT, he replied, "Of course, since it would be useless to negotiate without the CGT."

"If it is easy for the leaders at the top to refuse any dealings with the CGT," said a local FO spokesman, "do you think it is the same in the factories, the shops, or the office, where fellow-workers of the two confederations rub elbows—especially if the CGT local is the strongest in the shop or if the confessional unionists are allied with it?"[25] In general, however, the origins of FO dictate the outlook that its "first job is to destroy the CGT, to permit us then to rebuild a true union movement."[26]

The CFTC recognizes the possibility of joint action with the CGT under specified conditions. The confederation's right wing and left wing unions are in agreement on this tactic, although constantly warning against the dangers of a "pact with the devil." "On unity of action, everything possible has already been said," the confederation declared, associating its tolerance of joint action with its concept of separate Catholic unionism.

For the CFTC the justification of union pluralism is complete only with the corollary of the search for unity of action. . . . Unity of action can take place only when the objective is unquestionably a trade or industry issue, where the lines are clear and defined, after an agreement in proper form regulating in detail the means of joint action.[27]

The issue of whether or not to coöperate with the CGT introduces an added element of discord between the CFTC and FO. The free unions seldom coördinate their action in relation to the CGT. One of the few arrangements for coöperation is that in the St. Etienne area, where a formal committee is based on good personal relations and the habits of consultation among an energetic young group of FO and CFTC activists. The committee tries to coördinate the FO and CFTC positions on each bargaining situation and then to reach a common position with the CGT before tackling employers.

[25] Cottet, social security employees of Paris, FO, Informations, compte rendu du 3ᵉ congrès confédéral, 1952, p. 74.
[26] Cochinard, general secretary of federation of department of the Marne, Ibid., p. 27.
[27] CFTC, 27ᵉ Congrès Confédéral, 1953, La CFTC face aux responsabilités du syndicalisme moderne, rapport d'orientation . . , p. 70.
For a specimen of terms of an agreement at the national union level among the CGT, FO, and the CFTC, see the CFTC textile union's Inter-Textiles, August-September 1950.

The shifting bargaining alliances among the unions in almost every industry are like the meeting and parting of figures in a dance of changing rhythms and improvised steps. The attitudes of individual CFTC and FO unions toward various degrees of joint demands, negotiation, and strike action with the CGT have little relation to their characterization in other contexts as left wing or right wing. A few examples may illuminate a scene which defies generalization, varying as it does from union to union, locality to locality, and time to time.

In early 1951 the CGT and CFTC building trades unions agreed on joint demands for a master wage agreement for the Paris region. When the employers turned down their first demand, the CFTC proposed a lower raise, as agreed with the CGT. But the CGT representatives repudiated the lower demand, and remained in the bargaining sessions "only as observers." Finally the CFTC alone signed the agreement, followed the next day by FO. In the provinces, however, the CGT building trades union soon signed similar agreements.

Early in 1950 all the Paris transport unions negotiated through a joint committee with the management of the publicly-owned subway and bus system and the Ministry of Transport and Public Works. Negotiations were still at an indecisive stage when the CGT pushed for an immediate strike. At a joint mass meeting the CFTC, FO, and autonomous unions opposed the strike call. When their arguments were rejected, they pulled out of the committee. The CGT, intent on striking, in part to aid the simultaneous metal trades strike, went it alone—to defeat.

In the spring of 1950 all the Paris region metal trades unions collaborated in demands on their employers and in the strikes which followed. In the fall of that year, with the consent of the other unions the CGT was frozen out of negotiations, first with Renault, then with the Paris region metal trades association. A year later, the CFTC metal trades union was refusing to negotiate with the Paris region employers unless the CGT were a party to the bargaining.

From 1949 until 1951, all the national textile unions took part in joint negotiations with the employers association. The difficulties of coördinating union demands are clear in the CFTC's restrained account:

In the course of four meetings . . . we tried to reach a common union position on the various articles of agreement. This was very difficult because of the frequent absence of FO, and because the CGT had placed a new draft agreement before the employers without having had it considered jointly.[28]

---

[28] CFTC, Fédération française des syndicats chrétiens du textile, *Inter-Textiles*, no. 22, June 1950, Supplement, "Convention collective nationale des industries textiles," p. 2.

When an agreement was finally drawn up, the CGT refused to sign. A few months later it signed, but served notice at the same moment of a demand for termination of certain clauses. (A union or employer organization may add its signature to a registered contract, subsequent to its signing, whether or not it took part in the negotiations.)

The confusing patterns (or lack of pattern) of multi-union negotiation are summarized in Table 7, below, which shows the frequency with which unions of competing national centers have signed collective agreements and wage settlements. Figures are not available for the numbers of workers covered by the contracts.

In comparatively few cases did one organization sign alone. The highest rate of sole signatures was that of the CGT, but even its unions signed only about one tenth of all contracts alone. All three (CGT,

TABLE 7

PATTERNS OF UNION SIGNATURE OF COLLECTIVE AGREEMENTS AND
WAGE SETTLEMENTS,[a] 1950–1952

Unions signing	Number of collective agreements and annexes (February 1950–June 1952)	Number of wage settlements (September 1951 June 1952)
	Single union signatures	
CGT	44	102
FO	4	50
CFTC	8	53
CGSI	3	—
CGC	10	—
Miscellaneous	48	—
Total	117	205
	Multi-union signatures (major workers' confederations only)	
CGT-CFTC	25	134
CGT-FO	12	57
FO-CFTC	73	117
CGT-FO-CFTC	83	295
Total	193	603
	Total number signed	
CGT	164	588
FO	172	519
CFTC	189	599
CGSI	5	—
CGC	72	—
Miscellaneous	79	120
Unspecified	—	134

Source: Based on Ministry of Labor data, August 1952.
[a]For difference between collective agreements and wage settlements, see Chapter XII, *infra*.

CFTC, and FO) unions together signed over one fourth of both the collective agreements and wage settlements; this is the most frequent pattern. The CFTC and FO, without the CGT, were signatories of 23 per cent of the collective agreements and 11 per cent of the wage settlements. The CGT-CFTC combination, without FO, signed 8 and 12 per cent respectively. Least frequent is the CGT-FO juxtaposition, without the CFTC. The CFTC signed more contracts all in all than either the CGT or FO. This is an indication of the greater willingness of its unions to join with either or both its rivals in contract negotiation and signature.

Similar variations are found in almost every industry. Thus, in the building trades, in the series of wage settlements in most of the departments of France, in late 1951, 37 departmental contracts were signed by all three unions (CGT, CFTC, and FO), 10 by the CGT and the CFTC, 6 by the CGT and FO, 3 by the CFTC and FO, 4 by the CGT alone, 1 by the CFTC alone, and 4 by FO alone.[29]

In a period of rising wages, the unions signing an agreement when the CGT or another union refuses to sign do not run too great a risk. If wages should be falling, however, there would be a premium on intransigence; unions excluded or abstaining could capitalize on opposition to an agreement, while the unions signing it would not have any of the protection of exclusive representation rights.

UNION REPRESENTATIVITY

The theory of the law is that collective agreements are negotiated between "the most representative organizations of workers and employers," convoked in bargaining sessions by government officials. Despite the gaps between law and bargaining practice, the doctrine of "representativity" still regulates many aspects of union-employer and interunion relationships, and governs many of the rights of unions at all levels of the economy. "Representativity" is not an English or American term. But there is no more euphonious way of naming the doctrine than by transliterating the French term, and no simpler way of defining it than by explaining its application.

Employer representativity has raised no problems since the war. The occasional pluralism of the prewar period has almost entirely disappeared. The organizations affiliated with the CNPF are in fact as in theory most representative.

For the unions, the prevailing concept might more aptly be called that of "recognized organizations." When the 1936 laws launched the

---

[29] CFTC Fédération Française des Syndicats du Batiment, dv buis, etc., *Rapport sur les industries du batiment et travaux publics,* 1952, pp. 31-32.

doctrine of representativity, it will be recalled, the government decided that more than one organization might be designated as "most representative." In many sectors of the economy, however, the CGT unions then enjoyed almost exclusive rights. Now, union pluralism is the rule at every echelon in almost every industry. Union pluralism is associated with the intimacy of individual religious and political convictions. The CGT's politics, furthermore, mean that France does not even consider exclusive bargaining rights for majority organizations.

The CGT attempted to establish exclusive rights for itself after liberation. The CFTC, however, soon received recognition for its claims to representativity, which its resistance record and the political position of the MRP made it hard to deny. Later, over the opposition of both the CGT and the CFTC, the CGC won its fight to be recognized as a representative organization for the cadres. The CGT's reformist leaders had joined with its Communist leaders in opposing CFTC and CGC representativity. When FO was established, it could, thanks to the acceptance of union pluralism, quickly be recognized as another "nationally representative" organization.

Actually, the CGT, the CFTC, and FO all continue to enjoy general recognition as "nationally representative."[30] More limited representativity may be granted, for a single occupational category or for a single industry, on a national or a local basis. The CGC, which does not claim to represent production workers, is nationally representative for its constituency, the cadres.

The prewar tests of union representativity were membership, independence, dues income, and "experience and seniority." These were expanded shortly after liberation to add those of "patriotic attitude during the occupation" and conformance with purge ordinances. Attempts at negotiation under the 1946 collective bargaining law brought innumerable controversies over representativity rights. The government at one time proposed to apply the test of "membership" quantitatively; that is, to grant representativity only to unions whose membership included at least specified percentages of the organized workers in the industry or occupational category concerned. The requirements were complex, the membership data impossible to obtain. They would have fallen of their own weight had not CFTC protests and legislative activity by its MRP friends caused the government to abandon its quantitative formulas.[31]

---

[30] See declaration of Pierre Segelle, Minister of Labor, Assemblée Nationale, *Débats*, December 16, 1949, 1st session, p. 6952.

[31] For negotiation of agreements covering all occupational categories of an industry, a union had to number 10 per cent of the industry's organized workers, and 25 per cent

The criteria of representativity, already embodied in administrative practice, were given legislative sanction for the first time in the 1950 collective bargaining act.[32] In interpreting the criterion of membership, numbers are significant but not decisive. Only the CGT makes a show of offering to open its books to comparison with its rivals. "Independence" refers to freedom from employer domination. This, and the criterion of dues income, are meant to exclude company unions. "Seniority" or age ("ancienneté") is the vaguest in application. Gaullist friends of the CGSI, newest of the union centers, failed to smoke out any definition in the parliamentary discussions. Apparently "seniority" is relevant for the light it may throw on the other requirements, notably independence. Some anti-Communist legislators made a vain attempt to change the final criterion to read not "patriotic attitude during the occupation" but simply "patriotic attitude." This would have thrown into question CGT behavior at the time of the Nazi-Soviet pact and since 1947.

Employees never vote directly on representativity, although shop and social security elections are indirectly votes toward this purpose. As the Minister of Labor remarked, "These criteria are neither mandatory nor rigidly fixed. They are simply elements of judgment."[33] After all the attempts to set precise qualifications, what inevitably remained, given the relations among the unions, was the old administrative discretion.

The rights which representativity confers run the gamut of union

---

in one of the categories. For agreements covering a single category, it had to show either: a) 10 per cent of the organized workers in the whole industry and 25 per cent of those in the category involved; or b) 33 per cent of the organized in the category. Decision of Premier and Minister of Labor, March 13, 1947, *Journal Officiel*, March 15, 1947. See also Georges Scelle, "La Notion d'organisation la plus représentative et la loi du 23 décembre 1946," *Revue française du travail*, vol. 2, no. 15-16, June-July 1947, pp. 529-539.

The MRP group in the National Assembly introduced a bill, which was not passed, to select worker representatives for bargaining committees by proportional representation in referendum vote among four categories of personnel: (1) production workers, (2) clerical workers, (3) foremen, (4) engineers and "cadres."

For the government's retreat, see Circular TR 97/47, Dec. 4, 1947, *Revue française du travail*, special no. 1, 1948, pp. 75-77.

[32] For a detailed administrative exposition of the criteria later set forth in the 1950 law, see Ministry of Labor Circular TR 21/48, January 26, 1948, *Ibid.*, pp. 78-82. See also the "conclusions" of the government "commissioner" in the controversy over FO's claim to a seat for farm labor on the National Commission on Collective Agreements. These "conclusions" (recommendations to the Conseil d'Etat, the nation's highest administrative court) are a valuable resumé of the criteria of representativity. "La composition de la section agricole de la commission supérieure des conventions collectives et la représentation de Force ouvrière," *Droit social*, vol. 15, no. 2, February 1952, pp. 110-115.

[33] Assemblée Nationale, *Débats*, January 3, 1950, 1st session, p. 29.

participation in economic life from the plant to the national economy. The most representative unions have the right to take part in government-convoked contract negotiations and to ask the extension of collective agreements. Only they put up slates in the various shop elections— stewards, plant committeemen, rail and mine delegates, and so on. They nominate worker representatives on the directorates of public enterprises and on public regulatory and consultative bodies, notably the National Economic Council and the National Commission on Collective Agreements.[34]

From these forms of representativity in turn flow great practical advantages: the control of the payrolls of plant committees, the payment of members of social security boards, the payment of unionists in many public and private concerns for time spent on union business. A single example: it was estimated in 1953 that about 50 communist unionists were thus supported by the Paris public transport system.[35]

The system of representativity is one neither of exclusive majority representation nor of real proportional representation. In public organisms where labor has seats, it is an attenuated form of proportional representation favoring the weaker of the major unions. In collective bargaining it permits equal representation of all recognized unions, regardless of relative strength. All representative unions have a right to participate in government-convoked bargaining sessions. But nothing in the law forces an employer to bargain with all of the most representative unions, or only with them, outside such sessions. Employers and unions may bargain as they choose privately. Many contracts are signed with the unions which are, at least numerically, least representative.

So far the government has not used its discretion to deny representativity to any major organization. Minor organizations charge a monopoly by the three main workers' confederations. The CGSI, the chief claimant knocking at the door for several years, alleges political discrimination. Granted significant recognition locally and in single industries, it was in a fair way to obtain full national recognition in 1952 when the resounding split in its own ranks made the government draw back.

Its most important political prejudice the government has not yet attempted to enforce. The question of the CGSI has been minor, that of the CGT crucial. "It is appropriate that the government refuse to

---

[34] For a brief summary of rights of the most representative organizations, see André Rouast and Paul Durand, *Précis de législation industrielle (Droit du travail)* (3d ed.), (Paris, 1948), pp. 200-201.

[35] Pierre Felce, general secretary of FO national transport union, "Les Révolutionnaires professionnels et la représentativité syndicale." *Air-Terre-Mer,* April 1953, p. 8.

deal with the CGT, but it is not appropriate that it refuse to deal with all the non-Communist workers who support the CGT," remarked a high official of the Ministry of Labor. The government has not tried to extend the criterion of "independence" to include independence of political party control.

The system of representativity does not take from workers the right in considerable measure to indicate, by membership and by various forms of elections, what unions shall speak for them. It makes it more difficult for any new organization to enter upon the scene, if it does not have government favor—or easier, if the government smiles upon it. It gives the government a veto power over union performance of most of the functions of employee representation, a veto power the government finds it easier to use over new entrants than over established organizations.

EXTENSION OF AGREEMENTS

By the process of extension, first introduced in 1936, the state may in effect permit trade associations and unions by collective bargaining to fix wages and other conditions binding on all employment within the industry and the area covered by the original agreement. Government sanction thus elevates the terms of a negotiated agreement from private contract to public regulation. Searching for some analogy in the United States, one might compare extension to the process by which railroad union-management agreements on labor relations and pension systems have been enacted by Congress into legislation binding on the whole industry.

In terms of coverage, extension has less potential importance than before the war, now that employer organization is so widespread. The degree of union organization is not formally determining in the application of an agreement, since an employer covered either through his own signature or that of his trade association is required by law to apply its terms to all his employees. In industries of many small dispersed employer units, such as road transport, however, the unions do not know which employers are association members and which therefore are covered by the agreement. Extension can solve this problem for them.

For unions and management concerned with equalizing certain minimum competitive conditions, the chief value of extension lies in its enforcement feature. The clauses of an extended agreement are subject to inspection by Ministry of Labor inspectors and enforcement in the same way as statute law or administrative regulation.[36] Only if it has

---

[36] Enforcement of extended labor agreements in agriculture is by labor inspectors of the Ministry of Agriculture.

been extended does the government police the terms of an agreement, and then for firms covered by the original agreement as well as those to whom it has been extended. The whole wage rate system of an industry may be enforced through the extension of an agreement: in the silk industry the complicated piece-rate scales depend for enforcement largely on the labor inspectors' checking the payrolls of many dispersed small units, including numerous outside contractors, in a way neither the unions nor even the employer association can do.

Only full collective agreements may be extended. Extension may be demanded by one of the "most representative" organizations or by the Minister of Labor. The government then consults the National Commission on Collective Agreements, whose opinion is advisory. The government itself decides whether to extend the agreement, in whole or in essential part.

The requirements for a collective agreement are so complicated that the first extensions, two years after the law's passage, covered agreements which, on important points, as the CNPF remarked, "because of the nature of things, took liberties with the letter of the law."[37] As of the end of 1952, there had been extended only 6 national agreements, 14 annexes to national agreements, 3 regional agreements and 32 annexes to the cadres' national pension agreement.[38]

The theory of extension assumes agreements between organizations genuinely representative of the employers and employees involved. There are sectors of the economy in which no union, nor even all the "most representative" union organizations together, can fill that requirement. Unorganized workers may often be presumed to be represented by the unions of those who are organized. Under current conditions in some industries or localities, extension may give the force of law to contracts of unions which are not only minorities but obviously unrepresentative. Where a major union opposes the extension of an agreement (as the CGT unsuccessfully did in the case of textiles), the relationship between the parties contracting and the parties covered is doubly tenuous.

When the collective bargaining law was under debate, its extension provisions were considered, both by those hopeful and those fearful of their effects, of major consequence in creating the "regime of collective bargaining." The government made a determined and successful attempt to retain the power of discretion in extending agreements. So far the provisions for extension have played, not the significant role ex-

---

[37] *Bulletin du CNPF,* vol. 6, no. 78, February 20, 1952, p. 33.
[38] Letter from Ministry of Labor, January 25, 1953. See Pierre Fournier, "L'Extension des conventions collectives," *Droit social,* vol. 15, no. 4, April 1952, pp. 242-247

pected, but a minor role in regulating conditions of employment. The unions' weakness in bargaining, hence the sketchy nature of most contracts, makes extension possible in comparatively few cases. The government may be willing to extend more agreements, but the rigidities it imposed on the contents of such agreements nullify the flexibility to intervene which it thought to keep for itself.

CHAPTER XII

THE CONTENT OF COLLECTIVE BARGAINING

When one tries to define the attitude of French employers toward collective agreements, one must avoid two errors. One would be to conclude, after having noted some resistance or hesitations, that our employers are opposed in principle to collective agreements. The other would be to believe, that, like their opposite numbers in the United Kingdom or other countries, they see in collective agreements the essential element in the mechanism of labor relations.

—Pierre Waline, French employer delegate to the ILO, *Revue Economique,* February 1951.

No great innovations have ever been introduced into French labor relations by collective agreement. Collective bargaining is not the main process for determining conditions of employment in France. The unions exist more for reasons of political protest and political pressure than for economic bargaining. Legal enactment and many forms of government intervention preëmpt much of the field which, historically, the resistance of employers and the character of unionism have denied to collective bargaining. This framework determines the content of collective bargaining, which is discussed in this chapter. The following chapter considers labor disputes; Chapter XIV, labor relations at the plant level.

COLLECTIVE AGREEMENTS AND WAGE SETTLEMENTS

The French distinguish sharply between the contracts which the law terms "full collective agreements" ("conventions collectives") and those it terms simple "wage settlements" ("accords de salaires"). It spells out the subject matter which a full-fledged collective agreement must cover. The obligatory clauses, in the sequence and for the most part in the wording of the law itself, concern:

1. Trade union rights and workers' freedom of opinion.
2. Wages:
   a. Wage of the unskilled worker.

      b. Skill differentials, applied to (a) as base.
      c. Differentials for heavy, dangerous, or dirty work.
      d. Methods of application of the "equal work, equal pay" principle for women and young workers.
3. Conditions of hiring and firing, without infringing on workers' free choice of a union.
4. Dismissal notices.
5. Shop stewards, plant committees, and financing of welfare schemes operated by the plant committees.
6. Paid vacations.
7. Procedure for revision or termination of all or part of the agreement.
8. Procedures for conciliation of collective disputes.
9. Apprenticeship and vocational training.
10. Conditions of work of women and young workers.

The law also enumerates various categories of optional clauses; the list is not limiting. Again in the sequence of the law, these are:

1. Special conditions of work: a. Overtime, b. Shift rotation, c. Night work, d. Sunday work, e. Work on paid holidays.
2. Incentive payment systems.
3. Bonuses for seniority and diligence.
4. Allowances for occupational expenses.
5. Moving allowances.
6. Part-time work.
7. Arbitration of collective disputes.
8. Supplementary pension plans.

If a trade or industry has a national collective agreement, regional or local agreements may simply implement that agreement, or they may grant more to employees. If there is no national agreement, regional or local agreements must cover the required subject matter to qualify as full collective agreements.

This listing measures the expectations of the unions and of the parliamentary majority which voted the 1950 law. Actually the obligatory clauses hampered the writing of any real collective agreements. The attempt to define the content of bargaining was not accompanied by any requirement that the parties bargain. A requirement to bargain in good faith is difficult to enforce. But the lack of any such requirement is made all the more conspicuous by the portentous specification of the contents of the bargain. Partly as a result, most of the contracts signed have been simple wage settlements—whose contents are not specified by law—rather than collective agreements. There has been little to bridge the gap between the rudimentary wage settlement and the ambitious collective agreement.

For the unions the compulsory clauses were to be the opportunity for improving the rights they already had by legislation, both on pecuniary questions and on representation rights. Employers have taken a different view. The law already requires a great deal of them. In the area of wages and fringe benefits, it provides for a minimum wage which affects wages at all levels, it sets overtime rates over the basic 40-hour week, it calls for vacations with pay, dismissal notices, and dismissal wages. It sets requirements (hardly enforced now) for government approval of work schedules over forty hours a week and of layoffs. For certain industries it adds special requirements, for example, in the building trades, the payment for time lost by bad weather. In the area of employee representation, it requires the election of shop stewards and plant committees.

"We are already hemmed in by a system of regulation which we no doubt owe as much to the excessive power of government bureaus, encouraged by the war, as to our national mania to legislate on everything and for everybody," complained Pierre Waline, leading official of the national metal trades association, one of the ablest and most reasonable exponents of the employer position.[1] "The competition of our political parties in the pursuit of social progress," he noted, with irony, as another reason for the amount of legislation. Why, he asked, did the 1950 law "add to rules of our labor code, which are considered 'untouchable,' contractual requirements which would make their load even heavier? Instead of forcing the parties concerned to build monuments for which they do not have the materials—these having already been employed in the construction of an imposing legislative edifice—logic would have indicated leaving the greatest latitude to the parties concerned so that they might profit by every occasion to build a few more modest but useful structures, and thus to resume the habit of collective bargaining."

Given the power relations since bargaining resumed, few of the "monuments" Waline decried have been built. The most common structures have been simple wage settlements. The 1936 collective bargaining law had been followed by the writing of thousands of collective agreements. The 1950 law resulted in comparatively few. As if to underline the inability of the unions to win agreements, agreements of the 1936 period remained nominally in force in many industries and many areas of the country.[2] They had become, however, statements merely of customs and usages, where the law had not gone beyond their provisions; of course they no longer regulated wage scales. It was hardly of good

---

[1] Pierre Waline, "Le Patronat français et les conventions collectives," *Revue économique*, vol. 2, no. 1, February 1951, pp. 25-34.

[2] They had remained in force, except for wage and other provisions contrary to the law or official regulation, since the beginning of the war.

augury that the first agreement negotiated in 1950 was not in trade or
industry but between the Archbishopric of Paris and a CFTC union representing the sacristans of the diocese.[3] More than three years of intermittent negotiation all over France produced not a single collective
agreement in the most important branch of private employment; the
first metal industries agreement was not signed until mid-1953 (in the
Lille area). And this agreement was signed by only one of the workers'
unions plus the CGC. By June 1953, only 169 collective agreements and
306 annexes had been signed,[4] and a number of these covered fields of
slight industrial importance.

The national collective agreements and even the regional and local
agreements have to a considerable extent merely codified the usages of
the industry, and repeated the provisions of legislation and regulation
with what a union leader called "grammatical improvements." The chief
gains made by the unions have been in fringe benefits: added dismissal
pay, dismissal pay for production workers equal to that already given
white collar employees, longer paid vacations, and other advantages associated with seniority. Some agreements call for consultation on the
necessity for layoffs, and engagements by employer associations to make
an effort to find employment for displaced workers. A rare gain was the
provision in the national oil agreement (signed by the CFTC, FO, and
the CGC in 1953) for overtime pay higher than the legally required
premium rates. In many cases the employers have insisted that the
collective agreement exclude wage rates, leaving those to determination
by wage agreements or unilateral decision at lower levels. "It is true
that this collective agreement has no wage schedule," said the CFTC
union after signing the national chemical industries agreement. "Why?
The reason is known to all our comrades who have taken the trouble to
analyze the situation: the weakness of the unions."[5]

The 1946 collective bargaining law had been still-born because it permitted no wage bargaining. Under the 1950 law, employers were at first
willing to negotiate on little but wages. As they surmised, wages were
what really interested workingmen. When they received wage adjustments, workers, including most union members, showed little determination to press for the institutional content of agreements about which
their leaders talked.[6] Most contracts have been brief and rudimentary

---

[3] The CFTC had to explain to the archbishop that the closed shop clause he sought
was against the law.

[4] Information from the Ministry of Labor, June 1953.

[5] *Chimie: Informations,* January 1953, p. 11.

[6] For one union leader's candid appraisal of the situation, see Charles Savouillan
(CFTC metal workers), "Hausse des prix et conventions collective," *La Vie intellectuelle,* June 1951, pp. 75-78.

wage settlements. The text of a typical agreement is given in Appendix F. The law's provision for such contracts was rather an afterthought. It had been contemplated that they would serve as a stop gap pending the conclusion of collective agreements, not as the common form of contract. By June 1953, the number of wage settlements recorded was 3,467.[7]

The large number of wage settlements gives a false idea of the extent to which wages are really determined by contract. The settlements, mostly area-association-wide, give only minimum wage scales. In certain areas and industries, particularly those which pay chiefly by the hour, actual wages remain close to the contractual scales. In others, particularly where various forms of bonus and incentive pay systems are in effect, as in the metal industries, actual wages are considerably above the contract minima. In areas with a high percentage of skilled labor, such as the Paris Region, the gap between contract minima and effective wages is highest. During the life of an agreement many raises may be given by individual employers. These may follow union agitation and stoppages, but they are most often accorded unilaterally by the employer, or stated in a purely verbal "agreement," not contractually negotiated. The Paris metal trades employers in September 1951, failing to sign a wage settlement with the unions, adopted association "recommendations" for increases to bring the minimum rates for skilled labor to 155.25 francs an hour. By February 1953, although there had been no new recommendation or contract, skilled workers were averaging 190.49 francs.[8]

WAGE BARGAINING

Area bargaining fortifies the tendency to align the contract wage scales (or unilateral recommendations) of employer associations on the wages of the marginal concern. More successful or forward-looking enterprises, or firms facing stronger unions, may grant larger fringe benefits or higher wages, either in straight rates or—more frequently— through incentive payment schemes and bonuses. But in general association wage rates are set in line with the ability to pay, real or fancied, of the marginal enterprise. Even where there are departures from such minima, association rates give the tone to actual wage rate movements.

Information on wage rates and earnings is, like other business information, usually well-guarded. What Alfred Sauvy calls a "sort of property right in figures" is extended from the single firm to the trade asso-

---

[7] Ministry of Labor, June 1953.
[8] *L'Usine nouvelle*, May 14, 1953, data of the employer association.

ciation.[9] "The freedom of the secret is perhaps the freedom French firms cherish most."[10] (As one consequence, the public may get the idea that profits are larger than they are.) "On the employer side," wrote a leading industrialist, "we have always attached excessive weight to secrecy. This is the heritage no doubt of a peasantry for centuries exploited by an insatiable fisc."[11] The heritage is also that of the family-structured firm, which inspires many an entrepreneur to keep three sets of books, one for the state and other outsiders, one for his family, and one for himself.[12] "The resemblance between the entrepreneurial techniques of the large impersonal corporation and the modest family based firm" is so great, David Landes points out, that "one is tempted to describe the former as the latter writ large."[13] A change in businesss attitudes is hopefully affirmed by a new business publication: "People have understood that by wishing to hide everything, they have concealed the very reason of the enterprise, which is to serve."[14]

Price policy parallels employer wage policy. In practice inefficiency as well as smallness, low wages as well as high profit margins, have been protected by "a policy of excessive prudence."[15] With competition feeble, the capacities of the marginal firm are often determining. Despite the great disparities in costs of production, the more efficient do not displace the less efficient. "By price agreements or more frequently still by unconscious adaptation to the social milieu," the best equipped firms sell at prices permitting the marginal firms to survive.[16] The practice has been encouraged by the government's criteria in price-fixing: "Prices must correspond to the average necessary to all enterprises to live," ac-

[9] *Le Pouvoir et l'opinion* (Paris, 1949), p. 76.
[10] Louis R. Franck, "Planisme français et démocratie," *Revue économique*, vol. 4, no. 2, March 1953, p. 217.
[11] M. Detoeuf, *Figaro*, May 5, 1945. Detoeuf added: "The passion, the mania even, of secrecy is not restricted to employers. It corrupts all groups."
[12] David S. Landes, "The Statistical Study of French Crises," *Journal of Economic History*, vol. 10, no. 2, November 1950, p. 202, note 18. His remark is based on long study of family business archives in France.
[13] "French Business and the Businessman: A Social and Cultural Analysis," *Modern France*, pp. 346-347.
The importance of secrecy in French business is underlined by contrast in the comments of French visitors, notably employer and technician members of ECA-MSA technical assistance teams, on the comparative openness of communication of American business with workers, government, and other business concerns. For a published statement, see Première Mission aux Etats-Unis de la Construction Electrique (Matériel d'Equipement), *Rapport présenté à M. le Commissaire Général du plan de modernisation et d'équipement* (Paris, 1949), p. 13.
[14] "Pourquoi nous lançons *Entreprise*," advertisement in *Le Monde*, March 31, 1953.
[15] See the searching analysis of the economy in Ministry of Finance, *Rapport sur les Comptes Provisoires de la Nation . . . , 1951 et 1952*, (Paris, 1953).
[16] Louis R. Franck, *Revue économique*, March 1953, p. 218.

cording to the Director of Price Control.[17] Business practice and government policy combine in what Premier René Pleven, a conservative businessman, called "the worst form of controlled economy, which permits inefficient producers to exist without seeking progress, and others to make excessive profits, all to the detriment of the community. The price of liberty is competition."[18]

The problem is perhaps even graver in distribution than in production. "Let us face it sincerely," said a leader of the National Council of Commerce, "what has been the line of trade association policy for years now? Whether on taxes, on legislative regulation, or on the obstacles put in the way of initiative, it is for the benefit of the laggards that we have done our utmost to delay the march of progress, to bar innovations."[19]

Against this "marginalism in reverse"[20] the unions have done little, even less than they might do. The CGT seeks to identify itself with small business against large, and with domestic firms against any foreign competition. FO and the CFTC have passed resolutions condemning to extinction the inefficient enterprises, particularly in distribution, which drag down the standards of wages and slow down the economy, but these declarations remain platonic. Moreover, the unions are seldom strong enough to push wages up to a point where they threaten the unfit enterprises. Wage pressures toward greater efficiency are usually nullified by price rises; there is not enough competition in the economy, nor consumer resistance after years of inflation, to prevent the price rises. "The undifferentiated character of wage increases," said the *Report on the National Accounts*, "leads the firms capable of absorbing these raises without a modification of their selling prices to align themselves on the increased prices of the marginal firms."[21]

Unions anywhere must consider the possible effects of wage increases on the volume of employment. The French unions have an acute concern about the possible shutdown of any marginal enterprise. They have a fundamental pessimism, not altogether unwarranted, about the ability

---

[17] "The price fixed is a limit, a maximum price, which generally reflects the average weighted cost of production of a group of 'specimen-firms'; in theory it is too low for the badly equipped firms and rather generous for the best equipped: but, as a whole, it must correspond to the average necessary to allow all enterprises to live. Such a price is not an instrument of selection. . ." *Ibid.*, p. 211.

[18] Speech of investiture as Premier, National Assembly, August 8, 1951, *L'Année Politique, 1951* (Paris, 1952), p. 374.

[19] Pierre Benaerts, general manager of the National Council of Commerce, "Un Quart d'heure d'autocritique," *Bulletin du CNPF*, vol. 7, no. 93, February 5, 1953, p. 55.

[20] Maurice Duverger, "Les fonctionnaires du capitalisme," *Le Monde*, September 2, 1951.

[21] *Rapport sur les comptes provisoires de la nation . . , 1951 et 1952*, p. 105.

of individual employers to make adjustments to avert laying off help and about the ability of the economy as a whole to absorb those laid off. "Full employment is obtained at the expense of the standard of living."[22]

There is little of the geographic mobility which might make layoffs more supportable. The housing crisis deepens this immobility. Unemployment assistance is low and uncertain, going to only one in every four or five unemployed. Interunion competition increases the risk for any organization signing an agreement followed by layoffs. Employers naturally find their bargaining power enhanced by the shadows of unemployment falling across the union side of the bargaining table.

The extent to which collective bargaining alters the long-run distribution of real income among economic classes may be a subject of argument in any economy. In France the real income of the wage earning group as a whole, even in the short run, is determined more by price changes and the incidence of indirect taxation than by money wage readjustments. Employers and employer organizations often attach more importance to the level of prices than of wages. "The powerlessness of the opposing forces to fix real wages is an essential aspect of our economy," says a French economist. "An explanation appropriate to our special [economic] structure must be developed to take account of this 'fatality' which we call the wage-price spiral or the brake on increases in real wages."[23]

Bargaining on money wages is to a great extent a form of political and economic competition among different groups within the working class. It is also a baffled search by unions for the real sources of power to determine wages.[24] Individual employers frequently argue powerlessness to change wages in the face of association decisions. Associations insist they can bargain only on minima, and that actual rates can be determined only by each firm. Wage decisions may be taken out of the hands of both by government determination of the general minimum wage.

MINIMUM WAGE DETERMINATION

The legal minimum wage is vastly more significant in France, given its low wage levels, than in higher wage countries or in countries where collective bargaining is better developed. It is a basis for discussion of

---

[22] Pierre Uri, "France: Reconstruction and Development," in *The Economics of Freedom,* ed. by Howard Ellis (New York, 1950), p. 287.

[23] Pierre Bauchet, "Evolution des salaires réels et structure économique," *Revue économique,* vol. 3, no. 3, May 1952, pp. 301, 321.

[24] I am indebted here to a paper read by Daniel Bell at the Industrial Relations Research Association meeting in New York, May 1952, "Is American Management Mature?"

contract scales, even in the better paying industries, rather than a bare minimum for those unable to defend themselves by trade union action. An increase in the minimum evokes adjustments all along the line of the wage hierarchy.

The setting of the minimum wage itself turned out to be a matter of government decision rather than the collective bargaining process envisaged by framers of the 1950 law. The law empowered the National Commission on Collective Agreements to draw up a "standard budget to serve in the determination of the national guaranteed minimum wage." The cabinet itself was to set the final wage figure, in the light of the National Commission's recommendations and of "general economic conditions." The employer and union representatives who made up most of the commission's membership[25] were expected to agree upon the items in a standard budget and their cost. But with contract negotiations almost suspended awaiting a minimum wage determination, the parties were being asked, in effect, to agree on the key figure in the bargaining to come.

The possibilities of disagreement were maximized by the commission's undertaking two jobs better left to impartial technicians. One was the composition of the budget. First the commission labored to define its purpose. It came up, by a majority vote over employer opposition, with a definition which left everything as subjective as before: "a budget which assures, under all circumstances, and as a minimum, the satisfaction of those individual and social needs of the human person considered elementary and incompressible." This was to be a budget for an individual worker, not a family. From the theoretical "human person" the commission moved to a "man doing light unskilled labor," the hypothetical Paris "manoeuvre ordinaire" who soon became a stock character of social humor and pathos. Passions flared as employers and unionists debated his "elementary and incompressible" needs. On both sides there were experts, but they spoke as advocates. The atmosphere of future negotiations was envenomed by debates as to the need for an inside faucet or whether pajamas were a needless luxury in workers'

---

[25] Of the 36 members of the commission there are:

    15 Employers: 9 for private industry and commerce
                  1 for public enterprise in the competitive sector
                  2 artisanal employers
                  3 agricultural employers
    15 Workers: 6 CGT
                  4 CFTC
                  4 FO
                  1 CGC
    3 Representatives of "family interests"
    3 Government representatives, including 1 as nonvoting chairman.

budgets. Or: why a "good suit" if a "worker wore it only twice in his life, once to get married in, and once to get buried in?" Making up a standard budget in a country with the social residue of a feudal system was no task for a commission of the parties.

A second thorny subject, equally inappropriate for commission debate, was that of price quotations. The government, although maintaining several confidential series for its own use, then published no official cost-of-living index, even for Paris. Finally, Paris provided the only usable consumer price data.[26]

Naturally the parties could reach no decision, in a three-cornered fight among the CGT, FO and CFTC, and a fight of all three against the industrial and agricultural employers. With another cabinet falling apart on the wage-price issue,[27] the new government of René Pleven took the responsibility of setting a minimum of its own.[28] When the minimum was raised, twice in 1951, the government each time had to resolve deadlocks in the commission on the amount of the increase. The commission's inability to agree on any recommendation was labeled by some observers a failure of collective bargaining and democracy in industrial regulation. But those processes were hardly meant to determine the type of issues thrown to the parties in the commission.

Employers had resisted the idea of the minimum wage, arguing (with reason) that it would set off changes all the way up through the wage structure. They claimed, however, that substandard earnings were restricted to a tiny proportion of wage earners—5 per cent, President Villiers told the CNPF, and many of those only because of partial unemployment.[29] A government-fixed minimum, the CNPF said, would mean a continuation of government decision rather than freedom of wage bargaining. If fixed too high, it would be inflationary.

Of the several rounds of wage increases under collective bargaining, the magnitude of the first was determined by CNPF policy, the second by the initial minimum wage determination, the third and fourth by the increases in the minimum wage; the 1952 stability was a result (and

---

[26] For a summary of the commission's work, see "Les Travaux de la commission supérieure des conventions collectives tendant à l'élaboration d'un budget-type," *Revue française du travail*, vol. 5, no. 9-10, September-October, 1950, pp. 355-428; and Claude Lapierre, "L'Elaboration du budget-type et la fixation du salaire minimum garanti," *Droit social*, vol. 14, no. 6, June 1951, pp. 380-387. Since then the government has published cost-of-living figures.

[27] The Bidault government fell on the specific issue of government workers' salaries.

[28] For decree and circular of application, see "La Fixation du salaire national minimum interprofessionnel garanti," *Revue française du travail*, vol. 5, no. 9-10, September-October 1950, pp. 429-450.

[29] Report to general assembly of CNPF, *Bulletin du CNPF*, vol. 4, no. 54, July 20, 1950, p. 3.

cause) of the government's holding the price line. At the resumption of
wage bargaining in 1950, the CNPF offered figures of 5 to 8 per cent as
the maximum employers could afford without price increases; these indeed were the limits of most settlements. For the first half of 1950, the
general wage index showed a rise of 6 per cent.[30]

The first minimum wage was followed by a round of increases in the
latter part of 1950.[31] The increase in the minimum in March 1951 by
12 per cent followed an equivalent increase in the cost of living. The
September 1951 minimum wage increase was almost 15 per cent: the
amount exceeded cost of living changes, avowedly to discount future
rises. The anticipated price rises were not slow in following. Meanwhile
the general wage index rose with the minimum but went slightly farther: 15 per cent during the first half of the year, 16 per cent during the
second half.[32]

The president of the CNPF protested early in 1951 that: "In the
name of a minimum wage which concerns an infinitesimal number of
Frenchmen, the government is putting pressure on all the contracts concluded since last September, whatever their form or their date. The law
of February 11, 1950, officially supposed to free wages, has managed
to maintain under hidden forms a system of tenacious controls. The
utilization the government has just made of the 1950 law leads to a control of wages, blended with a sliding scale in fact, which is perhaps less
apparent but more dangerous than the post-liberation wage decrees."[33]
The increases in the minimum did indeed seem to govern the frequency
of wage settlements and the magnitude of wage movements. Put another
way, however, these were governed by the price increases which—once
again—dominated the French economy from the latter half of 1950 to
early 1952. Wage increases were largely a periodic catching up with
price changes; real wages were doing little more than holding their own.

Most contracts did not provide automatic escalation; the printing and
leather trades were two exceptions, although a number allowed a wage
reopening when the cost of living index went up "in a significant and
lasting manner," often defined as 5 per cent or more. The connection between the government minimum and private wage scales was neverthe-

---

[30] The index (with January 1946 as 100) stood at 297 on January 1, 1950; 309 on
April 1, reflecting most of the first round increases; and 315 on July 1, 1950. *Revue
française du travail,* vol. 6, no. 3-4, March-April, 1951, p. 245.

[31] The increases brought the general wage index at the beginning of 1951 to a point
12 per cent above July 1, 1950. *Revue française du travail,* vol. 6, no. 10-12, October-
December 1951, p. 557.

[32] Raymond Lévy-Bruhl, "L'Evolution des salaires en 1951," *Revue d'économie
politique,* vol. 62, no. 3-4, May-August 1952, p. 557.

[33] Georges Villiers, "Salaire minimum garanti et conventions collectives," *Bulletin
du CNPF,* vol. 5, no. 65, March 20, 1951, p. 1.

less clear. The minimum exercised a function "not of correction, but of impulsion."[34] One dramatic example: on Wednesday, March 21, 1951, the Paris metal trades association signed a wage agreement with several unions. On Friday the government raised the minimum wage. By Saturday the employer association raised the wage scales in the 3-day-old contract.

SLIDING SCALE LAW

The increases in the minimum wage came to a halt for a time in 1952, with the government's success in holding down, even slightly rolling back, prices.[35] To make his policy more effective, Pinay overtly opposed wage increases. He instructed the prefects to discourage wage increases or price rises allegedly based on wage increases.[36] With the temporary price and wage stability, Pinay enacted the sliding scale law.

The law of July 18, 1952 concerned only the government-fixed minimum wage. It provided for adjustments in the minimum wage in response to rises of 5 per cent or more in the Paris cost of living index. It did not require adjustments in case of comparable declines, nor did even strong imaginations contemplate such declines, despite the price stability of the moment. The law made it almost certain that the widespread tacit escalation in privately negotiated wage scales, of which the CNPF complained, would continue.

Years of agitation for the sliding scale illustrated the modest immediate expectations which went along with the millenary dreams of French labor. To be sure, the union and political leaders who had been demanding a sliding scale law were not enthused about it. The Socialist deputy Coutant, reporting for the Assembly labor committee, concluded: "The sliding scale, like the injection of morphine, never has cured the ailment. But giving the patient relief, giving him hope again, it can avert an attempt at suicide and, with strong medicine, offers a chance to save him definitively."[37]

Union leaders felt powerless to get the measures they thought of more fundamental value in redistributing income and increasing total national income. So they turned to the defensive operation represented by a sliding scale. They tried to do what every other group in an old, tired society did: protect the positions already acquired. On many occasions, with

---

[34] "Grèves de mars," *Reconstruction*, No. 37, March 1951, p. 3.

[35] The Paris consumer price index (1949=100) had reached its high of 148.5 in February 1952, just before Pinay took office. In July it reached its 1952 low, 142.8. (By December it stood at 145.4).

[36] *Le Monde*, April 17, 1952. See also Pinay's statement to a union-management delegation from the Lorraine steel industry, *Le Monde*, March 23-24, 1952.

[37] *Le Monde*, September 13, 1951.

seven rounds of wage increases between 1944 and February 1950 and four more by the end of 1951, workers had shown a proper skepticism about money increases which were bound to be nullified soon by price rises. But the only economic decisions they seemed able to influence were those of money wages. A CFTC leader of vision put it in these terms: "How can you hold it against people who have to work to live that they follow only short-run policies? In order to exist, wage earners yield to the temptation to demand wage increases. But other people, who are responsible for the country's destiny, follow policies of the same sort on a scale much larger and far more dangerous for the country. Don't they, for less noble motives, yield to the demands of vineyard owners, sugar beet growers, highway truckers, the CNPF?"[38] It is always possible to demand greater civic virtue or economic wisdom of labor than of other groups, but hardly reasonable or effective.

"Minimum" has been used here, as it was in the collective bargaining law, in the singular. Despite the law's apparently clear prescription of a single national minimum, the government in 1950 retained the five zones from the period of wage fixing. "Decidedly," a business journal wryly commented, "pluralism has become one of the essential traits of our social life."[39]

TABLE 8

ZONE DIFFERENTIALS IN MINIMUM WAGES AND AVERAGE WAGES, JANUARY 1, 1953
(IN PERCENTAGES BELOW PARIS RATES)

Zones	Legal minimum rates[a]	Average wage rates
Paris	—	—
1st Zone	3.75	11.7
2d Zone	7.50	17.8
3d Zone	11.25	21.7
4th Zone	13.50	25.0

Source: Ministry of Labor, *Enquête sur l'activité économique et les conditions d'emploi de la main d'oeuvre au 1er janvier 1953*, p. 9.
[a]See note 40, *infra*. The minimum wage for the Paris area in 1953 was 100 francs per hour.

Unionists demanded that the government abandon the system of zones. The government reduced the number of zones and several times narrowed zone differentials. But inequalities in bargaining power made inequalities in wages as a whole between the provinces and Paris much greater than those in the minima. At the beginning of 1953, the differentials for all wages were twice as high as those in the government-set

[38] Charles Savouillan, "Hausse des prix et conventions collectives," *La Vie intellectuelle*, June 1951, pp. 76-77.
[39] Max Réville, *La Semaine économique, politique et financière*, August 25, 1950.

minima, as Table 8 shows.[40] "There are no longer wage zones," a union leader said. "All that remains is the weakness of unions in the face of the employer desire to reëstablish them."[41]

Public discussion and the debates in the National Commission had all been in terms of monthly wages. The government announced the first minima chiefly in monthly figures, the latter based on the current average 45-hour week.[42] Actually, the only relevant minima could be the hourly rates, in the absence of guaranteed monthly employment.

SOCIAL WAGES

A large element removed from the realm of contractual relations is that of "social" and "deferred" wages. The postwar governments increased social insurance benefits, notably health insurance, and enlarged family allowances in scope and size to make them perhaps the most extensive in the world. Social security transfer payments, which had been 1.4 per cent of national income in 1938, rose to 4.6 per cent in 1946 and 10.1 per cent in 1951.[43] Employer contributions for social insurance (including workmen's compensation) and family allowances before the war amounted to about 10 per cent of payrolls. In 1952 they were about 28 per cent of payrolls.

French employers include a number of other labor costs with social insurance and family allowances when they speak of "social charges." Table 9 shows social charges, as defined by the Paris metal trades employers, paid in 1952. These amount to almost 43 per cent of the amount

---

[40] Differentials were actually higher than those shown in Table 8 because a transportation allowance paid to Paris workers (but not elsewhere) should be added to the nominal Paris minimum rate shown. The legal differentials shown in Table 8 were those fixed by decree June 13, 1951.

If one calculates from the lowest zone up, instead of from Paris down, the spread is much greater. E.g., if the figure for all wages in the fourth zone be taken as base, the spread between it and Paris (still not counting the transportation allowance) is 33 per cent rather than 25.

[41] Charlot, food workers' union, at FO national committee meeting, *Force ouvrière*, May 10, 1951.

[42] This included overtime at the legally established minimum premium rate of 25 per cent additional between 40 and 48 hours.

[43] Ministry of Finance, *Rapports . . . sur les comptes provisoires . . . 1951 et 1952*, p. 41, n. 2. Social security resources in 1951 were made up to the extent of 17.4 per cent by wage earners' payments and 82.6 per cent of payroll taxes paid by employers, p. 43.

For comparisons between France and other countries, see *International Labour Review*, vol. 67, no. 3, March 1953, "A Comparative Analysis of the Cost of Social Security," pp. 292-303. (The items included in the ILO's comparison are different from those used above, since they include public assistance and benefits to war victims and exclude certain French charges.) French expenditures were 13.7 per cent of national income in 1949, as compared with 11.3 per cent in the United Kingdom, 17.1 per cent in Western Germany, and 4.8 per cent in the United States (p. 297).

TABLE 9

"SOCIAL CHARGES" IN THE PARIS REGION METAL-WORKING INDUSTRIES, 1938 AND 1952
(EMPLOYER CONTRIBUTIONS AS PERCENTAGES OF DIRECT WAGES)

Category of Payment	1938	1952 (4th quarter)
A. Social Security		
Old age and health insurance	4.00	9.30
Family allowances	3.20	15.58
Workmen's compensation	3.00	3.02
Total social security	10.20	27.90
B. Other payments		
Apprenticeship tax	0.20	0.40
Payroll tax	—	5.00
Paid vacations	4.69	6.64
Paid holidays	—	0.40
Transportation allowance	—	2.38
Total other payments	4.89	14.82
Total	15.09	42.72

Source: *Bulletin mensuel de statistique,* Supplement, April-June 1953, p. 53, Paris Region Metal Trades Association data.

paid out in direct wages, or almost 30 per cent of the total of direct plus social wage payments.

The designation of certain labor cost elements as social charges requires explanation. The 5 per cent charge shown in Table 9 was formerly one type of income tax, withheld from the employee at the source, which in 1948 was turned into a payroll tax upon employers, in order to grant a scarcely disguised wage increase. The transportation allowance (required only in Paris) was another disguised wage increase granted by the government in 1948, when Paris bus and subway fares were raised. Like the 5 per cent shift from income to payroll tax, it has been merged into the wage structure. Paid vacations and the one paid holiday might be treated, as in the United States, as fringe elements of wages rather than as social charges, even though they are required by law. If the paid vacations be considered as an element of wages, the social charges become 32.4 per cent (of the enlarged wage base) instead of 42.7 per cent. Some employers have even classified overtime pay differentials, since they are required by law, as social charges. The assignment of certain payments to social charges can be debated only in the light of the use of the data. In terms of employers' total wage cost calculation, it does not matter how the individual components of the wage bill are designated.

There are, as a matter of fact, other items which might be included in the social charge calculations. These are the expenditures for plant medical and social welfare activities, which come to about 2 per cent of payrolls. The law requires employers to support these activities; some employers go much farther than the law's requirements.[44] Perhaps the highest percentage of such expenditures, the heritage of a long history of company welfare work, is to be found in the textile industry of the north. The Roubaix-Tourcoing textile association in 1950 estimated its voluntary "social charges" at 12 per cent of payrolls, for housing projects, supplementary family allowances, supplementary pensions and dismissal wages, apprenticeship programs, plant medical services, and so on.[45] It proposed to reduce these expenditures to 8 per cent, a figure almost attained by 1952.

Despite understandable employer complaints about the burden of social charges, the increased benefits have come, not out of profits, but essentially out of a redistribution of income within the working class, as between direct wage and social wage recipients. Bachelors and small family heads have seen their real incomes drastically cut to pay for the increased benefits to large families, the healthy to pay the medical costs of the ailing. "The working class functions as a vast mutual aid association in which . . . the poor help out the poorer."[46]

This phenomenon is made clearer by the fact that both (1) the total of real income going to wage earners (in the form of direct wages and social wage payments) and (2) wage earners' share in national income are about the same as in 1938. "Since the total mass of wage income, made up of the sum of direct wages and indirect wages (i.e., social or transfer payments) has remained stable in real value despite the considerable increase of the latter, it is evidently because the first have contracted to almost the same extent," as the *Report on the National Accounts for 1951 and 1952* points out.[47] As for wage earners' share of national income, since 1947 that has hovered at about the same figure (50 per cent) as in 1938.[48] (The wide margins of error in calculations

---

[44] See *Revue française du travail,* "L'Importance des compléments sociaux de salaire pour l'année 1950," vol. 7, no. 7-9, 1952, pp. 49-68; A. Devaux, "Comparaison des charges sociales dans quelques pays d'Europe occidentale," *Droit social,* vol. 14, no. 5, May 1951, pp. 329-335.

[45] Syndicat Patronal Textile de Roubaix-Tourcoing, *Année 1949-1950* (President's report to annual meeting), p. 5. A number of these activities—notably the housing program—were carried on in collaboration with the unions.

[46] Michel Collinet, *Lettre aux militants,* no. 1, November 20, 1950, p. 2.

[47] Ministry of Finance, *Rapports sur les comptes provisoires de la nation . . . de 1951 et 1952,* p. 46. See table page 45, n. 1, for estimate of real value of mass of direct wages and transfer payments, 1938 and 1946-1951. According to this estimate the total in 1951 was 104 per cent of the 1938 total, estimated in francs of constant value.

[48] J. Marczewski, *Rapport sur la comptabilité nationale française.* Organisation Européenne de Coopération Economique, (Paris, 1952); Pierre Bauchet, "Evolution des salaires réels et structure économique," *Revue économique,* vol. 3, no. 3, May 1952, pp. 312-313; Conseil Economique, *Revenu national et conjoncture économique, 1952,* p. 218.

of the mass of wage earner income and of shares of national income make refinements of observation of 1 or 2 per cent out of place.) The constant share of national income, however, has been earned by a work force about 10 per cent larger than before the war, representing a larger fraction of the population, working longer hours—a scheduled work week averaging over 45 hours in 1952, as compared with less than 40 hours in 1938.

Not only has social security not redistributed income from other classes to the wage earning group, but there has been a significant (though not statistically measurable) redistribution in the other direction. The agricultural family allowance system (including proprietors) has been financed largely from consumption taxes because of the government's failure to collect contributions from farmers. Many "pseudo-wage earners" have profited by the options of social insurance coverage: notably wives of business men insuring themselves as employees of their husbands and in effect determining their own contribution rates, and the large number of entrepreneurs disguised as wage earners for fiscal and other reasons.[49] On the other hand, to the extent that deficits of nationalized industry, for example, the railroads, arise from more generous than average retirement and welfare plans, other classes share the burden as taxpayers.

Family allowances are financed by payroll taxes. The weakness of the fiscal system would have made it difficult to finance them, as in the British Commonwealth countries, out of general taxation. With payroll levies for the various programs, there have been widespread delays and frauds in employer remittance of their own and employees' contributions. The Court of Accounts found that among small employers (less than 10 employees) more than half were delinquent in their payments. Among employers of over 10 employees, it found that as of February 1951, one sixth still had not made their December 1948 payments.[50]

The expansion of social security had come when employers were without effective voice in the nation. The CGT assured its 1946 convention: "The social security ordinances and decrees, except for a few shadings of difference, reflect the opinions expressed by the CGT."[51] The postliberation government, reflecting the community's bad conscience about workers' insecurity and low wages in the past, avowed the

[49] See for example Jean-Jacques Ribas, "Sécurité sociale et classes sociales en France," *Droit social*, vol. 15, no. 7, July-August 1952, pp. 477-484; Report of the Cour des Comptes, cited chapter VII, note 15, *passim*.

[50] Report of the Cour des Comptes, 1952 (chapter VII, note 15), pp. 156-160. See also Etienne Antonelli, "La sécurité sociale en 1951," *Revue d'économie politique*, vol. 62, no. 3-4, May-August 1952, p. 606.

[51] *Voix du Peuple*, January 1946, *XXVIᵉ Congrès ... rapports confédéraux*, p. 73.

desire to redistribute the national income in their favor, as well as enhance their security against the risks of illness, accident, and old age. In the family allowance program it was moved by the considerations of population policy as well as social justice. It was not in a mood to listen to arguments as to the cost of the programs in relation to the age profile of the population[52] and the nation's likely capacity to produce.

A few years later, with the power relations reversed, employers and the political parties of the right attacked the benefits and the administration of the social security program. After 1949, chronic deficits in some of the funds, for which the reasons were complex,[53] furnished the chief argument for those seeking to "reform the reforms." Employers complained that social security burdens were ruining their international competitive position, that the government was crushing them beneath a burden of taxation, in which they lumped the "parafiscal" social charges with regular fiscal burdens.

Social security inevitably became more than ever a political issue. A few industries or occupational categories bargained out medical, welfare, and pension benefits above the general levels. The most important agreement in private industry was the over-all contract between the CNPF and the CGC, implemented by a series of specific industry agreements, for supplementary pensions for the cadres. But many of the industries with ambitious private plans had been nationalized. The advantages their employees had obtained under private ownership were retained and extended under public ownership: notably, railroads, mines, gas, electricity, Paris transport. Where the industry's cost structure did not cover these benefits, most conspicuously the railroads, the deficits became lively political issues. The pension and welfare plans have been the subject of negotiations and strikes, of administrative and legislative action, in that twilight realm of collective bargaining and politics wherein are determined the conditions of employment in nationalized entreprise.

For several years before the return to free collective bargaining, government wage setting had been a cause of cabinet crises. In 1952, however, two cabinets fell, at least nominally, on social security issues. The Pleven government fell, at the beginning of the year, when it proposed to revise the railroad workers' benefits. The Pinay government fell, at the end of the year, when it proposed to meet deficits in the general so-

---

[52] Setting the retirement age at 60 in France was equivalent, in terms of the ratio of active to retired population, to setting it at 57 for England, 55 for the United States, and 51 for the USSR. Alfred Sauvy, *Les Chances de l'économie française* (Paris, 1946), p. 208.

[53] The old-age insurance program is on a pay-as-you-go basis. Fund accumulation would hardly be feasible at the rate of inflation in France.

cial security system by a transfer of funds from the family allowance system.

Higher benefits appeared to have a negligible effect on labor relations, unless it was to create dissatisfactions among workers in different industries as a result of the many complicated differences in health, welfare, and pension benefits. The industries with the highest benefits have had some of the worst industrial relations and strike records. The reasons were to be found, not in their levels of benefits, but in the key economic position and national operation which made them targets of union political drives. At any rate, in these industries high benefits have been powerless in themselves to improve industrial relations.

OTHER CHANGES IN WAGE STRUCTURE

Government wage-fixing policies, inflation, and social reform brought other great changes in the postwar structure of wages, so far much more important than those brought by collective bargaining.[54] Perhaps the most striking change was the decline in the position of the bachelor or small family head as compared with that of the head of larger families. The impact of family allowance increases on workers of varying responsibilities may be seen in Table 10, which compares a bachelor's earnings with those of heads of families of different sizes before and after the war. Family allowances begin to be important only with the second child. An important part of the allowance is that for the non-wage-earning wife.

TABLE 10

CHANGES IN AVERAGE MONTHLY EARNINGS, INCLUDING FAMILY ALLOWANCES,
OF PARIS METAL TRADES WORKERS, BY FAMILY SIZE, 1939–1949
(INDEXES, BACHELOR = 100)

Year	Bachelor	Head of family, with dependent wife and:			
		2 children	3 children	4 children	5 children
1939	100	109	120	130	141
1949	100	142	174	198	223

Source: INSEE, *Etudes et conjoncture: économie française*, November-December 1949, p. 73.

The spread in rates between the provinces and Paris was halved in the period of wage-fixing. The lowest areas, more than 50 per cent be-

---

[54] See the periodic wage studies in the INSEE's *Etudes et conjoncture: économie française*, notably "Taux, masse et disparité des salaires en 1949," November-December 1949, pp. 58-74; the quarterly surveys in the Ministry of Labor's *Revue française du travail;* the monthly economic surveys by Alfred Sauvy in *Droit social;* and annual surveys by Raymond Lévy-Bruhl in the *Revue d'économie politique,*

low Paris before the war, were by 1953 some 25 per cent lower. In real wages, their relative improvement was far less, however, for the cost of living rose even more steeply in provincial cities than in the capital.

Women's wage rates moved up in comparison with men's. The differentials were about 30 per cent of men's rates before the war. By 1946, when the national policy of equal pay for equal work was promulgated, the spread was about 15 per cent. At the end of 1952, it was 8 per cent. Women also benefitted from the general improvement in the position of the less skilled categories.

There was an improvement in the relative positions of such low-paid industries as textiles and agriculture as a result of concern with meeting minimum subsistence needs under wage fixing in the years of the worst inflation. Agriculture and mining gained during the early postwar years too, as industries with great labor shortages.

Changes in the position of workers at various skill levels were due both to the growth of family allowances and the compression of rate differentials. The latter are hard to measure, in the imperfect state of wage data, and at that can be seen only in hourly rate figures.[55] Where in the hierarchy of skills and occupations, and by how much, differentials were compressed is hard to measure. The effect of family allowances can be seen most clearly. The allowances, graduated only by family size and responsibility (and varying slightly by area), are the same at all wage and salary levels. They add relatively small amounts to the highest paid workers' incomes. But a worker employed at the minimum wage, supporting a wife and three children, in 1952 received about the same amount in family allowances as in direct wages. Table 11 shows the narrowing of the gap in earnings (including family allowances) between skilled and unskilled, and between the provinces and Paris.

The percentage of workers who receive family allowances is small. About 3.3 million out of 12 million wage earners receive some allowances, and of these 1.25 million receive negligible sums.[56] Given low

[55] On the types of wage data collected by the government, see Georges Lutfalla, in discussion of national income calculations, Conseil Economique, *Etudes et travaux*, No. 18, *Etude sur le revenu national* (Paris, 1951), pp. 57-58; A. Aboughanem, "L'Organisation et développement des statistiques sociales en France," *Revue française du travail*, vol. 6, no. 7-8-9, July-August-September 1951, pp. 405-436; and Raymond Rivet and Raymond Dumas, in Robert Mossé, *Les Salaires* (Paris, 1952), pp. 170-179.

[56] Estimate of the Union Nationale des Associations Familiales (National League of Family Associations), using figures for 1947, 1949, and 1950 for the various family allowance systems. According to another estimate, in the general family allowance system (which excludes agriculture and many special industrial systems), of the 8,300,000 persons covered—employers as well as workers—only 1,931,000 or 23.3 per cent receive any family allowances. *Droit social*, "Etude comparative des caractéristiques démographiques du régime général et du régime agricole des prestations familiales," vol. 15, no. 10, December 1952, p. 698.

wage levels and insecurity, there was little question of the need for the "socializing" of a certain proportion of wages in the interest of larger families, the aged, and the sick. But changes in relative positions in the wage hierarchy probably increased social tensions and may be presumed to have lowered individual incentives to acquiring greater skill and responsibility.

TABLE 11

CHANGES IN MONTHLY EARNINGS OF
SKILLED AND UNSKILLED WORKERS (INCLUDING FAMILY ALLOWANCES),
IN PARIS AND IN THE PROVINCES, OCTOBER 1950 AS COMPARED TO 1938
(INDEXES, OCTOBER 1938 = 100)

Family responsibility	Unskilled worker		Skilled worker	
	Paris	Provinces	Paris	Provinces
Bachelor	1341	1583	1207	1501
Father of 2 dependent children, wife not working	1733	2121	1536	1956
Father of 5 dependent children, wife not working	1994	2661	1784	2453

Source: *Bulletin mensuel de statistique*, quarterly supplement, April-June 1951, p. 48.

In labor relations, the expansion of social insurance and family allowances broadened the area of political decision at the expense of labor-management determination. This is an effect of any great enlargement of social security; the defects may be inherent in the purposes. In France the defects have been enhanced by the relatively low direct wage base, by inflation, and by the rigidities of the economic structure. At the same time, the importance of the minimum wage, the influence of government employment, and the intervention of public officials in labor disputes combine to make the government the chief arbiter of wage levels. All this further restricts the private collective bargaining function and sends the unions, as the party desiring change, to the government—or against the government.

Although employers deplore the expansion of the state's role, they do not mind having some union pressures and workers' resentments shifted from them to the government. Despite labor leaders' complaints, the state, even under conservative cabinets and parliaments, has been more responsive than employers to labor demands. So every group turns to the state, whose authority is omnipresent yet everywhere weak, by all held in disrepute yet sought by all.

CHAPTER XIII

LABOR DISPUTES

With us, the strike is the final resort, always used to win legitimate demands. The right to strike is therefore sufficient unto itself, and there is no need of any regulation which might diminish its significance.

> —Laurent, general secretary of FO railway workers national union, *Force Ouvrière,* June 12, 1952.

Regulation of the strike? It has been talked of for a very long time, that is true. . . One must conclude, however, that the question is not as easy to handle in practice as in the oratorical enthusiasm of the parliamentary tribunes, for up to now no cabinet has succeeded in resolving the problem.

> —M. Menu, in the Council of the Republic (Senate), January 28, 1950.

French workers, who received the right to strike twenty years before they received the right to organize, have long given the strike a special and symbolic place in their thinking. To be sure, the labor movement has changed vastly since the days when the general strike was to achieve the supreme social transformation, the days when syndicalism could be called only a philosophy of strikes.[1] But the doctrine of a living social movement is never homogeneous. Even then not all unionists saw strikes in the same syndicalist light; many saw them simply as a last resort in economic relations with employers.

The myth of the revolutionary general strike has been dead a long time. Yet the strike is much more than an occasional test of force, or a necessary threat of force, in bargaining relations. Table 12 (page 234) shows the extent of strikes in the postwar years. But the importance of strikes can hardly be judged in terms of man-days lost or of output lost

---

[1] Félicien Challaye, *Syndicalisme révolutionnaire et syndicalisme réformiste* (Paris, 1909), p. 8, cited by Leroy, *La Coutume ouvrière,* vol. 2, p. 638.

TABLE 12

MAN-DAYS LOST THROUGH STRIKES, 1946–1952
(IN THOUSANDS OF MAN-DAYS)

Year		Quarterly losses	Annual losses
1946			312
1947	First quarter	157	
	Second quarter	7,020	
	Third quarter	670	
	Fourth quarter	14,827	
			22,673
1948	First quarter	235	
	Second quarter	325	
	Third quarter	1,430	
	Fourth quarter	10,049	
			12,039
1949	First quarter	498	
	Second quarter	1,063	
	Third quarter	340	
	Fourth quarter	5,225	
			7,129
1950	First quarter	10,332	
	Second quarter	1,067	
	Third quarter	128	
	Fourth quarter	202	
			11,729
1951	First quarter	1,655	
	Second quarter	611	
	Third quarter	488	
	Fourth quarter	717	
			3,471
1952	First quarter	898	
	Second quarter	541	
	Third quarter	119	
	Fourth quarter	173	
			1,731

Source: *Revue française du travail*, various issues.

or deferred. Strikes are important (1) as a symbol, (2) as a political weapon, (3) as a source of constant uncertainty in labor relations, and (4) as a factor of confusion in interunion relations.

In any country unions have to know how to strike. In France, industrial relations retain so much of the character of class combat, rather than economic adjustment for "mutual survival," that the strike has an almost mystical value to many workers, noncommunist as well as communist. The strike is an affirmation of class consciousness and class action. It is an act of revolt, a moment of dissociation of the worker from the capitalist system.

Excessive use and misuse wear down the sharpness of the symbol, to be sure. Unionists know the ambiguities of the strike as a weapon; workers know the difficulties of long or excessively frequent stoppages. Free trade union leaders are aware of their own weakness in the face of employer resistance on the one hand and communist manipulation on the other. Yet the high regard for the occasional strike manifests the low regard for continuing organization.

The strike is important for its political uses. To the communists it is one means of waging the political battle on the terrain where they are strongest. The Communist Party disproves the old distinction that "the weapon of a party is the election; the weapon of a union is the strike." All the party's major drives have been carried on more or less through strikes and agitation in the workplace. In communist tactics, industrial war and peace are analogous to international war and peace. And, "to the Soviets, international war and peace are not two diametrically opposed and mutually exclusive phenomena, but two equally important means, supplementing each other in the Communists' advance toward their revolutionary goal."[2]

In times of civic decay, the strike is not the method of labor or of extreme leftist politics alone. It is an expression of the lack of consensus in the community, a form of warfare by the "feudal powers" within the state. Restraints on production and the flight of capital are more subtle forms of strike. Overt strikes are common too. Taxpayers' associations threaten tax strikes. Storekeepers, some of whom regularly hold back part of the sales taxes they collect, lower the iron shutters of their shops in protest strikes. Farmers and vineyardists strike or threaten strikes against government controls when prices are rising, for government supports when prices are falling. Mayors and town councils go on "administrative strikes" against national regulation unfavorable to local interests. Prelates in the Catholic west have called upon parents to withhold taxes until the church schools received subsidies. Group after group calls for some form of state action in behalf of interests no doubt legitimate. While awaiting justice, it strikes against the community.

Work stoppages are an irritant beyond their actual incidence. The overhanging strike threat adds one more element of insecurity to the lives of management and labor. Strikes are often part of negotiations

---

[2] T. A. Taracouzio, *War and Peace in Soviet Diplomacy* (New York, 1940), p. 219.

rather than a recourse when negotiations fail. The CGT, in particular, considers it legitimate to strike an employer at any moment and for any reason. It has denounced other unions for betrayal in agreeing to the short strike notice clauses (4 days, more usually, or 10 days) in contracts. Any strike is legitimate in the communist tactic of "transferring the center of gravity from the masses and placing it in the struggle of the classes."[3] Since the employer cannot free Jacques Duclos or end the war in Indo-China, such stoppages are a social abrasive. Seldom in France does a strike serve to clear a troubled industrial atmosphere.

With multi-union organization at every level, the strike contributes to the confusion of interunion relations. In most communist political tests by strike, the free unions—immediately or after a certain hesitation—have opposed the CGT. But where the political issue is not explicitly clarified, the other unions have often found it natural to associate themselves with the CGT in strike action and in joint strike committees. This is the result of rank-and-file pressure on the free unions, their desire to win economic demands and not to appear lacking in militancy, and their natural reluctance to take on the role of strike-breakers.

The strike highlights the uncertainties of union action. Leaders of any single organization cannot be sure their own followers will go out on strike when called out or go back when urged to. Unorganized workers and members of other unions may be among those who will follow a strike call. In a situation of clear union jurisdiction this might make for cautious leadership. In the French situation of rival unionism, it makes for irresponsibility. It invites minority organizations to call strikes which others may follow. It permits organizations to compete in militancy by frequent short strikes or scattered stoppages, then feel their way in the course of events they find it hard to predict or control.

FORMS OF THE STRIKE

Strikes take the forms which correspond to the structure and aims of the unions and the state of labor relations. Many forms are better adapted to political than to economic action. Although the conventional work stoppage is the most common, the sit-down strike[4] occupies a great place in labor thinking. The 1936 sit-downs remain the greatest and easiest triumph of labor memories. In recent years the CGT has tried to launch sit-down strikes to foster analogies with 1935-1936.

[3] Resolution of eighth plenary session of executive committee of the Comintern, cited in Taracouzio, p. 219.

[4] The French term is literally "occupation strike" ("grève d'occupation") or "strike on the heap," i.e., pile of work ("grève sur le tas").

Such strikes serve its "unity" campaign, for the recollections of 1936 are those of working class unity as well as working class power.

Although some sit-downs have taken place, the circumstances of 1936 cannot be reproduced in times when labor hopes are waning, not rising. There has been no wave of sit-down strikes. Nor have the post-war sit-down strikes had any of the quality of psychic release and folk rejoicing which made the 1936 wave "festival" or "kermesse" strikes.[5] They have been not spontaneous occupations of plants by the mass of their own workers, as in 1936, but mostly planned maneuvers by picked groups or commando raids with the aid of trusty characters from the outside.

A CGT handbook of documentation for union officers insists: "The right to strike carries with it the right to make the strike effective— otherwise it would be altogether platonic—therefore the right to occupy the premises."[6] As to the lockout, however, the CGT readily concludes that it is illegal as an infraction of the "right to work."[7] The sit-down, although not illegal as such, is not protected by the constitutional right to strike; the right of property is also inscribed in the Constitution.[8] The employer may go to court and ask for an order of expulsion, by force if necessary, of the sit-down strikers.[9] Or the public authorities may intervene on their own.

Strikers have remained in plants or mines without hindrance in a number of strikes. Since mid-1948, however, the police and, chiefly, the security troops ("Compagnies Républicaines de Sécurité"), the CRS, have usually cleared out sit-down strikers. It was the socialist Minister of the Interior, Jules Moch, who took the energetic steps of the first postwar evacuation of a struck plant. The evacuations have naturally been accompanied by some violence. Except in a few crises, the CRS have appeared with more than enough force to overawe the strikers. In recent years the strikers have seldom been sure enough of themselves to offer more than token resistance. In some cases non-strikers have themselves cleared out strike commandos who have forced their way into plants.

"Quickie" strikes, walkouts or demonstrations of short or almost momentary duration, are a stock in trade of the CGT. They are particu-

[5] The term is that of Collinet, *Esprit du syndicalisme,* part III, chapter I.
[6] *Cahiers d'information du fichier confédéral de documentation,* July 27, 1948, section 12a, 11, paragraph 38.
[7] *Ibid.,* Section 12b, paragraph 6.
[8] René Drouillat and Georges Aragon, *Code du travail annoté* (Paris, 1950) p. 25, section 49.
[9] Pierre Juvigny, "Les conflits collectifs: la grève et le lockout," in *Jurisclasseur du travail,* 1953.

larly suitable for a rapid succession of political agitations. They also
reflect the inability to wage decisive strikes. Other unions, too, have
in recent years taken part in numerous short stoppages, for economic
reasons: strikes of a day, two hours, one hour, even half an hour or
ten minutes. Among the strikes reported in government statistics, in the
first half of 1952, out of every ten strikes, 8 lasted less than a week, 5
less than a day, and 2 less than an hour.[10] Brief stoppages are sometimes
called to add pressure when a union delegation or a group of stewards
or plant committee delegates is meeting with the employer. There is
even an occasional brief strike whose first demand is payment for time
lost by the strike. These brief stoppages are probably self-defeating.
Employers usually refuse to continue discussions with a plant delegation
when notified their employees have walked out for the moment. More
important, the value of the strike for serious tests with employers is
degraded by its nagging overuse on minor occasions. The concept of
the strike as an ultimate force to be held in reserve is superseded by a
repetitive ritual concept: the enemy must be annoyed at any and all
times. The right to strike is frittered away by the rite of the strike.

The slowdown, rule-book, or nuisance strike is a natural in government administration. Customs officials a few years ago staged two
strikes within a period of months. In the first, they hit the government
by simply omitting inspection for customs or for the currency control
then required. In the second, they enforced the regulations with a
thoroughness that clogged all the inspection points. Paris traffic police-
men on one occasion in 1950 manifested their impatience with delays in
reclassification by excessively zealous observation of the book of rules,
snarling traffic hopelessly at a well-chosen series of bottleneck intersec-
tions. In a postal workers' slowdown, the FO union urged its followers
to hold up only official, not private, letters.

Frustrated with the long wait for promised pay raises, a group of
teachers in 1951 called an "examination strike." They refused to give
or grade the examinations for those *lycée* (secondary school) graduates
who, having failed the university qualifying examinations in the spring,
are permitted a second try in the fall. The incident, with the plight of
its third party victims, caused bitter but inconclusive argument over
the right to strike and the duties that accompany public employees'
rights. In the traditional language of the democratic French left, the
Paris *Franc-Tireur* had affirmed: "The rights of the State can be
invoked only when the State is right."[11] But the question put by a

---

10 *Revue française du travail*, vol. 7, nos. 7-9, 1952, p. 103.
11 March 11-12, 1950.

group of the striking teachers summed up the social impasse: "How can we make effective our rights, which are systematically disregarded, without infringing on the duties which balance them?"[12]

Violence is more often a matter between strikers and troops or police than between strikers and nonstrikers. In the general strike of 1947 and the coal strike of 1948, however, there was considerable violence by roving squads of strong-arm men, strikers and others, against opponents of the stoppages. The CGT and the Communist Party have made considerable use of foreigners—Poles, North Africans, and Spanish republican exiles—as shock troops and rioters. Many of them, particularly the Spaniards, had extensive experience in the French resistance as well as in the Spanish civil war. Tough, rootless, and discontented, these men are—in the Communist calculation—expendable.[13] The response of the authorities has been to deport considerable numbers of noncitizens caught in riots or suspected of rough work in strikes or of conspiratorial activity.[14]

One Communist aim has been to induce repression and create martyrs. When a building trades worker was killed in the course of an unauthorized protest parade during a strike in Brest, the government was accused of "shooting down Frenchmen with the arms furnished by the American imperialists."[15] This could be hailed as proof of "the haste with which the war-mongers have recourse to fascist methods to prepare their anti-Soviet aggression."

The police and security troops have not been entirely unhelpful to this obvious aim. Often under considerable physical provocation, they have been rough—by the testimony of non-Communists—on demonstrators and strikers. The police beat up several worker-priests, who, in their usual workingmen's clothes, joined in the anti-Ridgway demonstrations in 1952. In a sharp exchange of letters with the prefect of police, the archbishop of Paris, although regretting the presence of worker-priests at such a manifestation, "refused to admit that men, whoever they might be, should after their arrest suffer treatment unbefitting human dignity."[16] Considering the bitterness of feeling in France, it is perhaps remarkable that the outbursts of violence, at least of fatal violence, in the years since 1948 have been no greater and Communist martyrs no more numerous.

---

[12] Le Monde, October 11, 1951, letter to the editor.
[13] Especially since many of the Spanish exiles have shown an inferior adaptation to Communist discipline.
[14] Spanish refugees have been deported not to Spain but to eastern Europe.
[15] L'Humanité, April 18, 1950.
[16] Communiqué of archbishopric of Paris, Le Monde, June 13, 1952.

The extent of sabotage is of course not public knowledge. As an adjunct to strikes there have been only a few spectacular instances. The worst was that in the 1947 general strike which wrecked the Paris-Tourcoing express. The CGT has proved to its own satisfaction that damage to plant or property in strikes is always a matter of "provocation." Thus when police and troops cleared the Bergougnan plant in Clermont-Ferrand after a week's occupation in 1948, the CGT claimed the plant was pillaged by those who cleared out the strikers. One of the reasons for the use of the sit-down strike, the CGT declares, is that "it permits the guarding of the factory and machines against any provocation."[17]

No legal requirements surround the strike call, except for the conciliation requirements, generally honored in the breach. A preferred method of the CGT (after it has taken its own decision) is the mass meeting open to all workers regardless of union affiliation or nonaffiliation. Such a meeting lends itself to control by vigorous orators, well-placed activists, and show-of-hands voting. Mass meetings give opportunity for manipulation of the unorganized, a raw material to whose working the CGT has long addressed itself, and for CGT appeals over the heads or under the noses of rival union leaders to their members.

Strike votes seemed for a few years to be growing into a standard practice. After the CGT leadership set out to "consult all workers" in its own way in the 1947 general strike, FO and the CFTC countered by calling for secret ballots open to all employees. In 1950, the CGT, alone or with other unions, organized and ran numerous strike votes. Where it could, the CGT (with the aid of party factory cells) tried to stop work as soon as it could claim 51 per cent of any unit in a plant in favor of a walkout—pulling men off the job without waiting for plantwide or areawide returns.[18] In self-protection many employers called upon the Ministry of Labor inspectors to supervise voting, count the ballots, and in some cases to phrase or rephrase the strike questions; such voting was by secret ballot open to all employees. By permitting its labor inspectors to carry on this activity, the government gave quasi-official approval to the strike referendum. The practice has not been sanctioned by any law or regulation. It has been used much less fre-

---

[17] *Cahiers d'information du fichier confédéral de documentation,* July 27, 1948, Section 12a, 11, paragraph 36.

[18] See, for example, FO national metal workers' union, *La Métallurgie syndicaliste,* "Expliquons-nous," April 1950, p. 1. For an interesting discussion of the pros and cons of plantwide or areawide strike votes, see CFTC national metal workers' union, executive report to the 1950 convention, p. 65.

quently since 1950, usually at the demand of unions or of public authorities opposed to strike action.

When the referendum was in vogue, voting might determine the return to work as well as the strike call. The CGT, as part of the business of keeping things stirred up in the plants, has frequently demanded that the terms of settlement be ratified in open meetings of all workers, but this has been for purposes of agitation not ratification. By 1953 the practice of membership referenda, either for strike calls or on settlement terms, was no longer common.

FINANCING STRIKES

Labor is materially unprepared for long strikes: the organizations because of their low dues and financial anemia, the individual members because of the thin margin of economic safety on which most live.

The CGT's financing of strikes is naturally shrouded in considerable mystery. In the 1948 coal strike, Communists and anti-Communists gave publicity to financing from outside France. The Communists published figures from day to day on the millions of francs coming from all over the world (chiefly the Soviet orbit), to cheer the strikers with international proletarian solidarity.[19] The Minister of the Interior, Jules Moch, gave the National Assembly the details of transfers of money to French Communist sources through a medium remote from proletarian solidarity, namely the Banque Commerciale pour l'Europe du Nord, owned by two Soviet state banks.[20]

Some of the talk of vast sums being poured in from outside is no doubt exaggerated. Since 1948 the CGT and the Communist Party, which have had to curtail or suspend a number of publications, have had difficulty financing strike movements. That is one reason for their emphasis on short stoppages and nuisance demonstrations.

Neither the struggling new FO organization nor the CFTC has built up any real strike funds. The CFTC began to move in that direction when the confederation voted a small monthly assessment earmarked for organizing and strike funds. A number of national unions

[19] The CGT and party press reported donations from abroad totaling between 300 and 600 million francs, then equivalent to 1.4-2.8 million dollars at the official rate of exchange, or 1.15-2.3 million dollars at the "unofficial" or black market rate. Contributors included unions of Western countries, but the chief contributors were reported as the Czech unions. Despite the then recent Cominform breach with Yugoslavia, the Yugoslav unions were among the contributors listed.

[20] The largest number of French banks are still privately owned. Only the Banque de France and the four largest deposit banks have been nationalized.

For the mechanism and nature of the Cominform countries' contributions, see the report by Jules Moch, Assemblée Nationale, *Débats,* November 16, 1948, pp. 7005ff.; for the Communist Party reply, Jacques Duclos, *Ibid.,* pp. 7129ff.

have been following suit.[21] The metal workers' union launched its strike fund on the unsatisfactory basis of optional contributions, in addition to regular dues, by members wanting to receive strike benefits. The most important strike fund is the regional fund of the CFTC department federations of the Nord and Pas-de-Calais, started in 1950, with which the miners' and textile unions' funds are tied in.[22] It is backed by "reinsurance," the promise of support to meet its obligations, by the strong Catholic unions of Belgium. The CFTC in the north dropped about one-fifth of its members at first for nonpayment of the strike fund assessment, but by 1953 had recovered more than it dropped.

Strikes call forth no large publicity campaigns by unions or by employers. Unions put out only leaflets and relatively inexpensive posters. The union's chief problem is the staying power of its supporters and their families. The striker seldom has any cash savings to fall back upon. The inducement for workers to save, and the possibility of saving, have been drastically reduced by postwar inflation. Strikes may terminate with "the victory of the baker." Food is indeed the main consideration; other items are minor or postponable. Most workers pay very low rents (rent has a weighting of only 2.1 per cent in the French consumer price index), with payments generally due quarterly rather than monthly. In company-provided housing, neither public nor—in most cases—private employers are now likely to try to dispossess strikers. Workers seldom buy on the instalment plan, so there is no danger of missing payments on furniture or clothing. As for expensive consumer durables, the mechanical refrigerator or washing machine is as rare in a worker's household as the automobile. So there is no risk of having a valued possession recaptured by finance company or instalment dealer. In a long winter strike, fuel would be the only worry to rank with food.[23]

"Solidarity" is the classic, and often the current, answer to the question of how workers and their families can hold out during a pro-

---

[21] For an example of the statutes of a strike fund, see CFTC national textile workers union, *Inter-Textiles,* August-September 1950, p. 24-28. This fund proposed paying benefits, in strikes lasting more than three working days, which, in the highest of three categories, amounted to 200 francs a day plus 10 francs for the striker's wife and 5 francs for each dependent child. For a striker with a wife and three children, that would mean 225 francs, equivalent (at the then official rate of exchange) to the sum of 64 cents, a day.

[22] *Le Nord social* (CFTC), January 1953, p. 12, summarizes the first two years' use of the fund. One million francs were paid out; no large-scale strikes occurred during the period.

[23] Coal miners receive free coal, gas workers free gas, as part of the wage structure in those industries. Striking coal miners would therefore have some fuel, as would gas workers—unless they succeeded in shutting down the gas plant.

longed strike. Workers who are negligent about paying dues are willing to make sacrifices to hold out or help others hold out. One old, dramatic form of solidarity is the sending of children to the countryside or to a community that is not hit by the strike. This takes a terrible pressure from the strikers with children; in addition it stirs waves of sympathy where the children go. But the favorable connotations of the word cannot disguise the fact that "solidarity" in all its forms still meets only a small fraction of strike needs. Outside sources help make strikes possible. In the strikes waged by the CGT, CFTC, FO, and other unions in the Paris region between February and April 1950, outside aid of all sorts (including municipal strike relief funds) came, according to the CGT, to 500,000,000 francs ($1,400,000 at the then current official rate of exchange).[24]

Community collections in food and money are taken up in cities and surrounding farm areas. Merchants give goods or cash even if they hesitate to give credit. Temporary coöperatives may be launched to distribute necessities at or below cost.[25] Municipalities, even those under conservative administration, commonly vote strike relief funds; often they set up soup kitchens or dispense free school lunches.

The churches may also take up collections, tacitly making the distinction between strike issues and family distress. "The suffering which most in the world calls itself to the attention of the observer is beyond doubt that which weighs so heavily on a large part of the working class," wrote the Bishop of Tarbes and Lourdes, asking for collections in his diocese during a long-drawn-out strike.[26] In a church in Chambéry in 1950 the archdeacon announced:

This Sunday there will be two collections, one inside the church as usual, and one outside, for the needy families of strikers. There are complex economic issues into which we shall not enter. But everybody knows that strikers' families are in need; there are workers getting less than they need to live on even when employed. Of the two collections today, the one outside the church is the more important.

In the strikes of that period, such collections were particularly common. The French hierarchy had issued its moving plea for a living wage,

---

[24] L. Monjauvis, "L'Action pour les 3,000 francs dans la région parisienne," *Servir la France*, no. 59, June 1950, p. 31.

[25] In a St. Nazaire shipyard workers' strike, for example, a food distribution coöperative flowered suddenly, with branches in 40 of the nearby little communities from which workers commute to bombed-out St. Nazaire, did a 40 million franc business ($114,000), then folded up when the strike was over.

[26] Diocesan Bulletin of December 30, 1949, cited in "Histoire d'une grève" (anonymous but perhaps by a local priest), *Esprit*, vol. 18, no. 6, June 1950, pp. 1048-1049. Also cited by M. Menu in Conseil de la République, *Débats*, January 28, 1950, p. 383.

while the CGT carefully put forth only economic demands. Even in the general strike of 1947, however, Cardinal Gerlier had a collection taken up for the strikers of Lyon.[27] In order not to hinder such charitable efforts, it is common for headquarters of joint relief to be set up in CFTC rather than CGT or FO offices.

Family allowances continue to be paid during strikes, as they are during unemployment. "Even if the fathers are excited, the children should not suffer," the Minister of Labor is said to have remarked. Some of the pressure on the poorest workers and the largest families— frequently the two are the same—is thereby eased.

Employers, private and public, may subsidize strikes through the management-financed welfare facilities run by plant committees. The plant committees may continue the employee lunch rooms, perhaps at reduced rates, or operate soup kitchens. Factory coöperatives or buying clubs may extend credit. Sometimes a committee may even use its facilities and resources to help strikers elsewhere. In one strike wave, the overenthusiastic secretary of a plant committee called a meeting of its employee members to vote a contribution from its treasury for the children of strikers at another plant. He did not bother to notify the employer, chairman of the committee. As he explained in court, the employer would have been against the donation anyway; but his vote would not have mattered, nor would his arguments have swayed the other members, since they surely would have wanted to do the right thing.[28] The court did not take this matter quite as seriously as did the employer; it required only the return of the expended amount to the committee; a fine of 3,000 francs was suspended. In a concurrent civil suit, the employer was awarded one franc's symbolic damages.

The fact is that—in this land of class conflict—strikes are to a significant extent financed by the community, churches, government, and employers.

REGULATION OF THE RIGHT TO STRIKE

The 1946 Constitution, among the rights of the citizen, guarantees the right to strike "within the framework of the laws which regulate it." A formula "both pompous and obscure," Paul Grünebaum-Ballin, distinguished figure of the prewar arbitration court, called it. "It seems to promise everything, even the impossible, and leaves reality all in suspense."[29] It became standard practice after 1946 for new governments

---

[27] *Syndicalisme,* December 11, 1947, p. 2.

[28] "Jurisprudence récente en matière sociale," *Droit social,* vol. 15, no. 3, March 1952, pp. 181-182.

[29] Introduction to Charles Capeau, *Le Statut moderne du travail* (2d ed.) (Paris, 1951), p. ii.

to promise legislation on the right to strike. But seven years later, that legislation, for which the Constitution seemed to call, did not exist.[30]

The 1950 collective bargaining law made no attempt to regulate the right or practice of strikes, except for two provisions. One was the requirement for so-called compulsory conciliation. The other was a clause which, ending an old controversy in labor law, declared that striking did not constitute grounds for discharge.[31] In the absence of violence or similar misdeed, an employee did not sever his contract of employment by going out on strike. In the unfolding judicial interpretation of this important clause, its protection has been held not to cover slowdowns or political strikes.[32]

The chief restrictions on the right to strike are, naturally, found in government and in essential public services, although both doctrine and practice are far from clear or firm. Theoretically, civil servants have the right to strike. The 1946 civil service law was silent on the right to strike, although for the first time expressly granting government employees the right of union organization, which they had in practice enjoyed for two decades (except under Vichy). The Constituent Assembly specifically rejected the attempt to exclude civil servants from the Constitution's protection of the right to strike, which they had not previously enjoyed.[33] But the government may through ordinary administrative channels require them to work despite a strike call. The right to strike, even without regulatory legislation, is a general principle, modifiable like other general principles of the law. One modification may come through the application of the old principle of French administrative law of the "continuity of the public service." It is not clear whether the administrative courts (a separate and independent

---

[30] A 1947 law specified that the security troops (often used in strikes) did not have the right to strike. A 1948 law deprived the police of their usual guaranties in discipline cases in the event of a strike or "collective act of indiscipline." In 1950, in the face of Communist and CGT interference with French shipments to Indo-China and threatened interference with American military aid deliveries, the government enacted antisabotage measures more specific than the general criminal code provisions. None of these measures has had any significance for the general practice of strikes.

[31] Paul Durand, "Fin d'une controverse: les effets de la grève sur le contrat de travail," *Droit social,* vol. 13, no. 3, March 1950, pp. 118-126. However, for a recent decision allowing the employer permanently to replace striking workmen, see the Cour de Cassation's *Arrêt Spiteri, Droit social,* vol. 15, no. 10, December 1952, p. 582, and comment by P. D. (Paul Durand), *Ibid.,* vol. 16, no. 1, January 1953, pp. 29-31.

[32] For slowdowns, see Cour de Cassation decision in *Dunlop versus Plisson, Le Monde,* March 14, 1953. On political strikes, Paul Durand, "Le Régime Juridique de la grève politique," *Droit social,* vol. 16, no. 1, January 1953, pp. 22-29.

[33] *Journal officiel, Débats,* March 19, 1946, 3d session, p. 881; J. de Hulster, *Le Droit de grève et sa réglementation* (Paris, 1952), p. 192.

branch of the French judiciary) will uphold a government prohibition of a strike unless the government service in question is essential.[34]

The government seems to be moving towards a firmer distinction between permitted and prohibited strikes in the civil service based on strike issues. Economic strikes might be permitted, at least for lower-ranking civil servants. Political strikes would be banned, with severer sanctions for those disobeying orders to stay at work. The whole question remains wrapped in uncertainty, however. As the Conseil d'Etat, the highest administrative tribunal, was told by its "commissioner": "When . . . the constituent assembly has been purposely vague, the legislative authority systematically fails to act, the executive authority perpetually hesitates, then the judiciary alone cannot remedy the situation."[35] This is true particularly when the judiciary too is uncertain and divided, and responsive to a public opinion which tolerates civil servants' strikes.

In the whole area of strike control, the post-war experience indicates that the government can rely on its own administrative and judicial apparatus of repression only when the provocations of strike violence are extreme, as in the 1948 coal strike.

In nationally owned enterprise, as distinct from the civil service, the right to strike is theoretically complete. But in public utilities and essential services (public or private in ownership; most are public corporations), there is the sharpest restriction on the right to strike. Restriction comes from a law passed, not for the regulation of labor-management relations, but for industrial mobilization in time of war or the threat of war. The National Service Law was passed in mid-1938, after fourteen years' intermittent discussion.[36] Socialist and Communist Party deputies joined in the unanimous votes in both houses. The CGT dropped its earlier opposition to such legislation. It "approved of the law only inertly,"[37] but it failed to voice any criticism of those provisions which might be turned against legitimate union action.

The government was empowered to requisition all men over 18 and use them individually or collectively in public services or establishments functioning in the national interest. It could also requisition any individual or the entire personnel of a service or enterprise considered

---

[34] Jean Rivero, "Le Droit Positif de la grève dans les services publics d'après la jurisprudence du Conseil d'Etat," *Droit social,* vol. 14, no. 9, November 1951, p. 596.

[35] Conclusions of commissaire du gouvernement Gazier, *Arrêt Dehaene, Droit social,* September 1950, pp. 317-321.

[36] Law of July 11, 1938, *Journal officiel,* July 14, 1938.

[37] Ehrmann, *French Labor,* p. 87. For his discussion of the history and provisions of the law, see pp. 81-88, for its use in the 1938 general strike, pp. 118-120.

"indispensable to meet the needs of the nation." Severe penalties were possible for requisitioned personnel not reporting for work or quitting work. These measures the government might take in case of war or external tension. It was to act in consultation with the most representative organizations of labor and management. Four months after its passage, the national service law was used to break the CGT's 24-hour general strike. Applying the law for this purpose, the government of course did not consult with labor representatives. The 1938 precedent of nonconsultation has been followed since.

The government has used the law since the war in a number of gas, electricity, railroad, and flour mill strikes. In the most damaging strikes, however, it did not lean on this power. Probably it was too unsure of the response to apply requisitioning against the general strike of 1947 or the coal strike of 1948. Requisition orders since the war have been applied only to strikers; the struck industries have not been seized. Although the employees of public corporations do not have the status of government employees, seizure would not of itself strengthen the government's arm, since strikes against the government are not illegal.

By requisitioning, the government proceeds against the individual striker, not against the union as such. Requisitioning is often made deliberately suggestive of military mobilization, a government function for which workers still have respect. A gendarme delivers the notice to the requisitioned worker at his home, if possible early in the morning. It reaches him at a vulnerable moment, when he is sustained neither by the presence of his fellow-workers nor by assurance of how they will respond. Sometimes, however, orders have been simply posted on bulletin boards. For the worker who does not want to strike, the requisition provides a moral sanction; it interposes another discipline between him and that of the union.

The rank and file of workers have not protested violently against requisitioning as a curtailment of the basic right to strike. But, despite the attempted analogy with military duty, many workers have refused to comply. To take an example of the widest disregard, in the March 1951 railroad walkout only about 40 per cent of the 40,000 requisition orders were honored, the Ministry of Transport admitted. In the settlement between the Ministry and the free unions after the successful strike, the government agreed not to prosecute those who had disobeyed the orders. It seems impossible to apply penal sanctions in cases of mass disobedience, particularly if a strike is more or less effective. Although the administrative courts have upheld requisitioning as a proper exercise of administrative authority, the criminal courts have not been clear on the application of criminal sanctions to those disobeying requisition orders.[38]

The public is inured to partial breakdowns of government authority. Occasionally, too long or too frequently inconvenienced by strikes in the public services, it manifests a burst of impatience, as when a group of housewives in a working class quarter took a load of garbage accumulated during a CGT street cleaners' stoppage, and dumped it in front of the neighborhood Communist Party headquarters. But the public has shown little emotion against strikers' disregard for requisition orders.

With or without requisition, the authorities generally try to run struck utilities—railroads, communications, street cleaning, water, gas, and electricity services—of a health and safety character. Occasionally the government calls upon troops or police to handle the struck work, such as running trucks to replace the shutdown Paris bus and subway services. A Paris garbage collection strike in 1950 found the troops performing what an irreverent press called "maneuvers with pail and brush." In the coal strike of 1948, the troops not only protected miners willing to work but themselves took over some of the safety and maintenance functions halted by the CGT.

Picketing is less important in French strikes than in the United States. Meetings at the plant gate rather than picket lines are likely to be stressed. There is no special legislation which specifically refers to picketing. Regulation of picketing comes under the nature of police action. Its legal basis is in the old sections of the Penal Code on interference with the "freedom to work." These penalize threats, violence, assault, and what the law calls, in language which conservative political leaders long ago denounced as dangerously ambiguous, "fraudulent maneuvers." The law permits severe sanctions, but actually, when penal action is pressed, sentences are usually light and often suspended.

The courts have circumscribed the application of these restrictions, moreover. Peaceful picketing is held to be no "threat." False news is not a "fraudulent maneuver" unless accompanied by outward act. Interference with machinery is not necessarily an infringement of the liberty to work.[39] The highest civil tribunal, the Cour de Cassation, in 1951 reversed the conviction of a railroad worker for turning off the steam and stopping a train during the 1947 general strike. Although his act

---

[38] See Conseil d'Etat decision, *Fédération de l'éclairage* (CGT), *Droit social*, 1951, p. 597, upholding requisition of gas and electric workers in March 1950. The existence of a technical "state of war" has been held adequate to permit use of the 1938 law; this technical state has been repeatedly prolonged by Parliament, most recently, for an indefinite period, February 28, 1950. See comments by Rivero, "Le Droit positif . . . ," cited in note 34, *supra*.

[39] Juvigny, "Les Conflits collectifs," *Jurisclasseur du travail*, 1953.

might have been unlawful on òther grounds, it held, it did not frighten or coerce men who wanted to continue at work or resume work. This section of the Penal Code, said the high court, has as its aim "not the protection of the work in itself or the tools of work, but only the freedom of workers."[40]

THE REJECTION OF COMPULSORY ARBITRATION

When the Bidault government attempted to revive compulsory arbitration in its 1949-1950 collective bargaining bill, it met the opposition of both employers and unions. In no way surprising, employer and union objections arose out of different sets of memories and expectations.

Employers, looking back to the Popular Front, which had forced compulsory arbitration on them, and to the left-center governments of the first postwar years, assumed their customary role of defenders of laissez-faire. "Fervent partisans of liberty, we cannot tolerate the imposition of arbitration by law," affirmed the head of the CNPF committee on labor relations.[41] (At the same meeting of the CNPF, he suggested that the time had not yet come for a return to free collective bargaining.[42]) Employers felt that the unions would get more from the awards of government arbitrators "cutting the pear in half" than they could win by economic force. Although the government leaned less and less to the left, the calculation was sound.

Union leaders recalled that after they had hastily demanded compulsory arbitration from a Popular Front government, they had soon chafed under its application by an unsympathetic government. Now they feared impairment or loss of the right to strike. They feared too that compulsory arbitration would further reduce union functions and the economic reasons for union membership. Dissatisfied with government wage-setting, they—and even more their members—overestimated the gains they could make on their own. Employers and unions made their mood clear in the National Economic Council; for once the Council was unanimous. It strongly recommended to Parliament against the compulsory arbitration provisions of the government's bill.[43]

In the National Assembly, compulsory arbitration was deleted from the bill in committee.[44] Deputies praised the prewar system, but found the time was not ripe to renew it. "It must be in a climate of mutual

---

[40] Case of Gabillet, Droit social, vol. 14, no. 7, July-August 1951, p. 476.

[41] Bulletin du CNPF, vol. 5, no. 44, February 5, 1950, p. 16.

[42] Ibid., p. 17.

[43] Assemblée Nationale, December 15, 1949, first session, pp. 6894-6896.

[44] Under its rules the Assembly takes up, not the original bill, but whatever draft is brought out by the committee to which the bill is referred.

confidence, and that is not yet created," said a centrist deputy.[45] Compulsory arbitration is possible only in a régime of class collaboration, said a unionist from the MRP benches, "now we are in a régime of class conflict."[46] The Assembly buried an amendment to put compulsory arbitration back into the bill, by a vote of 176 to 417.[47]

The Council of the Republic (or "Senate"), less important of the two legislative chambers, amended the bill to require arbitration in disputes which "endanger the functioning of services and activities essential to the life of the nation."[48] This amendment the Assembly rejected lest it be interpreted so freely as to impair the right to strike.[49]

Some participants and observers could not help regretting that so little had been salvaged of the nation's prewar experiment in labor disputes arbitration. Probably, labor and management being opposed and the public indifferent, it was useless to try. With helpless indignation, Moro-Giafferi, renowned lawyer and Radical deputy, asked his fellow parliamentarians: "Do we legislate to lead or to follow?" Gazier, Socialist and former union leader, turned back the question: "Do you believe that the Assembly's sovereignty has anything to gain by laying down rules which are not applied?"[50] One authority expressed his profound melancholy at the spectacle of a Parliament which, he said, "confused the sense of realities with the refusal to act on realities." Contemplating the ground lost in the way of conciliation and arbitration since 1939, he put the peaceful solution of labor disputes down as one more on the list of war victims.[51]

Voluntary arbitration always remains a possibility. Outside of whatever contractual clauses the parties may agree on for arbitration of disputes—and so far they have agreed on almost none—the law invites them to submit to arbitration the points at issue when conciliation fails. To encourage arbitration by a background of agreed principles and the possibility of appeal from illegal or arbitrary awards, the law revived the National Arbitration Court ("Cour Supérieure d'Arbitrage"). It

---

[45] Degoutte, Radical, *Assemblée Nationale,* December 15, 1949, third session, p. 6928.

[46] Jean Dumas, *Ibid.,* p. 6934.

[47] *Assemblée nationale,* January 4, 1950, third session, p. 141.

[48] *Conseil de la république,* January 28, 1950, pp. 394-395.

[49] The power of the Council of the Republic to veto or amend legislation is only suspensive; it can be overridden by specified majorities of the National Assembly. The Council, elected by indirect suffrage, wields less power than the Senate of the Third Republic, although more power now than was contemplated by the framers of the constitution of the Fourth Republic.

[50] *Assemblée nationale,* January 4, 1950, second session, p. 121.

[51] Jean Rivero, "Conciliation et arbitrage dans la loi du 11 février 1950," *Droit social,* vol. 13, no. 4, April 1950, p. 151. See also articles of Adolf Sturmthal and Joel Colton, cited in Chapter VIII, n. 37, *supra.*

is composed of high officials, active and retired, of the administration and the judiciary.[52]

The court passes only on appeals. Those are appeals from private awards under a voluntary system, not (as before the war) from public awards under a compulsory system. Appeals may be taken only on legal grounds—"excess of power" or violation of the law—not on substantive issues. The court may quash a decision, whereupon the case goes back to the parties. Only if they go through arbitration again, and the second arbitrator's decision is likewise appealed, does the court itself—if it upholds the appeal—hand down a substantive award. This is not subject to review. The court closely resembles its active and successful predecessor under the 1938 law. The difference is that it has had no work to do; in its first two years it handled two cases.

Almost no contracts require arbitration of unresolved disputes; a few set up procedures which may be utilized if both sides are willing. The national job printing agreement sets up a joint arbitration board which attempts mediation first. For one of the rare instances of obligatory arbitration it is necessary to search as far as the contract of the Grenoble janitors; it designates the Labor Ministry inspector covering the trade as the arbitrator.[53] By mid-1953, a total of seven arbitral decisions under contracts had been recorded in all France.[54]

CONCILIATION

Having rejected compulsory arbitration, the Assembly wrote compulsory conciliation into the collective bargaining law. This has turned out to be compulsory in name only.

The obligatory conciliation procedures had been among the most successful features of the 1936-1939 labor relations system. In 1950, however, the Assembly refused to follow the government in specifying that disputes be submitted to conciliation, as under the 1936 law, "*before* any strike or lockout." Instead it declared that "all collective conflicts must be immediately submitted to the procedures of conciliation." The word "immediately" sounded peremptory, but it was far from clear as to whether there must be an attempt at conciliation before a strike or lockout.

The Assembly also rejected sanctions for noncompliance. The sanctions in the government bill were clearly too one-sided: possible loss of

---

[52] For organization of the court, Decree No. 50-320, March 15, 1950, *Journal officiel,* March 16, 1950.

[53] Renée Petit, "Le Contenu des conventions collectives," *Droit social,* vol. 15, no. 8, September-October 1952, p. 523.

[54] Information from Ministry of Labor, June 1953.

employment for workers, a mere token of disapprobation for employers. The Assembly was more sensitive to labor's objections than the temper of the times indicated; it had been elected in 1946, when labor and the left were powerful. It kept as the only sanctions for noncompliance those of public opinion. Even in countries of firmer social cohesion, such sanctions do not always compel respect for the agencies of conciliation or arbitration. In France, public opinion has not added much to the force of conciliation requirements.

The law envisages two possible channels for conciliation, one by agreement and one which it provides for. Each full collective agreement must include "conciliation procedures for the settlement of collective labor disputes which may arise between employers and employees bound by the agreement." The legislature pointedly refused to define "collective disputes." Some agreements refer to "individual disputes" as well as "collective disputes" (neither defined) arising out of application of the agreement. The collective agreements generally provide step-by-step conciliation procedure, an attempt to adjust disputes through bipartite boards at local or regional and national levels. The national textile agreement, for example, supplemented by regional agreements, provides that disputes not settled at the plant level go to a local or regional board for the textile industry as a whole or to a national board for the branch of the textile industry involved. The freight handlers and the road transport agreements take matters directly to national boards. In most cases there is no further procedure provided in the event of failure of the conciliation boards to reach agreement or to have their recommendations accepted. Multi-union signature of contracts is met by composing the conciliation boards of one representative of each union signing, plus an equal number of employer representatives. Ministry of Labor or other public officials are frequently designated chairmen of the boards.

The joint boards have accomplished a modest amount of useful work, but they have as yet played no important role. They suffer from imprecise definition of their terms of reference, an absence of community backing, and, more often than not, the lack of any willingness to compromise by the stronger party.

The law itself sets up machinery to supplement whatever the agreements may provide. There is no specialized conciliation or mediation service, although labor inspectors and ministry officials have a considerable amount of experience in mediation and conciliation. The formal machinery is that of tripartite boards, whose employer and union representatives (in equal numbers) are named by the Ministry of Labor from lists submitted by the most representative organizations. Officials of the Ministry, from the Minister down, preside over the boards. Below it are regional boards, which may have departmental sections.[55] Conciliation may be invoked by either party or by the government. Most often it has been invoked by the weaker side, the unions.

The tripartite boards have achieved little success in heading off or resolving important conflicts. They usually enter a conflict after it has reached the stage of strike or lockout.[56] They may provide an opportunity for face-saving by a party willing to settle; at other times they result in a public stiffening of positions as they are defined in formal meeting. The presence of several unions in many disputes complicates the task of the boards. The boards' record in terms of conflicts handled and settled is shown in Table 13; there are no data for the magnitude

TABLE 13
CONCILIATION BOARD RESULTS, MARCH 1950–MAY 1953

Jurisdiction	Number of disputes	Number settled	Number not settled
National	14	5	9
Regional	125	47	78
Departmental	281	92	189
Total	420	144	276

Source: Information from Ministry of Labor, June 1953.

of the conflicts involved. The statistics cannot take account of the conflicts attenuated by a clearer definition of issues or by the opportunity to get a public hearing, but not settled by the board; on the other hand, they tend to give disproportionate weight to minor settlements. In 1952 and 1953, the role of the boards was diminishing, not growing.

To its work on arbitration and conciliation, the 1950 legislature gave a curious quality of impermanence. The other provisions of the law were enacted into the Labor Code; the conciliation and arbitration provisions were deliberately omitted from the code. Sadly but hopefully one writer said, "Compulsory arbitration remains in the legislative mists, as long

---

[55] The boards are organized according to Decree No. 50-241, February 27, 1950, *Journal officiel*, February 28, 1950, with rectification March 5, 1950.

[56] The highest civil court has held that strikers' by-passing of the conciliation requirements of the law did not deprive them of their protection against discharge. *Etablissements B.A.C.C.I. vs. Barbanchon*, cited by P.D. (Paul Durand), "Nouvelles contributions au droit jurisprudentiel de la grève," *Droit social*, vol. 15, no. 8, September-October 1952, p. 533. Indeed the legislative history of the 1950 act indicates that the National Assembly specifically rejected such drastic penalties.

as the provisions excluding it are not graven on the brass tablets of the code."[57]

In the face of the weakness of the conciliation machinery and the inability of unions to slug it out with employers, there has been some increase of union sentiment, publicly or privately expressed, for compulsory arbitration. The CGT, of course, continues to be unreservedly opposed. At the other end of the scale, the CGSI since its origin has been in favor of arbitration, as a complement to its doctrine of superseding the class struggle with the "association" of capital and labor. The CGC has likewise supported compulsory arbitration; a strike of the workers' unions puts the cadres in an awkward position between the contending parties.

The CFTC gave support to a bill introduced by MRP deputies, which called for compulsory arbitration only in disputes where it was demanded by the union. One of the unions in a dispute might demand arbitration even if the others were opposed, leaving it to the Ministry of Labor to determine whether the union (or unions) demanding arbitration was sufficiently "representative" to justify the procedure. This would retain the best of both worlds for its union sponsors. But the temper of Parliament, as well as the opposition of employers to compulsory arbitration, made it unlikely that the bill would be acted on.

In FO, too, there were people prepared to accept compulsory arbitration as a lesser evil, as a means of "forcing employers to yield to the recognition of an injustice which an arbitrator would define." In 1953 the confederation again rejected the proposal, in what it termed "an act of faith and virility." But it noted that the rejection, "if it is not to remain a dead letter, requires powerful and enhanced methods of action from the unions."[58]

---

[57] Bernard Chenot, "Réflexions sur l'arbitrage," *Revue économique,* vol. 2, no. 1, February 1951, p. 11.

[58] *FO Informations,* no. 18, May 1953, "L'Arbitrage obligatoire," pp. 107, 109.

CHAPTER XIV

INDUSTRIAL RELATIONS AT THE PLANT LEVEL

> Every worker may participate through his delegates in the collective determination of working conditions and in the management of the enterprise.
>
> —Preamble to the Constitution of the Fourth Republic, 1946.

> Union action normally should not take place at the level of the shop. It should be placed at the level of the corresponding employer association, that is to say, at the local, regional, or national level.
>
> —National metal trades association, *La Discussion du projet de convention collective nationale dans les industries métallurgiques: Etat de la question en avril 1949.*

The least satisfactory aspect of labor relations in private industry is that at the shop level. In almost every shop or office of any size, there are several competing unions; very often a majority of the workers belong to no union. There is confusion between union tasks and those of the delegates—shop stewards and plant committeemen—elected by a vote of all employees. CGT politics makes the workshop a place of simmering agitation. Union officials schooled in the doctrines and experiences of conflict come up against employers stronger in concepts of authority than in wisdom of personnel practices. Employer hostility to unionism within the plant is both response to, and cause for, continued conflict.

GRIEVANCE CHANNELS

"It would be a good idea if we concerned ourselves in France with organization instead of hypnotizing ourselves with the *regulation* of labor," wrote Professor Scelle a generation ago.[1] The handling of griev-

---

[1] Georges Scelle, *Le Droit ouvrier* (Paris, 2d ed., 1929), p. 216. Underlining in original.

ances is a case of much regulation by law and little organization by labor and management. Few agreements specify any clear procedure. Full collective agreements must, by law, contain a clause relating to the "conciliation of collective conflicts." The formula is vague, and in practice it has not produced contractual procedures for the submission, processing, and final settlement of grievances.

There is no lack of grievance channels; in fact, there is a proliferation of channels created by government regulation. We may note first the shop steward and the plant committee, leaving both for discussion later. Although the plant committee is not supposed to handle individual grievances, it often does; even with good faith, the line between individual complaint and general condition is easily blurred.

For certain types of grievances, the worker may turn to the "conseil de prud'hommes,"[2] a local labor court whose origins go back to Napoleonic times. It is composed of an equal number of employer and worker members, elected by employers and workmen. In large cities there are specialized sections for major industries, or at least for production and clerical employees. The *prud'hommes* mediate, or if mediation fails, adjudicate "any disputes which may arise out of the *individual* contract of employment." This brings before them many disputes on dismissals, job classification, wage payments. Their broad jurisdiction stops short of "collective conflicts" or disputes arising out of collective agreements.

When the *prud'hommes* split evenly, a justice of the peace rehears the case with them and casts a deciding vote. In the many areas away from cities, where no *conseil de prud'hommes* exists (there are about 200 in the nation), the justice of the peace performs its functions of conciliation and adjudication.[3] The *prud'hommes*' or justice's decision may be appealed up through the regular court system. The union may help a worker prepare his case for the *prud'hommes*. In theory (often ignored in practice) a union official may appear in his behalf only if he works at the same trade: a throwback to the corporate origins of the institution. The *prud'hommes* on the whole function to the greater satisfaction of labor and management than almost any other institution in the process of labor relations.

For certain grievances, a worker may appeal to the Ministry of Labor

---

[2] Literally, the term means "council of wise men." The term is no longer literally correct: women have been eligible since 1908 to election as *prud'hommes*.

[3] For the functions of the *prud'hommes,* see *Revue française du travail,* vol. 5, special no., 1952, "Guide de Législation sociale: Les Rélations Individuelles entre employeurs et salariés," pp. 211-256; also Paul Durand, *Traité de droit du travail,* vol. 2, pp. 946-995. Specifically on the justices of the peace, see Michel Vasseur, "La Compétence des juges de paix en matière de contrat de travail," *Droit social,* vol. 15, no. 2, February 1952, pp. 106-109.

inspectors. The labor inspectorate has three quite different functions: regulatory, mediatory, and judicial. Its members inspect for the observance of all labor laws and regulations in industry and commerce, including health and safety, hours, and other protective labor legislation. They mediate and conciliate labor disputes informally, and preside over formal joint or tripartite conciliation boards. They exercise a quasi-judicial role in passing on the justification offered by employers for economic dismissals (for lack of work) and on the special cases presented by disciplinary dismissals, especially of plant committeemen or stewards.

The number of men carrying on these complex functions is comparatively small: in 1950 there were 343 members (including departmental and regional chiefs) of the corps of inspectors.[4] In the handling of grievances, the labor inspector often functions as might an impartial chairman, with a bent for mediation, under a contract in the United States, notably in cases of disciplinary dismissals.[5]

After unsuccessful strikes, the unions have repeatedly complained that employers were illegally discharging strike activists. In 1950, for example, the Minister of Labor instructed the inspectors to "use their influence to smooth out differences which arise." They could use their specific legal authority in reference to discharges of shop stewards and plant committeemen. For workers without such special protection, the inspectors were to examine individual cases brought to them "in a spirit of social conciliation, trying to intervene personally with the employer . . . to see to it that the penalties were not out of proportion to the gravity of the wrongdoing."[6]

The bipartite discipline committee is a grievance processing mechanism found chiefly in nationalized industry or public utility types of employment. Such committees, with employee representatives elected or named by the unions, are provided for by government regulation in nationalized industry, for example, the railways and mines. They are established by collective agreement in some industries, for example, the street railways and banking. In the mines there is a hierarchy of discipline committees, local, district, and regional, with a national committee at the top, to pass on appeals. The committees also have rule-making powers

---

[4] *Journal officiel,* October 21, 1950; *Droit social,* vol. 13, no. 10, December 1950, pp. 411-412. Inspections for labor law compliance are also carried on by some officials of other departments.

[5] For a good example, see "Décision de M. Megissier, inspecteur du travail, du 28 mai 1952," *Droit social,* vol. 15, no. 10, December 1952, pp. 688-689, and editorial reference by Paul Durand, pp. 653-655. The case involved a plant social worker, who has special legal protection against arbitrary dismissal.

[6] Circular of March 22, 1950, *Journal officiel,* March 29, 1950.

and conciliation functions.[7] In the street railways, the discipline committee has only advisory powers, and handles only cases involving penalties above a specified degree of severity.

Individual appeal to higher management is another possibility. Employers reiterate that "the door is always open" to individuals in personnel matters. Appeals may go directly to the top even in good-sized plants. Few employers have well-developed personnel departments; fewer give much latitude to the departments they do have.[8] Employers generally are not well disposed to the intervention of such "outside" agencies as the discipline committees or the labor inspectors. They prefer the worker's appeal and appearance in person before them. That "would seem to them a better protection of the worker's interests. It would guarantee that he would not be at the mercy of lower supervisory personnel, and that he would be able to present his case before the responsible head of the establishment."[9]

SHOP STEWARDS

The shop steward ("délégué du personnel") is normally the first resort of a worker with a grievance. The earliest stewards were the miners' elected safety delegates, established by law in 1890. Stewards were first set up in large numbers during World War I by the Socialist Minister of Munitions, Albert Thomas. The institution lapsed with the decline of unionism following the war. By the Matignon Agreement and the 1936 collective bargaining law, agreements were required to provide for the election of stewards. In the next three years, the stewards' functions and their hiring and firing were the cause of much conflict. With the war's coming and the CGT ouster of the Communists, the institution of elected stewards disappeared, nominally in favor of stewards to be named by the most representative unions. After Vichy, the institution was revived by legislation. A law of April 16, 1946 made the election of stewards compulsory in all plants and offices of over ten employees.[10]

---

[7] Statut du Mineur, Decree 46, 1433, June 14, 1946, as later modified. Drouillat and Aragon, *Code du travail annoté,* pp. 589-617. For a criticism of these and similar committees, see Adolf Sturmthal, "Nationalization and Workers' Control in Britain and France," *Journal of Political Economy,* vol. 61, no. 1, February 1953, pp. 43-79.

[8] For example, the head of a leading machinery construction concern, with 5,000 employees in an Alsatian plant, said he "really handled personnel matters" himself. Incidentally, the free unions in the city considered labor conditions in his plant quite good.

[9] André Rouast and Paul Durand, *Précis de législation industrielle (Droit du travail),* 3d ed., p. 123.

[10] Law No. 46-730, April 16, 1946, *Journal officiel,* April 17, 1946. See *Revue française du travail,* 1948, special no. 1, pp. 230-246, which includes the text of the law, and special no. 4, 1950, *Guide de législation sociale, les comités d'entreprise, les délégués du personnel;* International Labour Office, *Labour-Management Coöperation in France,* pp. 145-153; Rouast and Durand, pp. 149-156.

Since no collective bargaining was permitted at the time,[11] the law could not have restored the stewards via collective agreements, as in 1936, even had the unions been willing.

The scope of the stewards' functions is defined as the presentation of "individual or collective grievances which have not been directly satisfied, related to the application of wage rates and other occupational classifications, of the Labor Code, and of the other laws and regulations for the protection of workers, health, safety, and social insurance." Employers must give stewards fifteen hours a month on company time for their functions. The "head of the establishment or his representative" is required to receive the stewards at least once a month, and in "urgent cases" at their request. If they specifically request it, the stewards may bring with them a representative of their union.

More efficient grievance handling is secured in some plants by specialization of stewards. With management agreement, a number of stewards, usually those of a single union, assign their aggregate allowed time for grievance handling to one of their number. This gives him a substantial period, perhaps full time, to devote to grievance (and union) work. Similar arrangements may be made by plant committee members, who get twenty hours a month each on company time for that business. The worker may have the choice between taking his grievance to a steward elected from his own department, but belonging to another union, and taking it to one of his own union, but elected from another department. Management generally aims to establish the principle of grievance handling along lines of plant operations, rather than union affiliation.[12]

The methods of election and protection against arbitrary dismissal are almost the same for the two types of "delegates," the stewards and the plant committee members; they are therefore considered together here. The legislation is a compromise between the two extremes: making the delegates union representatives or making them independent of the unions. They are chosen by a secret ballot of all members of the work force, regardless of union affiliation or lack of it.[13] But it is the

---

[11] The collective bargaining law of 1946 was not enacted until December of that year.

[12] See report of national metal trades association (Union des industries métallurgiques, etc.), *La Discussion du projet de convention collective nationale dans les industries métallurgiques: Etat de la question en avril 1949* (Paris, 1949), employer draft of article 29, p. 21. This document, including both employer and union draft clauses for a detailed agreement, is a capital statement of the employer position. It is cited hereafter as *Etat de la question*.

[13] Election of stewards is by two units: 1, production and white collar workers; 2, foremen, supervisors, technicians and engineers. By agreement, management and unions may set up different election units. The number of stewards depends on the size of the establishment. There are slightly different requirements for the electoral units for the plant committees.

unions—the "most representative organizations"—which nominate the
slates of candidates. Only if a second ballot is required for lack of sufficient votes on the first, may individual candidacies be presented in addition to union nominations.

At first the stewards and plant committee members were elected by
majority vote. In 1947, the law was amended to provide for proportional representation of opposing union slates.[14] This not only gives the
minority unions representation, but also encourages workers to cast for
them the ballots they would hesitate, under majority rule, to "throw
away" on slates sure to be in the minority. Delegates are elected for a
term of one year.[15] The short term enforces the dependence of the delegates on the union, as does the possibility of recall. A union may recall
a delegate elected on its slate only if a majority of his constituency votes
approval.

The employer may not dismiss a delegate without asking the consent
of the plant committee. If the committee refuses its consent or if the
plant has no committee, the employer must ask the permission of the
Ministry of Labor inspector. Against the considerable possibilities of
discrimination other than firing, the delegates have no special protection.[16] Legal authorities attach great weight to recent jurisprudence
defining the legislative guaranty against arbitrary dismissal and the relief for the delegate dismissed in violation of the law.[17] But the courts
have also established their own supremacy in the matter of dismissals.
The plant committee and the labor inspector may exercise merely suspensive vetoes. From their refusal to approve a dismissal, the employer
may appeal to the *conseil de prud'hommes* and from that to a regular
civil tribunal; or (under a 1952 decision), he may go directly to them

---

[14] Law No. 47-1235 (stewards) and Law No. 47-1234 (plant committees) of
July 7, 1947, *Journal officiel*, July 7, 1947.

[15] A bill to lengthen the term of plant committee members to two years passed the
National Assembly early in 1953. *Le Monde*, February 5, 1953.

[16] A national conference of FO plant committee members, for example, charged
that some employers were "paralyzing delegates" by holding them responsible for the
same volume of production as other workers, despite time legitimately spent on plant
committee functions. *Force ouvrière*, June 26, 1952, p. 9.

[17] Paul Durand, "Les Problèmes posés par la protection des délégués du personnel
et des membres des comités d'entreprise," *Droit social*, vol. 13, no. 10, December 1950,
pp. 401-409. The law's remedies are viewed somewhat differently in René Drouillat and
Georges Aragon, *Code du travail annoté*, p. 732.

Almost every month's issue of *Droit social*, usually under the rubric "Jurisprudence
récente en matière sociale," contains recent decisions of the *prud'hommes*, civil courts,
or the two highest courts of appeals, the Cour de Cassation (for civil law) and the
Conseil d'Etat (for administrative law), giving the emerging jurisprudence on this
and related issues.

to ask annulment of the contract of employment. The courts pass on the facts as well as the law.[18] With the possibility of going directly to the courts, employers have been turning less to the plant committees and the labor inspectors, whose decisions in most cases favor the employee. This is in line with a principle stated by the most important national employer association: "It is finally the courts that should judge the validity of disciplinary punishments, not the plant committees or the persons concerned."[19]

The employer may suspend immediately a delegate charged with violence, sabotage, or similar illegal action, pending approval to dismiss. There are differences of opinion as to the gravity of the acts justifying suspension or dismissal. Wrongful dismissal of a delegate may be a cause for criminal prosecution of an employer for "wilful hindering" of the functioning of the institution of the shop steward or plant committee. Such prosecutions are rare, since they involve the difficult proving of intent.

For the delegate whose dismissal is held by the courts to be illegal, there are two forms of relief open. He may (1) get a court to pronounce the dismissal null and void, in which case the employer must continue to pay his wages. Or he may (2) accept the breach of his contract of employment as definitive, and claim damages. Neither remedy approximates that of reinstatement. The continued payment of wages, according to the emerging jurisprudence on the subject, appears to be required of the employer only for the unexpired term of the steward or committeeman. (Of course the employer may take him back on the job, and get some work for the wages paid.) The delegate's pay would thus be for a maximum of a year, often much less, depending on when in the course of his year's term he was fired. "We figure the head of a union activist is worth about 200,000 francs," bitterly remarked one union leader. If that is to be the law on continued pay, presumably the lump sum damages awarded under the other recourse will not be more.

No special guaranties protect the unionist who is not a shop steward or plant committeeman. His only recourse in case of arbitrary dismissal is to appeal to the *prud'hommes* and, if the employer refuses to reinstate

---

[18] Claude-Albert Colliard, "La Stabilité de l'emploi et les autorisations administratives devant le contrôle juridictionnel," *Droit social,* vol. 14, no. 4, April 1951, pp. 237-252. For a statement of the procedural requirements, see *Nicolas v. Michelin,* in which the Cour de Cassation upheld a civil court decision affirming a *prud'hommes'* decision to permit the employer to fire a shop steward for sabotage. *Droit social,* vol. 15, no. 4, April 1952, pp. 259-260.

[19] *Etat de la question,* p. 22.

him, to sue for damages for breach of his contract of employment.[20] Even if successful, this is usually a poor compensation for loss of a job.

In short, it may cost an employer a modest money payment and considerable effort to fire a shop steward or union activist. But if he is sufficiently determined, he can get rid of him. The relief for the individual is incomplete. The protection for the function of representation, while much greater than under the Popular Front legislation, is still minimal.

PLANT COMMITTEES

Another institution before which grievances may come, although that is not its purpose, is the "comité d'entreprise" or plant committee.[21] While the institution has given disappointing results, it is important as a major experiment in labor-management coöperation and industrial democracy at the plant level, whose functioning sheds light on the state of industrial relations and unionism in France.

The precursors of the institution were the employee "councils" set up about the turn of the century by a few socially-minded employers worried about the heightening of class antagonisms. The most famous were those created by the distinguished Catholic employer, Léon Harmel, as early as 1885. The CGT after the first World War emphasized the democratization of the economy at the industrywide and national level, but there was some demand for joint committees at the plant level. Different groups envisaged the plant committees then in different ways: Socialists and syndicalists as a means of training workers for larger responsibilities in the direction of the economy; Communists as a prelude to the seizure of plants in the Soviet manner; Catholic unionists as a means of collaboration with management. The most careful proposal was that of the metal workers' national union, under reformist leadership, which unsuccessfully proposed to the employer association that as a complement to agreements, union members designate committees in each plant to check on the enforcement of labor laws, the application of disciplinary measures and equity in hiring, and the application of wage scales.[22] The collapse of labor's power in the 1920's put to rest union demands and employer worries. In the Popular Front days, the CGT's

---

[20] For example, see *Rousseau v. Demoiselle Borgraeve, Droit social,* vol. 14, no. 7, July-August 1951, p. 474. The Cour de Cassation upheld a lower court award to a secretary who had been warned by her employer that union activity was incompatible with her job; she was demoted 48 hours after her election to the presidency of a CFTC union branch, and fired soon after. The amount of the award, 100,000 francs, was about three or four months' salary.

[21] The term "comité d'entreprise" has received a large number of names in English: "works council," "works committee," "labor-management committee," "joint production committee," and others.

[22] Gérard Dehove, *Le Contrôle ouvrier en France* (Paris, 1937), pp. 277-282.

demands for industrial democracy at the shop level stressed the institution of shop stewards, not joint committees.

Vichy produced, perhaps as its one constructive innovation, the plant social committees. Elected by workers or chosen by employers, they dealt with social welfare matters exclusively. They were forbidden to meddle with the employer's serious business of an economic or financial nature. In the hard times of the occupation, their efforts to eke out a food supply for workers earned them the title of "potato committees." By exertions and stratagems to keep plants operating despite shortages, they helped save workers from going off to labor, voluntary or forced, in Germany.

The ferment at the liberation did away with the Vichy social committees. In the south and center, dozens of workers' councils sprang up, to go farther than the resistance program had promised. Some dispossessed owners, proved or alleged collaborators, or took over after owners fled. Many of the committees, with a backbone of the resistance organization of engineers and technicians, proposed to run the plants themselves.

The Provisional Government of De Gaulle, fearing worse spoliation to come, acted to give regular status to the committees already set up and to steer the demands for a share in plant management into more respectable channels. This it did by an ordinance of February 1945[23] which instituted the "comités d'entreprise" and made them obligatory in every enterprise with 100 or more employees. Management was to have one representative on the committee, its chairman. The other members—in number depending on the size of the enterprise—would all be elected representatives of the personnel. The committees were given wide powers of administration of plant social welfare work, but only consultative powers in economic matters. The ordinance stressed labor-management collaboration to increase production, rather than labor participation in management prerogatives.

The unions and the left political parties pressed for an expansion in the committees' scope and coverage, which they received by a 1946 law.[24] Coverage was extended to all enterprises of over 50 employees.[25] The committees received more authority in economic matters, and the unions more power in relation to the committees. By the 1945 text the

---

[23] Ordinance No. 45-280, February 22, 1945, *Journal officiel*, February 23, 1945.

[24] Law No. 46-1065 of May 16, 1946, *Journal officiel*, May 17, 1946.

[25] The numbers of enterprises and workers covered remain shrouded in the mystery of French statistics. Among conflicting estimates, we may cite those of the ILO; 7,500 establishments and 2,500,000 workers under the 1945 ordinance; an additional 8,500 enterprises and 700,000 workers under the 1946 law. *Labour-Management Coöperation in France*, p. 171.

employer merely had to "inform," now he had to "consult," the committee on "all questions concerning the organization, the management and the general state of the enterprise." The phrase was as alarming as it was vague to the CNPF, which had warned that such a requirement would wreck managerial authority. Once the law was passed, the CNPF took a more hopeful line. "The law, powerless to create authority, cannot destroy it. With or without previous consultation of the committee, the power of decision of the head of the enterprise remains intact." But, it reminded its members: "A too slavish interpretation of a purposely uncertain statutory text could lead, through an excess of timidity, to hindrance of the progress of the enterprise."[26]

The 1945 ordinance had provided for election of the entire ticket which received the highest vote. The theory was that the CGT and the CFTC would, in a spirit of "resistance unity," agree on joint slates. Even in the first committee elections, however, a national agreement to this effect between the two confederations was not carried out in all regions; local rivalries produced a number of local contests.

The CFTC's skepticism increased when the most powerful CGT union, the metal workers, declared that joint slates should be only a prelude to "total trade union unity in the factory." Hinting that new CFTC locals were only breakaway organizations, the CGT union indicated it would combine slates only with well-established old CFTC locals.[27] Such declarations heightened fears of a CGT closed shop. The CFTC pushed for and obtained proportional representation of opposing union slates. There are now competing slates in almost all elections in plants of any size. In a smaller plant there may be a single formal or informal joint slate.

The committees' powers are clearly differentiated between the plant's "social" and "economic" activities. In the first, they have powers of decision or supervision. They run cafeterias, "coöperatives" or buying clubs, vacation camps, sports clubs, day nurseries, and other social welfare activities. They supervise housing projects, garden plots, and mutual aid societies. They exercise surveillance over plant apprenticeship and vocational training and administer safety and health committees.

In the domain of production, price, investment, and other economic problems, the committees' powers are advisory. They are supposed to be consulted on plans of organization and operation of the enterprise, and at least annually on its program for the ensuing year. They are to

---

[26] Philippe Bayart, *Comités d'entreprise: Expériences étrangères, législation française* (Paris, 2d ed., 1947), pp. 261-262.

[27] *Ibid.*, p. 233.

"study the suggestions of management and of employees for the increase of output and the improvement of productivity." They must be informed of the concern's profit position, and may offer suggestions on the disposition of profits. In a joint stock company, they have the right to see all documents submitted to stockholders' meetings, to send two delegates to board of directors' meetings, and to have a certified accountant examine the books.

The government had specified in the 1945 ordinance that the committees should not take up wage demands. The 1946 law gave them the right to take up wage questions "in relation to the economic and financial possibilities of the enterprise." The committees are consulted on group layoffs or dismissals.

In concerns with more than one establishment, the several plant committees send delegates to a central *comité d'entreprise*. Although it meets less frequently (twice a year instead of monthly) and has certain special functions of coördination, its basic problems are those of the single-plant committee. For comparative brevity, the discussion here is in terms of the single-plant committee; most of it applies also to the central committee of the multiplant enterprise.

The committee aims could be attained only if three elements were present: the capacity of workers to undertake their new responsibilities, employer acceptance, and a social and economic climate permitting collaboration. Although real success could come only in the long run, shortcomings could be observed soon. The committees have been hamstrung by (1) lack of qualified worker representatives, (2) employer hostility, and (3) a worsening social climate since the 1947 turn in the CGT line.

No group could suddenly produce representatives ready to exercise technical responsibilities to which it had previously been denied access. There are few manual or white collar workers able to cope with the technical production problems that come up in a plant committee or follow management explanations of an annual balance sheet. Nor can most of the national industrial unions give their local plant committeemen much help. If the unions are to make the committees work, they need continuing programs of training for the committee members. Particularly in the free unions, they require greater resources and more freedom from day-to-day crises.

The committees need more coöperation from the technicians, engineers, and accountants in their plants. But the cadres are closer socially and psychologically to their employers than to the other employees. Even when they are themselves committee members, they often regard the committee as short-circuiting their own lines of authority in the establishment. Their coöperation has been deterred on the one hand by CGT tactics, on the other by employer hostility to the committees.

Employer acceptance has been the exception. At first employers feared the committees would do away with their authority in the plant. Their fears can be understood in the light of the circumstances of 1945 and 1946, when the committee legislation was forced upon them. But most employers sooner or later ran the required committee elections.

The large plants were the first to set up committees; others followed suit, it seems, almost in direct proportion to size.[28] The committees exist in almost all large establishments, and in many of the medium-sized and smaller ones covered by the law. In some industries, notably the building trades and road transport, the dispersal of operations has made difficult the designation and operation of committees. In a number of small and medium-sized establishments, the unions have been unable to present slates; individuals have hesitated to single themselves out for possible employer disapproval. Committees in many of those establishments lack independence of their employers. Many such committees, once formed, later died, lacking candidacies for election or employer interest.[29]

Employer opposition has been directed chiefly at the "economic" role of the committees. In the less industrialized areas of the country, many employers still keep control even of social welfare activities, with the committees, if they exist, merely executing employer decisions. But generally employers have conceded the "social" functions, which had already been exercised within narrow limits by the Vichy social committees. In some firms management is not only reconciled, but even happy, to see the committee active on social welfare business. That leaves it with little time or energy to "meddle" with problems of production, price, and profit. The social welfare activities are, by law, financed by the employer. A skillful employer can keep the committee dangling on his generosity to bail it out of recurring deficits in the cafeteria, crèche, or vacation colony, so that it is most "reasonable" about making any economic demands.

The CFTC metal workers is one of the unions that has taken seri-

---

[28] For varying estimates of the numbers of committees set up, see M. Blanc, *Revue française du travail,* vol. 3, no. 7, July 1948, pp. 287-300; and Pierre Chambelland, *Les Comités d'entreprise: fonctionnement et résultats pratiques* (Paris, 1949), chapter III. Probably no one knows how many committees were set up or have been functioning at any given time. A Ministry of Labor official hazarded the guess of 7,000 committees set up, all in all (1953).

[29] Michel Collinet, in his brilliant and somber *Lettre aux militants,* no. 8, July 20, 1951, "Les Comités d'entreprise," p. 3, estimated that in 1951 there were only 2,000 committees left, including some with a paper existence. This figure may be too low.

ously the responsibilities of the new institution. When it expressed its considered disappointment, in 1950, it did not spare itself or its employers: "We have the impression that, as the saying goes, we have been 'had' by the employers. In giving us the social welfare projects, they have loaded us down with work. They have also turned our attention and efforts from the real work of the plant committee. In this they have been aided by the weakness of our training in this field, our lack of preparation to study and resolve these problems."[30]

Social welfare activities involve an obvious community of interest between management and labor and a minimum threat to managerial authority. The economic activities of the committees may promote the deepest joint interests, but they invade areas traditionally reserved to management.

THE CGT AND THE COMMITTEES

At first the CGT pushed the committees with the greatest vigor, especially in the larger plants. "Gain the battle of steel so that France may live!" was the keynote of a CGT national plant committee conference in the industry in which the committees were most important, metallurgy and metal-fabricating.[31] The committees, said Frachon in 1946, have been "motive forces of economic recovery, sometimes against the will of reactionary employers who were sabotaging production for political reasons."[32]

Even in this period, the CGT had one eye on the uses and potential uses of the committees as instruments of power. The metal workers' guide book on the committees, a basic text for CGT unions, urged that CGT activists:

fortify themselves against the "legalistic" myopia which, in closing their horizon, would lead them to act only within the closed terrain of the law and obtain only what it grants, exclusively by the means which it envisions. . . . Our activists of the local unions and the plant committees must in no case restrict the action of the committees toward management merely to the terrain of the law.[33]

After 1947, coöperation was no longer in order. "To new conditions

---

[30] CFTC, Fédération de la Métallurgie, *Rapport moral présenté par le bureau fédéral*, 1950, p. 85.

[31] CGT, Fédération des Travailleurs de la Métallurgie, *La Bataille de l'Acier: le Comité d'entreprise, organisme de l'avenir, première conférence nationale des comités d'entreprises de la métallurgie, des 22 et 23 février 1946* (Paris, 1946).

[32] *La Vie ouvrière*, October 4, 1946.

[33] CGT, Fédération des Travailleurs de la Métallurgie, *Les Comités d'entreprises: Principes d'orientation, d'organisation et de fonctionnement*, 2d ed. (Paris, 1947), p. 13. This edition appeared before the turn of the CGT line in May 1947.

must correspond new forms of activity," said Benoît Frachon in launching the CGT's monthly *Revue des Comités d'Entreprise* in 1948. "Above all, it is necessary to paralyze the effort of those who are leading the country to ruin, to chaos, to unemployment, to foreign domination and to war for the American expansionists. The plant committees can and must play a capital role in this action."[34]

In the big strike waves of 1947 and 1948 many of the *comités d'entreprise* were metamorphosed into strike committees. Again and again the plant committees have been "mobilized" against the political enemies of the CGT and the party. A convention of CGT plant committeemen promised to "mobilize the committees against the American imperialists' plan of enslavement,"[35] that is, the Marshall Plan. Against the Schuman Plan, the CGT urged its committeemen to "mobilize themselves for the creation in all enterprises of committees of defense of our industry and of the peace."[36] The committees were to settle the war in Korea, bring the French army out of Indo-China, and ban the atom bomb.[37]

They waged war on the cultural front too. For, as the CGT reminded them, they may run factory cultural activities. "Is it not true that until now these cultural activities—for they exist in many and many a committee—have had no rational orientation?" it asked.[38] It summoned them to clean the "trash" out of the plant lending libraries: "If the employer set up the library, it probably reflects his state of mind . . . Above all, we must absorb this reality, that there are *their* books and *ours*. When we say *their* books, we mean an American 'literature,' the books of collaborators, scandal writers, pro-fascists. When we say *ours*, we mean all the rest."[39]

The new line toward the committees encountered enough resistance in the shops to call for repeated admonitions from the higher CGT echelons. The Communist Party denounced "briefcase carriers" and other "opportunists" seduced by employers through the committees. Such an elite group as the Paris region metal workers had to thank Frachon and Monmousseau for "the aid which they brought to the correction of errors committed in the plant committees." Thus corrected,

---

[34] "Les Comités d'entreprise dans la lutte pour la démocratie," *Revue des comités d'entreprise*, no. 1, April 1948, p. 7.

[35] CGT, *XXVIIe congrès . . . 1948, compte rendu*, p. 262.

[36] *L'Humanité*, June 30, 1950.

[37] For a summary list of foreign policy issues on which the CGT has sought to rally the committees, cf. *Droit social*, "L'Expérience des comités d'entreprise. Bilan d'une enquête," vol. 15, no. 2, February 1952, p. 97.

[38] "Activités culturelles du comité d'entreprise: contre l'intoxication systématique des esprits," *Revue des comités d'entreprise*, no. 1, April 1948, p. 49.

[39] "Les Activités culturelles du comité d'entreprise: les bibliothèques d'entreprise," *Revue des comités d'entreprise*, no. 2, May 1948, pp. 45-46.

the delegates to a special convention promised to "extirpate from their midst the ferments of paternalism planted there by the employers and to make the committees arms of class combat . . . battling against the deviations which, in the course of collaboration with the employers, permitted the discrediting of this conquest of the workers."[40]

The only mutuality of labor and management interest the CGT granted was that in preventing plant shutdowns. Otherwise, "We repeat, the class struggle must be intensified in the plant committees. Our comrades must remember at every moment that they have opposite them a class enemy. They must . . . never forget that they have been delegated to improve the workers' lot, not to collaborate with management."[41]

The earlier coöperation to increase productivity had no place in the CGT line now. Not even if tied in by collective agreement with wage increases, Frachon told the 1951 convention:

In a capitalist regime and especially with reactionary governments . . . increasing productivity means increasing the profits of capitalists and the misery of workers. . .

Among those who pretend that under present conditions increasing productivity will increase wages, some are themselves fooled. But most of those who say that, the politician-lackeys of the American billionaires and their agents in the labor movement, are fakers trying to fool others.[42]

The CGT's intensified politicization of the committees coincided in time with the decline of labor's political standing and with the return of employer confidence. In this atmosphere, almost any chance that might have existed in the long run for employer acceptance of the committees evaporated.

UNIONS AND DELEGATES

The union as such has few functions which management recognizes within the plant. Collective negotiations scarcely involve the local or shop branch directly, for they are usually areawide and for broad industry groupings. Where contracts exist, they seldom include functions of administration for the local or branch. Local union functions are largely tied in with those assigned by law to the stewards and plant committees. It is thus essential for the union to guide and control the delegates, on pain of being a shadow in the plant.

---

[40] *Le Peuple,* February 24, 1949, p. 2.
[41] "Bénéfices avoués . . . bénéfices réels," *Revue des comités d'entreprise,* no. 28, July 1950, p. 11.
[42] *Le Peuple,* May 28, 1951, p. 3; in bold capitals in the original.

Control is aided by short terms of office and the possibilities of recall. Delegates are generally active unionists; overlapping of directorates aids control. But in areas where local leadership is scarce, the overburdening of activists with union, plant committee, and stewards' posts may leave them ineffective in all. The unions try to instruct their delegates and have them report back to union meetings, or more frequently, union executives. The CGT is most energetic in this direction, but it too encounters opposition. The plant committee delegates may identify themselves with the interests of their establishment in opposition to union interests, especially those of the national union or the confederation. Although the union has the right to a representative at committee meetings, the law requires that he be an employee of the plant.

A shrewd employer may deliberately play off the plant committee against the union, by making it a substitute in workers' minds for union action, for example, by formalizing profit-sharing arrangements. It is not surprising that one of the model concerns of France in efficiency and high wages, Télémécanique, although its main plants are in the "red suburbs" of Paris, has no real CGT organization, only an autonomous union working closely with the plant committee. The unions often find their activists diverted into the welfare jobs of the plant committee. The CGT has been most concerned about this danger, and has repeatedly reminded its people that they are not elected to the committees to spend their days poring over the books of the vacation camp or watching the unloading of potatoes and carrots for the cafeteria. FO too denounces "company committees" and complains that "the union activists transformed into grocers have deserted union work and forgotten that their field is economic action."[43] The CFTC adds the complaint that centering too many welfare activities around the shop may be to the detriment of the home.

The unions find a source of concern in increasing abstentions in the first round of plant committee elections. These are sometimes so high as to necessitate a second ballot, which opens the field to nonunion candidacies.

The unions carry on training programs, of which the most extensive are those of the CGT. The CGT has also done more than the other centers in coördinating the work of its delegates at the levels of the confederation, the national union, and the department federation. In 1948 the CGT claimed 8,707 committee members of all industries present at a national conference. Many, it did not hesitate to say, had their expenses

---

[43] "Pourquoi doivent fonctionner les comités d'entreprise," *FO Informations,* no. 18, May 1953, p. 100.

paid by their employers.[44] In 1952 a second national conference claimed no more than 4,000 delegates.[45]

The CGT views all its activities in the name of the working class as equally legitimate parts of one great effort. Although they are the elected spokesmen of all the workers, the CGT uses its stewards and committeemen as part of the party-union apparatus, for whatever job comes to hand, from promoting wage increases to fighting rearmament.

Control of a majority of the plant committees gives the CGT an important source of funds, equipment, and patronage. In large concerns, the committees' social welfare activities, financed by employers, involve considerable sums and sizable staffs.[46] The committee payroll can be used for union or party patronage. The Communists in control of the Renault committee, for example, have used it to make place for CGT activists discharged for violence and other misconduct.

Despite abuses and difficulties, some of the committees have real if limited achievements to their credit. Habits of coöperation have been built up here and there which have resisted the changes in the CGT line. Where management has been astute and forward-looking, the committees have stimulated output, helped increase productivity, and given workers a deeper stake in the industrial process. They have in many cases shown management how to avert layoffs. The committees have enlarged the technical qualifications of their members, particularly those reëlected year after year, and lifted their sights beyond their compartmentalized daily tasks. The committees have been vehicles for an exchange of ideas, and for innovation by a consent unknown before. "I can get the committee to put over many new ideas in the plant far better than I could do myself," remarked the head of a progressive electrical machinery concern employing about 250 workers. This despite the fact that in his plant the CGT is the only union with any effective organization.

In the realm of employee benefit plans, the committees have developed new programs and in a great many cases substituted worker management for company paternalism. The welfare activities are not only the least controversial; they demand the least technical knowledge, and

---

[44] Le Léap, "Les Conférences nationales des comités d'entreprise," *Revue des comités d'entreprise,* no. 2, May 1948, pp. 9-10.

[45] Special number of *Revue des comités d'entreprise,* no. 51-52, June-July 1952.

[46] For an example of the budget of a well-developed committee, see the 1947 Renault committee budget reproduced in ILO, *Labour-Management Coöperation in France,* p. 191.

In 1949, the Renault committee, carrying on probably the widest activities of any plant committee in the nation, employed 30 people in its administrative office alone, and a total of 600 in its far-flung activities.

can be run by hired staff. They are in many ways close to the workers, or at least to those workers who benefit from them. (Obviously not all do; many are left untouched by the factory sports club or children's vacation colony, for example, or even the lunch room, since food shortages ended.)

Some workers view the experience in running these social activities as training for larger tasks ahead. Others—and these are the majority of aggressive committeemen and unionists—feel that restriction to social welfare schemes denotes a status of inferiority. "All we get to do is run the Christmas tree." Or, "We're just lunch peddlers." These are frequent and deeply felt complaints. The feeling behind them is that management will not really discuss production processes or economic decisions with the committee members, that it shows them only as much of the books and as many of the stockholders' documents as it thinks "it is good for them to see."

The director of a large St. Nazaire shipyard—with a long record of troubled labor relations—retorted to the dissatisfied employees on his plant committee: "How are you going to manage shipbuilding problems if you can't even manage the lunch room?" The question was disparaging, but difficult to answer. Although French workers lack confidence in the managerial qualities of their employers, they know they are not ready to furnish these qualities themselves. Those who are in earnest about the committees' assigned purposes believe the committees might have furnished, and yet may furnish, an opportunity to enlarge the horizons of both management and workers.

Most workers see the experiment of the plant committees as another postliberation reform that has failed to come off. Workers' loss of interest in all their organizations since the war has affected the committees. And the committees themselves have contributed to that process of disillusionment. The rank and file had been led at first to expect so much from the committees that union leaders found it difficult to be candid about the reasons for the committees' shortcomings. It is easier for leaders to blame these on the limitation of committee functions, and demand fuller powers for the committees, than to face the problems of training men and developing programs to realize more of the functions the committees do have.

The committees have not altered managerial concepts of authority in the plant or reformed the temper of labor relations: it is too much to expect that they alone could do that. On the other hand, neither have they undermined the prerogatives and functions of management. It is not possible to say that the committees have "worked." It is too soon to say that they "cannot work." Even under favorable circumstances, such a reform would take decades to absorb. The circumstances have not been favorable. So far, therefore, the committees have disappointed the hopes of their friends and the fears of their opponents.

THE STATE OF PLANT RELATIONS

All the government's intervention in favor of the various forms of worker representation has not produced habits of union-management coöperation in the plant. It has been accompanied, on the contrary, by an employer stiffening against any form of collaboration not required by law. Union rivalries and the politicization of CGT activity add reasons for employers to resist recognition of the union within the plant. Union rights in the plant, employers feel, are "a domain where one may hold that the indirect intervention of the lawmaker has already gone beyond the bounds of the reasonable. It is an illusion to expect employers conscious of their responsibilities to freely admit rules which would prevent them from carrying on the normal functions of management in the enterprises for which they are responsible."[47]

Where a shop steward insists on calling in an outside union officer, management may insist on calling in an employer association official. Thus at least symbolically it reserves its rights against the union as an outsider in the shop. "Union action should normally not take place at the level of the plant," said the national metal trades association. "It should be placed at the level of the corresponding employer association, that is to say, on the local, regional, or national level."[48]

The "trade union rights" clauses have created vast difficulty in the negotiation of collective agreements. Employers concede union officers working at the trade some free time in the plant and leave of absence for union business, and rehiring priority for a certain period for those taking full-time union jobs. Other demands cause more difficulty. Plant bulletin board space is already provided by law for shop steward and plant committee business. Employers usually offer to grant space for union business if they can keep out political and polemic material. But employer precensorship would eliminate many announcements because items on union meeting agendas are called "derogatory of employer authority." This might be a minor matter if it did not typify an impasse in plant dealings. Despite its class struggle philosophy, the CGT argues

[47] Pierre Waline, "Le Patronat Français et les conventions collectives," *Revue économique,* vol. 2, no. 1, February 1951, p. 29.

[48] *Etat de la question,* p. 10. Note also the comment on the union proposal for union delegates in addition to the elected stewards and plant committees: "This supplementary institution of union delegates manifestly aims merely to pit against the authority of management an authority whose action could take place only to the detriment of the normal running of enterprises," p. 9.

for union meeting space inside the shop, as well as for collection of dues and distribution of union literature on the working premises. Only a rare collective agreement, like that for artisan shoemakers, permits these privileges.

The metal trades' unions at one time proposed that the local unions share with management in the establishment of production norms. The national employer association replied acidly, "the deplorable effects . . . of the intervention in this essentially technical domain by committees which are for the most part incompetent, and of the interminable discussions which would follow, are incontestable. On the other hand, one does not see what new protection would result for the workers."[49] The Lille textile industry has one of the rare joint employer-union agencies for the determination of work loads.

It is not only in France that employers still prefer to "deal only with their own employees," or that a union official may have a hard time getting into a plant he does not work in. But in France, the conception of authority remains a personal one, deeply rooted in the family structured business and the small and middle-sized concern. Some of its flavor is carried by the term "chef d'entreprise" and by the juxtaposition in employer conversation of the words "autorité" and "chef d'entreprise."

Concepts of authority show in the rules on hiring and firing. The unions have influenced hiring and firing comparatively little under collective bargaining. The exception is the CGT closed shop which prevails in newspaper publishing in most big cities; in addition the CGT has a practical closed shop in longshore hiring in a few ports, occasionally in the building trades, and in some cinema work. At one time after the war the CGT had what amounted to hiring hall rights in longshore employment, but the government has gradually whittled down its privileged position in most ports.

Most employers do not dismiss or lay off workers lightly; they often keep them on the payroll longer than there is work for them. Criteria for economic dismissal in the absence of any agreement were laid down in a 1945 government regulation as family responsibility, seniority, and performance: "not necessarily in that order of priority."[50] This is the language still found in a number of collective agreements, which do not spell out the criteria any further. The clauses for dismissal pay based on seniority in some agreements carry an inducement to use

---

[49] *Etat de la question,* p. 42.

[50] Ordinance 45-1030, May 24, 1945, *Journal Officiel,* May 25, 1945, with rectification, *Journal Officiel,* June 9, 1945; Paul Durand, *Traité du droit du travail,* vol. 2, p. 879. In theory dismissals must still be approved by the labor inspectors; usually this means simply the formality of employer notification to the authorities.

that criterion. Seniority and family needs are occasionally superimposed in more specific provisions: the national tramway agreement gives added seniority for each dependent child. But most agreements leave the criteria vague, hence up to employer decision in each establishment. Shop stewards and plant committee members have no "superseniority" in case of layoffs.

It is a comparatively low standard of living and a pessimistic economic outlook which puts family situation at the top of criteria for layoffs. It is a recognition of employer authority, made possible by family firms and the predominance of small and middle-sized shops, which allows employer evaluation of the private family responsibilities of the worker.

In dismissals ruled arbitrary, the law requires the employer to pay damages to the worker but not to reinstate him. Authority must not be shaken by requiring an employer to take back an employee he does not want in his shop. Legal doctrine, to be sure, says that neither party may be held to the performance of the employment contract against his will: either party may terminate the contract subject to the other party's possible claim for damages.[51] As we have seen, even the delegates' special legal protection against discriminatory firing is in practice transmuted into a money payment which minimizes the challenge to employers' authority.

Increased paternalism may appear an antidote to union encroachment. Most of what welfare work French employers did in earlier periods was socialized or submerged, with a few outstanding exceptions such as the textile industry of the north and the Michelin tire domain. Family allowances were socialized, with the unions sharing in their administration. The Vichy social committees were replaced by the plant committees. Many of the industries with housing and welfare benefits were nationalized. Recently, however, employers have shown a new interest in housing, in supplementary pensions and unemployment funds and wage payment methods tying the worker to the firm. In some cases these activities have been carried on jointly with employee representatives. A move back to paternalism has been noted by the CNPF, which refers to it in explaining the "partial failure" of collective bargaining.[52] This is "the increasingly important place which the enterprise has been able to recover in the consideration of its personnel. This evolution . . . tends to bring the head of the enterprise closer to his employees on the concrete level of their daily preoccupations . . . An immense field has

[51] Rouast and Durand, *Précis de Législation industrielle*, p. 378.
[52] Report of labor relations committee to CNPF general assembly, *Bulletin du CNPF*, vol. 7, no. 93, February 5, 1953, p. 38.

opened to all the efforts aiming to improve human relations in the enterprise." As the CNPF remarks, this movement has developed "to the detriment of collective procedures."

In sum, forced by law to deal in his plant with the elected representatives of the whole body of his employees, the employer has sought to keep the union *qua* union out of the determination of plant conditions. With the elected spokesmen among his own employees he can work, or at least cope. In the union he sees the greater threat to his authority, the greater risks of industrial anarchy—or industrial democracy. He tries to hold its functions in the shop to the minimum prescribed by "an invading social legislation."[53] In this effort, he may take practical comfort from the cleavages in the trade union movement, and moral support from the Communist character of its dominant wing.

As for the worker, he finds the functions, like the personnel, of stewardship, plant committees, and union overlapping and blurring into each other. Often he hardly distinguishes among them. If he has any contact with the union branch or local, it is not usually in a function of on-the-job protection for him. The multiplicity of grievance channels dilutes his potential loyalty to the union organization, as distinct from the peripheral attachment of periodic shop votes or the sporadic manifestation of strikes. Perhaps, as an employer association executive remarked, "Those workers who reflect are union members." The reflection and the loyalty are largely political, sometimes religious, a matter of ideology and class sentiment. These may be among the most valid reasons for union membership. But their inadequacy to sustain a functioning trade union movement seems clear both from the preponderance of the unorganized in private industry and from the frustration of unionism at the shop level.

---

[53] *Ibid.*

CHAPTER XV

UNIONS AND POLITICS

The guardians of trade union virtue are howling. They say we are meddling with matters that are not the business of the unions. . . The essential action must be organized and developed in the shops. But we make it a principle to fight the enemy wherever we get a chance. Above all, we are not so stupid as to let ourselves be turned from our duty by the "virtuous" indignation of hypocrites who no longer have the slightest bit of independence to lose.

—Benoît Frachon, CGT general
secretary, *Le Peuple,* March 17, 1949.

The unionism to which I have sacrificed 40 years of my life no longer has any vitality. It has been killed by the political parties, the odious political parties, which have degraded the masses and replaced the effort of wage earners to think with the desire to follow.

—Vallet-Sanglier, *Révolution
prolétarienne,* June 1950.

Unless we accomplish the political analysis which urgently demands our efforts, the active non-Communist workers will, in dealing with their government, do no more than forever alternate between the violent momentary reflex of strikes and the disappointments of beautiful ineffective resolutions.

—*Reconstruction,* June-July 1950.

In all countries, trade union movements have gone into politics on some level. Strictly economic activity was a luxury of unions in a society which, on the one hand, took its political institutions for granted and, on the other, had not yet assumed the welfare functions of the modern industrial state. The scene on which the modern American unions—a minority movement—operated before the great depression of the 1930's was altogether unique. Elsewhere, union movements sought not only political equality for workers and the right to exist and function—to organize and bargain collectively—but also the gains of wage and hour laws, social security, and varying degrees of reorganization of the economy and the polity. Some formed labor parties themselves; others worked closely with autonomous labor parties. The forms of political action were related—as they are in the United States today—to the peculiar history and institutions of each country and the expectations and dreams of its working people. In only two of all the industrialized nations of the free world has the main body of the union movement allowed a political party to take charge of its destiny. Their history explains why Italy and France are those countries and why in each case it is the Communist Party which has taken over.

The unions in France are less instruments of collective bargaining than of political action. Workers have joined unions in great part as a "reflex" of class consciousness rather than as a move for job control. The two major forces of the old CGT—revolutionary and reformist— have struggled for supremacy for the last thirty years; both have increasingly followed political channels. Revolutionary unionism fell into the hands of a political party; reformist unionism has tried to win from the state concessions which it could not command from employers. The political interests are most obvious in the CGT, manipulated by the Communist Party. The CFTC and FO have not yielded their independence to parties, but they look to political action to determine a large part of workers' income in the short run, and to the state in the longer run to expand the national income and enhance labor's share in it. All look to the administration for many of the conditions of union functioning and worker representation.

Politics has reasserted its primacy in the last decade, since the collapse of 1940, when the unions had to renounce political concerns. Under Vichy and the occupation, resistance activities became the unionists' title to glory. In the critical years after liberation, the unions dealt with government rather than with employers. Their chief concerns were with institutional reforms, achieved by legislation or decree; with wages, which the government set; and with prices and food supplies, which the government was supposed to control. The unions could see that politics was even more the cause of economic difficulties than economics the root of political stress. Both the government's immediate economic responsibilities and its promises of social justice demanded a cohesion and courage which no governmental coalition could muster. Rising prices and falling cabinets were visible signs of the interdependence of politics and economics.

For five years after liberation, there was no opportunity for real collective bargaining to develop members' interest in the bread-and-butter aspects of unionism as against the political interest. There was not enough independent force in their ideology, nor strength in the unions' structure, to withstand onslaught and envelopment by a political party which made the unions its first target. It seemed, as Simone Weil had written in London during the war, that "the union cannot live along-side the political parties. It is as impossible as if it were a law of mechanics."[1]

The unions now are not strong enough to compel respect from their employers or their members. Therefore, despite deep-seated hostilities to government and a skepticism about political parties, workers turn to party and government action. But the belief that things can be settled by reform is far from strong. Haunted by revolutionary reminiscences, many workers are inclined to expect improvement only by drastic change of the political and economic system.

COMMUNIST STRENGTH

The reasons for the Communist Party's speedy conquest of the CGT after liberation have already been examined (Chapter VII) in the light of the circumstances of those times. Despite all its setbacks, its hold has not been successfully challenged in the unions. The party and the CGT unions have lost members and strikes, but they have not lost the leader-ship of the most active and articulate segment of the industrial workers of France. In the politics of labor protest, all the advantages are with the Communist Party, and the CGT, as long as the party does not force things too far with the unions—which it periodically does. Party and unions have kept the initiative on symbols and slogans of economic disaffection and the fears of war. Other parties and other unions protest economic inequities and governmental deficiencies, but only the Com-munist Party and the CGT give the appearance of will and force to do something about them. That is not essentially a matter of program but of constant activity, emotional intensity, and militant organization.

In program the party outbids all competitors—in wage demands and social security claims, protectionism against imports, opposition to lay-offs and shutdowns. (At the same time it makes equally obvious and unqualified demands of higher prices for farmers, lower taxes for trades-men, and many other demands of a simple electoral type for many other special interests.) It holds out to workers the millenial hope of ending capitalism and wage slavery, and the promise of working class power and revenge for past defeats. But that chiefly by implication. Actually the Communist Party has talked little of Communism in the years since the war. Instead it has devoted itself to interweaving immediate political demands and peace slogans with simple economic agitation. With its avowed goals, almost no worker has disagreed.

---

[1] *L'Enracinement* (Paris, 1949), p. 32.

By contrast, the program and temper of the Socialist Party and the MRP invite workers to long effort in search of complex solutions. They and the FO and CFTC unions demand of workers a greater exercise of individual and collective responsibility. The Communist Party holds out more, now, in simple form, for less effort.

It is hard to evaluate the parts of faith and simple economic appeal. The Communist Party offers both, and it is the only one that can offer both to most workers. Communist ideology occupies a vacuum of faith. Religion in this nominally Catholic country ceased to be a living faith for most of the working class over a century ago. Perhaps the church never "lost" the workers, because the industrial working class became important only when the Catholic Church had already lost its hold over workers. Socialism lost its dynamism a generation ago. Defensive, respectable, "bourgeoisified," it represents a reasoned outlook or an habitual creed to its followers, but hardly a militant faith to compete with Communism. Belief in the republic is not strong enough to bring consensus in the community, let alone feed the ardors of faith. How lovely the Republic looked under the Empire, it used to be said in the days of the Third Republic. The Fourth Republic looked even more beautiful—under Vichy. Only in a crisis, as in 1934 and 1944, can workers' belief in the republic rise to the height of faith.

The franchise of working class representation is one the Communists have awarded themselves by ideology and propaganda, leadership origins and party structure. It is one their conservative enemies have conferred on them, too, by the nature of their own anti-Communism. The anti-democratic political movements of the right, the anti-unionism of employers except in moments of panic, seem to confirm the Communists' claims. The worker forgives the Communists much for the enemies they have made. On the other hand, some employers are apparently not above paying out money to Communist political or union organizations,[2] in what may be called protection against immediate difficulty or "social insurance" against eventual upheaval. The combination of intransigence and lack of self-confidence sets up poor defenses against a movement backed by social injustice, a sense of historic inevitability, and the chief continental power.

It is not easy for an American reader, accustomed to seeing the Communists as a tiny party on the lunatic fringe, to realize how "natural" it is for many European workers, especially in France and Italy, to be Communists, to vote Communist, or at least to be tolerant of Com-

---

[2] For one of the few references in writing to this phenomenon, see Pierre Drouin, "La France sous les feux croisés des propagandes," one of a series of articles on Communism and anti-Communism, Le Monde, June 12, 1952.

munism. They equate Marxism with class consciousness. They tend to regard Communism as simply one more of many shades of Marxism or, even more simply, as the farthest left of many shades of leftism. In France, where the Communist Party gets one vote out of every four cast in elections,[3] any worker is likely to work alongside, or live next to a Communist. He does not see them as set apart from their fellows in any way; on the contrary. It requires a heroic effort of the imagination for him to make the necessary jump from the normal daily behavior of Communist fellow employees to the final intentions of Communist leaders.

Regarded as one more shade of leftism, Communism benefits by the long French tradition—among other classes as well as the proletariat—that "you can never vote too far to the left." Regularly during the Third Republic many farmers, professional people, and lower middle class voters cast their ballots for the candidates successively occupying the extreme left of the political spectrum. Discounting the highly charged verbalism of these candidates, they expected no violence from them—especially if they were elected. The voter could thus register his protest with the government and feel "advanced" at no cost. "The elected did not really deceive the electors, except perhaps the *militants* of the left and the sincere pessimists on the right."[4] To a considerable extent, despite the closer danger of Soviet aggression in recent years, this has continued to be part of the voting pattern in both political elections and shop elections.

The slogan of "no enemies to the left," developed before the day of totalitarian parties, has long operated to the benefit of the Communist Party. Most Communist voters have been far from pro-Soviet convictions, even far from Communist convictions. A large proportion of the Communist vote, among workers as well as farmers, has represented not the interest in politics conventionally attributed to all Frenchmen, but

---

[3] The relative electoral strength of the parties, from presumed left to right, is shown by the votes obtained in the last *national* election, that of June 1951:

Registered voters	24,522,000
Communist Party	4,934,000
Socialist Party	2,784,000
MRP	2,454,000
Radicals and other Center Parties	1,980,000
Independents, Peasants, and other Right Parties	2,295,000
Gaullist Party	4,266,000
Miscellaneous	239,000
Abstentions	4,861,000

François Goguel, *France under the Fourth Republic* (Ithaca, 1952), p. 90.

[4] D. W. Brogan, Introduction to Alexander Werth, *The Twilight of France* (New York, 1942), p. xi.

an indifference to the real meaning of politics. In a nation noted for its Cartesian logic and the proliferation of parties in response to ideological differences, this has been only one of the contradictions of political behavior. It is not only the continued large Communist Party vote in national and municipal elections, but also its hold on the CGT, that reflects these considerations.

Another consideration is the party's organizational strength. The Communist Party is an incomparably better instrument in a power struggle than any of its competitors. If the party's discipline is not perfect at the lower echelons, it is immeasurably tighter than any other French party has ever achieved. Its leadership has—in Soviet terms— "passed the test of underground work," of "class battles," and of Soviet policy switches. It is experienced—almost every leading figure held a prewar leadership position—yet it is not overage.

The leadership is predominantly, and ostentatiously, one of working class origins. Such a leadership, at secondary as well as top levels, has not come naturally or easily, but as the result of constant stimulation and development. For respectability and decoration flattering to the party's followers, it parades a host of famous writers, artists, and scientists. In France these are "the parsley of all sauces," as Rossi puts it, "admired and exploited, used to dress up all enterprises, noble or shady."[5]

After the war, in contrast to the dissensions and purges which shook the party in the 1920's and 1930's, there was until mid-1952 no major dissidence. Whatever the inner debates between trade union leaders and purely political leaders, no echo reached a waiting public ear. The Communist Party achieved a coördination of union and party lines beyond anything its rivals could attempt. Had it remained in the government beyond May 1947, the unions' subordination to its governmentalism would have become an increasingly heavy mortgage. But it quickly rebuilt its union strength in opposition. Then it repeatedly led the unions too far in opposition. Even these demands on the unions drove no important Communist unionists out of the party nor—after 1948—any unions out of the CGT.

THE CGT IN COMMUNIST STRATEGY AND TACTICS

As the most important mass organization in France, the CGT has had a large role in the strategy and tactics of the Communist Party and the Soviet Union.[6] In the years from 1944 to 1947, when the Commu-

---

[5] *Physiologie du parti communiste français,* p. 333.

[6] Cf. Val R. Lorwin, "Communist Strategy and Tactics in Western European Labor Movements," *Industrial and Labor Relations Review,* vol. 6, no. 3, April 1953, pp. 383-390.

nist Party probably expected to take power within a near future, it used
the CGT to spur production and maintain work discipline, in a mild
forecast of unionism in a people's democracy. In opposition, the Communist Party has used the CGT for all its major purposes: to hamper
economic recovery and accelerate inflationary trends, to deepen the gulf
between working people and the government, to bring the party back in
a "government of democratic union," to support the long Soviet peace
offensive, to hamstring the integration of France into Western union
and Atlantic defense, to weaken the French will to fight if war should
come.

Its methods have ranged from straight wage demands to outright
political strikes, from the proliferation of committees to factory commando raids, coupling political and foreign policy themes with economic
grievances, to fight "the policy of misery *and* war."[7] Below the surface
of overt action, it has used the CGT as a base and cover to prepare for
the possibility of having to operate underground.

International pacificism has been blended with fighting appeals to job
and wage interests, the "defense of national independence" with "proletarian internationalism," and all with an increasingly crude and xeno-
phobic anti-Americanism. In the image the Communists have built up,
the enemy has been not just the American government or Wall Street,
but the United States and Americans. The similarity of much of this
propaganda to that of the Nazis is striking. The Marxian themes have
been the inevitability of capitalist crisis, and the inevitable war to avoid
the inevitable crisis—unless the inevitably victorious masses prevent the
inevitable war.

After Maurice Thorez shocked even a blasé public by his declaration
that the French people would welcome the Soviet Army if it occupied
Paris in righteous "pursuit of an aggressor,"[8] Frachon, Raynaud, and
other leaders at the CGT national committee sessions at once echoed the
statement, in slightly more veiled terms, as CGT policy.[9] The executive
board soon issued a "solemn declaration" that the working class of
France would "never consider itself bound" by the government's signature to the North Atlantic Treaty.[10]

The scope of party manipulation of the CGT for foreign policy demands may be seen, by way of illustration, in the agitation of a single
period of a few weeks in the summer of 1950. Unionists were called

---

[7] CGT Executive Board communique, *Le Peuple,* June 28, 1950. Underlining supplied. The significance of this propaganda line has been its strident repetition; specific
citations would be superfluous and boring.

[8] "Une Déclaration capitale de Maurice Thorez," *L'Humanité,* February 23, 1949.

[9] *Le Peuple,* March 3, 1949.

[10] *Le Peuple,* March 17, 1949.

upon to demonstrate or strike for the withdrawal of American troops from Korea, for the end of the war in Indo-China, for the acquittal of Partisans of Peace on trial for obstructing military shipments. They were to manifest against the lengthening of military service, against the Schumann Plan, and for a "government of democratic union." They were to organize Committees for the Defense of Peace, obtain signatures to the Stockholm Peace Petition, and promote the Youth Peace Relays. They were reminded to refuse to manufacture or transport armaments. They were asked to stop work in protest against the assassination of the head of the Belgian Communist Party. This listing, moreover, does not include the unions' economic demands, whose interweaving with the foreign policy issues was perhaps the most effective political action.

With those French union political actions which have taken the dramatic form of the general strike, history appears to have dealt rather consistently, according to their purposes. The strike of February 12, 1934, was a political demonstration to infuse courage into the threatened Republic: it succeeded. That of 1920 reflected a struggle for power within the CGT; those of 1938 and 1947 represented party manipulation of the unions against party enemies: they failed. The Duclos strike in 1952 was the most unabashed use of the CGT's forces for party maneuver; it was the most evident failure. It was unfortunate that the failures of the general strikes were at the expense not only of political manipulators, but also of rank-and-file workingmen, and of unionism itself.

MECHANISMS OF CONTROL

In a democratic community, the value of political control of unions is enhanced if it can be disguised. The CGT affirms its political independence on the strength of fifty years of "apolitical" CGT history, the membership of many non-Communists, and the votes in shop elections of many more non-Communist workers. All these have little to do with the facts of present control.

The mechanisms of control of the CGT by the party include interlocking directorates[11] at all echelons, the interchangeability of activists between party and unions, the party apparatus which parallels that of the CGT, fractions within the unions, and the party press. At the top, Benoît Frachon is one of France's most important Communists. He was responsible, perhaps more than any other one man, for the party's successful passage into clandestine operations after its outlawry in 1939.[12]

---

[11] Of course interlocking party-union directorates may be perfectly compatible with democratic control (as in Britain, Belgium, Sweden).

[12] Rossi, *Les Communistes français pendant la drôle de guerre*, p. 97.

During the clandestine period of 1939-1945, he and Jacques Duclos were the heads of the party. A prewar Politburo member, he now holds no official party post. The party hardly pretends that this is anything more than a formal concession to the rules of syndicalist virtue. As the names of the nominees to the central committee were read to the 1950 party convention, before their unanimous election, the convention was assured, "So that the CGT may unite the whole working class, we do not propose to you the candidacies of Benoît Frachon and Gaston Monmousseau. But we consider them members of the official leadership of our party."[13] Among the members of the central committee then chosen were eight top CGT leaders, including the general secretaries of the national metal trades, building trades, railroad, and gas and electric workers unions and the departmental federations of the Seine (Paris) and the Bouches-du-Rhône (Marseille).

The CGT in 1946 changed its statutes to permit members of the confederation's executive board to be members of party executives. It still prohibits them from holding political office. The French Communist movement is rich enough in men so that, unlike the Italian, it has enough to go around for both parliamentary and top trade union office. It does not suffer the diminishing of effectiveness which comes from too much doubling in union and parliamentary brass.

Party newspapers represent another form of interlocking directorate. Frachon and other top CGT leaders frequently use the Communist daily press, especially the Paris organ, *L'Humanité*, to discuss union problems and issue strike directives.

The confederation's most conspicuous non-Communist (or nominal non-Communist) is its cogeneral secretary, Alain Le Léap. Devoting most of his time to the confederation's foreign affairs, he has taken a spotlighted position in the international Communist peace front, the Partisans of Peace, as well as succeeding Jouhaux as the CGT vicepresident in the World Federation of Trade Unions. Several other non-Communists, none of real importance, have served on the CGT executive board since the FO split. Non-Communists have headed a few important organizations, notably Ehni, national leader of the printers' union at the time of the split. Most of his non-Communist associates in the printers' executive, however, were eased out of office. The several non-Communist department federation heads include the one outstanding pure syndicalist of the present CGT, Julien Forgues of Toulouse.

With the wide purge of the CGT in 1944-1946, FO's withdrawal

---

[13] *L'Humanité,* April 7, 1950. But the CGT's *Peuple* of that week did not mention this honor bestowed on its two leaders.

of leading non-Communists in 1947, and no desertions of the Communist Party by trade union leaders, there has been little need of political purging in the CGT. An exception was the case of Yves Dellac, which represented an amazing admission of the political obligations of the CGT. Dellac was one of the non-Communists on the executive board, first chosen after the FO split. When he was reëlected in 1948, "no one had any illusions about his real worth," Le Léap later admitted. But Dellac had only two weeks before been elected a member of the executive committee of the Socialist Unity Party, a feeble fellow-traveling group attempting to duplicate the role of the Nenni Socialist Party in Italy. For the CGT not to have reëlected him then, said Le Léap, "would have been an affront to the Socialist Unity Party, which would have been prejudicial to working class unity."[14] All this came out because Dellac in 1950 became tainted with Titoism, and was expelled from the Socialist Unity Party. "Working class unity" was then served by turning him out of CGT office.

The parallel apparatus of the party can observe and direct the unions from the national level down to the local. At the intermediate levels of the union structure, control is exercised not only from above through the confederation and national union, but by the departmental secretary ("secrétaire fédéral") of the party. His opposite number in the CGT is the department federation secretary, in practically all cases a Communist, usually a member of the party executive of the department. As Thorez reminded a conference of party departmental secretaries, they are "responsible for the *work in the factory, and not only that which concerns the organization of the party.*"[15]

A number of non-Communists occupy department or local union positions, mostly unpaid. Some are identified as Catholics or as Socialists, others with no party. Their value for demonstration purposes is obvious. Thus Frachon was able to beam from photographs at a national convention with one arm around a Socialist postal worker, who had resigned his FO job, and the other arm around a Catholic worker-priest, an official of the Paris metal workers' union.[16] While a few of the non-Communists retain some liberty of personal action, they cannot influence major policies. Their value for demonstration purposes, their personal following, or the noncritical industrial positions they control have given them temporary immunity from the choice between conformity and removal.

---

[14] *Le Peuple,* October 4, 1950. Cf. *Force ouvrière,* October 12, 1950.
[15] Maurice Thorez, "Le Rôle du secrétaire fédéral," *Cahiers du communisme,* vol. 26, no. 4, April 1949, p. 439. Underlining supplied.
[16] *Le Peuple,* June 7, 1951.

The union fraction is not an organizational unit of the party, but a group of its members boring from within the union organizations at a given echelon.[17] It is most important when the union or federation is the theatre of struggle, when tactics have to be concerted against the enemy Where no organized opposition lifts its head, there is less work for the party fraction.

The factory cell works outside the local union, at the place of work. It can arouse pressures within the plant to undermine a CGT local or section not in the hands of the faithful, or propel it in the direction desired by the party. Where the local is Communist-controlled, the cell can make the most, for political purposes, of its action.

The factory cell, as distinguished from the geographic unit of organization of the socialist and other parties, is one of Communism's major organizational innovations. The "organizational Bolshevization" of the party has been going on ever since Zinoviev, head of the Comintern, told the French delegates to the 1924 World Communist Congress, "Factory cells and committees, here are the first requirements we put to the Communist Party of France."[18] This process had to be resumed after liberation,[19] and again after the 1947 change in line. The leadership has frequently manifested vexation with the factory cells' weaknesses in number, membership, and activity.[20] After weeks of "self-criticism" by middle rank party officials for the deficiencies of the cells, Lecoeur, organization secretary, reminded the 1950 convention that "first place must go to the question of the functioning and the setting up of factory cells."[21]

Many CGTU locals in the early 1930's were reduced almost entirely to party members; cells and local unions simply overlapped. Both in membership and the support of nonmembers the CGT is much stronger than the old CGTU, but there are signs of the difficulties of a generation ago. A party leader warned: "It is difficult for the workers in many factories to tell what differentiates the Communist cell from the union

---

[17] On both fractions and cells, see Collinet, *Esprit du syndicalisme,* esp. pp. 92-99.

[18] *Bulletin communiste,* August 1, 1924, p. 733, cited by Walter, *Histoire du parti Communiste français,* p. 166.

[19] In December 1946 there were 8,363 factory cells as compared with 15,860 local (geographic) cells and 12,060 rural cells. Einaudi and others, *Communism in Western Europe,* p. 84. For numbers of factory cells in relation to local cells at various periods from 1937 to 1946, see Maurice Duverger, *Les Partis politiques,* pp. 51-52.

[20] The highest percentage of serious activists is to be found in the factory cells, less in the area cells of the cities, and least in the rural cells, concludes a recent student of Communist Party organization, Charles Micaud, "Organization and Leadership of the French Communist Party," *World Politics,* vol. 4, no. 3, April 1952, p. 334. See also Maurice Duverger, *Les Partis politiques,* pp. 45-55, 68-70.

[21] *L'Humanité,* April 4, 1950.

local."[22] Extensive centralization of work and control of offices in the unions have added to this confusion. "Because of a centralization pushed too far and leading to union activities of a general nature," said a party and CGT leader, "confusion is easily possible with the higher organization of the working class: the Communist Party."[23] Despite numerous admonitions by party heads, the confusion has persisted, "aggravated by the composition of the executive bodies of the union movement, which at all echelons, do not include a sufficient number of nonparty union cadres."[24]

Within the CGT membership, Communist influence is of the order of a widening series of circles. First, there is the small hard core of Communists-through-thick-and-thin, which probably includes most of the full-time paid officials of the unions. Second, there are the union members who are also party members. Their loyalty to the party may be unshaken in so-called normal times, but in a crisis would depend on the way in which the issues were presented, on the loyalties and pressures opposing those of the party and the Soviet Union. Third, there is the circle of CGT members who vote Communist as a matter of course and class conformity but are not party members. Fourth, there are those who remain within the Communist-dominated unions while themselves either non-Communist or specifically anti-Communist. Obviously no one can give numbers for these categories. The hard core might be of the magnitude of 5 or at the most 10 per cent of the CGT membership. As union membership falls, the hard-core percentage rises. In the second circle would be a large number of the nearly half a million members of the Communist Party. The third, with their families, form a high percentage of the five million men and women who have voted Communist since the war.

The French workers to whom the Communist Party appeals are not, in general, the most depressed.[25] In the 1930's it reached many unemployed; since the war, however, there have been comparatively few workers unemployed. The party has shown concern about its failure to attract the worst off. "Profound misery does not 'spontaneously' create the conditions favorable to the struggle," the Seine department execu-

---

[22] André Souquière, "Après la conférence fédérale de la Seine," *Cahiers du communisme*, vol. 29, no. 2, February 1952, p. 185. See also Auguste Lecoeur, "Parti et syndicats," *Servir la France*, No. 59, June 1950, p. 9.

[23] Arrachard, "Pour une structure syndicale plus efficace," *Servir la France*, no. 41-42, November-December 1948, p. 42.

[24] André Souquière, as cited in note 22, this chapter.

[25] Cf. Rossi, *La Physiologie du parti communiste français*, pp. 331-333; Collinet, *Lettre aux militants*, no. 3, February 15, 1951, "Les Causes de l'Influence communiste en France," pp. 4-5.

tive committee observed, complaining of local elections "marked by the abstention of numerous workers belonging to the poorest categories." Yet certain comrades "persist in remaining indifferent to the growing misery of workers, their brothers"; some "even overtly show scorn for these unfortunate people whom they regard as 'not worth much.' "[26]

Among young workers, the Communists have achieved a fairly high degree of success. Since liberation they have not revived the Communist Youth. They have operated through the party itself, the CGT, and special interest fronts: a workers' sports organization ("Fédération Sportive et Gymnastique du Travail"), a workers' travel organization ("Tourisme et Travail"), a girls' organization ("Union des Jeunes Filles de France"), and the general youth front ("Union de la Jeunesse Républicaine de France"). A centralized and disciplined party can train, place, and promote young people in a way which the decentralized democratic Socialist Party, encrusted with seniority rules and local jealousies, finds impossible.[27] The same possibilities, used more discreetly because of election requirements, are available for the promotion of youth in the CGT. At the 1951 CGT convention, the average age of delegates and alternates was only 33½ years. Less than 10 per cent were over 50 years of age; over half were under 35.[28] But neither party nor CGT has permitted itself to be carried away by a surge of new blood; both organizations have kept the top positions in the hands of tested leaders with prewar experience.

It has, however, been difficult to interest young rank-and-file workers in the routine business of party and union. "The young people come out in strikes and demonstrations, not to the meetings," said the Communist, André Tollet, in charge of CGT youth activities. "They are active when they feel that their activity serves some purpose."[29]

COMMUNIST WEAKNESS

For all its seeming inevitability, the Communist hold on workers remains conditional and vulnerable. The interests of the Soviet Union,

---

[26] Maurice Colin, *L'Humanité,* March 10, 1950. Cf. the fragmentary but interesting findings of Bettelheim and Frère in their recent study of a "French Middletown," Auxerre. They found a very low percentage of political interest or party membership in the categories of domestic servants and unskilled laborers. A higher percentage of interest was shown by the category of "workers" above the unskilled level. Out of discretion, the questionnaire did not ask the names of parties. Charles Bettelheim and Suzanne Frère, *Une Ville française moyenne; Auxerre en 1950, étude de structure sociale et urbaine* (Cahiers de la Fondation Nationale des Sciences Politiques, No. 17), (Paris, 1950), pp. 236-238, 264.

[27] Cf. Duverger, *Les Partis politiques,* pp. 189-197.

[28] *Le Peuple,* June 7, 1951, p. 4.

[29] Youth committee, CGT convention, *Le Peuple,* May 31, 1951, p. 2.

hence those of the French Communist Party, are basically incompatible with those of French workers. If workers have been generally unaware of that incompatibility, it has emerged in crises. For all the damage they did, the big strikes of late 1947 and 1948 collapsed, not so much because of police action, but finally because of workers' opposition.

In democratic countries, Communist Party recruitment is a revolving door. Since 1947, the French party has lost hundreds of thousands of workers and active unionists who joined it after 1944 out of admiration of its work and sacrifices in the resistance, comradeship born in that experience, a feeling that it was the wave of the future, or the pressures exerted in a period of confusion. Thorez tried to dismiss membership losses as merely the dropping away of fair weather friends: "We have lost some of the adherents who came to us in the years of relative facility, on the morrow of liberation. These people recoiled from the difficulties of our task."[30] Some did. But many recoiled rather from the party's relationship to the unions and the French Republic, as they saw it clarified after 1947.

Defeats in strikes and politicization of union activity have driven millions from the CGT unions, and dulled the confidence of those who remain. Economic demands assert themselves in conflict with the more flagrant political demands made of the unions, in a way the party periodically brands as "economism." This is the sin defined by Lecoeur, miners union leader and party organization secretary, in terms typical of its Leninist origins: "It is only when the trade union organization does not carry on, together with the political fight, the campaign of explanation to show the close tie which exists between the difficult material situation of the workers and the reactionary policy of the government which is its cause, and only when the struggle for peace . . . is not carried on with vigor, that the trade union organization can be charged with economism."[31]

This is the dilemma of the party leaders in the CGT. If they push the unions too far in political strikes, they weaken them and "confuse their role with that of the party." For many workers, as a party leader complained, "fail to see that under present historical conditions the struggle for peace is the most effective struggle we can wage for the workers' vital interests."[32] But if the leaders avoid political issues, making possible joint economic action with other unions and breaking the CGT's

---

[30] Speech at twelfth party convention, 1950, cited by Auguste Lecoeur, "Lettre aux secrétaires et trésoriers de cellule," *Cahiers du communisme*, vol. 29, no. 2, February 1952, p. 188.

[31] "Parti et syndicats," *Servir la France*, no. 59, June 1950, p. 8.

[32] Souquière, as cited in note 22, this chapter.

isolation, one of the periodic shifts in the party's emphasis is bound to bring them rebuke for lapsing into "economism." "The obstacles are sometimes within ourselves," said Hénaff, head of the Paris region CGT. In the campaign for signatures to the Stockholm Appeal to outlaw the atom bomb, Hénaff cited the "stupefying" answer of the Paris transport union officers: "Oh, we have not yet begun to work on that. We are too busy preparing for our convention next month." Here, he said, "these officials of an important union . . . continue to sleep on the edge of the volcano. How can they imagine the preparation of their convention without active and daily participation in the great fight to prevent war?" His advice was categorical: "Not a single leader of a local union or branch, not a shop steward or plant committee member, not a single dues collector, man or woman, should say a word, write a line, issue an instruction, which is not in this direction."[33]

From this obsessional propaganda many workers turn in boredom. A state of tension cannot be maintained indefinitely, when the enemy is not at the gates. Workers may by custom and by class be so cut off from contacts with the rest of the community as to be almost completely swathed in Communist-controlled activities and sources of information. But the party and the CGT cannot in the French democracy create a closed society around them. Nor can the party exert its full force in the demonstrations of strength and the perpetual agitations it asks of unionists. That it might do only in a bid for power which the international situation has not allowed it to make.

FO AND THE SOCIALIST PARTY

Long-continued communist inroads on its industrial labor constituency have not dimmed the Socialist Party's assertions to representation of the working class: on the contrary. Shortly after liberation it toyed vaguely with the idea of a Labor Party along British lines. But it soon perceived that it lacked the essential element; it could not compete with the Communist Party for the support of labor unions. But the party, which is close to the FO unions, still has significant minority support in labor ranks. Its appeal to workers is compounded of its leftist tradition, a program slanted toward labor, a temper of reasonableness, and the long practice of machine politics.

The party's leftist heritage and a mild form of class conformity keep some workers in the Socialist Party or at least voting Socialist. In doctrine, the party offers a humane version of Marxist emancipation, to be achieved by democratic action. Its immediate program offers current

---

[33] *L'Humanité,* May 20, 1950.

satisfactions to labor, all the more freely since the party left the government. It has been vocally anticolonial, except in conduct of the Ministry of Colonies when it held that post. Its old pacifism and internationalism divide it deeply between European responsibility and the more popular neutralism. But neither on workers' material interests nor the hope of peace can it compete effectively with the lack of scruple of communist propaganda. Only in its anticlericalism does it make a comparable polemic appeal. Otherwise there is a mild ineffectuality, a routine and doctrinaire quality, to all its attempts at opportunistic agitation.

The contrast between Socialist and Communist Party leadership is obvious to workers. As against the Communist Party's many leaders of proletarian origin, the executive committee of the Socialist Party (in 1950) showed not a single member who had been a manual worker or had even come from a family of manual workers. In leadership, as in following, it is largely a party of civil servants (FO's chief constituency also), white collar, and professional people—doctors, lawyers, journalists, engineers, teachers. Out of every 100 Socialist voters, a recent poll found, 13 were civil servants, as compared with 5 among Communist voters. The Socialists counted 21 production workers out of 100 voters, the Communists 38.[34] Only 30 per cent of its voters were under 35 years of age, as compared with 42 per cent for the Communist Party.

The Socialist Party suffers from lack of an effective youth movement which might be a source of renewal and leadership for the FO unions as well as for the party. A purely electoral party like the Radicals may wait for the members' beards to grow, but not a mass party, allied with labor organizations. This weakness is both sign and cause of the "crisis of socialism" of which Socialists constantly talk. The outward manifestation of this crisis was a decline in popular vote from 4,561,000 in 1945 to 2,784,000 in 1951; and in membership from the high of 335,000 in 1945 to less than a third of that number in 1952.[35]

The slipping of support in the nation and especially among workers caused a six-year debate in the Socialist Party over the issue of its participation in the government. Its anxiety was increased when the Com-

---

[34] *Sondages: Revue française de l'opinion publique,* vol. 14, no. 3, 1952, special number. A recent study by a critical second-rank Socialist leader adds quantitative data about the social composition of the party leadership at the department level. Pierre Rimbert, "L'Avenir du parti socialiste," *Revue socialiste,* n. s. no. 54, February 1952, and no. 55, March 1952.

[35] In 1953 the party itself claimed only 110,000 members. *Le Monde,* July 4, 1953, quoting Guy Mollet, general secretary. For a good brief summation, see Henry W. Ehrmann, "The Decline of the Socialist Party," with extensive bibliography, in *Modern France,* pp. 181-199. See also Adolf Sturmthal, "Democratic Socialism in Europe," *World Politics,* October 1950, vol. 3, no. 1, pp. 88-113; Jacques Fauvet, *Les Forces politiques en France,* 2d ed. (Paris, 1951), pp. 56-95.

munists resumed their freedom of attack outside the government. "The greatest service we can render the Communist Party," said a former Socialist cabinet minister, "is to give the impression that to break with it is to move to the right." [36] To regain some of the industrial workers it hoped to represent, and to help the civil service workers it did represent, the Socialists in the government brought on five cabinet crises in four years over wage and salary issues. In 1951-1952 the party definitely moved into the opposition. Because of the need to distinguish its own "loyal opposition" from the Communist opposition, however, the Socialist Party could enjoy no more than a restricted freedom of action. Whatever the chances for a Socialist revival—and they were not brilliant—they were bound up with those of the non-Communist union movement.

The relations of FO and the Socialist Party are relations of equality and mutual respect—or mutual despair. The Socialist Party could not control FO, even if it wished to. It has neither the philosophy nor the mechanism to do so. Despite a few sporadic attempts, the Socialists have never suceeded in developing factory cells. To their organization on a geographical basis, they tried in the late 1930's to add "Socialist shop groups." These were revived after the war as they took belated alarm over the Communist conquest of the CGT. But the shop groups gave the Communist factory cells little competition. Some were active at the period of the FO split from the CGT; most have withered away since then. Shop groups are the device of a disciplined party; most of the Socialist comrades would rather spend their spare time at home or at the café tables than in organizational drives or shop meetings.

The Force Ouvrière banner bears the motto, "Against any political control." This is a throwback to FO's origins in protest against Communist methods. It corresponds also to a sensitivity, by unions often on the defensive against Communist attack, on the score of involvement with the Socialist Party. The constitutions of the confederation and of many national unions and department federations forbid any member of the executive to hold or even run for political office.

FO is not, as is often said for the sake of an easy pigeonhole, "socialist." Almost all FO leaders who are politically identified are Socialists. But no member of the confederation's executive board is at all conspicuous in the Socialist Party; about half are not members of any party. One leading FO official, Capocci, head of the clerical employees, was for a time a member of the Socialist Party executive committee, but resigned to make clear FO's independence. Jouhaux is essentially Socialist

---

[36] Edouard Depreux, "Le Vrai problème: L'autonomie socialiste," *Revue socialiste,* n. s. no. 42, December 1950, p. 473.

in outlook and occasionally refers to himself as a Marxist, but he has always avoided party ties, making it easier for him to work with those both to the right and the left of the SFIO. Bothereau is unaffiliated politically. Some lower rank FO leaders are officers and candidates of the Socialist Party, but relations vary greatly from region to region. FO leaders both inside and outside the Socialist Party do not hesitate to criticize it vigorously.

The Socialist Party's attempts to obtain outright support from FO have usually brought irritated protests by Socialists as well as non-Socialists in the labor organization. (In part this has been due to the lack of preparation and maladroitness of the overtures.) There has been a close parallel for years between almost all the positions of the two organizations; the FO program of economic reform is a broad one of generally socialist planning and economic control and development; nationalization is hardly an issue now with either, except to defend existing nationalizations.

The party in 1952 reminded FO that "the isolation and lack of contacts limit and retard results, risk paralyzing and making anemic our respective movements, reinforce the positions of capitalism and totalitarianism. Union independence, necessary as it is, which we intend to respect, must not . . . end in a repudiation of all contact with the only democratic party of the working class."[37] In 1953 the party made a broader attempt; it launched the idea of a "democratic and socialist front." The free unions were invited to help form a new political alignment, which would awaken the masses, end the rightist control of government, and resume the march of social reform: in short a Popular Front without Communists or the CGT. Only if the realignment should show a broad political base, going well beyond the Socialists, could it meet with the desire of FO to head off the danger of a Communist-style Popular Front. Otherwise FO fears it will be increasing its own weakness, rather than strengthening itself or the party, by overt ties with the Socialist Party.

THE CFTC AND THE MRP

The relations of the CFTC to the MRP, like those of FO to the Socialist Party, are the relations of independent centers of power with a community of interest and overlapping of constituency. Most European Catholic union movements have been associated with national Catholic parties. Before World War II, the CFTC, although working actively in Parliament with deputies friendly to Catholic unionism, avoided close

---

[37] *Le Populaire,* May 27, 1952.

ties with the small Popular Democratic Party or the smaller, more left-ish Young Republic. Temptation to political commitment was minimized by the weakness of these parties (the Popular Democrats had 2 per cent of the vote in 1936). Since the war the CFTC has avoided commitment to the far stronger MRP.

The renewed vitality in postwar France of Catholic faith, intellectual life, and unionism has made Catholic politics more important than it has been for generations. The new Popular Republican Movement blossomed suddenly after liberation as one of the big three parties of the government. It drew strength from the resistance activity of many of its moving spirits, their youth and energy, and a vague social idealism suited to the period. It profited from the temporary eclipse of the old right parties. A coalition of different social views, like most parties on a religious base, it was the farthest left of all the European Catholic or Christian political parties. The MRP went along with the social and economic reforms of 1944-1946 : a matter more of humanitarian temper than of specific program; a large streak, but not a foundation, of Christian socialism.

In the June 1946 elections the MRP was for a moment the largest party in popular vote. Many who then voted for it as the best bet against the Communists or the party closest to De Gaulle soon deserted it for the new Gaullist party or the revived parties of the "classical right." Its vote dropped from its dazzling 1946 height of 5,590,000 to slightly more than half of that five years later. The losses were not only on the right. The support of the MRP among Catholic workers was eroded by its years as part or head of successive governments. Its confusion in the attempt to recover labor support (and retain middle class urban and rural voters) was typified in the party's three-way split in the final Assembly vote on the minimum wage sliding scale bill.[38] By the close of 1952, some of the MRP deputies made protection of the family allowance funds an issue for their break with Pinay, forcing his resignation. But they were back in succeeding conservative governments, torn between the governmental participation to which they had been accustomed since the party's origin and the hope of recovering popularity in the opposition. An MRP senator stated his party's dilemma : "Doubtless the misfortune of the times may be so great that participation in the government majority does not carry with it any real influence—and opposition does not carry any hope of victory."[39] The gloomy charac-

---

[38] Forty-six MRP deputies voted for the bill, 10 against it, and 30 abstained from voting. *Le Monde,* July 10, 1952.

[39] Léo Hamon, "Lutter dans la majorité ou se replier dans l'opposition," *Le Monde,* January 16, 1953.

terization almost summed up the situation of the free unions as well as of the MRP and Socialist parties.

Within the CFTC, voters of every party are to be found. The majority leadership has been close to the MRP, as a matter of spiritual affinity and personal relationships. Some MRP leaders, including half a dozen prominent deputies, but none of the party heads, have come up through the ranks of labor and CFTC unionism, including Paul Bacon, for many years Minister of Labor. No less than 38 CFTC officials were elected to the first Constituent Assembly. These included four executive board members given special dispensation by the 1945 convention to retain their posts.[40] But the confederation ruled that full-time officers of the CFTC or presidents and secretaries of its affiliates could not at the same time hold political office.[41]

At the time when the CFTC removed the reference in its statutes to the papal encyclicals, it would hardly have been consistent to commit itself to a Catholic political party, even one of faint confessional tinge and bold social program. If in the first flush of MRP success, some of the right wing considered doing so—the railroad workers, with six MRP deputies in the Constituent Assembly, and the white collar employees—the left wing successfully opposed the idea. In 1946 a resolution for a political tie with the MRP was decisively defeated.[42] The next year the convention unanimously amended the constitution to declare: "Trade union organizations must differentiate their responsibilities from those of political groups, and the CFTC intends that its action shall be entirely independent with regard to the state, cabinets, and parties . . . Strictly limiting its action to the representation and defense of the general interests of labor, the confederation determines this action on its own responsibility and in full independence of all outside organizations, political or religious."[43]

The CFTC has refused to take a stand with the MRP on the issue which has so often divided Catholic from non-Catholic France, that of state subsidies to church schools. This old question, arising from what seemed like history's scrap heap, in 1951 dislocated the Socialist-MRP modus vivendi which had made possible the Third Force cabinets. In the face of national and international problems of political and economic survival confronting France, the intransigence on both sides

---

[40] *Syndicalisme*, September 22, 1945.

[41] CFTC, *22ᵉ congrès, rapport moral*, 1946, pp. 51ff.

[42] *Syndicalisme*, June 15, 1946.

[43] *Syndicalisme*, May 29, 1947. For an account of the change in the statutes, from the point of view of a union which pushed for the changes, see CFTC, Syndicat Général de l'Education Nationale, Commission de formation sociale, note no. 2, January 15, 1951, "Documents et remarques sur l'histoire du syndicalisme français de l'inspiration chrétienne."

of this fight might seem like the most despairful illustration of the historical-mindedness of French politics—or the alarmed search for electoral support. Although the CFTC refused to take part in this debate, the bitterness between the MRP and the Socialist Party could not help being reflected in revivals of anticlericalism in FO and greater difficulties of coöperation between FO and CFTC unions.

The left wing of the confederation, which had pushed for neutrality vis-à-vis the MRP, sought vigorously for other forms of political action. For several years its members have discussed, with a rare willingness to begin from scratch, the bases and forms for the political activities of free trade unionists. While talking of a "new left," they have also viewed with sympathy the pragmatic approach of the AF of L and CIO political groups in the United States, sounding an empirical note which contrasted—for some of them—with moments of doctrinaire anticapitalism.[44] For they have been convinced of the necessities for positive political relations with government and democratic parties, going beyond bursts of special pressures or of impotent rage.

The confederation as a whole has moved from fear of the state (along with lobbying activities) to a broad concept of political action, whose goals are more clearly seen than its methods. While continuing to emphasize the necessity of social transformation in relations at the level of the single enterprise, the CFTC has given added emphasis to national goals requiring essentially political action. "The indispensable perspectives of economic and social transformation" included a broad degree of economic planning under a firmer state impulsion, with trade union participation, government investment and public direction of the investment of private funds, and the universally demanded and always distant tax reform.

"It is up to us to think through the problems of the effectiveness of the union movement in terms of the nation as it is organized in 1953 and not as it functioned in the nineteenth century," said the CTFC's new general secretary, Georges Levard.[45] And the new president, Maurice Bouladoux, declared that "Union independence in politics must not become union impotence in the face of the political activities directed against the most essential interests of the working class . . . One might conceive of understandings with political groups to the extent that one

---

[44] The *Reconstruction* group of the CFTC left is not to be confused with the small fellow-traveling group of the Christian Progressives. Their bulletin *Reconstruction* has carried many severely critical articles on the Soviet state and its world outlook, on French communist and CGT ideology, strategy and tactics. See, for example, the declaration of Paul Vignaux at the 1949 CFTC convention, reproduced in "A propos d'une déclaration: Rappel de notre orientation," *Reconstruction*, no. 23, July-August 1949, pp. 1-5.

[45] *Syndicalisme-Magazine*, June 1953. Report of convention.

or more of them would clearly undertake by a precise agreement to pursue in common the realization of this or that point or all of the union program."[46] He conceived of the setting up of local or regional "centers of political study and training" of CFTC and other interested people which might "gradually get our positions accepted by political organizations at the base."

These official remarks in 1953 indicate the early stages of a reformulation of political policies and methods. There was a feeling that whatever winds were to lift the unions out of five years' doldrums, and the nation from economic stagnation, would have to blow first from political quarters. There was also a fear—as in FO—that if workers' apathy gave way to an explosion against the failures of collective bargaining and the drab conservatism of government, in a "new 1936," only the Communists would profit, unless there were a vigorous democratic alternative to a Popular Front. To this danger the CFTC was particularly sensitive because so many of its leaders were of an age which had first known union responsibilities in 1936, when they had fought for the right of the CFTC to exist.

In the CFTC program, the element that was Catholic was not any specific economic or political proposal, but the preoccupation with moral values and the concern for the individual and the family. The Church could not be praised or blamed for the program, which the CFTC tried to derive from its experience in the temporal realm. This originality and independence were stated by a St. Etienne leader in words whose pungency the majority might not have approved, but whose philosophy was becoming accepted: "We do not want to be, and we are no longer, merely foot soldiers occupying the terrain after it has been made safe by a bombardment of papal encyclicals."

THE CGSI AND THE RPF

The newest of the trade union centers, the General Confederation of Independent Unions, has had the most confused political relations. The CGSI brought together Gaullists, ex-Vichyites, and ex-Communists. Before they joined in forming the CGSI, the Gaullists had blown hot and cold on the idea of forming a separate labor federation of their own. They were the one organized partisan political force in the CGSI.

The Gaullist labor, social and economic program has been so cloudy as to defy analysis. Nobody other than the General, and probably not even he, knows what he would try to do if he returned to power. He has deplored the class struggle, urged profit-sharing, and spoken of an un-

---

[46] 27ᵉ Congrès Confédéral, 1953, *La CFTC face aux responsibilités du syndicalisme moderne, rapport d'orientation*, pp. 72, 24. (Report as outgoing general secretary.)

defined "association" between capital and labor.[47] Gaullists have offered a hodge-podge of warmed over guild notions, the older hierarchic Catholic social doctrine, scraps of Italian and Vichy corporatism, all served up with a hot sauce of anti-Communism. Most workers have found this indigestible. Nor has it attracted many employers; they have preferred the traditional right to the uncertainties of Gaullism, particularly as the domestic Communist tide receded.

The RPF has been keenly aware of its weakness among workers. It has maintained RPF factory groups, noted for their toughness against the Communist "separatists," as De Gaulle calls them. It has also tried to win labor support by such symbolic efforts as May Day celebrations. Its clientele, however, includes few proletarians, but many white collar workers, artisans, and shopkeepers, who "fear the proletarian condition and reject it spiritually although they are not far from it materially."[48]

Unionists suspect in the General and his entourage both the old-fashioned trappings of the military and the clerical and the possibilities of a more up-to-date fascism.[49] The very vagueness of his social policy is alarming, nor are they reassured by the attempts of several brilliant ex-leftists in his following to give Gaullism a social philosophy. The exigencies of maintaining power might lead him to suppress first the CGT and then other unions, they fear; that in itself would give the Communists the leadership of an anti-Gaullist movement. He might be led step by step toward a one-party state, they think, and might conceivably restore, with greater success, the universal obligatory unions which Vichy tried to set up.

Within the CGSI, conflict between the Gaullists and other elements reached the stage of hand-to-hand battle in 1952. Amidst mutual recriminations of the suspicious origin of financial support, the confederation split at its 1952 convention, leaving neither wing with more than scattered membership. The two splinter confederations claiming to be the CGSI continued to occupy different floors in the same building. At the head of each was a former Communist deputy.

By 1953 the defections in the Gaullist parliamentary group, followed by De Gaulle's attempt once more to take the Rally of the French People out of party politics, lessened the thrust of his movement. Meanwhile one more labor confederation which had summoned the workers of France to independent trade unionism and unity above party lines had been torn apart by party politics.

---

[47] For De Gaulle's most important statement on the "association of capital and labor," see *L'Année politique, 1948,* edited by André Siegfried and others, p. 324, and brief discussion in François Goguel, *France under the Fourth Republic,* pp. 49-50.

[48] Jacques Fauvet, *Les Forces politiques,* p. 239.

[49] See for example, Raymond Aron, *Le Grand Schisme,* pp. 225-226; "Pour l'action politique des salariés," *Reconstruction,* no. 39, June 1951, p. 1.

CHAPTER XVI

SUMMARY AND CONCLUSIONS

It is too bad that, revolutionaries that we are, we are at the same time such traditionalists.

—Robert Bothereau, at Force
Ouvrière convention, 1950.

From time to time, the working class appears more revolutionary, at other times more reformist. Under the reformism, one must know how to perceive the latent revolutionary feeling, and under the bursts of extremism, rediscover the stable elements of permanent reformism.

—Maxime Leroy, *Les Techniques
nouvelles du syndicalisme*, 1921.

Labor organization first took hold in modern France in the skilled artisanal trades; the workers in factory employment and mines came later to unionism. A series of promising starts at workers' organization was wrecked by government repression, in the early 1830's, in 1848, in the prosecution of the moderate French leaders of the First International, in the tragedy of the Paris Commune. Union organization was postponed and turned into more radical channels. But the unions rejected the control of the many socialist parties which were, until 1905, furiously divided among themselves.

The local Bourses du Travail and the struggling national unions joined at the turn of the century to create the General Confederation of Labor, the CGT, which has since, through all its changes, remained the main body of organized labor. Revolutionary syndicalism was the most original French contribution to labor doctrine and practice. The syndicalist outlook on the world corresponded to the state of the unions; decentralized and financially ill-nourished, weak in the face of employers, the minority unionism of an individualistic élite of skilled workmen chafing under social and economic inequality. The unions responded to the character of the economy and the behavior of employers. With population hardly growing, France's balance between agriculture and industry allowed it to avoid modernizing more rapidly in either agriculture or industry; social stability was purchased at the cost of progress. Industrial employers, with a high share of small enterprises and family firms, remained in spirit close to their peasant and commercial middle-class origins, seeking security above expansion. This social and economic climate made workers pessimistic about improving their levels of living through evolutionary processes. In the tradition of the country's political changes since 1789, they substituted the easier dream of a sudden sweeping change. But even in the decade before the first World War, in the "heroic period" of syndicalism, there were less spectacular unions in the CGT with stronger structures, a reformist approach, and collective bargaining relations; by 1914 there were probably as many reformists as revolutionaries.

Syndicalism—practice and prediction—collapsed the moment France mobilized in 1914. The CGT leaders rallied to the coöperation with government which has since characterized reformist unionism. As the war dragged on, and particularly after the Russian Revolution, revolutionary sentiments revived. For a moment after the war the CGT took on mass membership and embarked on extensive collective bargaining. But the Communists and syndicalists brought on a disastrous general strike in 1920, and a schism which left both wings of the union movement feeble for the next fifteen years. The Communists readily took control of their labor organization, the CGTU, from the syndicalists, but they drove most workers out of it. The reformist CGT, a minority at the split, soon was much stronger than its Communist rival. But reformist unionism became chiefly a movement of public service and white collar employees. The CGT was reunited at the time of the Popular Front, in which it was a moving element. With the electoral victory of the Popular Front parties and the sit-down strikes, the CGT in 1936 attained its first real mass membership. Among the newly enrolled millions of factory workers, the Communists in the CGT took a preponderant role. Supported by the Blum government, the unions received long overdue representation and bargaining rights. The reluctance of employers to accept the new state of affairs led to compulsory arbitration of labor disputes. But this last chance of the Third Republic for social peace was lost because of the economic failure of the Popular Front, political strife in the unions, and the menace of international fascism. When war came, the government ended collective bargaining and compulsory arbitration. The CGT, weakened by the Communist-promoted general strike of 1938, was by then only a shadow of its 1936 organization.

War and the Nazi-Soviet pact split the CGT a second time. The Communists managed to recover strength with the failure of the reformist unions to receive a place in the war effort, and with the physical and moral failure of the war effort itself. In the resistance labor took a leading part. Responding once again to a new international situation, the CGT was reunited underground. The Communists, devoted French patriots after the Nazi invasion of Russia, with the most effective clandestine organization, took control of the CGT soon after liberation.

The labor movement in 1944-1946 reached new heights of membership, power, and prestige. With the traditional élites discredited, labor won important institutional changes—nationalization of key industries, the expansion of social security, and rights of representation at plant, industry, and national levels. For almost three years the Communist Party led the unions' coöperation in the reconstruction effort, then suddenly turned them against the government and the European Recovery Program. With the general strike of 1947, it split the CGT for the third time in a generation—once again in response to Soviet international policy. But the Force Ouvrière Confederation created by the reformists failed to rally more than a fraction of those disgusted or disheartened by the politicization of the CGT. The Confederation of French Catholic Workers, the CFTC, although stronger than ever before in its history, was also distinctly a minority movement.

When the return to free collective bargaining came in 1950, the unions were too weak to exercise any real control over wages or the conditions of employment. Their defensive fight was illustrated by their stress on the passage of a law providing a sliding scale for the government-fixed minimum wage.

In form union structure remains almost as decentralized as it was in the syndicalist period. In fact, the Communist Party centralizes decision-making in the CGT through the apparatus of both the unions and the party. All the confederations suffer from the reluctance of workers to pay dues high enough or regularly enough to sustain the organizations needed to deal with well organized employers in a modern labor market and with the government of a welfare state. The very concept of union membership is imprecise and fluid. The electoral loyalty manifested in shop elections and social security board votes shows the contours of the relative influence of the competing unions. The CGT, despite the loss of a series of disastrous political strikes, and the loss of over half its postwar membership, retains its apparatus intact. In the basic industries it is not only the strongest union, but leads both the CFTC and FO together. The CFTC is a distant second, FO close behind the CFTC. A separate General Confederation of Technical and Supervisory Employees predominates in its field. Several splinter movements and a number of unaffiliated unions further complicate the labor scene. The majority of workers in private industry are unorganized.

Employers are far better organized and employer association discipline is better than ever before. Negotiation is industrywide, mostly by area associations, occasionally by the national associations; seldom by single plants or firms. On the union side there is a kaleidoscopic shifting of alliances among the CGT, the CFTC, and FO. The most highly developed industrial relations are to be found in the government-owned industrial enterprises, but the spirit of relations there, despite greater union rights and higher pension and welfare benefits, is no better and often worse than in private employment. Government industries have borne the brunt of the heaviest strikes, because of their stronger unionism, key industrial positions, and CGT political aims.

In private industry, the elaborate legal requirements for what is called a full "collective agreement" are unaccompanied by any obligation on the parties to bargain. Comparatively few collective agreements are signed and even those add little to what the law demands. The common form of contract is a skeletal wage settlement setting only minima. Actual wages are determined by a multitude of complex special arrangements, often unilaterally, by individual employers, in the light of trade association minima and the government minimum wage. With social security and family allowance benefits greatly enlarged since the war, direct wages have fallen sharply in real value, thus redistributing income within the working class rather than among social classes. The unions find it hard to locate the sources of power to determine real wages.

The strike holds a symbolic importance in labor thinking. But the unions' lack of strike funds and individual workers' lack of resources make it difficult to sustain serious long strikes. The unions launch innumerable brief and partial walkouts, with union leadership uncertain of how its own followers or other workers will respond. It is often the contributions, direct and indirect, of community, government, church, and employers which make strikes possible.

The chief limitation on the right to strike comes from the government's power to requisition workers in essential public services, privately or publicly owned. This power has been weakened by the failure to apply sanctions in cases of widespread disobedience of requisition orders. Labor and management successfully opposed the government's attempt to reinstate compulsory arbitration via the 1950 collective bargaining law. Conciliation is theoretically compulsory, but actually strikes and lockouts occur without much regard for the conciliation requirements. The right and practice of strikes are in a twilight zone between freedom and regulation.

At the plant level, the multiplicity of competing unions in plants of any size complicates industrial relations. Shop stewards, elected by all workers regardless of union affiliation or lack of it, are only one of many grievance channels. Few contracts provide specific forms of grievance processing, almost none for any final arbitration of unresolved grievances. The plant committees have failed to induce labor-management coöperation because of their lack of qualified worker representatives, the hostility of employers to their economic role, and their use by the CGT for wage demands and political warfare. The worker's loyalty to the union is diluted by the proliferation of grievance channels and the lack of union functions of job protection. The declining power of unionism has encouraged the resistance of employers to union encroachments.

The unions have, historically, made their greatest gains at moments of political upsurge and through legislation rather than collective bargaining. Yet they have never developed satisfactory working relationships or organic ties with the political parties claiming to represent labor. Now the most important segment of the union movement is controlled by the most exigent of political parties. Communist party control and manipulation of the CGT have caused withdrawals, discontent, apathy—but no effective protest since the FO schism. Many non-Communist workers, even many Socialists and Catholics, remain in the CGT; but those who hold office in it do not influence its major policies.

The FO is close to the Socialist Party, the CFTC to the Catholic MRP, but neither is controlled by the party. Both confederations have been reaching for broader and more constructive forms of political influence. As yet no wing of the union movement has developed fruitful or effective forms of political action. Nor has any since the war developed the sort of ideological basis for daily union action which French workers demand. The concept of class, once creative of solidarity and generous vision, now breeds sterile resentments. The union movement, once so rich in ideas if not in bread-and-butter achievements, now has little of either to show.

France, hence French labor, still suffers from the bloodletting, the destruction of cities, the inflation, and the shocks to old values of two great wars in one generation. This convalescent society bears the physical and moral strains of a profoundly unpopular war in Indo-China, of colonialism in Africa, of rearmament in Europe. Neutralism is a form of the escape it seeks. Perhaps no group is more fatigued than the urban workers who bore so much of the weight of postwar reconstruction. The energies of the largest number and some of the best have been turned into the negative fight of the CGT against the recovery of a democratic France. The free unionists have had to spend much of their energies in what often appears like negative battle too, against the power of attraction of the Communist CGT, the shortsightedness of employers, and the "immobilism" of government.

The hopes with which French workers greeted the liberation in 1944 and the peace a year later may or may not have been reasonable, as the hopes of men go. One after another, these hopes have been dashed or deferred beyond the visible future. In the years since the war's end, labor has become increasingly frustrated. Without the unity, the program, or the capacity to give the nation leadership, without confidence in those who have resumed France's political and industrial leadership, labor has felt a sense of historic mission miscarried in what should have been its greatest hour.

Henri Bergson tells the story of the one man in a French village church who sat unmoved through a sermon which had everyone else in tears. As they walked out of the church, one of the other worshippers asked him how he had been able to remain unmoved. He answered, "I am not from this parish."

It would be idle to argue that we can see detailed analogies between the problems of the French unions and our own, that we can see a clear line between all that happens in Paris and St. Etienne and what may happen in Washington and St. Louis. But in the French union movement there is much of absorbing interest for us. Its destiny is not foreign to our own. Our oldest ally is the only major power on the continent of Europe with a tradition and long experience of freedom. Its influence has long been greater than its material power. Should democracy fail to provide solutions for French problems, its attraction for the rest of the continent would sink much below its present precarious level. If French democracy reasserts its vitality, it will lift democratic forces everywhere. That vitality is sapped as long as the alienation between the working class and the national community continues.

It is easier to visualize continued stalemate or sudden catastrophe than the infinitely varied possibilities of social adjustment. Certainly long and difficult years of adjustment are required of employers, government, and the unions.

Can employers give a new impulse to the private enterprise which remains in France? "French employers must develop the thirst for success," remarked the energetic executive of a big French chemical company, much influenced by his several stays in the United States. It is the definition of success, perhaps, which needs broadening. More risk-taking and less huddling close to security, a more dynamic concept of the market in preference to the philosophy of "small deals but good deals" would produce a less defeatist capitalism and one capable of recovering the respect of its workers. It was a conservative manufacturer, Premier Antoine Pinay, who said, "The world will soon cease to doubt France when France ceases to doubt herself."[1] The willingness of employers to share authority responsibly with unions would be part of that faith in France.

Will workers achieve a unionism that can recover the best in their traditions and represent them constructively in an industrial nation's life? Again, one can only ask the question. They may see through the CGT's cloak of militant unionism to the realities of political subservience. They may develop a freely consented discipline to democratic labor organizations rather than alternating between anarchistic individualism and abdication of responsibility into the hands of totalitarians. They may devote more effort to making the present institutions of industrial representation work before demanding new interventions of the government. Perhaps they will see beyond the simple fixed imagery of class struggle constructions to the complex changing economic situation of companies and markets. Workers will somehow have to reconcile union pluralism with effectiveness in labor representation and greater stability in relations with management.

The government will have to learn how to intervene in industrial relations so as to promote independent dealings between unions and management rather than further dependence on its own intervention. Since some of the essential conditions for economic expansion can be created only by the government, any government will have to find the courage to make difficult choices and enforce decisions. Can it reform tax assessment and tax collection as well as forgive tax arrears? It will have to allocate consciously and more equitably the sacrifices hitherto left by default to the play of pressure groups and the hazards of inflation. "If it is better to be rich in France, it is better to be poor in England," said a politician of unusual courage.[2] The sense of injustice is the worst poverty of a richly endowed land. On this sense of injustice Communism has fed. "Perhaps," said the Cardinal Archbishop of Toulouse, in a pastoral letter, "the working class has suffered more in the past. But never has it had so sharp a feeling of being the victim of injustice."[3]

These are some of the problems of the times. They involve the capacity of social groups to turn their backs on a long heritage of conflict and work out solutions of common survival. It has been done in other coun-

---

[1] At meeting of Société Française de Géographie Economique, *Le Monde,* April 30, 1952.

[2] Pierre Mendès-France, *Assemblée nationale, Débats,* December 21, 1947, 2d session, p. 6033.

[3] *Le Monde,* March 5, 1953.

tries, although never with the weight of so much history to overcome. Can change be achieved without the compulsions of war or dictatorship, in a country whose premier, the very moderate businessman René Pleven, said: "France has not recoiled before any sacrifices for its recovery, except those which would imply a change. France has been willing to do without, but not to change itself."[4]

Change is all the more difficult because it must come on so many fronts at once. The CGT will not wait with its demagogy until the free unions develop the strength to meet its competition. The government cannot hold back asking sacrifices from wage earners until economic development catches up with social aspirations. And the tensions of the cold war, the pulse of nationalism in overseas France, the demands of European integration will not stop while France engages in the great adventure of "turning its back on decadence."[5]

Whatever the solutions which emerge (if positive solutions happily do emerge), they will be as distinctively French as the difficulties which now crowd the scene. A new French unionism would be different from the unionism of other countries as it would be from today's unionism. Each country's unions are the product of the curious complex of all the factors whose cluster is unique to that country: its history and politics, its economic development and social structure. Only this complex and not any one factor, no matter how brilliant the one-cause explanation, explains the unions or any other social movement.

Yet even the problems which are peculiarly French depend, for such is the French situation, in part upon what the rest of the free world does (as well as what the Soviet Union does). Comprehension by the free world and especially the United States is part of the problem of France; France's comprehension of the rest of the world is another large part of her problem. Charles Péguy, French Catholic and patriot, once wrote: "It's annoying, says God; when the day comes when there are no more Frenchmen, there are some things I do which no one will any longer understand."[6] Sometimes it may seem as if there are some things Frenchmen, and French unions, do which only God could understand. But for us it remains a rewarding task as well as a responsibility to try to understand.

---

[4] October 21, 1951, *L'Année politique, 1951* (Paris, 1952), p. 377.
[5] The phrase "France has turned its back to the decadence which threatened her" is that of the Monnet Planning Commission. *Rapport du commissaire général sur le plan du modernisation et d'équipement de l'union française: Réalisations 1947-1949 et Objectifs 1950-1952* (Paris, 1949), p. 8.
[6] Charles Péguy, *Le Mystère des saints innocents* (Paris, 1929), p. 105.

CHRONOLOGY OF FRENCH LABOR AND SOME PARALLEL POLITICAL DEVELOPMENTS, 1789-1952

1789   Beginning of French Revolution.
1791   Guilds and corporations abolished.
       Le Chapelier Law, forbidding workers' and employers' organizations.
1799   Napoleon Bonaparte's coup d'état.
1810   Penal Code provisions against strikes.
1815   Restoration of Bourbon monarchy.
1830   "July Revolution" dethrones Charles X; proclaims Louis Philippe king.
1831   Lyon silk weavers strike.
1834   Strikes and revolt in Lyon and Paris.
1841   First factory legislation: child labor law.
1843   First collective agreement setting wage rates, between Paris printers and employers' association.
1848   "February Revolution" overthrows Louis Philippe; proclaims republic.
       "June Days," suppression of workers' protest at closing of national workshops.
1851   Coup d'état of Louis Napoleon, president of republic.
1862   Delegation of Paris workers to London Exposition.
1864   Ban on strikes lifted by law.
       International Workingmen's Association (First International) set up.
1868   Tolerance of labor organizations promised by government.
1870   Franco-Prussian War, collapse of Second Empire, republic proclaimed.
1871   Paris Commune.
1874   Law on women's and children's work.
1876   First "national workers' congress."
1879   First national union (hatters) formed.
       First Socialist Party (Guesdist).
1884   Law permitting freedom of association.

1886   First national trade union center (Fédération Nationale des Syndi-
       cats Ouvriers).
       First Bourse du Travail (Paris).
1887   First Catholic local union (clerical workers, Paris).
1889   Second International organized.
1891   First collective agreement in mines (of north).
1892   Law on voluntary conciliation and arbitration.
       National Federation of Bourses du Travail founded.
1895   CGT (Confédération Générale du Travail) created.
1898   First general railroad strike; failure.
       Law on employer liability for work accidents.
1899   First company ("yellow") union.
1902   CGT and Federation of Bourses du Travail merge.
1905   Unification of Socialist parties of France into SFIO.
1906   Charter of Amiens voted by CGT.
       Ministry of Labor created.
1909   First major strike of government workers: PTT (Postal, Telegraph,
       and Telephone) workers.
1910   Railroad strike broken by Briand's mobilization of rail workers.
       First old-age pension law; boycotted by CGT.
1912   CGT eliminates its separate section of Bourses du Travail.
1913   First national union of Catholic workers (clerical workers).
1914   August 3: Germany declares war on France.
1917   Wartime ban on strikes, compulsory arbitration in munitions in-
       dustries.
1918   CGT "Minimum Program."
1919   CGPF (Confédération Générale de la Production Française) set up.
       March: law on collective agreements.
       April: eight-hour-day law.
       June: Paris metal industries strike.
       November: CFTC (Confédération Française des Travailleurs Chré-
                 tiens) set up.
       Labor and Socialist (political) International reconstituted.
       International Federation of Trade Unions revived; CGT a member.
       Third (Communist) International set up.
1920   General strike, beginning with rail strike; failure.
       Socialist Party split, majority becoming Communist Party.
1921   CGT ordered dissolved by court (decision never carried out).
       Red International of Labor Unions set up.
1921-1922   CGT splits; Communists and syndicalists create CGTU (Con-
       fédération Générale du Travail Unitaire).
1923   CGTU affiliates to Red International of Labor Unions.
1926   CGTU syndicalist minority forms CGTSR (Confédération Générale
       du Travail Syndicaliste Révolutionnaire).
1927   Federation of civil service unions votes to reaffiliate with CGT.
1930   Social insurance law in effect (voted in 1928).

1932 First family allowance law.

1934 February 6: fascists (and Communists) riot against Chamber of Deputies.

February 12: General strike against fascist danger by CGT; CGTU joins in.

1935 CGT and CGTU decide on reunification.

1936 March: unity congress of CGT and CGTU.

May: Popular Front election victory.

Sit-down strikes begin.

June 7: Matignon agreement.

June 20: paid vacation law.

June 21: 40-hour-week law.

June 24: collective bargaining law.

December 31: temporary legislation on compulsory conciliation and arbitration.

1938 March 4: new law on compulsory conciliation and arbitration.

July 11: National Service law.

November 30: general strike; failure.

1939 September 1: government suspends arbitration law.

September 3: declaration of war on Germany.

September 18: CGT Executive Board begins expulsion of supporters of Nazi-Soviet pact.

1940 June 22: armistice with Germany.

July 10: Pétain voted full powers by Parliament.

November 9: dissolution of CGT, CFTC, and CGPF.

November 15: "Manifesto of the Twelve" trade union leaders.

1941 October: Vichy Labor Charter.

1943 April: agreement of Le Perreux reuniting CGT (underground).

1944 July: provisional government decrees restoration of trade union liberty.

August 25: liberation of Paris.

September 26: CFTC Executive Board declines CGT unification proposal.

December: nationalization of coal mines of North.

1945 February: decree instituting plant committees.

September: Socialist Party convention rejects unity with Communist Party.

October: World Federation of Trade Unions (WFTU) constituted; CGT a member.

Decree reforming social security system.

1946 January: De Gaulle resigns as President-Premier.

April: nationalization of gas and electricity industries.

First CGT congress since 1938, shows overwhelming Communist majority.

Law reinstituting shop stewards.

May: nationalization of all coal mines.

Law strengthening powers and extending coverage of plant committees.

June: CNPF (Conseil National du Patronat Français) organization completed.

July-August: first significant postwar schism in CGT (Post, Telegraph and Telephone workers union splits).

October: Constitution of Fourth Republic adopted by referendum.

November: First National Assembly of Fourth Republic elected.

December: Law permitting resumption of collective bargaining, except on wages.

1947   April-May: first wave of postwar strikes. Communists out of government in May.

November-December: CGT "generalized" strike.

December: FO (Force Ouvrière) splits off from CGT.

1948   October-November: CGT coal strike.

1949   January: WFTU splits; CGT remains a member.

October: CTI, later called CGSI (Confédération Générale des Syndicats Indépendants) set up.

November: International Confederation of Free Trade Unions (ICFTU) created; FO a member.

1950   February: collective bargaining (and minimum wage) law; wages decontrolled.

1951   June: Second National Assembly elected.

1952   July: Sliding scale minimum wage law.

APPENDIX B

THE CHARTER OF AMIENS
Adopted by the CGT Convention of 1906

The convention of Amiens reaffirms Article 2 of the CGT statutes, which says: "The CGT unites, regardless of political belief, all workers conscious of the struggle to be carried on for the disappearance of the wage system and the employing class."

The convention believes that this declaration is a recognition of the class struggle which, in the economic realm, places the workers in revolt against all forms of capitalist exploitation and oppression, material and moral.

The convention clarifies this theoretical affirmation by the following specific points:

In its day-to-day demands, the union movement seeks the coördination of workers' efforts, the increase of workers' well-being by the achievement of immediate gains, such as the shortening of hours, the raising of wages, and so forth.

This effort, however, is only one side of the work of the union movement. It prepares for the complete emancipation which can be achieved only by expropriating the capitalist class. It endorses the general strike as a means of action to that end. It holds that the trade union, which is today a fighting organization, will in the future be an organization for production and distribution, and the basis of social reorganization.

The convention declares that this double task, the day-to-day task and that of the future, arises from the position of wage earners, which weighs upon the working class and creates for all workers, regardless of their political or philosophical opinions or attachments, the duty to belong to their basic organization, the trade union.

As far as the individual member is concerned, therefore, the convention affirms his complete liberty to take part, outside of his union, in whatever forms of action correspond to his philosophical or political views. It merely asks him not to bring up in the union the opinions he holds outside it.

As for affiliated organizations, the convention declares that, since economic action must be directed at the employers if the union movement is to attain its full results, the unions should not concern themselves with the parties and sects which, outside and parallel with the unions, may in their own free way strive for social transformation.

APPENDIX C

THE MATIGNON AGREEMENT

Between the General Confederation of French Production (CGPF) and the General Confederation of Labor (CGT)

June 7, 1936

The delegates of the CGPF and the CGT have met under the chairmanship of the Premier (Léon Blum) and have concluded the following agreement, after arbitration by the Premier:

Article One—The employer delegation agrees to the immediate conclusion of collective agreements.

Article Two—These agreements must include, in particular, articles three and five below.

Article Three—All citizens being required to abide by the law, the employers recognize the freedom of opinion of workers and their right to freely join and belong to trade unions established in conformity with Book III of the Labor Code.

In their decisions on hiring, organization or assignment of work, disciplinary measures or dismissals, employers agree not to take into consideration the fact of membership or nonmembership in a union.

If one of the contracting parties claims that the dismissal of a worker has been caused by a violation of the right to organize and belong to a union stated above, the two parties will seek to determine the facts and arrive at an equitable solution of the case in question. This does not prejudice the rights of the parties to obtain reparation at law for the damage caused.

The exercise of trade union rights must not give rise to acts contrary to law.

Article Four—The wages actually paid to all workers as of May 25, 1936 will be raised, as of the resumption of work, by a decreasing percentage ranging from 15 per cent for the lowest rates down to 7 per cent for the highest rates. In no case must the total increase in any establishment exceed 12 per cent. Increases already granted since May 25, 1936 will be counted toward the increases indicated above. But higher increases already granted will remain in effect.

The negotiations, which are to be launched at once, for the determination by collective agreement of minimum wages by regions and by occupations must take up, in particular, the necessary revision of abnormally low wages.

The employer delegation agrees to carry out the adjustments necessary to retain a normal relationship between salaries of nonproduction employees and hourly wages.

Article Five—Except for special cases already regulated by law, in each establishment with more than 10 workers, after an agreement between labor and management organizations (or, in the absence of those, between the interested parties), there will be two shop stewards or more (stewards and alternates), in accordance with the size of the establishment. These stewards will have the right to present to management individual grievances which have not been satisfactorily adjusted relating to the application of laws, decrees, regulations of the Labor Code, wage scales, and health and safety measures.

All workers, men and women, aged 18 and over will be eligible to vote for shop stewards, if at the time of the election they have been employed at least 3 months in the establishment and if they have not been deprived of their civil rights.

All those eligible to vote will be eligible for election as stewards if they are French citizens, at least 25 years of age, and have been continuously employed for at least a year in the establishment. The last requirement shall be lowered if it reduces below 5 the number eligible to election.

Workers carrying on any sort of retail business, either themselves or through their spouses, may not be candidates.

Article Six—The employer delegation promises that there will be no sanctions for strike activities.

Article Seven—The CGT delegation will ask the workers on strike to return to work as soon as the managements of establishments have accepted this general agreement and as soon as negotiations for its application have begun between the managements and the personnel of the establishments.

Paris, June 7, 1936

(Signed)
Léon Blum

(CGT)	(CGPF)
Jouhaux	Duchemin
Belin	Dalbouze
Frachon	Richemond
Semat	Lambert-Ribot
Cordier	
Milan	

APPENDIX D

"THE MANIFESTO OF THE TWELVE"
French Trade Unionism, What It Still Is, What It Must Become

November 15, 1940

French trade unionism is still alive, despite its internal difficulties, despite the defeat of the nation, despite the suffering of the working class. But it does not know in what direction and according to what principles its action today should be carried on, for it to resume the place to which it is entitled in the economic and social activity of France. It is to these essential questions that a group of French trade unionists wants to reply, without sectarian spirit, without political preoccupation, without consideration of any external pressure.

THE PAST

First of all, there can be no question of denying the past.

Trade union action, under diverse forms, has determined an evolution of the French working class towards a continual betterment of the conditions of existence. This evolution has included periods of advance and periods of stagnation; but if one makes a comparison over many years, it cannot be denied that the evolution has been favorable to the workers.

The war and the defeat have dealt a terrible blow to the work of the trade union movement. But can one say that the trade union movement is responsible for the disasters which have struck our country:

When none of the solutions and reforms which it called for were applied by any government when they should have been?

When no French trade union group was called upon to take its part in the responsibilities of power?

When trade union action was hamstrung in our country at the very moment when the unity of Frenchmen and the collaboration of workers in the national task were more than ever necessary?

When the CGT and Christian trade union organizations never ceased to affirm that peace should and could be preserved through an international collaboration based on the spirit of justice?

We can go further.

Who first criticized the excesses of capitalism?

Who denounced the dangers of an excessive laissez-faire and individualism at a time when the national economy needed energetic direction on the part of the State?

Who foresaw the consequences of the armaments race, begun at a period when peace could still have been preserved?

Who denounced the errors of the foreign policy of most of the governments which have followed one another in France since 1919?

Who, if not the French trade union movement?

To convince oneself of these elementary truths, one has only to read the resolutions of the various conventions of the CGT and the CFTC, as well as the "Plans"[1] drawn up by these two confederations.

The French trade union movement is not responsible for the present situation. It remains none the less true that it committed errors. Some of its members tied the existence of the trade union movement too closely to that of the political parties and of a discredited parliament. The trade union movement, particularly at its base, too often sacrificed the search for general economic solutions and structural reforms to the satisfaction of immediate demands. The existence of competing caucuses and personal politics destroyed the solidarity of workers and lessened the effectiveness of union action.

THE PRESENT

What is the present situation of the trade union movement?

We must have the courage to recognize it: the majority of workers have lost interest in their organizations to the extent that they feel that those organizations bring them neither a satisfactory ideology, nor a program adapted to present circumstances, nor an effective defense of their job interests.

On the other hand they will not recognize as genuine labor organizations those whose leaders are not freely chosen by them and whose activity is carried on under government control.

If one wishes to regroup the workers around their unions, it is necessary to: affirm or reaffirm the ideological principles of French trade unionism; clarify the relationships between the trade union movement and the state; establish the framework within which trade unionism may evolve and the methods it can employ.

---

[1] The reference is to the CGT Plan of 1934 and the CFTC Plan of 1934-1935.

PRINCIPLES OF FRENCH TRADE UNIONISM

The French trade union movement must take its inspiration from six essential principles:

A. It must be anticapitalist and in general opposed to all forms of oppression of the workers;

B. It must accept the subordination of special interests to the general interest;

C. Within the state it must assume its full place and only its place;

D. It must affirm respect for the individual without considerations of race, religion, or opinion;

E. It must be free, in its collective activity as well as in the exercise of the individual liberty of each of its members;

F. It must seek the international collaboration of workers and peoples.

Anti-Capitalism—The trade union movement was the first to understand and denounce the responsibility of capitalism in the economic crises and the social and political convulsions after the first World War.

The international financiers and trusts, big corporations, employer groups —real feudal economic powers, bodies directed by a small number of irresponsible men—too often sacrificed the interests of the nation and of the workers to the maintenance or the increase of their profits. They systematically held back the development of French industrial production by their monetary operations, their exports of capital, their refusal to follow other nations along the road of technical progress. They are more responsible for the defeat of our country than even the most tarnished or incompetent political leader.

A planned economy in the service of the community must succeed the capitalist regime. The notion of collective gain must succeed that of individual gain. Enterprises must henceforth be managed in line with the general directives of a plan of production, under the supervision of the State, and with the coöperation of technicians and production workers' unions. The management or direction of an enterprise will carry with it, as a matter of law, full responsibility for all errors or abuses committed.

It is thus and only thus that unemployment can be wiped out and working conditions improved in a lasting way, leading to the well-being of the workers, the supreme aim of trade unionism.

Subordination of Special Interests to the General Interest—This subordination must be carried out in all domains and in particular within the union organizations themselves.

The excess of individualism in our nation has always prevented any coördinated collective action, each one believing that he had the right, after expressing his point of view, to hamper by his personal action the execution of necessary decisions taken by the majority.

Trade unionism is a collective movement; it is not the sum total of a great number of little individual movements. Individuals have value for it only to the extent that they serve its cause and not their own. The whole history of trade unionism, moreover, proves that collective action is the best defense of individual interests.

Place of Trade Unionism in the State—The trade union movement cannot try to absorb the state. Neither must it be absorbed by the state.

The trade union movement, which is an occupational and not a political movement, must play only its economic and social role of defense of the interests of production. The state must play its role of sovereign arbitrator among all interests concerned. These two roles must not be confused.

Union action and the sovereignty of the state will function all the more easily when the various trades or industries are organized.[2] This indispensable industrial organization must not block the action of an interindustry organism capable of taking an over-all view of economic and social problems and carrying out a policy of coördination. The organization of trades or industries in too rigid a framework would lead to a completely state-run and bureaucratic system.

The definitive suppression of the great national inter-industry confederations[3] would in this connection be a mistake.

It is not necessary to choose between unionism and corporatism. Both are equally necessary. The formula of the future is: The free union, in the organized industry, under the sovereign state.

On the sovereignty of the state and its efficacy as an arbitrator depends the elimination of the strike as a means of defense of the workers. It would be iniquitous to deprive the workers of all means of action, if the state does not make itself responsible to them for the strict application of social legislation and the reign of equity in social relationships.

The class struggle, which has hitherto been a fact more than a principle, can disappear only through the transformation of the profit system; the equality of the parties to collective dealings; a spirit of coöperation between these parties, for the lack of which must be substituted the impartial arbitration of the state.

Respect for the Individual—In no case, under no pretext, and in no form, can the French union movement admit distinctions among individuals based on race, religion, birth, opinions, or wealth.

Every human being is equally deserving of respect. He has a right to his free and full development as far as that does not oppose the interest of the community.

In particular the French union movement cannot admit: anti-Semitism; religious persecution; the punishment of opinion; the privileges of wealth.

---

[2] "Organization" here refers not to unionization but to the corporate reorganization then vaguely envisaged.

[3] A reference to the dissolution of the CGT and the CFTC (and that of the CGPF and several other employer bodies), foreshadowed by a law of August 16, 1940, and specifically decreed November 9, 1940.

Furthermore it rejects any regime which makes of man a machine, incapable of thought or of personal action.

Liberty—Trade unionism was and remains founded on the principle of liberty. It is false to claim today that the defeat of our country is due to the exercise of the liberty of its citizens, when the domestic causes of defeat are the incompetence of our general staff, the weakness of our administration, and the disorder of industry.

Trade union liberty must include: the right of workers to think what they please, and to express themselves as they wish, in the course of union meetings on the problems of the trade; the right to be represented by delegates of their own election; the right to belong to a union organization of their own choice or to belong to no organization; the right to privacy in their personal lives, free from the meddling of the union organizations.

Liberty may bring abuses. It is less important to punish them than to prevent their recurrence. In this connection, workers' education is better than threats or constraints. It must give workers the knowledge and the methods of action and of thought necessary for an awareness of the general interests of the country, of the interests of the industry, and of their own real interests. It will be up to the industry to organize this workers' education, under the supervision of the unions and of the state.

International Collaboration—If the trade union movement must not intervene in place of the state in the policy of the nation, it must nevertheless be concerned with: international conditions of production; the fate of the worker all over the world; collaboration among the peoples, which generates greater well-being and progress.

It would be senseless to think that tomorrow our country could live within itself, isolate itself from the rest of the world, and refuse to concern itself with the great international economic and social problems.

THE FUTURE OF FRENCH TRADE UNIONISM

The future of French trade unionism depends on the future of France; its economic and social organization; the men who will be at the head of it.

Of the future of France, we must not despair. We must not consider ourselves, because of the accident of a military defeat, an inferior nation or people. We shall resume our place in the world to the extent that we are aware of the place that we can take.

The economic and social organization of France must wipe the slate clean of the mistakes of the past. We have given the essential principles of that new organization.

As to the men who can assume the leadership of the trade union movement, they must fulfill the following conditions: not have the mentality of the defeated; put the general interest ahead of their personal interest; respect the working class and have the will to serve it; have the general and technical knowledge needed to face present problems.

French workers will unite to save their interests: to defend the French
trade union movement, its traditions and its future, to defend their job
interests, to avoid unemployment and suffering.

[Signed]

M. Bouladoux, ex-deputy-secretary of the ex-CFTC
O. Capocci, general secretary of the Clerical Workers' National Union
(ex-CGT)
L. Chevalme, general secretary of the Metal Workers' National Union
(ex-CGT)
A. Gazier, general secretary of the Paris Region Council of the Cleri-
cal Workers' Union (ex-CGT)
E. Jaccoud, general secretary of the Transport Workers' National Union
(ex-CGT)
R. Lacoste, ex-secretary of the Federation of Civil Servants' Unions
(ex-CGT)
P. Neumeyer, ex-secretary of the Federation of Civil Servants' Unions
(ex-CGT)
Ch. Pineau, secretary of the department of Bank and Stock Exchange
Employees, Clerical Workers' National Union (ex-CGT)
L. Saillant, secretary of the Building and Wood. Workers' National
Union (ex-CGT)
G. Tessier, ex-general secretary of the ex-CFTC
Vandeputte, general secretary of the Textile Workers' National Union
(ex-CGT)
J. Zirnheld, ex-president of the ex-CFTC

Paris, November 15, 1940 [mimeographed]

Source: CFTC, *Unité Syndicale ou Unité d'Action: Recueil des Textes et
des Documents* .., Paris, CFTC, n.d. (1945?) pp. 5-11.

APPENDIX E

GOVERNMENT ENTERPRISES NOT COVERED BY THE COLLECTIVE BARGAINING LAW

List of enterprises not covered by the collective bargaining law of February 11, 1950, because they are regulated by "statute," legislative and/or
administrative:

Bank of France
Bank of Algeria and Tunisia
Central Fund for Overseas France
Air France (air transport)
Paris airport
National Railways of France

Algerian Railways
Mediterranean-Niger railroad
Corsican railway network
Paris Transport Authority (bus and subway)
Transatlantic Steamship Company (office personnel)
Mediterranean Steamship Lines (office personnel)
Coal mines of France : central office
Regional coal mine authorities
Coal mines of Southern Oran
Potash mines of Alsace
Autonomous oil authority
National company for oil research and development in Algeria
National electricity company
National gas company
Algerian electricity and gas company
Autonomous national fund for miners' social security
National immigration bureau
National surplus liquidation company (salaried personnel)

Source : Decree 50-835, June 1, 1950, *Journal Officiel,* June 7, 1950.

APPENDIX F

WAGE SETTLEMENT FOR PARIS REGION METAL TRADES, PRODUCTION WORKERS, OCTOBER 31, 1950

Between the GIMMCRP (Association of Metallurgical, Mechanical and Allied Industries of the Paris Region)
and
CFTC
FO

It has been agreed as follows :

Article 1. The present contract, concluded in accordance with articles 31, a, b, c, d, and e of Book I of the Labor Code, applies to the production workers employed by the establishments belonging to the GIMMCRP.

I. MINIMUM WAGE SCALE

Article 2. The minimum wage scales of production workers maintained in effect by the law of February 11, 1950 until the signature of a contractual agreement[1] are replaced by the new scales shown in annex one of the present agreement.

---

[1] The reference is to the wage rates fixed by the government before the enactment of the collective bargaining law of February. 11, 1950.

Article 3. The minimum rates referred to above are the guaranteed minima below which no adult wage earners, as defined by the collective agreement of June 12, 1936, of normal physical capacity, shall be paid.

Article 4. The signatory parties agree to continue the various differentials called for by government wage regulations, as set by the ministerial decrees issued before the promulgation of the law of February 11, 1950.

II. ADJUSTMENT OF EFFECTIVE WAGE SCALES

Article 5. The application of the guaranteed minima and the possible changes resulting therefrom within enterprises will lead to an increase of wages effectively paid on August 23, 1950,[2] in accordance with the rates annexed to the present contract.

Article 6. The wage to take into account for the determination of the applicable increase is that in effect on August 23, 1950. It includes all elements entering into the wage, except bonuses having the character of reimbursement of expenses and indemnities corresponding to special conditions of dangerous or dirty work.

Article 7. The increases will be applied after deduction of:

    a. increases resulting from application of the new minimum rates.
    b. increases resulting from the application of the decree of August 23, 1950.
    c. increases granted by member establishments since August 23, 1950.

Article 8. The increase of effective wages for the categories of personnel paid at substandard rates because of age, physical handicap, or geographic situation will be applied in the following manner:

The wage which the employee would receive if he were paid at the standard rate will be determined. The increase corresponding to the theoretical wage thus obtained will be granted, after application of the reduction corresponding to the differential for the wage earner in question.

Article 9. The lunch bonus provided for in article 25, c of the collective agreement of June 12, 1936, is set at 80 francs.

III. GENERAL CONDITIONS OF APPLICATION

Article 10. In case of collective grievances concerning the application of the present agreement, involving the personnel of one or several establishments, which are not satisfactorily settled at the level of the establishment, the signatory organizations will attempt to work out in common a solution to the conflict.

In any case, no strike or lockout may be decided without four full working days' notice.

---

[2] Date of promulgation of the first government minimum wage under the law of February 11, 1950.

Article 11. The signatory parties expressly declare that the present contract in no way constitutes an obstacle to the work of the subcommissions studying the clauses of a collective agreement to be concluded under the terms of articles 31, h and i of Book I of the Labor Code.[3]

Article 12. The present contract is effective as of October 1, 1950.

Article 13. The text of the present contract and the annexed wage scales will be filed with the appropriate *conseils de prud'hommes,* in accordance with article 31, d of Book I of the Labor Code.

Article 14. In accordance with article 31, c, Book I, of the Labor Code, any organization or employer not a party to the present agreement may sign it subsequently. Such signature will take effect as of the day following that of the notification of the signature to the secretary of the *conseil de prud'hommes* where the contract is filed.

Article 15. In accordance with article 31, c, of Book I of the Labor Code, it is specified that termination or revision of the present contract requires a minimum advance notice of two months. This notice is valid only if given by registered letter with return receipt.

Paris, October 31, 1950

GIMMCRP
Rouillier

CFTC, Paris Metal Workers' Joint
Council
Morin
Dubois
Michelet
Gillot

FO, Metal Workers' Union of the
Paris Region
Bouché
Durand

ANNEX ONE

SCALE OF MINIMUM WAGES, FIRST ZONE OF THE PARIS REGION
(BASE: 40 HOURS, ADULT EMPLOYEES)(IN FRANCS PER HOUR)

Categories	Minimum Rate	Effective Guaranteed Rate
Unskilled	72.00	81.00
Unskilled, heavy labor	77.76	84.00
Semiskilled, grade 1	87.12	—
Semiskilled, grade 2	91.44	—
Skilled, grade 1	100.80	—
Skilled, grade 2	111.60	—
Skilled, grade 3	122.40	—

[3] A full collective agreement, subject to extension. References here to the Labor Code are to sections incorporated into the Code by the February 11, 1950 law.

ANNEX TWO

SCALE FOR ADJUSTMENT OF EFFECTIVE RATES (ARTICLE 5)

Present Rate	Increase (in francs per hour)
68 francs	13
69 francs	12
70 francs	11
71 to 74 francs	10
75 to 80 francs	9
81 to 85 francs	8.50
86 to 90 francs	8
91 to 95 francs	7.50
96 to 99 francs	7
100 and over	6

APPENDIX G

CLAIMED MEMBERSHIP OF NATIONAL UNIONS OF THE CGT, MARCH 1936, 1937, AND 1946
(NUMBERS ROUNDED OFF TO NEAREST THOUSAND IN ALL BUT TWO CASES)

Note that numbers are claimed figures.

National Union	March 1, 1936	March 1, 1937	March 1, 1946
A. Private industry (or with membership predominantly in private industry)			
Agriculture	12,000	156,000	290,000
Barbers and hairdressers	3,000	22,000	20,000
Building trades and wood	65,000	540,000	700,000
Chemicals	4,000	190,000	160,000
Clerical workers	15,000	285,000	200,000
Clothing	6,000	110,000	74,000
Coopers	1,000	18,000	18,000
Designers and technicians	500	79,000	—
Food industries, hotels, and restaurants	15,000	300,000	300,000
Glass	3,000	30,000	23,000
Hatters	3,000	10,000	10,000
Jewelry	2,000	12,000	8,000
Leather and hides	10,000	88,000	86,000
Metallurgy and metal-working	50,000	775,000	912,000
Paper and cardboard	1,500	72,000	40,000
Pharmaceuticals and drugs	2,000	47,000	19,000
Ports and docks	20,000	92,000	90,000
Pottery	3,000	36,000	20,000
Printing trades	25,000	60,000	55,000
Seamen	13,000	38,000	50,000
Textiles	47,000	360,000	270,000
Theatres and motion pictures	8,000	14,000	45,000
Traveling salesmen	—	6,000	20,000
Transport (excluding railroads and docks)	53,000	150,000	120,000
Total, private industry	362,000	3,490,000	3,530,000

MEMBERSHIP OF CGT UNIONS (*Continued*)

National Union	March 1, 1936	March 1, 1937	March 1, 1946
B. Public utility industries (Nationalized during this period)			
Gas and electricity	35,000	80,000	105,000
Mines	75,000	270,000	287,000
Railroads	165,000	320,000	394,000
Total, public utilities	275,000	670,000	786,000
C. Government Workers			
Air, war, and navy ministries	14,000	16,000	15,000
Education	90,000	101,000	150,000
Finance ministry	46,000	55,000	40,000
General administration (various ministries)	14,000	23,000	—
Other unions in general federation of civil service unions[a]	—	—	245,000[a]
Matches	11,000⎱	14,000	12,000
Tobacco	1,000⎰		
Communications (postal, telegraph and telephone)	75,000	119,000	150,000
State industrial workers (arsenals, navy yards, etc.)	40,000	75,000	156,000
Municipal, communal, departmental services	90,000⎱	180,000	290,000
Hospitals	25,000⎰		
Total, government workers	406,000	583,000	1,263,000
Grand total	1,043,000	4,743,000	5,579,000

[a]In 1946, the General Federation of Civil Service Unions, composed of seven national unions (1. Air, War, and Navy, 2. Education, 3. Finance, 4. General Administration, 5. Ministry of National Economy, 6. Ministry of Public Works, and 7. the newly formed Police union), claimed a total membership of 450,000.
The list does not include all the smaller national unions. Totals therefore are not complete totals of claimed membership of the CGT.

Sources: For 1936 and 1937, Montreuil, *Histoire du mouvement ouvrier en France*, p. 488.
For 1946, *La Vie ouvrière*, April 4, 1946, and other issues of *La Vie ouvrière* and *Le Peuple* of March and April 1946. (In some cases conflicting figures were published.)

APPENDIX H

INITIALS IN COMMON USE: LABOR, EMPLOYER, AND POLITICAL ORGANIZATIONS[1]

FRENCH LABOR ORGANIZATIONS

CFTC—Confédération Française des Travailleurs Chrétiens (French Confederation of Catholic Workers).

CGC—Confédération Générale des Cadres (General Confederation of Technical and Supervisory Employees).

---

[1] This is not a directory, but only a listing of those organizations frequently referred to by their initials.

CGSI—Formerly CTI—Confédération Générale des Syndicats Indépendants (General Confederation of Independent Unions) ; formerly Confédération du Travail Indépendant (Independent Confederation of Labor).

CGT—Confédération Générale du Travail (General Confederation of Labor).

CGTU—Confédération Générale du Travail Unitaire (Unified General Confederation of Labor), 1922-1935.

CNT—Confédération National du Travail (National Confederation of Labor).

FO—Force Ouvrière (Workers' Force). Full title: Confédération Générale du Travail—Force Ouvrière.

FRENCH EMPLOYER ORGANIZATIONS

CGPF—Confédération Générale de la Production Française (General Confederation of French Production), 1919-1936; later, Confédération Générale du Patronat Français (General Confederation of French Employers), 1936-1940.

CNPF—Conseil National du Patronat Français (National Council of French Employers).

CPME—Confédération des Petites et Moyennes Entreprises (Confederation of Small and Middle-sized Enterprises).

FRENCH POLITICAL PARTIES

MRP—Mouvement Républicain Populaire (Popular Republican Movement), Catholic.

RPF—Rassemblement du Peuple Français (Rally of the French People), Gaullist.

SFIO—Section Française de l'Internationale Ouvrière (French Socialist Party).

FRENCH GOVERNMENT AGENCIES

INSEE—Institut National de la Statistique et des Etudes Economiques (National Institute of Statistics and Economic Studies).

INTERNATIONAL LABOR ORGANIZATIONS

ICCTU—International Confederation of Christian Trade Unions.

ICFTU—International Confederation of Free Trade Unions.

IFTU—International Federation of Trade Unions (pre-1944).

RILU—Red International of Labor Unions, or Profintern (inter-war period).

WFTU—World Federation of Trade Unions.

BIBLIOGRAPHY

A. JOURNALS, NEWSPAPERS, REVIEWS

I have referred to parliamentary debates by the date of the debate, not the date of the issue of the *Journal Officiel* (usually the following day) which prints the debates. Most union weeklies and some other periodicals bear a double date, giving the time span of each issue, e.g., "Week of November 8—November 15, 1947"; I have referred only to the first of the two dates, e.g., November 8, 1947. The pages of *Révolution prolétarienne* bear a double numbering, that of the issue and that of the volume, e.g., 11-238, followed by 12-239, and so on; I have used only the issue pagination. *Le Monde,* the leading daily newspaper of the period following World War II, bears the date of the following day; e.g., the issue which appears on the streets the afternoon of Thursday, June 12 is dated "Friday, June 13"; I have used the latter date.

Union Journals:

The CGT issues *Le Peuple,* which was before the second World War a daily, after the war a weekly, and which in 1952 became a semimonthly, devoted to internal organization matters. At the same time in 1952, the CGT declared the Communist Party's trade union weekly, *La Vie ouvrière,* an official journal, concentrating on the mass propaganda at which it had evidently been more successful than the *Peuple;* it continues as a weekly. The *Revue des comités d'entreprise* is a CGT monthly whose subject is indicated by its title.

The CFTC publishes the weekly *Syndicalisme,* and a semimonthly in slightly more popular vein, *Syndicalisme-Magazine.* For officers and activists, its educational bureau issues the monthly *Formation.*

Force Ouvrière issues the weekly *Force Ouvrière* and the monthly bulletin *FO Informations.* Its education center issues the *Cahiers Fernand Pelloutier* irregularly.

Other official organs of the trade union centers are:

> CGC, *Le Creuset des cadres,* bi-monthly.
> CGSI, *Travail et liberté,* weekly.
> CNT, *Combat syndicaliste,* weekly.

The reports and proceedings of conventions are published in separate volumes by the CGT and FO; the CFTC publishes some officers' reports as such, but the conventions are covered in the regular CFTC press. There are in addition journals of national unions, regional papers, and so on.

Several journals on the labor side, unidentified with unions, are of importance. The *Révolution prolétarienne,* monthly, issued by pure syndicalists of the old school, some connected with FO, is valuable for its current commentary on the CGT and FO. *Reconstruction,* issued by the study groups of that name, monthly since 1953, is chiefly the work of the left wing of the CFTC. It presents unusually candid and self-critical analyses of economic, political, and organizational problems from the general trade union and Catholic point of view. Michel Collinet issues the *Lettre aux militants,* a short monthly bulletin ably analyzing a single subject in each issue. The *Revue Syndicaliste,* monthly, is issued by a number of trade union or extrade union figures, such as René Belin.

The Communist Party puts out an important monthly journal of trade union organizational and theoretical matters, rather oddly entitled *Servir la France.*

Management Reviews:

The most important available employer journal is the biweekly, *Bulletin du CNPF.* The Young Employers' Center issues the monthly, *Jeune patron.*

A valuable journal for documents and the employer point of view is the weekly, *L'Usine nouvelle,* published commercially.

Newspapers and Reviews of Political Parties:

Among the political party papers, *L'Humanité,* the Communist Party's official daily, is most useful. CGT leaders publish signed articles in it, and during strikes it gives directives to the rank and file and activists. The Socialist daily, *Le Populaire,* because of financial difficulties, has appeared in such reduced format as to leave little space for labor reporting. *L'Aube,* the MRP daily, naturally giving attention to the CFTC, has been discontinued. The monthly, *Cahiers du Communisme,* devoted chiefly to Communist Party organizational—less to doctrinal—questions, frequently covers issues of union policy.

The SFIO's *Revue socialiste,* monthly, has more general and theoretical articles, with less of the flavor of orthodoxy, than the *Cahiers du Communisme.*

General:

The daily, *Le Monde,* the nearest French analogy to the *London Times* or the *New York Times,* is indispensable.

Among other daily papers, *Figaro* is a distinguished conservative paper; *Franc-Tireur,* independent leftist journal, has a wide working-class readership in the Paris region.

Among the general reviews, the most frequently useful are the *Revue économique, Revue française de science politique,* the *Revue d'histoire économique et sociale, Population, Revue d'économie politique,* the left-wing Catholic *Esprit,* the Catholic *Revue de l'action populaire.*

The *Revue française du travail* is issued irregularly about five or six times a year, by the Ministry of Labor and Social Security. It carries signed and unsigned articles, in addition to current statistical surveys. The government's chief statistical agency, INSEE (the Institut National de la Statistique et des Etudes Economiques) issues the valuable *Etudes et Conjoncture: Economie Française,* every few months, in addition to the weekly and monthly *Bulletins de statistique* and their supplements. The May-June 1951 number of *Etudes et conjoncture,* vol. 6, no. 3, devoted to "La France et l'Inflation," is a useful survey of production, price, wage, and other developments of the past generation.

The private Institut d'Observation Economique publishes the monthly *Observation Économique,* which carries its own real wage figures, with cost-of-living indexes calculated for three different types of employees, as well as discussion articles.

Droit social is a monthly, privately published, with articles on labor and social security developments, social and economic as well as strictly legal, and a lively current economic survey in each issue by Alfred Sauvy.

B. BOOKS AND ARTICLES

This part of the bibliography is divided into the following general headings:

1. General trade union and economic history.
2. Labor history and background, 1789-1914.
3. Historical background and trade union developments, 1914-1952.
4. Collective bargaining and industrial relations.
5. Political parties.

1. General trade union and economic history:

Bothereau, Robert, *Histoire du syndicalisme français* (Paris: Presses Universitaires, 1945). A brief sketch by the present general secretary of Force Ouvrière.

Chaumel, Guy, *Histoire des Cheminots et de leurs syndicats* (Paris: Rivière, 1948). Stops short of the second World War; skimpy on unionism; interesting introduction by Dolléans.

Clark, Marjorie R., *History of the French Labor Movement, 1910-1928* (Berkeley, University of California, 1930). Competent, though not as good on the political aspects of union action as Saposs.

Collinet, Michel, *Esprit du syndicalisme* (Paris, Editions Ouvrières, 1952). An important critical work on union doctrine and union practice.

Dolléans, Edouard, *Histoire du mouvement ouvrier,* vol. I, 1830-1871, vol. II, 1871-1936 (Paris, Colin, 1948). (A reissue of the 1936-1939 edition.) This semistandard history of the trade union movement is written with great verve and emphasis upon the personalities of some of the leading figures (but none of the contemporaries), who are sketched with color and sympathy. Not attempting to be complete, it skips over some periods. Parts of the two volumes cover other countries. A third volume is in press.

Dolléans, Edouard and Michel Crozier, *Mouvements ouvrier et socialiste: Chronologie et bibliographie, Angleterre, France, Allemagne, Etats-Unis (1750-1918)* (Paris, Editions Ouvrières, 1950).

Duchemin, René-P., *Organisation syndicale patronale en France* (Paris, Plon, 1940). Useful source materials for the history of employer organization between the wars, by the ex-president of the General Confederation of French Employers.

Duroselle, Jean-Baptiste, *Les débuts du catholicisme social en France (1822-1870)* (Paris, Presses Universitaires, 1951).

Ehrmann, Henry W., *French Labor: from Popular Front to Liberation* (New York, Oxford, 1947). A richly documented and thoughtful work. Most valuable on the national and international politics and labor relations of the period from 1934 to 1940.

France. Ministry of Commerce, Office du Travail (predecessor of the Ministry of Labor), *Les Associations professionnelles ouvrières* (Paris, 1899-1904, 4 vols). A basic compilation on the history of the early unions.

Goetz-Girey, Robert, *Pensée syndicale française: militants et théoriciens* (Paris, Colin, 1948). A survey of labor union doctrine.

Halévy, Daniel, *Essais sur le mouvement ouvrier en France* (Paris, Société Nouvelle de Librairie et d'Edition, 1901). A beautifully written and perceptive work.

Hoog, Georges, *Histoire du Catholicisme social en France, 1871-1931* (2d ed.) (Paris, Domat-Montchrestien, 1946).

Lefranc, Georges, *Histoire du mouvement syndical français* (Paris, Librairie syndicale, 1937). A valuable general history written when the author was education director for the CGT. Lefranc has carried his work forward in two important later volumes. One was published under the nom de plume of Jean Montreuil: *Histoire du mouvement ouvrier en France des origines à nos jours* (Paris, Aubier, 1946). This halts in 1939, with a chronological listing of events of 1940-1944. The other is *Les Expériences syndicales en France de 1939 à 1950* (Paris, Aubier, 1950). Among other things, it makes as able a defense as it is possible to make of René Belin, former CGT secretary, Minister of Labor under Pétain from 1940 to 1942. It gives extensive citation of documents.

Leroy, Maxime, *La Coutume ouvrière* (Paris, Giard et Brière, 1913). 2 vols. A most substantial and illuminating description and analysis of organization and philosophy, with a great deal of history. A monumental pioneering work.

Lorwin, Lewis L., *Syndicalism in France* (2d ed.) (New York, Columbia University, 1914). One of the best analyses of the philosophy of revolutionary syndicalism, related to the history and structure of the CGT.

Louis, Paul, *Histoire du Mouvement Syndical en France,* vol. I, 1789-1918, vol. II, 1918-1948 (Paris, Valois, 1947-1948). A semistandard history, it has a mass of useful detail, put together in a disheveled chronological way, often strung along in catalog form. The author's preoccupation with "working class unity" distorts his emphasis.

Piat, R. P. Stéphane-J., *Jules Zirnheld, président de la CFTC* (Paris, Bonne Presse, 1948). This biography is a work of piety rather than an objective account, but it is usefully documented.

Saposs, David J., *The Labor Movement in Post-War France* (New York, Columbia University, 1931.) Describes the trade union, coöperative, and political organization of labor with thoroughness and insight.

Thorel, Guy, *Chronologie du mouvement syndical ouvrier en France, 1791-1946* (Paris, Editions du Temps Présent, 1947). Brief paragraphs in chronological form.

Vial, Jean, *La Coutume Chapelière: Histoire du mouvement ouvrier dans la Chapellerie* (Paris, Domat-Montchrestien, 1941). Perhaps the best of the few histories of individual unions, although helter-skelter in its construction.

Vignaux, Paul, *Traditionalisme et syndicalisme, essai d'histoire sociale, 1884-1941* (New York, Editions de la Maison Française, 1943). A spirited and reflective book by a leader of the "CFTC left," written in patriotic exile; most valuable on the roots of corporatism and the fight against it in the CFTC.

Villey, Etienne, *L'Organisation professionnelle des employeurs dans l'industrie française* (Paris, Alcan, 1923). Covering the early period, this is still the only systematic work on employer organization.

Weill, Georges, *Histoire du mouvement social en France, 1852-1924,* (Paris, Alcan, 1924). A solid history of the unions, political parties, and coöperatives.

Zirnheld, Jules, *Cinquante années de syndicalisme chrétien* (Paris, Spes, 1937). A valuable book by the CFTC'S founder and first president, with almost all the personal element unfortunately suppressed.

ON ECONOMIC DEVELOPMENTS

Beau de Loménie, E., *Les responsibilités des dynasties bourgeoises (de Bonaparte à Poincaré),* 2 vols. (Paris, Denoël, 1943-1947) A stimulating book on the relations of business and govenment by a nonprofessional economic historian, a monarchist in persuasion.

Clapham, J. H., *The Economic Development of France and Germany, 1815-1914* (4th ed.) (Cambridge, Cambridge University Press, 1936, reissued 1948). Deservedly a classic.

Clough, Shepard B., *France: a History of National Economics, 1789-1939* (New York, Scribner's, 1939).

Collinet, Michel, *Essai sur la Condition Ouvrière (1900-1950)* (Paris, Editions Ouvrières, 1951). An analysis of changes in class structure, the distribution of national income, the composition of wage payments, and so on.

Earle, Edward M., ed. *Modern France: Problems of the Third and Fourth Republics* (Princeton, Princeton University Press, 1951). Contains many useful articles on social, economic, and political issues.

Louis, Paul, *La condition ouvrière en France depuis cent ans* (Paris, Presses Universitaires, 1950). A compilation, chiefly on wages, prices, and hours.

Ogburn, William F. and W. Jaffé, *The Economic Development of Post-War France* (New York, Columbia University, 1929).

Sée, Henri, *Histoire économique de la France, vol. 2, Les Temps modernes (1789-1914)* (Paris, Colin, 1942).

2. Labor History and Background, 1789-1914:

(See references under 1 to works of Maxime Leroy, Lewis L. Lorwin, Daniel Halévy)

Barthou, Louis, *L'Action syndicale: Loi du 21 mars 1884, Résultats et Réformes* (Paris, Rousseau, 1904). An interesting volume by a distinguished conservative statesman.

Blum, Léon, *Les Congrès ouvriers et socialistes français* (Paris, 1901).

Duveau, Georges, *La Vie ouvrière en France sous le second Empire* (Paris, Gallimard, 1946). An invaluable work of scholarship and imaginative insight.

Kelso, Maxwell R., "The French Labor Movement during the Last Years of the Second Empire," in Donald C. McKay, ed. *Essays in the History of Modern Europe* (New York, Harpers, 1936), pp. 98-113.

Kelso, Maxwell R., "The Inception of the Modern French Labor Movement (1871-1879): a Reappraisal," *Journal of Modern History,* vol. 8, no. 2, June 1936, pp. 173-193.

Leroy, Maxime, *Syndicats et services publics* (Paris, Colin, 1909). Valuable for the early struggle to organize in public employment.

Levasseur, Emile, *Histoire des classes ouvrières et de l'industrie en France, de 1789 à 1870* (2d ed.) (Paris, Rousseau, 1903), 2 vols.

Maitron, Jean, *Le syndicalisme révolutionnaire: Paul Delesalle* (Paris, Editions ouvrières, 1952).

Maitron, Jean, *Histoire du Mouvement Anarchiste en France de 1880 à 1914* (Paris, Sudel, 1951).

Mason, Edward S., *The Paris Commune, An Episode in the History of the Socialist Movement* (New York, Macmillan, 1930).

McKay, Donald C., *The National Workshops* (Cambridge, Harvard University Press, 1933). An authoritative account of the 1848 events.

Pelloutier, Fernand, *Histoire des bourses du travail* (Paris, Costes, 1946 ed). A classic work in the history and philosophy of unionism. This edition includes a preface by Georges Sorel and biographical note by Pelloutier's brother. Pelloutier, Maurice, *Fernand Pelloutier, Sa Vie—Son Oeuvre, 1867-1901* (Paris, Schleicher, 1911). A full-length life, useful but not satisfactory.

Rigaudias-Weiss, Hilde, *Les Enquêtes ouvrières en France entre 1830 et*

1848 (Paris, Alcan, 1936). A useful summary, with a mildly Marxist slant, of the most significant inquiries of the early industrial era.

Rude, Fernand, *Le Mouvement ouvrier à Lyon de 1827 à 1832* (Paris, Domat-Montchrestien, 1944).

Seilhac, Léon de, *Les Congrès ouvriers en France (1876-1897)* (Paris, Colin, 1899).

Sergent, Alain and Claude Harmel, *Histoire de l'anarchie* (Paris, Le Portulan, 1949), vol. 1 (to the late 1870's).

Séverac, J.-B., *Le Mouvement syndical,* Vol. 7 of *Encyclopédie socialiste, syndicale et coopérative de l'Internationale ouvrière* (Paris, Quillet, 1913).

Sorel, Georges, *Reflections on Violence* (Glencoe, Ill., Free Press, 1950). Sorel, the subject of many books and articles, has had only one work translated into English. This reissue of a 1915 translation by T. E. Hulme has an excellent new introduction by Edward A. Shils.

3. Labor History and Background, 1914-1952:

a. 1914-1944

(See references under 1, to Saposs, Ehrmann and Lefranc.)

Baudin, Louis, *Esquisse de l'Economie Française sous l'Occupation Allemande* (Paris, Librairie de Médicis, 1945). Esp. pp. 41-56.

Bloch, Marc, *L'Etrange défaite* (Paris, Société des Editions Franc-Tireur, 1946). Translated as *Strange Defeat: a Statement of Evidence written in 1940* (Oxford University Press, 1949). Contains some acute observations on workers' attitudes. This sober yet deeply moving book is probably the best single analysis of the "collapse" in 1940. The author, a great historian, was later active in the resistance and killed by the Nazis.

Danos, Jacques and Marcel Gibelin, *Juin '36* (Paris, Editions Ouvrières, 1952).

Dehove, Gérard, *Le Contrôle ouvrier en France* (Paris, Sirey, 1937).

France Economique de 1939 à 1946, La (Paris, Sirey, 1948). "Questions sociales," pp. 721-887, especially Gérard Dehove, "Le Mouvement ouvrier et la politique svndicale," pp. 748-785.

Gignoux, C.-J., *Patrons, soyez des patrons!* (Paris, Flammarion, 1936). A brochure in which the head of the CGPF sounds a call to employer action.

Jouhaux, Léon, *Le Syndicalisme et la CGT* (Paris, Editions de la Sirène, 1920). Gives the program of the CGT turned reformist, including the text of its famous 1918 Minimum Plan.

Jouhaux, Léon, *La CGT, ce qu'elle est, ce qu'elle veut* (Paris, Gallimard, 1937). History and program of the organization at the time of the Popular Front.

Navel, Georges, *Travaux* (Paris, Stock, 1946). *Parcours* (Paris, Gallimard, 1950). Two autobiographical books interesting for the attitudes of a nonconformist worker who labored at many trades, indoors and outdoors.

Philip, André, *Trade-unionisme et syndicalisme* (Paris, 1936).

Philip, André, "France," in Marquand, H. A., ed. *Organized Labour in Four Continents* (London, Longman's, 1939), pp. 3-59.

Picard, Roger, *Le Mouvement syndical durant la guerre* (Paris, Presses Universitaires, 1927).

Pickles, Dorothy M., *France between the Republics* (London, Contact Publications, 1946).

Pipkin, Charles W., *Social Politics and Modern Democracies* (New York, Macmillan, 1931), vol. 2, on France.

Rosmer, Alfred, *Le Mouvement ouvrier pendant la guerre: de l'union sacrée à Zimmerwald* (Paris, Librairie du Travail, 1936). A careful and documented account by a partisan, a man who opposed the war; reproduces many of the relevant documents of the period.

Sturmthal, Adolf, *The Tragedy of European Labor, 1918-1939* (New York, Columbia University Press, 1943). Reprinted with new introduction in 1951, has excellent chapters on France.

Weil, Simone, *La Condition ouvrière* (Paris, Gallimard, 1951). Has some poignant observations on factory life before the Popular Front, as lived by an ardent, mystical, self-centered intellectual who tried to throw in her lot with the working class.

Werth, Alexander, *The Twilight of France* (New York, Harper's, 1942). Several of Werth's books are brought together in this volume. The atmosphere of France in the Popular Front and Munich periods is well conveyed, with much lively detail (for example, on the sitdown strikes).

b. 1944-1952.

For this period most of the relevant works are cited under other headings. The annual volumes of *L'Année politique,* edited by André Siegfried and others, are useful reference works on economic as well as political happenings. Current economic data and analyses are to be found in the statistical sources referred to elsewhere (*Revue Française du travail,* the INSEE's *Etudes et conjoncture: économie française,* etc.), in reports and debates of the National Economic Council (Conseil Economique National) on national income, housing, etc., and periodic reviews of the economy by the Ministry of Finance and the Monnet Planning Commission (Commissariat Général du Plan de Modernisation et d'Equipement). See also reports of the U.S. Economic Coöperation Administration and the Mutural Security Agency; the Organization for European Economic Coöperation; and the United Nations Economic Commission for Europe, especially its annual economic surveys. Note Lefranc, *Les Experiences syndicales,* cited under 1. An annual review of social and economic questions, including an article on trade union developments (by Gérard Dehove), is given by the *Revue d'économie politique.*

Brousse, Henri, *Le Niveau de vie en France* (Paris, Presses Universitaires, 1949).

Ehrmann, Henry W. "Recent Writings on the French Labor Movement," *Journal of Modern History,* vol. 22, no. 2, June 1950, pp. 151-158. A thoughtful bibliographical article, of use for the author's reflections as well as for his references.

Lubell, Harold, *The French Investment Program: A Defense of the Monnet Plan* (photo-offset, Paris, November 1951). By a former ECA official.

Realités, "Condition du salarié français," January 1950. A good case study of a worker in one of the better-paid mechanics' brackets and his family.

Romeuf, Jean, *Evolution du pouvoir d'achat en France, 1938-1949* (Institut d'Observation Economique, étude speciale, no. 4), 1950.

4. Collective Bargaining and Industrial Relations.

Bayart, Philippe, *Comités d'entreprise: expériences étrangères, législation française* (2d ed.) (Paris, Rousseau, 1947). Valuable citations of the attitudes of various groups.

Capeau, Charles, *Le statut moderne du travail: la convention collective du travail, la conciliation et l'arbitrage* (2d. ed.) (Paris, Dalloz, 1951). Compares the Popular Front and 1950 legislation. A vigorous preface by Paul Grünebaum-Ballin.

CGT Metal Workers' National Union. *Les Comités d'entreprise, principes d'orientation, d'organisation, et de fonctionnement* (2d ed.) (Paris, 1947). An important work, published when the CGT was still coöperating with the committees.

Chambelland, Pierre, *Les comités d'entreprise: Fonctionnement et résultats pratiques* (Paris, Rousseau, 1949). Unlike most French studies of labor legislation and labor problems, not essentially juridical but an account of the workings of the institution. Written in a lively vein, illuminated by case studies, largely from the point of view of the technicians and middle rank supervisory personnel.

Colton, Joel, *Compulsory Labor Arbitration in France, 1936-1939* (New York, King's Crown, Columbia, 1951). An excellent monograph.

Droit social, "L'Expérience des comités d'entreprises. Bilan d'une enquête," January, February and March 1952, vol. 15, nos. 1, 2, and 3, pp. 14-33, 92-104, 163-179.

Drouillat, René and Georges Aragon, *Code du travail annoté* (Paris, Sirey, 1950). Much legislation applied to labor relations, notably on the right to strike, is not in the Labor Code, and is not discussed by the authors.

Dubreuil, Hyacinthe, *Employeurs et salariés en France* (Paris, Alcan, 1934).

Durand, Paul, et. al., *Traité du droit du travail* (Paris, Dalloz, 1947-1950), 2 vols. Excellent historical sections as well as many passages of general interest. A third volume is to deal with collective labor relations.

Hamburger, Ludwig, *Les Procédures de conciliation et d'arbitrage en France* (Geneva, 1938).

Hulster, J. de, *Le Droit de grève et sa règlementation* (Paris, Médicis, 1952). A strong plea for the outlawing of public service strikes.

International Labour Office, *Labour-Management Coöperation in France,* (Geneva, ILO, 1950). Summarizes union representation in the management of nationalized industry and in economic planning, shop stewards, plant committees.

James, Emile, *Les Comités d'entreprises: Etude de l'ordonnance du 22 février 1945* (Paris, Librairie Générale de Droit, 1945). An excellent background sketch.

Lambert, Edouard and Louis Cluzel, *Conventions collectives, jurisprudence arbitrale; recueil méthodique des décisions de la cour supérieure d'Arbitrage* (Gap, Ophrys, 1950), 2 vols.

Laroque, Pierre, *Les Rapports entre patrons et ouvriers* (Paris, Aubier, 1938). The best single book on the subject, by a chief architect and theoretician of the "new order" of labor relations of the Popular Front period. Also covers other countries.

Lorch, Alexander, *Trends in European Social Legislation between the Two World Wars* (New York, Editions de la Maison Française, 1943). Compares French and German collective bargaining and workers' representation.

Oualid, William, "L'Arbitrage obligatoire en France," *Revue d'économie politique,* vol. 53, 1939, pp. 665-711.

Rouast, André and Paul Durand, *Précis de législation industrielle (Droit du travail)* (3d ed.) (Paris, Dalloz, 1948). A fourth edition has just appeared (1953).

Scelle, Georges, *Le Droit ouvrier* (2d ed.) (Paris, Colin, 1929).

5. Political Parties

Aron, Raymond, *Le Grand schisme* (Paris, Gallimard, 1948). Acute analysis by a nominal Gaullist.

Borkenau, Franz, *World Communism: A History of the Communist International* (New York, Norton, 1939). Considerable discussion of France.

Brogan, D. W., *France under the Third Republic* (New York, Harper's, 1940). Penetrating, learned, and witty.

Duverger, Maurice, *Les Partis politiques* (Paris, Colin, 1951). Valuable factual and theoretical study.

Earle, Edward Meade, ed., *Modern France: Problems of the Third and Fourth Republics* (cited under 1).

Ehrmann, Henry W. "Political Forces in Present-Day France," *Social Research:* vol. 15, no. 2, June 1948, pp. 146-169.

Ehrmann, Henry W., "The French Peasant and Communism," *American Political Science Review,* vol. 26, no. 1, March 1952, pp. 19-43. Valuable for the study of urban communism too.

Einaudi, Mario, et al., *Communism in Western Europe* (Ithaca, Cornell University Press, 1951). Section on France by Jean Marie Domenach.

Einaudi, Mario, and François Goguel, *Christian Democracy in Italy and France* (Notre Dame University Press, 1952). On the MRP, section by Goguel.

Fauvet, Jacques, *Les Forces politiques en France* (2d ed.) (Paris, Editions *Le Monde,* 1951). By the astute political analyst of *Le Monde.* It includes some but not all of his sprightly earlier short work, *Les Partis politiques dans la France actuelle* (Paris, Editions *Le Monde,* 1947).

Goguel, François, *France under the Fourth Republic* (Ithaca, Cornell University Press, 1952).

Goguel, François, *La Politique des Partis sous la Troisième République* (Paris, Editions du Seuil, 1946). Already a classic, this remarkable work was written in a German PW camp. Stresses the dichotomy between the parties of "Movement" (the left) and of "Order" (the right).

Goguel, François, *Géographie des élections françaises, de 1870 à 1951* (Paris, Colin, 1951). No. 27 of Cahiers de la Fondation Nationale des Sciences Politiques. Valuable for its maps of electoral strength by departments, as well as for the author's informed comment.

Goguel, François and Georges Dupeux, *Sociologie électorale, esquisses d'un bilan guide recherches* (Paris, Colin, 1951). Cahiers de la Fondation Nationale des Sciences Politiques, No. 26. Lists major sources, and the main published works, as well as studies in progress, on electoral sociology. So far these have dealt chiefly with rural rather than with urban areas.

Halévy, Elie, *Histoire du socialisme européen* (Paris, Gallimard, 1948). Edited from students' notes of his lectures, after his death. Good chapters on France.

Louis, Paul, *Histoire du socialisme en France* (5th ed.) (Paris, Rivière, 1950).

Marabuto, Paul, *Les Partis politiques et les mouvements sociaux sous la IVᵉ République* (Paris, Sirey, 1948). The work of a high police official.

McKay, Donald C. *The United States and France* (Cambridge, Harvard University Press, 1951). A balanced general survey. Includes considerable bibliography.

Micaud, Charles A., "Organization and Leadership of the French Communist Party," *World Politics,* vol. 4, no. 3, April 1952, pp. 318-355.

Le Nef, Special issue on "Le Socialisme français, victime du Marxisme?" vol. 7, nos. 65-66, June-July 1950.

Rossi, A., *Physiologie du parti communiste français* (Paris, Editions Self, 1948). Translated in slightly abridged form as *A Communist Party in Action: An Account of the Organization and Operations in France* (New Haven, Yale University Press, 1949). A major study of general importance. Its wealth of factual documentation is concerned with the behavior of the French Communist Party just before and after the German attack on Russia.

Rossi, A., *Les Communistes français pendant la drôle de guerre* (Paris, Les Iles d'Or, 1951). Covers the "phoney war," with many reproductions of party literature.

Rossi, A., *Les Cahiers du bolchevisme pendant la campagne 1939-1940* (Paris, Wapler, 1951). Reproduces—with illuminating notes—the one issue of the official Communist Party organ to appear during the period, of which practically all copies have disappeared.

    These three volumes of Rossi, covering the crucial years 1939-1942, are carefully documented, profoundly hostile to the Communist Party. The author, now a French Socialist, was at one time an Italian Communist leader.

Spire, Alfred, *Inventaire des socialismes contemporains* (Paris, Librairie de Médicis, 1946).

Sturmthal, Adolf, "Democratic Socialism in Europe," *World Politics,* vol. 3, no. 1, October 1950. pp. 88-113.

Taylor, O. R., *The Fourth Republic of France: Constitution and Political Parties* (London, Royal Institute of International Affairs, 1951).

Thomson, David, *Democracy in France* (Oxford, Royal Institute of International Affairs, 2d ed., 1952). A thoughtful and vigorous essay on the Third Republic and the beginnings of the Fourth.

Walter, Gérard, *Histoire du parti Communiste français* (Paris, Somogy, 1948). Rather sympathetic in parts to his subject. Invaluable bibliography and documentation. Goes only as far as early 1940.

Wright, Gordon, *The Reshaping of French Democracy* (New York, Reynal and Hitchcock, 1948). A lively account of the Fourth Republic in search of a constitution.

Zévaès, Alexandre, *Histoire du socialisme et du communisme en France de 1871 à 1947* (Paris, Editions France-Empire, 1947). A useful account for the earlier period by a onetime Socialist deputy. The later period is distorted by the author's pro-Communist bias.

INDEX

Wertheim Publications in Industrial Relations

PUBLISHED BY HARVARD UNIVERSITY PRESS

J. D. Houser, *What the Employer Thinks*, 1927*

Wertheim Lectures on Industrial Relations, 1929

William Haber, *Industrial Relations in the Building Industry*, 1930*

Johnson O'Connor, *Psychometrics*, 1934*

Paul H. Norgren, *The Swedish Collective Bargaining System*, 1941*

Leo C. Brown, S.J., *Union Policies in the Leather Industry*, 1947

Walter Galenson, *Labor in Norway*, 1949*

Dorothea de Schweinitz, *Labor and Management in a Common Enterprise*, 1949

Ralph Altman, *Availability for Work: A Study in Unemployment Compensation*, 1950*

John T. Dunlop and Arthur D. Hill, *The Wage Adjustment Board: Wartime Stabilization in the Building and Construction Industry*, 1950

Walter Galenson, *The Danish System of Labor Relations: A Study in Industrial Peace*, 1952

Lloyd H. Fisher, *The Harvest Labor Market in California*, 1953

Theodore V. Purcell, S.J., *The Worker Speaks His Mind on Company and Union*, 1953

Donald J. White, *The New England Fishing Industry*, 1954

Val R. Lorwin, *The French Labor Movement*, 1954

Philip Taft, *The Structure and Government of Labor Unions*, 1954

George B. Baldwin, *Beyond Nationalization: The Labor Problems of British Coal*, 1955

Kenneth F. Walker, *Industrial Relations in Australia*, 1956*

Charles A. Myers, *Labor Problems in the Industrialization of India*, 1958

Herbert J. Spiro, *The Politics of German Codetermination*, 1958*

Mark W. Leiserson, *Wages and Economic Control in Norway, 1945–1957*, 1959

J. Pen, *The Wage Rate Under Collective Bargaining*, 1959

Jack Stieber, *The Steel Industry Wage Structure*, 1959

Theodore V. Purcell, S.J., *Blue Collar Man: Patterns of Dual Allegiance in Industry*, 1960

Carl Erik Knoellinger, *Labor in Finland*, 1960

Sumner H. Slichter, *Potentials of the American Economy: Selected Essays*, edited by John T. Dunlop, 1961

C. L. Christenson, *Economic Redevelopment in Bituminous Coal: The Special Case of Technological Advance in United States Coal Mines, 1930–1960*, 1962

Daniel L. Horowitz, *The Italian Labor Movement*, 1963

Adolf Sturmthal, *Workers Councils: A Study of Workplace Organization on Both Sides of the Iron Curtain*, 1964

Vernon H. Jensen, *Hiring of Dock Workers and Employment Practices in the Ports of New York, Liverpool, London, Rotterdam, and Marseilles*, 1964